The Struggle for Order

How has world order changed since the Cold War ended? Do we live in an age of American empire, or is global power shifting to the East with the rise of China? Arguing that existing ideas about balance of power and power transition are inadequate, this book gives an innovative reinterpretation of the changing nature of U. S. power, focused on the 'order transition' in East Asia. Hegemonic power is based on both coercion and consent, and hegemony is crucially underpinned by shared norms and values. Thus hegemons must constantly legitimize their unequal power to other states. In periods of strategic change, the most important political dynamics centre on this bargaining process, conceived here as the negotiation of a social compact. This book studies the re-negotiation of this consensual compact between the U. S., China, and other states in post-Cold War East Asia. It analyses institutional bargains to constrain and justify power, attempts to re-define the relationship between a regional community and the global economic order, the evolution of great power authority in regional conflict management, and the salience of competing justice claims in memory disputes. It finds that U. S. hegemony has been established in East Asia after the Cold War mainly because of the complicity of key regional states. But the new social compact also makes room for rising powers and satisfies smaller states' insecurities. The book controversially proposes that the East Asian order is multi-tiered and hierarchical, led by the U. S. but incorporating China, Japan, and other states in the layers below it.

The Struggle for Order

Hegemony, Hierarchy, and Transition in Post-Cold War East Asia

Evelyn Goh

OXFORD
UNIVERSITY PRESS

Great Clarendon Street, Oxford, OX2 6DP,
United Kingdom

Oxford University Press is a department of the University of Oxford.
It furthers the University's objective of excellence in research, scholarship,
and education by publishing worldwide. Oxford is a registered trade mark of
Oxford University press in the UK and in certain other countries

© Evelyn Goh 2013

The moral rights of the author have been asserted

First published 2013
First published in paperback 2015

All rights reserved. No part of this publication may be reproduced, stored in
a retrieval system, or transmitted, in any form or by any means, without the
prior permission in writing of Oxford University Press, or as expressly permitted
by law, by licence or under terms agreed with the appropriate reprographics
rights organization. Enquiries concerning reproduction outside the scope of the
above should be sent to the Rights Department, Oxford University Press, at the
address above

You must not circulate this work in any other form
and you must impose this same condition on any acquirer

Published in the United States of America by Oxford University Press
198 Madison Avenue, New York, NY 10016, United States of America

British Library Cataloguing in Publication Data
Data available

Library of Congress Cataloging in Publication Data
Data available

ISBN 978–0–19–959936–3 (Hbk.)
ISBN 978–0–19–875331–5 (Pbk.)

Links to third party websites are provided by Oxford in good faith and
for information only. Oxford disclaims any responsibility for the materials
contained in any third party website referenced in this work.

For Rosemary Foot

Preface to paperback edition, 2015

WRITING about the contemporary international relations of East Asia is a hazardous task, not least because of the risk of being overtaken by fast-changing events. In this crowded, noisy and partisan field, advancing a complex analysis can also be tricky. I am, therefore, grateful for this opportunity to contextualise the findings of *The Struggle for Order* against the backdrop of developments in the region since the first edition went to press in May 2013. I should note at the outset that this book's primary purpose is analytical rather than predictive. It analyses strategic developments in East Asia since the end of the Cold War, and offers an interpretation of what I call the 'order transition' (as opposed to power transition) that regional states have been negotiating for over 20 years. In unpacking the evolutionary nature of regional order, the book reveals important continuities as well significant areas of challenge and potential change in the region. The layered hierarchical order I identify as marking East Asia is an *interim* order – it has been forged from over two decades of struggle among the greater and lesser regional powers, but this is an order that is still in transition.

The book's endeavour to understand East Asia's order transition by taking into account non-great powers has been relatively well-received. The questions that have been raised have tended to focus upon the great powers. First, what explains the U.S. hegemony I see as prevailing in the region? The substantive bulk of the book is in fact about how the terms of the social compact underpinning U.S. hegemony in the region have been revised after the Cold War. Regional complicity with U.S. hegemony is sustained largely by the potent mix of the United States' preponderant power and the deficiencies of regional options. I have peddled this book to policy and academic audiences across the Asia-Pacific over the past 20 months, and two key claims have been universally endorsed: (1) "regional states consent to support or tolerate US hegemony because of their belief that the distribution of benefits, while not ideal, is preferable in this pluralist order to any alternatives they can devise" (p. 206); and (2) "U.S hegemony has been established in post-Cold War East Asia not in spite of, but partly because of, China's resurgence" (p.13). It is worth reiterating that instrumental and normative motivations are closely intertwined on the part of supporter states; complicity with the U.S. stems from both power and value considerations.

Fundamentally, U.S. hegemony is resilient because it is open to negotiation and consent—the book fleshes out how: (a) the East Asian states have managed to negotiate with the United States key means of committing and channelling the latter's power in reciprocal institutional bargains, not just within regional multilateral institutions, but also in revising the terms of bilateral alliances; (b) Washington has been responsive to allied and broader regional demands for its political, economic and military interventions in response to tensions in regional flashpoints and systemic economic crises; (c) U.S.-led global financial institutions have been adaptive and responsive to backlashes and criticisms after the Asian financial crisis; and (d) the U.S. has so far facilitated East Asia's incorporation of China into the regional order.

The key 'values' element of my story lies in understanding the U.S.' position as one of *hegemony*, "because U.S. leadership extends beyond preponderance and is characterised by consensual normative structures and a more accessible process of negotiation involving other great powers and smaller states in regional society" (p. 206). Thus, regional states, with the partial exception of China, buy into the 'guarantor' understanding of the U.S. and treat it as security provider and lender of first resort because they still trust in its benignity and openness to being persuaded to commit to their strategic imperatives. However, this is not the same as saying that U.S. hegemony is secure. Rather, whether this hegemony can be sustained will depend on Washington's ability to continue cultivating complicity and managing resistance.

This leads us to the second question that crops up regularly: how durable is this interim hierarchical order, especially in light of China's growing challenges to it? This query comes naturally to those who believe that the U.S. is in gradual decline as China grows stronger and more assertive. As Antonio Gramsci observed in a different context, "[t]he crisis consists precisely in the fact that the old is dying and the new cannot be born; in this interregnum a great variety of morbid symptoms appear."[1] And observers of East Asian security today see China as presenting some of the most notable of such morbid symptoms. At base, *The Struggle for Order* suggests that China has thus far acquiesced to—or at least has not been able to resist successfully—U.S. hegemony in the region. I analyse the contentions China has had with other regional states over regional hotspots and over historical memory, and China's support and initiation of alternative institutions and

---

[1] Antonio Gramsci, *Selections from the Prison Notebooks*, ed. and trans. by Quintin Hoare and Geoffrey Nowell-Smith (London: Lawrence & Wishart, 1971), p. 276.

Preface to paperback edition

exclusive regionalism. However, the limits of these Chinese contestations were clear up to 2013—notably, China eventually acquiesced to inclusive regional multilateral institutions and in sharing authority with Japan in regionalism; and China's assertiveness over territorial conflicts also generated regional backlash in the form of even stronger reliance upon the U.S. in the security sphere.

Yet, does China's continued 'assertiveness' since 2013 indicate the end of its unwilling hierarchical deference? Notable developments include rising tensions with Japan and other regional states since Beijing's November 2013 declaration of an Air Defence Identification Zone over parts of the the East China Sea; China's ostentatious placement of a giant oil rig within Vietnam's Exclusive Economic Zone in May to July 2014; and U.S. media coverage in early 2015 about China's reclamation and construction work on atolls in the South China Sea.

The South China Sea disputes are particularly vexing because the strategic calculations of the parties involved have thus far resisted linear logic. Certainly, China appears to be systematically testing the limits of rival Southeast Asian claimants, and more importantly, of U.S. tolerance and the scope of U.S. security commitments in maritime Southeast Asia. This Chinese opportunism would seem to stem from a reading that Washington is less willing to spill blood here than in the East China Sea, where the Obama administration has publicly assured Japan that their bilateral alliance would cover contingencies in which Japanese-held territory is attacked. Policy-makers in Southeast Asia are torn between two fears: on the one hand, they perceive China to be gradually but surely acting to 'change facts on the ground' and thereby expanding the foundations for its future claims and power projection. On the other hand, many Southeast Asian elites are also wary about turning the South China Sea into a cauldron of great power conflict if they should explicitly seek U.S. military commitments against China. The result is that U.S. military commitments have not yet been tested here because—apart from the limited case of the Philippines—Southeast Asian supporter states have not asked for these disputes to be included in their current strategic compact with the U.S. The ball thus remains in China's court and we shall have to wait to see how China's cumulative actions will impact upon regional order.

The situation is different in the East China Sea. Notably, the ratcheting up of tensions with China over the Senkaku Islands/Diaoyutai have reinforced Japan's current of strategic normalisation and regional activism under Prime Minister Abe Shinzo's leadership. Since 2013, Abe has been garnering domestic political support for various constitutional reforms to ease the conditions under which Japan might engage in foreign arms transfers and potential terms of engagement in conflict, and completed negotiations for new guidelines for the U.S. alliance. Japan has also upgraded its military-to-military exchanges and provision of coast guard and strategic development assistance to key maritime Southeast Asian partners. As a result, China's testing of Japan's limits in the East China Sea has intensified the kind of upward resistance from Japan in the middle of the regional hierarchy that I identify as particularly salient for regional order at the end of the book. These developments also highlight further my argument that the future of East Asia's order hinges upon whether China and Japan are able to negotiate a new strategic bargain between themselves.

Developments since 2013 would seem to support my approach, which emphasises the centrality of a social compact that underpins regional order. I chose to privilege the notion of a social compact so as to stress that the hierarchical regional order rests upon social foundations beyond mere one-way consent. Rather, the social compact framework captures the notion of a reciprocal and conditional exchange of promises and binding agreements—one party agrees to its part of the bargain as long as the other parties abide by theirs. Great powers are conceded their privileged positions and special rights by weaker states within international society in return for, and only if, they perform special duties or provide public goods that uphold the international order. Herein lies China's problem: it has thus far been unsuccessful in trying to convince many East Asian states that it can provide sufficiently compelling special functions in upholding regional order in exchange for the latters' support of China's elevated position within the regional hierarchy.

In this regard, the debate about various new international institutions China has promoted since 2013 is instructive. A common question I face is: do these alternative institutions—such as the Asian Infrastructure Investment Bank (AIIB), the BRICS New Development Bank, and President Xi Jinping's 'One Belt, One Road' initiative—represent Beijing's exit options towards an alternative order? My brief answer is, not yet—the reason being that China's approach to institutional creation differs from what we have come to expect. International Relations scholars tend to regard institutions as arenas in which to generate collective norms that would then shape behaviour and thus govern developments on the ground. In contrast, China is constructing institutional chapeaux to justify already changing facts on the ground—either to coordinate and channel its greatly increased economic capacity and influence, or to provide vision for China's greater international footprint. For instance, Beijing's plans to offer significant infrastructure funding through the AIIB serve to meet a huge unmet demand in the developing world, but also to leverage China's stark need for markets to absorb its excess capital. Deng Xiaoping's dictum of *yousuo zuowei* has truly come into its own in recent years as Beijing has pursued a 'do first' policy of 'striving for achievement'. Yet, in the process, China has exhibited a blind spot about

Preface to paperback edition

how to achieve sustainable legitimacy and cultivate supporter states beyond the 'win-win' or 'mutual benefit' rhetoric. Because it is not clear what reciprocal bargain China is offering potential supporter states, suspicions and anxiety will prevail.

However, the notion of bargains or social compacts is not alien to Chinese strategic thinking. Chinese explanations for Beijig's hardening stance towards maritime disputes in East Asia centre on claims that the other side reneged on previous bargains—for instance, that the Noda government broke the Sino-Japanese agreement forged during normalisation of relations in 1972 by nationalising the Senkaku Islands in 2012, and that the U.S. reneged on its longstanding policy of neutrality on the South China Sea territorial disputes when then-Secretary of State Hillary Clinton weighed in on the issue in 2010. Leading Chinese scholars have also publicly argued the need for a new, more equal great power bargain between U.S. and China that would capture a new set of mutual understandings about their respective spheres of dominance and influence in Asia and the world.

In order to understand the effects of these recent developments on East Asia's order transition, we shall need to apply to current and future analyses a more strategic understanding of social compacts—the multiple audiences involved, the basic mutual understandings that get re-negotiated, and the key bargains entailed. The myriad tensions over nationalist conflicts and rival organisations are but the "morbid symptoms" of the ongoing transition; fundamental changes to regional order can only be perpetuated when the 'deep' institutions and bargains that make up the existing social compact are altered.

Evelyn Goh
May 2015

Acknowledgements

There is a Chinese saying that one ought always to reflect upon the source of one's drinking water (*yinshui siyuan*). This admonishment occurred to me repeatedly in the process of writing this book.

In trying to formulate the often elusive strands of the conceptual framework, I drew from a number of deep wells—scholars who have been engaged in related intellectual enterprises far longer than I have. Ian Clark has been unstintingly generous and encouraging throughout, dispensing vital advice and providing incredibly fast feedback on the manuscript. Muthiah Alagappa, Barry Buzan, Andrew Hurrell, Peter Katzenstein, Rana Mitter, and Chris Reus-Smit provided very important comments and suggestions at various stages of the project. With his path-breaking work and engaging interest, David Kang inspired some of my best ideas and shared generously his research and contacts. Throughout this project and my career, Rosemary Foot has been a pillar of moral and intellectual support and a continual source of inspiration by example. I hope to live up to her scholarly standards one day. Meanwhile, this book is dedicated to her.

I was also very fortunate to be able to tap upon large wellsprings of goodwill among colleagues and friends. My editor Dominic Byatt showed remarkable patience and confidence in shepherding through to publication the book I wanted to write. I am grateful, too, to three anonymous reviewers for OUP; to Alice Ba, Ralf Emmers, John Ravenhill, and Jamie Reilly who critically reviewed and helped me to improve the empirical chapters; and to Brendan Taylor for forcing me to think harder about Japan.

In the course of this project, I was fortunate to be able to spend extended amounts of time in the field. Between 2008 and 2012, many officials, policy-makers, and analysts in the United States and East Asia generously shared their experiences and views with me in person and in written communications, for which I am very grateful. At the end of 2008, I received a Public Policy Scholarship at the Woodrow Wilson International Center for Scholars, which supported a two-month research stint in Washington DC, where I particularly wish to thank Robert Hathaway and Larry Reynolds. An East Asia Institute Fellowship enabled me to spend a month in Northeast Asia in the autumn of 2011. In Seoul, I am grateful to Moon Chung-In at Yonsei

Acknowledgements

University for his long-standing support and help with gaining access to policy-makers and scholars, and to Sheen Seongho at Seoul National University for opportunities to present my ideas. In Tokyo, I must thank Yoshihide Soeya at Keio University for his help and interest, Jun Tsunekawa at NIDS for arranging interviews with policy-makers, Kiichi Fujiwara at Tokyo University for introducing me to his graduate students, and Ken Jimbo at Keio for his insights. In China, Zhu Feng at Peking University and Cai Penghong at the Shanghai Academy of Social Sciences were particularly generous in sharing their time and ideas. My research in Southeast Asia was greatly facilitated by visiting fellowships at the Rajaratnam School of International Studies and the Lee Kuan Yew School of Public Policy in Singapore in 2011 and 2012. I thank their respective Deans, Barry Desker and Kishore Mahbubani, as well as Bilahari Kausikan and Tommy Koh for their friendship and help over the years.

I gratefully acknowledge the support of the UK Economic and Social Research Council in the form of a two-year Mid-Career Development Fellowship in 2011–12 (RES-070-27-0042), which provided the crucial time and headspace for writing this book, and Ian Clark for agreeing to be my mentor for the fellowship. For other funding for fieldwork and research, I thank the British Academy, the OUP John Fell Fund in Oxford, and Royal Holloway, University of London. I am grateful to colleagues at the Department of Politics and International Relations at Royal Holloway, where I worked between September 2008 and August 2013, for their warm support. Nigel Bowles at the Rothermere American Institute in Oxford very kindly hosted me at an important juncture of the writing, and William Tow at the Australian National University provided me with numerous opportunities for keeping up with developments in the Asia-Pacific by inviting me to participate in his exciting projects. In addition, I received efficient and expert assistance from Lu Caixia and Amy King for some of the Chinese material.

Finally, this endeavour was sustained throughout by a rich reservoir of groundwater. My friends Joyce Chen, Michelle Chew, Chin Chuanfei, Angeline Chua, Tim Kennedy, George Khelashvili, and Shelwyn Tay ensured that I stayed sane. My parents and my brother Edwin organized holidays, laughed at me, and generally kept me grounded. Through it all was Jochen Prantl, who asked the critical questions about my initial proposal that turned the project around, inspired me by his own research on global governance, read chapters, cooked for me, and laboured to make our life together possible. Thank you.

Evelyn Goh
December 2012

Contents

List of Figures	xvii
List of Tables	xix
List of Abbreviations	xxi
1. Introduction: Order Transition in East Asia	1
2. Institutional Bargains: Taming and Legitimizing Unequal Power	28
3. Authority and Public Goods: Managing Regional Conflicts	72
4. Regionalism and Community: Renegotiating Regional and Global Economic Order	118
5. Order and Justice: Contesting the Collective Memory Regime	159
6. Conclusion: The Hierarchical East Asian Order	202
Bibliography	227
Index	261

List of Figures

5.1	The collective memory regime	165
6.1	The East Asian hierarchical order	212
6.2	The vertical dimensions of hegemony with hierarchy	214

List of Tables

1.1	Analysing the normative structure of regional society	23
2.1	Proposals for multilateral security institutions involving East Asia, 1989–93	47
3.1	Analysing authority over the management of key East Asian regional conflicts	79
5.1	The collective memory regime and its challenges	173
6.1	The social dynamics of a layered hierarchical order	213

List of Abbreviations

6PT	Six Party Talks
9/11	Al-Qaeda terrorist attacks on New York and Washington, 11 September 2001
ADB	Asian Development Bank
AFC	Asian financial crisis
AMF	Asian Monetary Fund
AMRO	ASEAN Plus Three Macroeconomic and Research Office
APEC	Asia-Pacific Economic Cooperation
APT	ASEAN Plus Three
ARF	ASEAN Regional Forum
ASEAN	Association of Southeast Asian Nations
AWF	Asian Women's Fund
BRIC	Association of emerging national economies: Brazil, Russia, India, China
BRICS	BRIC economies plus South Africa
CBM	Confidence-building measure
CCP	Chinese Communist Party
CEPEA	Comprehensive Economic Partnership Agreement in East Asia
CLCS	Commission on the Limits on the Continental Shelf
CMI	Chiang Mai Initiative
CMIM	Chiang Mai Initiative Multilateralization
CoC	Code of conduct
CSBM	Confidence- and security-building measure
CSCE	Conference on Security and Cooperation in Europe
CVID	Complete, verifiable, and irreversible dismantlement (of nuclear facilities)
DMZ	Demilitarized zone
DoC	Declaration on the Conduct of Parties in the South China Sea
DPRK	Democratic People's Republic of Korea (North Korea)
EAC	East Asian Community
EAEG	East Asian Economic Group
EAFTA	East Asian Free Trade Area
EAS	East Asian Summit

List of Abbreviations

EEZ	Exclusive economic zone
EU	European Union
EVSL	Early Voluntary Sectoral Liberalization
FDI	Foreign direct investment
FSB	Financial Stability Board
FSF	Financial Stability Forum
FTA	Free Trade Agreement
G7	Finance ministers from United States, UK, France, Germany, Italy, Canada, Japan
G8	G7 plus Russia
G20	Finance ministers and central bank governors from twenty major world economies
GATT	General Agreement on Tariffs and Trade
GFC	Global financial crisis
GWOT	Global war on terrorism
IAEA	International Atomic Energy Agency
IFI	International financial institutions
IMF	International Monetary Fund
IMTFE	International Military Tribunals for the Far East
IR	International relations
JABF	Japan Association of Bereaved Families
JDD	Joint Declaration on the Denuclearization of the Korean peninsula
JSDF	Japanese Self-Defence Forces
JSHTR	Japanese Society for History Textbook Reform
JSP	Japan Socialist Party
KEDO	Korean Energy Development Organization
KMT	Chinese Nationalist Party (Kuomintang)
LDP	Liberal Democratic Party
LWR	Light-water reactor
METI	Japanese Ministry of Economy, Trade and Industry
MOFA	Ministry of Foreign Affairs
NAFTA	North American Free Trade Area
NATO	North Atlantic Treaty Organization
NIE	Newly industrialized economy
NPT	Treaty on the Non-Proliferation of Nuclear Weapons
OECD	Organisation for Economic Co-operation and Development
OEG	Operational Expert Group
PLAN	People's Liberation Army Navy
PMC	Post-Ministerial Conference
PRC	People's Republic of China
PSI	Proliferation Security Initiative
PTT	Power transition theory

List of Abbreviations

RMB	Renminbi, the Chinese currency, of which the yuan is the primary unit
ROC	Republic of China
ROK	Republic of Korea (South Korea)
SCAP	Supreme Commander of the Allied Powers
SCS	South China Sea
SDR	Special Drawing Right
SFPT	San Francisco Peace Treaty
SLOC	Sea lines of communication
TAC	Treaty of Amity and Cooperation
TPP	Trans-Pacific Partnership
UEP	Uranium enrichment programme
UN	United Nations
UNCLOS	United Nations Convention on the Law of the Sea
UNESCO	United Nations Educational, Scientific and Cultural Organization
UNSC	United Nations Security Council
US	United States
WMD	Weapons of mass destruction
WTO	World Trade Organization

1
Introduction: Order Transition in East Asia

Questions of power, purpose, revolt, and order have dominated the international political agenda since the end of the Cold War. While these themes have always lain at the heart of strategic imagination, the uncertainties attending triumphant unipolarity, the rapid rise of new great powers, and unprecedented globalized interdependence have turned them into sites of particular discursive struggle over the last two decades. In East Asia, debates about power and order congregate around two looming trends: the changing character of American preponderance, and the resurgence of China. Because so much of the focus is on China as an actual or potential challenger to US preponderance in the region—and increasingly in the world—these twin concerns merge in three prominent alternative narratives about the future global order and the role of Asia as a whole within it.[1]

First is the 'Asian century' narrative, premised on an 'irresistible shift of global power to the East', driven by 'the rapid and massive redistribution of world industry and economic power' towards the newer industrialized economies in East and South Asia.[2] This narrative contains civilizational overtones, recalling an older order, prior to Western industrialization, when Asian civilizations were among the most advanced in the world. At the regional level, some observers already see elements of the reconstruction of a Sino-centric system as East Asian states reorientate their economies and grand strategies to align with China's. As China's economic and political influence expands, strategically, neighbouring states will be more

---

[1] This study focuses exclusively on East Asia, defined to include principally the Northeast Asian security complex (China, Taiwan, Japan, and the two Koreas) and the Southeast Asian political and security complex (with specific focus on the most strategically active states, Indonesia, Singapore, the Philippines, Thailand, and Vietnam, and the collective ten-member Association of Southeast Asian Nations). The United States is treated as a part of the East Asian order because of its security and economic commitments, key role in providing public goods, and widespread regional ascription to and participation in its strategic agendas since 1945.
[2] Mahbubani 2008; Gilpin 1997, 23.

1

eager to accommodate Chinese interests and to avoid outright containment of China's power.³ Because of the unstoppable economic logic, the United States (and 'the West') must make room for and share power with China and other Asian rising powers, or risk conflict and even war.⁴ There remains, though, some disagreement about whether this shifting balance of power will be accompanied by a radical ideological challenge from 'the East'.⁵

The second, 'liberal hegemony' narrative presumes no radical changes in the ideological underpinnings of the global order in spite of rising powers in Asia and elsewhere. Rather, the main focus is on the continuing hegemonic role that the United States has played since the end of the Second World War, and the results of the 'extraordinary rise of the liberal democratic states from weakness and obscurity in the late eighteenth century into the world's most powerful and wealthy states, propelling the West and the liberal capitalist system of economics and politics to world pre-eminence'.⁶ The firm normative and institutional foundations of this liberal order ensure that, while rising powers may alter the material distribution of power in the world, the centre of normative and military power remains the United States.⁷ What will change are the means by which this liberal hegemony is exercised: the United States would increasingly share power with its democratic allies around the world. It might even yield some of its political and economic authority to accommodate rising powers, and if these secondary powers share sufficiently in the liberal orthodoxy, there might even arise a collective hegemony or concert of liberal great powers to orchestrate international order. The implication is that China would be given a seat at the great power table, and Asia would truly have risen, only if they successfully made the liberal transition.

In contrast, the final narrative of realist power balancing firmly identifies Asia as a whole as the locus of power politics in the post-Cold War era, because it is the region that contains the most promising rising powers that can challenge the United States. All rising powers will seek to maximize their power. China is the most prominent and powerful aspiring hegemon in the world and as it grows more powerful, it will first seek regional hegemomy. Thus China will try to dislodge the United States from Asia at the same time

---

³ Kang 2003a.
⁴ Goh 2005a; White 2012.
⁵ E.g. Mahbubani 2008 controversially suggests that Asian states are rising successfully precisely because they have assimilated the 'seven pillars of Western wisdom'—the rule of law, free markets, science and technology, meritocracy, education, adaptability, and a pacific culture. For some suggestions of China posing alternative ideologies of development, see e.g. Kurlantzick 2007; Ramo 2004.
⁶ Ikenberry 2009, 71.
⁷ Ikenberry 2011 is the most prominent of the liberal institutionalists who propound this narrative, but others who see a gradually expanding realm of liberal capitalist states acting according to the precepts of democratic peace include Friedman 2005.

Introduction: Order Transition in East Asia

as it tries to maximize the capabilities gap between itself and its neighbours such as Russia, Japan, and India. China's neighbours will take fright and begin to arm themselves; eventually they will have to choose between allying with the United States to contain China, or bandwagoning with China as it challenges the United States. At the very least, an unstable multipolar system will result, and at the most extreme, a global power transition may occur if China and the United States go to war.[8]

The Puzzle

All of these narratives echo variations of a theme about changing power distributions and worries about a potential power transition between a declining United States and a rising China. Yet they are somewhat too categorical in the face of significant empirical challenges facing scholars of international relations trying to make sense of what is going on. Over the last two decades, the United States' military preponderance has increased, and it is still functioning as the classic hegemon in the international political economy. However, its leadership has come under increasing scrutiny, first over Washington's general commitment to underwriting international order once the Cold War had ended, then over its legitimate exercise of power after the invasion of Iraq in 2003, and over US capacity for underwriting the global economic order after the global financial crisis of 2008–9. The hegemon appears to have suffered a severe crisis of identity and authority that the 'liberal hegemony' school is perhaps too sanguine about. In parallel, China's remarkable economic growth has been accompanied by inflated expectations, increasing military expenditure, and a growing international political profile. Yet Beijing has been more diplomatic, more cooperative, and less overtly challenging of most international norms than many would expect from a rapidly rising power.[9] This key rising challenger would need to take up greater responsibilities in maintaining the existing order or evince greater revolutionary zeal if the 'Asian century' expectations are to be fulfilled. At the same time, smaller states and non-state actors now play a more significant role in shaping international order, partly because of globalization and partly because of the plural nature of US hegemony. Non-great power states in East Asia also do not seem to conform to theoretical expectations in their

---

[8] Friedberg 2011; Mearsheimer 2006; Betts 1993/4.
[9] A range of careful scholarship has converged on this notable conclusion in recent years, be it regarding China's record regarding fundamental international norms like sovereignty, or key international regimes governing arms control, nuclear proliferation, finance, human rights, and climate change. See especially Carlson 2005; Kent 2007; Johnston 2008; Foot and Walter 2011.

strategic choices. Rather than balancing or bandwagoning, they hedge and try to lead multilateral institutions.[10] If international order is widely supposed to be created by great powers, then these small states seem to have taken too much advantage of the voice opportunities offered in exchange for their acquiescence.

How can we analyse these complex empirical trends within a coherent conceptual framework that does not resort to polarizing theoretical positions? How do we account for the continuing though changing character of US preponderance, and the extent, potential, and meaning of China's rise? Is the centre of geopolitical gravity indeed shifting, and if so, where, how, and to what effect? What do non-great powers have to do with it? Ultimately, what kind of change is afoot—the overthrow of the world as we know it, or an adjustment in the membership of the great power club that will continue to institutionalize unequal power in the world?

The Argument

Focusing on East Asia—where important legacies of the Cold War endure and where the strategic interests of China and the United States most overlap—this book aims to provide the definitive account of what has been going on in strategic terms since the end of the Cold War. It begins with a clear recognition that power—particularly grossly unequal, preponderant power wielded by the United States and potentially by China—has crucial social foundations. Great power projects are mediated through social frameworks, often of a normative nature, that other states must acquiesce to. As important as their superior material resources, therefore, is how other states perceive and receive their unequal power. This leads us to questions about negotiation, consensus, and legitimacy that stem from the social nature of claims to power. In unpacking these issues, this book presents a fundamentally different narrative about the changing international order since the end of the Cold War. It argues that the most important strategic changes have reflected not balance of power challenges to US primacy, but rather a complex process of renegotiating the consensus on values, rights, and duties that underpins US hegemony vis-à-vis other states. This hegemony has been consolidated, but at the expense of significant alterations to its underlying normative terms and social structure.

In explaining post-Cold War East Asia, this book presents a distinct narrative of 'parallel resurgence'. Over the last two decades, alongside China's rise,

---

[10] Goh 2007/8; Kang 2003a.

the United States has recovered the strategic initiative in East Asia that was undermined by its defeat in Vietnam and undercut by the disappearance of the Cold War rationale in 1989. Thus we are dealing not with the rise of one great power and either the static incumbency or decline of the other; instead, East Asia faces the active dynamics of a parallel strategic resurgence of both the United States and China. These dynamics cannot be understood simply in terms of Washington marshalling its material superiority to hold China at bay while Beijing rushes to convert its economic capabilities into military might and political clout to out-compete the United States. Just as significant are the processes by which both have been trying to institutionalize, to legitimize, to make desirable and 'normal' their unequal power vis-à-vis each other and their constituencies of other states in the region. The most crucial strategic developments in East Asia thus reside in these wider negotiations and contestations over ideas, collective beliefs and bargains about power, authority, security, and community; in other words, about the character of regional order. These discursive contests and normative practices make meaningful the complex material changes that have occurred, and it is by getting to grips with this struggle for order that we make sense of the nature of the ongoing transition in East Asia, and its global implications.

This book finds that US hegemony has been established in post-Cold War East Asia not merely as a result of its preponderance of power, but mainly because of the complicity of key regional states, which prefer to sustain a regional order underpinned by US primacy and leadership. Washington has been able to contain resistance by being relatively open to renegotiating the terms of its hegemony. One of the most prominent debates in the existing literature relates to the extent to which the United States is hegemonic, and whether it enjoys the ability to determine which rising powers to co-opt and accommodate, and how. Many existing works, however, focus on the material condition of primacy and unipolarity rather than the social relationship of differentiated authority that accompanies hegemony.[11] Others who have recently studied US hegemony tend, on the other hand, to rely on ideological assertion rather than empirical demonstration. This book contributes to the debate by providing an empirical study that substantiates and explicates the claim of continuing US strategic hegemony in East Asia. It also explores the instrumental as well as normative underpinnings to this hegemonic authority. Hegemony is, as always, accompanied by active resistance, but in East Asia, such resistance has been ultimately limited by co-optation, voluntary

---

[11] For these authors, e.g. Brooks and Wohlforth 2008, US preponderance of material power has a tendency then to become both the dependent and the independent variable. On the distinction between primacy and hegemony, see Clark 2011, 23–8.

and otherwise. Working from the understanding of hegemony as unequal power backed by a greater portion of consent than coercion,[12] this study emphasizes that consent to hegemony is negotiated and obtained for both material and ideational reasons. Even instrumental logic is underpinned by normative beliefs: for instance, the decision to rely on the United States as a regional security guarantor is based on calculations of US force projection capabilities in the region, but also on belief in the 'offshore power' narrative that portrays the United States as a benign external power that does not harbour any territorial ambitions in the region, but would agree with regional states on interpretations of critical crises and intervene in them to uphold values shared with regional states.

Finally, this book argues that hegemonic orders are not of a type, and provides an innovative analysis of how the character of the US-centred hegemonic order in East Asia is changing. It proposes that hegemonic order is produced and maintained by the negotiation of a social compact between the hegemon and other states. This compact is subject to renegotiation in the event of significant systemic changes such as the dissolution of the bipolar superpower conflict. The hegemon risks decline if these negotiations are unsuccessful; conversely, its authority is reified if these negotiations succeed. The analysis shows that even though a dramatic power transition has not occurred, many crucial battles have already been fought over the basic conceptual pegs, social norms, conflict management, justice claims, and institutional bargains that constrain power, justify inequalities, and permit governance, not just coexistence, in the region. In this process, the regional social compact that defines and sustains the hegemonic order is being renegotiated. The prevailing accounts of developments in East Asian security typically focus on outcomes and present curiously linear analyses that do not reflect the interactive ideational, discursive, and normative dynamics of change.[13] In contrast, this book unpacks the myriad processes of interpretation, contestation, and adjustment that have characterized the region in the last twenty years. Together, they constitute an ongoing transitional process that is neither linear nor simple, and certainly has not yet led to definitive outcomes in terms of war or the emergence of a new hegemon. Instead, the region has been undergoing a transition since the dissolution of the Cold War, which left an uncertainly committed but preponderant United States within an East Asian regional security complex containing a number of other major and rising powers. During this time, the locus of regional power has

---

[12] Thus I lean towards the neo-Gramscian emphasis on international hegemony as resting on legitimate consent, as opposed to materialist accounts that stress preponderance of power. Contrast, for instance, Cox 1987; Augelli and Murphy 1993, with Keohane 1984.

[13] E.g. see many of the essays in three important volumes: Alagappa 2003; Ikenberry and Mastanduno 2003; Suh, Katzenstein, and Carlson 2004.

been variously consolidated, diffused, shifted, or shared unevenly across a range of issues and crises. This book makes explicit the critical processes by which regional states are negotiating a new social compact that would consolidate US hegemony but also make room for rising powers and satisfy the insecurities of the smaller states, while promoting common interests and shared understandings of what constitutes 'the good life' in terms of regional international relations. It proposes that in this process, East Asian states have reconstructed the US hegemonic order to incorporate a layered hierarchy with more complex social processes of maintenance. In so doing, the contention is that post-Cold War East Asia has been undergoing not a power transition, but something more ambitious yet tenuous: an order transition.

Conceptual Framework

International Order

This study works from an 'international society' perspective associated with Hedley Bull and other scholars of the English School. This approach emphasizes the fundamentally social nature of the international system, in which shared norms, rules, and expectations constitute, regulate, and make predictable international life. As such, this study has two preoccupations: its starting point and key conceptual lens are order, and it regards ideational and normative contestation as crucial processes in negotiating order. 'Order' is encumbered with a plethora of possible definitions, but essentially, international order is a pattern or arrangement that sustains the primary goals of a society of states.[14] It must involve limits on behaviour, the management of conflict, and the accommodation of change without undermining the common goals and values of society. There is a strong normative element, since international order as rule-governed interaction must be underpinned by an inter-subjective consensus about the basic goals and means of conducting international affairs.[15] These shared understandings are historically contingent, evolving, and grounded in practice. They originate as shared ideas among actors, which are manifested in 'historically constructed normative structures—in international legal rules and practices, international political

---

[14] Bull 2002, 8. The common goals of international society that Bull identifies are the preservation of the state system and the society of states; maintenance of the external sovereignty of individual states; international peace; limitation of violence in international interactions; honouring of agreements; and observation of the rules of property (mutual recognition of territorial jurisdiction of states).

[15] There is a fairly extensive literature addressing variations on these themes in defining international order. For two useful critiques and refinements, see Alagappa 2003, 33–69; Rosenau and Czempiel 1992, 10–18.

norms, and in the dominant ideologies and practices that animate them'.[16] The process of creating these shared understandings involves contention, conflict, and negotiation, within which disparities of capability and influence exert their impact.

Unequal Power in International Society

Indeed, the practices by which states collaboratively protect and maintain the goals and values of international society encompass these inequalities of power, and privilege great powers. Crucially for this study, within international society, the privileged position of great powers is not just based on the structural logic of material superiority, but is substantiated and sustained by a reciprocal agreement between them and the smaller states—great powers are conceded special rights in return for performing special duties that uphold international society. From this perspective, the strategic conundrum in post-Cold War East Asia is an intensified version of the long-standing dilemma of how to tame on the one hand, and to legitimize on the other, unequal power. For powerful states, there is a constant need for what Martin Wight called 'the justification of power': the drive to turn brute ability for coercion into legitimate authority, because force alone is a costly and ultimately unreliable instrument of power.[17] A significant portion of a great power's foreign policy construction and behaviour is thus devoted to legitimizing and normalizing inequality, and especially stark superiority. For smaller states, the preoccupation is with how to bind powerful states, to ensure limits to the potential use of great power so as to maximize gains in terms of public goods but minimize costs in terms of disruptions to the rules and institutions that regulate international life and grant protection and voice to the weak.

Furthermore, in a variegated region like East Asia, there are two key levels of unequal power—the special position of great powers above the rest, but also the power differential between the United States as the incumbent dominant power and secondary or rising powers such as China, Japan, and India. Justifying and sustaining this hierarchy of unequal power require a complex set of shared understandings and bargains about differentiated rights, responsibilities, spheres, functions, conflict management, and social preservation.

But this book makes a bolder claim about the unequal structure of East Asian international society: the core analysis suggests that in the post-Cold War period, the United States has not only been resurgent but has managed to establish hegemony in the region. This is reflected in its military

---

[16] Hurrell 2007, 17.
[17] Wight 1991, 99.

preponderance and its near-monopolistic role as public goods provider, but even more importantly in the American ability disproportionately to determine regional order. The core values and goals of East Asian regional society are deeply defined by liberal US principles, including the rule of law and an open economic system; the core institutions of this society include US alliances and war-making but also cooperative enterprises defined by American principles and commitment. This book works from the recognition of hegemony as an institution of international society, 'an institutionalized practice of special rights and responsibilities, conferred by international society or a constituency within it, on a state...with the resources to lead'.[18] Hegemony is thus understood here in its classical sense, as being marked by superior capability, order provision, and the legitimate consent of followers. Legitimacy is the hallmark of hegemony as a social relationship, and what distinguishes it from preponderance or primacy; and hegemonic legitimacy derives in large part from the hegemon's willingness itself to be constrained by norms and rules, which are derived by negotiation with others rather than by imposition.

Bringing together these twin elements of order and hegemonic inequality suggests that while China's ascent and the consolidation of US hegemony represent a significant redistribution of power, the issue is not simply or even primarily the need to countervail overweening power with similar opposing capabilities. Rather, from an international society perspective, the main challenge is how to harness great powers to some collective authority, or to embed them within stable structures of interstate cooperation—not just to prevent war between them, but more to prevent the 'pathologies of power' from undermining the orderly functioning of international life along agreed rules and norms.[19]

Hegemony and Social Compact

Taming and legitimizing the deeply unequal power within post-Cold War East Asia thus depend upon negotiating new common understandings of values and rights and duties between the hegemon, the great powers, and other states. To capture the idea that the legitimacy of an existing order is underpinned by these negotiated understandings, it is useful to conceive of a social compact that exists between the hegemon (or great powers more generally) and other states. While social contract theories have been applied mainly to domestic political systems,[20] they are often referred to in

---

[18] Clark 2011, 4.
[19] Hurrell 2007, 31–2.
[20] See e.g. Lessnoff 1990.

international relations studies when alluding to the consensual nature of unequal power relations or institutional binding. Yet the idea of a social compact goes beyond consent, which might be a rather unilateral concept; instead, a compact refers to a reciprocal and conditional exchange of promises and binding agreements, whereby one party agrees to her part of the bargain as long as the other parties abide by theirs.[21] Similarly, it is more accurate to understand great powers as being conceded their privileged positions and special rights by weaker states within international society in return for, and only if, they perform special duties or provide public goods that uphold the international order. The specifics of these special rights and duties come under constant negotiation, since 'the legitimacy of the institution of the great powers depends upon how far their special privileges are made acceptable to others'.[22] But this compact is especially and inevitably subject to renegotiation in the event of significant systemic change; and the hegemon's role—indeed the hegemonic order—depends upon it.

Renegotiating Order: Contestation and Change

In formulating the problem this way, I am mainly influenced by the work of English School scholars such as Andrew Hurrell and Ian Clark, who have developed Bull's international society approach by sharpening the focus on the dilemmas of managing unequal power and mediating between conflicting values within international society.[23] My aim is to explicate the management of these dilemmas by uncovering the ideational and normative contestation in the collective processes of negotiating the social compact that would legitimize the changing character of the hierarchical regional order in East Asia after the Cold War. There have been other prominent studies of hierarchical orders as social contracts, but they have been essentially rationalist in that they are based on the logic of consequences, and this logic is either imposed by the powerful or somehow pre-understood between the powerful and the weak.[24] In contrast, my focus is on precisely the processes by which agreements about the particular social compact that determines

---

[21] Hence, with the exception of Hobbes, other political theorists have tended to present contractarian accounts of resisting or limiting rulers.

[22] Bull 2002, 194–222; Dunne 1998, 147.

[23] Others include Buzan 2008 and Dunne 2003.

[24] A good example is Lake's (2007, 54) extrapolation of international hierarchical relations from the domestic analogy of 'a bargain between the ruler and the ruled premised on the former's provision of a social order of value sufficient to offset the latter's loss of freedom'. Ikenberry's 2001 thesis about how victorious states exercise voluntary restraint to reassure weaker states and gain their support is similarly based on an unproblematic—indeed ideological—assumption that these actors somehow arrived at the shared belief that liberal institutions are the best means to achieve this bargain.

the nature and mechanisms of international order are forged discursively and normatively.

As Alagappa put it, 'the construction of order is a historical process in which inter-subjective understandings and their translations into institutions are reached through struggle, conflict, accommodation, and cooperation'.[25] But more than that, the creation and maintenance of international order involve constant negotiation and struggle to mediate between conflicting values and between competing priorities in the hierarchy of values that underpin international society. After all it is, as Hurrell notes, 'the very clash of meanings, ideologies, and claims to justice, interacting with patterns of unequal power, which makes stable cooperation so problematic'.[26] It is on the overtly contested and negotiated dimension of international order that this book concentrates. The strategic transition that has taken place in East Asia since the end of the Cold War has been critically constituted by the 'clash of meanings' over the changing patterns of unequal power, and the struggle for regional order has been about mediating between these competing meanings and claims to achieve a new regional social compact. This process resembles the 'serial negotiation' to try to achieve satisfaction with the status quo, which needs to occur between incumbent and rising powers if a violent trial of strength is to be avoided during power transitions.[27] This book shows, though, that the negotiation about order is an endeavour involving not only the great powers but also other key states and actors in the security complex.[28]

Certainly, the privileges accorded great powers include a more significant role in negotiating regional order. In East Asia, thinking about order after the Cold War was explicitly dependent upon the contingent nature of US hegemony henceforth. Washington's strategy in the world and in the region would create the opportunities for and delineate the limits of regional order. From 1989, its material and ideological victory from the Cold War combined with China's international disgrace after the Tiananmen massacre to put the United States in a position of potential hegemony in East Asia. This grave inequality of power gave Washington a unique capacity to shape collective beliefs by dominating and normalizing understandings about regional order, including the nature and organizing principles of its own benign hegemony, what the shared goals and values of regional society were, what the

---

[25] Alagappa 2003, 39.
[26] Hurrell 2007, 39.
[27] This aspect of power transition theory is discussed below.
[28] Having said that, this book adopts a generally state-centric focus, reflecting the prevailing world view of East Asian policy-makers. In cases where non-state or sub-state actors clearly play a prominent role in the analysis—such as in the sections on models of political-economic regionalism, and collective memory and historical narratives—they are privileged accordingly.

key potential challengers and challenges were, who and what needed to be secured, and how security would be achieved. For a powerful state, this capacity to shape others' beliefs and desires—what Steven Lukes called the 'third dimension of power'—is the most important aspect of its international power.[29] That this process is often insidious and unclear has been highlighted prominently by Antonio Gramsci: referring to the transnational and societal structures of capitalist domination, his 'consensual hegemony' points to a particular universalized power structure that manifests less as domination of the subordinate classes than as the necessary order of things.[30] 'Consent' to hegemony flows from a profound sense of obligation, an internalization of dominant values and definitions, or a partial internalization of values that is at once uncomfortable with the existing status quo yet accepting of it as the only viable option for society.[31]

However, my approach is as intent upon revealing the discursive power emanating from the dominant state as it is on analysing the reactions from its key audiences. Appropriately for a study of hegemony, this turns our analytical attention towards the reception to power and the conditions for followership.[32] Less ambitious than critical theorists' studies of structures of societal domination, though, this book focuses on the ultimately interactive processes by which the social structures of regional strategic order are challenged or reproduced. In exploring this interrelationship, it shows that the entire power/knowledge process of constructing dominance through monopolizing meanings is less straightforwardly oppressive than Gramsci or Foucault, for instance, suggest.[33] The audiences are not passive takers of these new meanings, but they can be a series of differentially active recipients who respond with selection, rejection, adaptation, localization, extension, and negotiation of different elements of these understandings. Moreover, they do so depending upon their own existing identities and interests, for instrumental as well as normative reasons. Thus, the renegotiation of order is a more interactive, contested process with real prospects of change.

---

[29] To the extent that it explicitly analyses the processes of negotiating and contesting collective beliefs about regional order within the context of unequal power, this study picks up the challenge set by Lukes 2005 to analyse exercises of the third dimension of power.

[30] Gramsci 1971.

[31] Lukes 2005, 8.

[32] Others have made this point particularly following reassessments of US global leadership post-2001, e.g. Reus-Smit 2004; Buzan 2008; Lee 2010.

[33] Some see Foucault as creating a 'bleak political horizon on which the subject will always be an effect of power relations, and on which there is no possibility to escape from domination of one sort or another'—Patton 1998, 64. However, Foucault 1986 does examine how individuals might resist or mediate—though not escape—relations of domination. Many applications of Foucauldian analysis also uncover resistance and negotiation by subjects—e.g. Duncan 2002; Chatterjee 2005.

So What?

Understanding the negotiation of order in East Asia this way allows us to situate China's rise properly within the context of US hegemony being consolidated in the region. Indeed, taken to its logical conclusion, the upshot of this book is that United States hegemony has been established in post-Cold War East Asia not in spite of, but partly because of, China's resurgence.

As the dominant power at the end of the Cold War, the United States could exercise its prerogative to define the goals and values of regional international society, against which meanings would be ascribed to China's rise. The story over the subsequent twenty years, though, is one of how China and other East Asian states resisted US discourse and power, exploited the inconsistencies of its normative aspirations and conduct, and countered with their own representations and practices to shape and reshape collective understandings of China's changing character and role, and of the necessary strategic alterations in bringing about peaceful transition in the regional order. The combination of unequal power and the imperative for justifying power meant that these dynamics of contestation resulted in negotiation with the US as well as China. One important function this book performs is to conduct the legwork to demonstrate for this vital region the liberal claim that US hegemony is resilient because it is open to negotiation and consent. The core analysis in this book examines the negotiating process over the revised social compact and social structures that would constitute the new regional order. But the renegotiation of core strategic beliefs and the proliferation of a larger number of 'belief brokers' in a system do not necessarily amount to a power transition. Instead, describing and explaining the processes of order negotiation help us to explain what, if not power transition, is taking place, and to assess the changing character of the post-Cold War order.

Why Order Transition?

The key contention of this book is that post-Cold War East Asia is undergoing an order transition instead of a power transition. However, the notion of order transition is not posed as a stark alternative to power transition theory (PTT), but rather as the logical research avenue for developing qualitative analysis of strategic transitions. The power transition framework is intuitively attractive because it directly addresses the central preoccupation in the literature about US–China relations specifically: the framework allows us to begin with American hegemony, and to test the proposition that China is the key rising challenger. PTT posits that the international system has been characterized by a succession of predominant states, and that periods of greatest stability coincide with the undisputed preponderance of one state, while the risks of instability and systemic conflict are greatest at times of power parity, when a rising challenger catches up with or overtakes a declining hegemon.[34] The central claim is that the incongruity between a rising power's capabilities and its continued subordinate position in an international order dominated by another erstwhile hegemon will trigger a security dilemma that can only be resolved by major war.

Indeed, the bulk of the PTT literature concentrates on explaining the incidence of war, rather than strategic transitions per se.[35] Scholars have expended significant effort in the largely quantitative exercise of determining the relationship between power transition—when an incumbent power's culmination of resources and attributes is surpassed by a challenger—and the outbreak of war, testing different power indicators and the relative rates and timing of changes in relative power.[36] Yet qualitative elements are crucial to PTT: power parity is most likely to lead to war only if the rising challenger is unwilling or cannot be persuaded to accept the existing order. Indeed, early statistical tests found that power parity provides the necessary condition for war—no major power wars took place without power transitions—but dissatisfaction with the status quo provides the *sufficient* condition for willingness to fight, since only half of the cases of observed power transition were accompanied by war.[37] And yet this vital explanatory variable remains undertheorized. The scope and domain of the status quo variable are unclear: does it refer simply to the distribution of power (in which case quantitative models of relative material power will suffice to decide when wars will occur), or more generally to various central elements of the international order? If the latter, analyses of transition will have to study not just relative positions of rising and declining powers in the hierarchy but also their relationships with other powers, the rules of the game, and prevailing institutions of international society.

PTT scholars have advanced a number of proxy measures for satisfaction. On the one hand, extraordinary military build-ups and arms races have been posited to reflect dissatisfaction of the challenger and its attempts to close the military gap more quickly.[38] On the other hand, satisfaction has been deduced from similarity of alliance portfolios and domestic political

---

[34] The classic works in power transition theory are Organski 1958; Gilpin 1981; Gilpin 1988; Modelski and Thompson 1989.

[35] In their seminal review of the field, DiCicco and Levy (2003, 144) observed that the PTT research programme 'has done a better job of specifying the structural conditions conducive to war than of explaining the causal mechanisms that drive this process'.

[36] De Soysa, O'Neal, and Park 1997; Organski and Kugler 1980, 13–63; Kim and Morrow 1992; Lemke and Werner 1996.

[37] Organski and Kugler 1980; Most and Starr 1989.

[38] Werner and Kugler 1996.

systems,[39] or economic interdependence.[40] But these quantifiable methods have limitations. For instance, the extrapolation of shared principles and preferences in domestic political systems to preferences regarding hierarchy, norms, and institutions in the international system requires demonstration, not just assertion. Similarly, long-term alliances by themselves do not tell us much beyond the directly war-related elements of international order. Interdependence, meanwhile, is a partial and unsatisfactory way of studying how states calculate the distribution of benefits during times of systemic change.[41] The further qualitative query is whether satisfaction and relative parity might be co-constitutive: when does power parity begin to alter mutual identification?

Ultimately, the empirical data suggests that dissatisfaction to the point of war occurs only in one in two power transitions; in the remaining instances, great powers apparently try to negotiate mutual satisfaction. Indeed, because wars destroy resources and fighting always leads to inefficient outcomes, one would expect the incumbent hegemon and challenger state to seek a mutually agreeable settlement that avoids war.[42] As Powell observes, 'the fact that fighting is costly ensures that a bargaining range always exists'.[43] The basic difficulty in reaching and sustaining such agreement revolves around expectations about continuing changes in distribution of power and thus bargaining strengths.[44] These commitment dilemmas are greatly exacerbated in situations of large rapid shifts in the distribution of power.[45] But commitment problems do not render bargaining impossible between major powers; rather, it consigns incumbent hegemons and potential challengers to 'serial negotiation', an intervening process that has been inadequately studied in PTT.[46]

Understanding power transition as a bargaining process entails asking what the bargain is about. At one level, rising and declining powers are clearly concerned about the relative distribution of power and the speed with which the distribution is changing; hence negotiations over arms control and limitations on the development of critical offensive hardware and software are to be expected. Negotiations about limiting domestic sources of economic growth would be more difficult, although agreed adjustments to terms of trade and financial exchange are possible. Beyond dyadic

---

[39] Kim 1991; Lemke and Reed 1996.
[40] E.g. de Mesquita 1990 uses money market discount rate to measure interdependence.
[41] See O'Neal, de Soysa, and Park 1998.
[42] A review of formal modelling approaches that treat war as a bargaining process is found in Powell 2002.
[43] Powell 2006, 171.
[44] Levy 1987, 96; DiCicco and Levy 2003, 145.
[45] On the commitment problem, see Fearon 1995; Powell 1999.
[46] Chan 2004, 116; DiCicco and Levy 2003, 145.

distributions, though, is the question of satisfaction with the systemic status quo. A hegemon creates an international order that ensures disproportionate gains to itself.[47] Thus, hegemonic challengers necessarily dispute not only the incumbent's hierarchical position, but, more importantly, seek to revise the existing structure of differential benefits. Other authors have studied the relationship between the incidence of war and this struggle for payoffs and privileges quantitatively.[48] But a wider concern with transition necessitates specifying the social and normative elements of international order that critically manifest the distribution of benefits and that ought to then come under negotiation when power distributions change. These are questions of 'who governs the international system and whose interests are primarily promoted by the functioning of the system':[49] representation in key international organizations; the rules and institutions that govern the most important aspects of international life; and mutual understandings about internationally legitimate modes of conduct, especially those relating to management of disputes. In other words, much of the serial negotiation attending power transitions centres on the qualitative question of the legitimacy of the international order.

In trying to move forward the qualitative study of strategic transitions, therefore, this book suggests that a broader focus on order transition is due. Beyond power distribution, an order transition involves significant alterations in the common goals and values, rules of the game, and social structures of international society. While the transition may be accompanied by armed conflict, these normative changes must be the result of bargaining and negotiation. Order transitions are more encompassing and challenging to analyse because they may be relatively drawn-out and non-linear processes, but they are less controversial to identify. Pre-eminent examples in the international realm are found in course of the spread of the Westphalian order of sovereign states, the most recent of which were decolonization and self-determination in the first half of the twentieth century, and the post-Cold War universalization of the Westphalian system and spread of liberal hegemony. The most revolutionary regional order transitions have taken place in Europe, with the twentieth-century European integration project transcending the Westphalian order. But the nineteenth-century Concert of Europe provides perhaps the best illustration of the key elements of international order that have to be negotiated during times of transition. Following the Napoleonic wars, the European Concert was distinguished by 'an unusually high and self-conscious level of cooperation', in which the great powers concerned

---

[47] Organski 1958, 327–8; Norrlof 2010.
[48] Powell 1999.
[49] Gilpin 1981, 29.

agreed on key common values regarding the avoidance of major war and a shared stake in economic prosperity. As 'statesmen thought more in terms of the international system and what was necessary to keep it functioning', the process was accompanied by a 'change in [their] values and beliefs about how politics can and should be conducted'.[50] This led in turn to the negotiation of a system whereby the great powers would maintain post-war international order using the key norms of crisis management through conference diplomacy, sanctioning territorial change only by consensus, protecting essential members of the system, and granting each other due respect.[51]

Analysing order transitions requires three levels of extension to PTT. The first two levels help us to investigate the question of negotiating satisfaction, beginning with how to understand the status quo that changes and is negotiated during power transitions. PTT studies have touched on wider notions, including the distribution of benefits, hierarchy of prestige, and alliance patterns and choices, but the qualitative analysis of these variables requires a direct engagement with the social foundations of international relations. Here, the English School version of order is helpful. It posits that international order involves more than just a simple hierarchy; it is a web of norms and rules underpinned by agreement about values among member states, consisting of a social structure that is not easily subverted or overthrown, and through which significant systemic changes must be mediated. This approach allows us to tackle directly two issues: first, the elements of the international (and regional) order in terms of norms, rules, and membership that lead to dissatisfaction and must be negotiated; and second, the extent to which a challenger can be incorporated (or co-opted) into the existing international society led by the incumbent.[52] Deriving mainly from Western international society of the nineteenth and twentieth centuries, the English School literature suggests investigation into negotiations between the incumbent and challenger(s) on the following aspects of the international order: membership and status in international society, spheres of influence, agreement about trade and use of force, and modes of conflict management.[53] The challenge here is to derive a relevant set of core negotiating themes for the East Asian case.

The second level of extension involves a closer concern with analysing process. Since creating and sustaining international order requires 'explicit and self-conscious management' by key states,[54] the ability of rising and

---

[50] Jervis 1992, 723.
[51] See Elrod 1976.
[52] The international society as conceived by Bull is largely a Western European society of states, for which expansion is always through the selective co-optation of new members. See Bull and Watson 1984.
[53] This is a broadly classical realist list of concerns, echoed for instance in Gilpin 1981.
[54] Jervis 1992, 724.

incumbent powers to negotiate acceptable revisions to the status quo turns on critical political processes (as opposed to the issues) of mobilization, negotiation, and implementation. The potential for altering state preferences and therefore their satisfaction often depends upon domestic and regime politics, which in turn affects these states' balance of motivations. At the same time, international interaction and socialization may incrementally alter state actors' preferences and identities.[55] At different junctures, material gain calculations, normative causes, mutual identification, and even social order goals may influence state choices to varying degrees, driving either reformist or revolutionary impulses. Moreover, in very few transitions may great powers be isolated from their wider international constituencies: allies, rogue states, and other actors may facilitate or impede great power negotiation. Indeed, one major insight of PTT is that the dynamics of power transition are by no means simple: there are often multiple rising contenders and simultaneous power challenges, and the outcome of these conflicts may be unpredictable. As constructivist studies have demonstrated, a more explicitly process-oriented approach would take into account these multiple dynamics and processes of argumentation and persuasion that constitute negotiations about values and interests that may not lead to linear outcomes.[56]

The final, and in some ways critical, extension lies in 'speaking power' back into an analysis of how states negotiate satisfaction. Beyond simple distribution are two related aspects of unequal power critical in an order transition. First is the control that an incumbent hegemon wields over the transition process. Significant attention is paid to rising challengers in power transitions, but the conflict potential of the transition dynamic depends on the threat perception of the incumbent.[57] Indeed, the incumbent has great latitude in determining the nature of the transition because it can exercise choices about making allies or enemies out of secondary great powers.[58] Because the incumbent chooses towards which states it will make how much concession—for instance, the United States chose to make Japan an ally after the Second World War and India a major strategic partner in the last few years, but did not extend such relations to China either in the post-Second World War or post-Cold War periods—it can determine the degree of potential dissatisfaction with the status quo that these various other powers may feel. Furthermore, we might ask about revisionism on the part of the incumbent hegemon. Prospect theory suggests that incumbents may be more willing to take risks precisely to avoid loss and to maintain the status quo.[59] Powerful

---

[55] On China's socialization into international regimes, see particularly Johnston 2008.
[56] See e.g. Weldes 1996; Kornprobst 2007; Goh 2005b.
[57] Rapkin and Thompson 2003, 335–6.
[58] Chan 2004, 124.
[59] Levy 1996; Levy 1987, 88.

states with increasing capabilities are most likely of all to seek change to further increase (rather than simply maintain) benefits to themselves. On this basis, Palmer and Morgan identify the United States today as the most change-seeking country in the world, regardless of its existing leadership.[60]

Paying more attention to the hegemon highlights the dynamics of justification and consent to its strategic choices, bringing us to my starting preoccupation with the social dimensions of material as well as ideational power. In negotiating order transitions, leading states trade on their capacity to shape collective beliefs, specifically by dominating and normalizing representations of core strategic understandings about how the international system is characterized; who and what the key potential challengers and challenges are; who and what need to be secured; and how stability is to be achieved. Post-structuralists would argue that this 'productive capacity' is the most important dimension of hegemonic power.[61]

But these understandings are negotiated through discourse and practice, and remain open to material calculations such as perceptions of the hegemon's ability to provide public goods, and to negative reinforcements such as the inability of other great powers to collaborate. In addition to the wider material, social, and normative structures associated with hegemonic leadership, these conditions suggest that an existing hegemony—both the identity and the order—would be difficult and costly to overturn.

In sum, the order transition framework centres on the premise that the process of systemic transition that accompanies a significant shift in relative power distribution is marked throughout by mutual adjustment and negotiation between the incumbent hegemon, the challenger, and surrounding states about key aspects of the international order. It is not simply a material evolution in which the capabilities gap between the incumbent and the challenger narrows to the point of war. Neither does it necessarily lead to the simple replacement of one hegemon by another. Transitions of order are by definition more complex.

Analysing Order Transition in East Asia

In what follows, this book tackles the challenge of analysing a major ongoing process of order transition. In East Asia, as elsewhere in the world, the end of the Cold War was widely perceived as the most significant systemic change since 1945. Because the Cold War partially transposed two separated and competing international orders into East Asia, the disappearance of the

---

[60] Palmer and Morgan 2007.
[61] See especially Foucault 1970.

Soviet Union entailed a fundamental alteration in the nature of regional order. East Asia's acute strategic uncertainties centred on the knowledge that the social compact that restrained and legitimized unequal power would have to be renegotiated, depending upon what role the United States chose to play as the sole remaining superpower. In this context, the Cold War's ending coincided with one of the most vitriolic ruptures within US politics on foreign policy after the Chinese communist government's violent crackdown on student protesters in Tiananmen Square in June 1989. The ensuing discursive tensions and policy incoherence within the United States about China policy and the associated reassessment of its East Asia strategy reverberated in the region.

Within the domestic political realm in the United States, there competed multiple representations of the China threat in the 1990s, variously coalesced around principles of human rights, free trade, political reform, and economic transformation, as well as apparent evidence of growing Chinese military development and aggression. Both the George H. W. Bush and Clinton administrations failed to exercise leadership in this discursive process. Both were seriously disconnected with prevailing domestic political sentiment about China and unable to construct convincing strategic and tactical rationales for the China policies they adopted. Supported by big business interests looking for access to the China market, Bush wished to continue the grand rapprochement with China begun by Nixon. But he could not adapt his strategic vision to cope with the moral blow of the Tiananmen massacre and the visceral disgust of the US public, and with the subsequent disappearance of the strategic logic when the Cold War ended shortly thereafter. Clinton began by reflecting public abhorrence about China in linking China's status of most favoured trading nation with its human rights record, but this policy failed in part because of commercial pressures. Yet when the Clinton administration turned in 1994 to rapprochement with Beijing, it did not construct a reliable strategic explanation for the new policy. The Clinton administration's flirtation with the strategy of 'democratic enlargement' did not include a plan for how transition economies would evolve into liberal democracies, at a time when dissenting voices preaching the China threat began to regain dominance in US domestic politics.[62]

The Bush and Clinton administrations did not manage firmly to re-inscribe China's new identity in the post-Cold War world in relation to national and regional security and to US identity. They thus ceded initiative first towards domestic critics, then to some East Asian states, and finally to China itself to define what China's rise meant. The lack of a clear US discourse making sense

---

[62] The best accounts of US China policy and the associated domestic ruptures are in Tyler 1999 and Mann 1998.

Introduction: Order Transition in East Asia

of the new strategic situation and its implications for regional order fuelled resistance and self-help from East Asian states. There were clear instances of regional attempts to resist and destabilize certain US understandings of China: the growing East Asian assertion that China was an opportunity as well as a threat; arguments about 'the shadow of China' on its immediate neighbours; the narrative of historical regional stability correlated with China's strength; and the notion of China as an 'inevitable power'. But there was also significant discursive and policy activism from regional actors, who strategically exploited the tension and uncertainty to reshape substantively collective understandings about the region and the roles of the United States, China, and other major powers within it.[63]

This book aims to study the broader processes of contestation and negotiation about regional order in East Asia, not simply competing interpretations of and reactions to China's rise. In so doing, the order transition framework is operationalized in the following way. International order is understood to be the product of a constant negotiation among the members of the society of states. Under negotiation are two bundles of shared understandings related to the normative and social structure of regional society, which together form the key elements of order. By normative structure I do not refer to what is the common focus of constructivist works, the sets of norms, rules, and values by which regional order is maintained. Rather, the focus here is on the contested process by which states come to a shared understanding about a set of core strategic understandings specific to the region. The social structure of regional society refers to its membership composition and collective understandings about position and status, rights and responsibilities. The social structure is derived from the normative structure and sustained by distinct social processes. With this focus, this book is primarily interested in the construction of the social compact that *creates* regional order, as opposed to other studies interested in the *maintenance* of order.[64]

The first and main task of this study, then, is to analyse the negotiations and contestations over the new normative structure in post-Cold War East Asian regional society. I propose that there are four core themes in the renegotiation of this normative structure: institutional bargains; authority and public goods provision; regionalism and community; and collective memory

---

[63] With this explicit focus on the preferences, reactions, and activism of a range of East Asian states vis-à-vis shaping and changing the regional order, this study addresses a significant gap in the existing literature which tends to ignore the role played by these medium and small states. Kang 2007 examines China's rise from the point of view of its Asian neighbours, but does not study systematically their contributions to creating regional order. This book builds in part on my earlier work on Southeast Asian states' strategies for managing great power relations for regional order—see Goh 2007/8.

[64] For instance, Bull 2002 is unclear about how international society came into being in the first place; one study that addresses this gap is Watson 1992.

revision.[65] The first two themes address the drive to power within a social context, highlighting the consensual and bounded nature of hegemony and the implications for the nature and extent of the challenge that rising powers can pose. First, institutions form the nexus of addressing the central conundrum of how to justify as well as tame power; bargains struck within institutions critically constitute international order because they provide a normative-contractual means of constraining and legitimizing unequal power. As sites of codified norms for regional interaction and governance, regional institutions are unique manifestations of the social compact being renegotiated. Second, the privileged role of great powers within an international order derives from their claims to special responsibilities, which are accepted by other states. Their central special responsibility is the provision of public goods, the critical assessment of which provides a key means of analysing changing patterns of great power authority—not just capability—within the region.

The next two themes focus on the dynamics of resistance and contestation within an international order undergoing transition. On the one hand, intensifying globalization after the Cold War has been accompanied by more localized trends of integration, generating expectations of eventual global fragmentation due to deepening regional identification and exclusive interactions. Regionalism and other political projects to create regional identities and ideologies, therefore, are key means of resisting the global US-led hegemonic orthodoxy. This is particularly salient in East Asia, where the United States is geographically and perceptually an 'offshore' great power. On the other hand, the most durable international orders are the ones that are also perceived by their members to be just. As for other major conflicts, the end of the Cold War has generated intense contestation over the peace settlement. Conflicting justice claims related to the collective memory of war make up a critical element of the moral negotiations over a new regional order. They also carry strong prescriptive implications for the viability of any new social compact between old enemies.

The bulk of what follows is devoted to analysing and evaluating transitions in each of these elements of the normative structure of the evolving East Asian regional order. As outlined in Table 1.1, each of the four chapters that follow selects specific sites of contestation and reveals the main competing strands of US and East Asian discourses and practice, and the contestations and interactions between them that give rise to new collective understandings. The latter in turn warrant, constrain, or reform national strategies and policies that embody the evolving new social compact.

[65] While these themes might be argued to be foundational beliefs for many international orders, I do not claim that my four themes here are universal, merely that they are applicable to East Asian order. Different themes would have to be identified and justified for other regional orders.

Introduction: Order Transition in East Asia

Table 1.1. Analysing the normative structure of regional society

Normative processes	Social dimensions of power		Resistance and contestation	
	Taming and justifying unequal power	Great power authority	Identity and resistance	Order and justice
Core themes in East Asia	Institutional bargains	Public goods provision	Regionalism and community	Collective memory revision
Cases used in the book	Bilateral and multilateral economic and security institutions in East Asia and the Asia-Pacific	Regional conflict management in the Korean peninsula and South China Sea	Financial regionalism after 1997	Post-Second World War collective memory regime contestation in NE Asia

Chapter 2 sets the scene by examining the plethora of East Asian regional institutions as the key means of articulating the taming but also legitimizing of unequal power. It argues that these institutions are codifications as well as instruments of the social compact being renegotiated. While it pays attention to the range of key regional economic and security institutions, from formal bilateral alliances to free trade areas to cross-regional political dialogues, this chapter focuses on 'institutional bargains' rather than the usual questions relating to the design or operations of these institutions per se. It investigates regional policy-makers' contesting and changing collective beliefs about what institutions are and what they are for, specifically their role as a means of constraining and justifying power and permitting regional governance. The central question here targets the institutional bargain encompassed in the leading competing institutions: how is unequal power restrained by being institutionalized? What rights and duties, what assurances from great powers do other states accept in exchange for their deference? What do different key states think they are getting out of it, and how are these reciprocal rights and duties supposed to be attained? What norms and rules regulate this bargain?

Given the rapid dissolution of the Cold War strategic bargains between East Asian states and the superpowers, this chapter investigates how the spate of new institution-building in the economic and security realms were attempts to renegotiate new bargains, especially among the United States, Japan, China, and ASEAN. How did US terms change, what did China offer, and how did other regional states resist or adapt or negotiate? The East Asian institutional landscape is crowded and supports the uncomfortable coexistence of exclusive and inclusive arrangements—if these competing efforts embody putative bargains, what are the main competing visions of the social compact, and why does there appear to be a stalemate? This analysis tries to move us beyond the cosy liberal institutionalist vision of constitutionally constrained power by deliberately reflecting the central preoccupation with power and by foregrounding the politics and instrumentality of many institutional enterprises in East Asia. In contrast to Ikenberry's relatively straightforward model of exchanging hegemonic self-restraint for followership, my institutional bargain framework stresses the multiple reciprocal compacts sought within these complex institutions. These include small states' selective security binding of great powers and subcontracting of the mutual constraint of regional great powers to cultivated processes of institutionalized balancing.

Shifting even more overtly towards the social underpinnings of power, *Chapter 3* focuses on the management of major regional conflicts to evaluate the degree to which hegemonic and great power authority has been shared or diffused or challenged in East Asia since 1989. Public goods provision is a key marker of hegemonic authority, and conflict limitation and management specifically are one core task within classical notions of great powers' special responsibilities vis-à-vis international order. This chapter analyses the two critical conflicts with systemic impacts on regional peace and stability—those on the Korean peninsula and in the South China Sea. While paying attention to the complexities involved in each case, the analytical focus is on the ability of the United States as the incumbent superpower to determine the key parameters of these conflicts. The authority framework here is disaggregated into three abilities: to define and prioritize the public goods at stake in the conflict; to organize and mobilize support or consent from other regional states to provide the public goods (thus determining the prevailing mode of conflict management); and to discipline dissenters. These two cases are salient for wider regional security, and they also provide some variation in terms of public goods at stake and key disputants to allow a comparison to evaluate American, Chinese, and other sources of authority in East Asia. The Korean peninsula conflict has spawned the clearest instance of great power coordination in the region in the form of the Six Party Talks—does this reflect power sharing particularly between Washington and Beijing and how does this relate to the re-legitimation of US preponderant power in the region? The South China Sea territorial disputes appear to be a less severe contest because of the grave asymmetry of power between China and the Southeast Asian claimants. Does the fact that the United States is not directly involved present China with a golden opportunity to establish authority in managing this conflict?

Concentrating on authority necessitates a focus on legitimizing preponderant power and on winning consent from follower states. Of special importance here is the extent to which the United States has adjusted the terms of its preponderance by involving China in its conflict management efforts. Of equal significance for legitimizing its power, though, is whether Washington has been successful at managing its allies' divergent interests and garnering the support and consent of other states to its preferred modes and goals of conflict management. For China, the key question is whether it has stepped up to Washington's invitations to be a 'responsible stakeholder' within the existing order, or whether Beijing has tried to chip away at US authority by resisting or revising the latter's prioritization of public goods and preferred modes of conflict management. For each of these great powers, to what extent is the basis of their authority their material capability, the appeal of their normative leadership, or their ability to discipline dissenters? Ultimately, this chapter critically assesses the state of US authority using its core identity as East Asia's regional security guarantor.

Following these analyses of constraining and developing legitimate power, the two subsequent chapters turn to the more overt elements of functional and moral resistance, and the potential for regional powers to develop greater authority within the renegotiations of post-Cold War East Asian order. Reflecting on the widespread notion that the removal of the Cold War divide and the rise of China have stimulated a greater sense of East Asian regional identity, *Chapter 4* studies the functional development and political construction of a regional community by focusing on its most substantive manifestation, financial regionalism after the 1997 Asian financial crisis. Distinctive practices of economic development and integration are some of the most obvious ways in which regional identity and a regional 'community' can be asserted. Against the background of China's spectacular economic ascendance, East Asian states have concentrated on recreating an economic compact in the process of renegotiating regional order. As covered in Chapter 2, China's rise had already caused its neighbours to consider more exclusive endeavours at forging exclusive East Asian institutions and enterprises that pointed towards the possibility of an alternative Sino-centric order. The major regional trauma of the 1997 Asian financial crisis further strengthened the political appeal of resisting hegemonic economic ideology and institutions by forging distinctive regional alternatives. In the process, potential future resistance to US hegemony may turn on the degree to which East Asian states can forge regional coherence and cohesion.

This chapter critically evaluates East Asian responses to the financial crisis in 1997, paying particular attention to the proposal for an Asian Monetary Fund and the process of creating the Chiang Mai Initiative monitoring and currency swap arrangements. The financial crisis provided an unparalleled opportunity for China and Japan, as the second and third largest economies in the world, to demonstrate to their regional constituency that they would be willing to provide critical public goods in the financial realm. This would have been their first step towards claiming regional leadership, and pushing forward potential challenges in the global economic order. To assess the viability of East Asian financial regionalism as a form of resistance to the US-led Western liberal order, the chapter also unpacks the relationship between regional renegotiation of financial governance and ongoing debates about reforming the global economic order. To what extent are China and Japan's regional leadership agenda connected to their aspirations at the global level? To what extent does the development of financial regionalism signal the strengthening of an East Asian order that could resist and potentially replace the neoliberal economic orthodoxy and the norms and practices of international financial institutions?

Chapter 5 shifts the book's focus further along the normative spectrum by exploring regional disputes about history and memory that debilitate key bilateral relationships between the indigenous great powers. In contrast to prevalent analyses of the domestic politics of these conflicts, however, this chapter stresses that these memory problems are in fact competing justice claims. Justice concerns tend to traverse both the vertical relationships between the great powers and smaller states, and the horizontal relationships among great powers, and previous chapters indirectly touch upon the former. Here, however, the justice concerns occur not between subordinates and the hegemon but rather horizontally among the key regional powers in Northeast Asia. In addressing the conundrum between order and justice, this chapter conceptualizes the relationship as a negotiated bargain between the demands of order and those of justice, which can shift during strategic transitions when the social compact is renegotiated.

Going against the grain of the existing literature, Chapter 5 firmly identifies Japan as the major variable in the ongoing East Asian order transition. At the heart of the East Asian history disputes are two unresolved core issues of order and justice: the longer-running Japanese challenge of and subsequent alienation from the Sino-centric East Asian order from the late seventeenth century onwards; and the pending settlements of the great war that culminated this conflict between Japan and its neighbours in the twentieth century. Employing a 'collective memory regime' framework that encapsulates the negotiated and contingent nature of shared memory, the analysis focuses on the disputes within Japan and between Japan and China and Korea in the contests over Japanese history textbooks, Yasukuni shrine, and restitution for comfort women. It unpacks the varied sources of resistance and contestation of the post-Second World War collective memory regime, and attempts to renegotiate the balance of justice and order in this vital moral realm. Moreover, this chapter explicitly connects these normative contests to the vital strategic role of the United States in interposing itself between Japan and its neighbours in post-war East Asia. The ongoing order transition requires a mutual reckoning between China and Japan about the terms of Japan's reintegration into contemporary regional society, for which a better reconciliation of demands for justice is crucial. In closely analysing the regional contestation over the collective memory regime negotiated after the Second World War between US occupation authorities and the Japanese elite, the chapter asks whether there has been evolution towards a more inclusive and just memory regime. It also investigates the effects of this contentious renegotiation of the moral order on the prospects of a Sino-Japanese social compact, and thus a transition away from US hegemony.

The multiple negotiations over the normative structure of regional society feed in turn into a developing social structure, which is addressed in the final chapter. *Chapter 6* pulls together the findings from the foregoing analyses and in reviewing the complex negotiation processes and outcomes across these realms, it strives to provide an answer to the central question of what has been happening to East Asia's regional order since the end of the Cold War. This concluding chapter interprets the book's complex findings about the renegotiation of the regional social compact by proposing that a layered hierarchical order is being created in East Asia. This order is hierarchical in the sense that US hegemonic authority persists; but it is also hierarchical in that it contains a rank ordering of other major powers below the United States. Critically, this hierarchy integrates China as a constrained, pro-status quo second-ranked great power. This hierarchical order represents an order transition rather than a power transition because the vital alterations reside in the terms of the social compact that underpins US hegemony, not in power distribution per se. The chapter explains and explores some of the explicitly social processes associated with this hierarchical order, with reference to the foregoing analysis. The layered hierarchy framework is not presented as a rigid model, but rather as the interim outcome of the ongoing order transition in East Asia. It acts as a useful touchstone upon which we might identify critical variables, stress points, and trajectories for the future evolution of regional order. Thus the book ends by highlighting key avenues for further research based on questions that arise from its analysis and conclusions.

2

Institutional Bargains: Taming and Legitimizing Unequal Power

This book explains the nature and processes of the order transition that has occurred in East Asia since the end of the Cold War. Conceiving of order as norm-governed interaction produced by a social compact among members of the regional society of states, it focuses on the renegotiation of this compact in reaction to post-Cold War systemic disruptions. This social compact serves to mediate between contending interests, beliefs, and values held about power and authority, and security and community. International institutions play a unique role in the manifestation as well as constitution of such changing social compacts: institutions provide a normative-contractual means of constraining and legitimizing unequal power, but institutions are also sites of codified norms for governance which can provide building blocks for security communities that are the ultimate expression of solidarist international society.

There is a large literature on regional institutions in East Asia, pertaining both to the governance of regional political-economic issues, and to the so-called 'regional security architecture'.[1] However, the focus here is neither on questions of institutional choice, design, or efficacy, nor on the stale debate about whether it is norms or power that explain regional cooperation. Instead, this chapter analyses regional institutions as codifications as well as instruments of the social compact being renegotiated. While it studies the key political, economic, and security institutions, this chapter focuses on *institutional bargains* rather than the institutions themselves. That is, it investigates regional policy-makers' contesting and changing collective beliefs about what institutions are and what they are for, specifically their role as a means of constraining and justifying power and permitting governance, not just coexistence. It asks: how

---

[1] E.g. Khong and Nesadurai 2007; Acharya and Goh 2007; Tow and Taylor 2010.

is great power supposed to be constrained by the various institutional arrangements; what duties and assurances from great powers do other states accept in exchange for their deference; how are these reciprocal rights and duties supposed to be attained; and what norms regulate this bargain? But the renegotiation of institutional bargains since 1990 has been a contested process, and this chapter reveals the competing bargains that were and are being sought and how these differences have been mediated.

The following analysis is in two parts. The first, conceptual part discusses the relationship between international institutions and order, and between institutional bargains and the regional social compact. The second, empirical part is organized within two temporal frames: the early post-Cold War period (1989–97) and the period since the Asian financial crisis (1997–2012), which marked a significant turning point in regional discourse and negotiations about the institutional bargain. The empirical analysis demonstrates how the content and nature of the institutional bargains have evolved from their initial nature as largely regulative features that specified the delivery of pre-agreed principles. Because many post-Cold War institutions were created precisely as sites for negotiating the new regional order, these institutions are constitutive of the new social compact. The analysis highlights competing conceptualizations of the institutional bargain put forward by key states—the United States, the Association of Southeast Asian Nations (ASEAN), China, and Japan—and explores how these differences were mediated and what their implications were for regional institutional development.

The analysis in this chapter presents three key findings. First, the institutional bargain has become increasingly constitutive of the renegotiation of the regional social compact because institutions are a key means of addressing the imperative of how to channel and constrain not just unequal power but also a changing *hierarchy* of power. Second, the most interesting aspect of this renegotiation is the attempted layering of institutional bargains—not just the competition between institutions, or the simple revolt against Cold War institutions—in order to mediate the multiple unequal power relationships and clashing beliefs about how to constrain and legitimize them. Third, the thinness of China's vision, the continued centrality of alliances and hegemonic concerns in the American view, and hesitant Japanese involvement, have allowed ASEAN to lead institutional activism, with the result that the broader regional renegotiation of the institutional bargain is constrained by ASEAN's own disagreements and transitions. In sum, while institutions are often regarded as important reflections of the regulative order codifying agreements about rules of the game, focusing on the changing institutional bargains allows us to see that what is primarily being renegotiated in post-Cold War East Asia is the more fundamental distributive order, that is, the division of material benefits and social authority.

Institutions and the Social Compact

Bull describes the institutions of international society as 'an expression of the element of collaboration among states in discharging their political functions—and at the same time a means of sustaining this collaboration'.[2] Institutions are vital to the cooperative endeavour that underpins a society of states and allows the maintenance of social order. While the regional institutions referred to in this chapter are the interstate regimes that English School scholars identify as 'secondary' institutions, they also reflect, facilitate, and constitute international order.[3] International institutions are commonly portrayed as both an instrument of domination by great powers and a means for smaller states to constrain preponderant power. How one conceives of the role of institutions in international order, however, depends upon one's particular theoretical and ideological inclinations. The common approach in the literature is to begin by drawing on the mainstream International Relations (IR) theories as proxy for the structural conditioning of international orders. For instance, Ikenberry distinguishes between balance of power, hegemonic, and constitutional orders; Mastanduno uses geo-economic, balance of power, and unipolar orders; and Alagappa identifies hegemony-with-liberal-features, balance of power, and normative-contractual conceptions of order.[4]

Within existing works, there are four general categorizations of the relationship between the type of international order and the role of institutions. First, the 'hegemonic' category, within which there is a preponderant power and hierarchical international relations. For Gramscians and other critical theorists, international institutions are instruments of domination, facilitating and legitimizing the hegemon's power.[5] For a liberal institutionalist like John Ikenberry, hegemonic orders are the result of unchecked dominance, within which hierarchy is created and sustained mainly by coercive power—this rules out any significant role for the type of institutions that he studies.[6] In his analysis of the contemporary East Asian order, Alagappa recognizes that the United States as hegemon does use particularly liberal multilateral institutions, but only as supplements to the primary instrument of its bilateral alliances.[7] This is related to the second, 'balance of power' category, within which institutions are another power instrument which multiple

---

[2] Bull 2002, 71.
[3] Buzan 2004.
[4] Ikenberry 2001, 22–44; Mastanduno 1999; Alagappa 2003.
[5] E.g. Cox 1983.
[6] Ikenberry 2001, 26. For a more subtle conceptualization of hegemony itself as an institution of international society and analysis of different institutionalized forms of hegemony, see Clark 2011.
[7] Alagappa 2003, 74–5. In my analysis, I treat bilateral alliances explicitly as security institutions; this removes them from the implied realm of coercive instruments.

great powers can use to check each other's power. This is a conception shared by realist scholars[8] and policy-makers. Alagappa, for instance, ascribes this view to Chinese leaders, who wish fundamentally to 'balance American power through the construction of a multipolar world' and regard international institutions as an important means of forging a counter-hegemonic coalition.[9] The other two categories allow for a more normative role for institutions. The third, 'constitutional' category is that advanced by Ikenberry in his definitive account of how a successful hegemon can perpetuate its favoured order beyond its material preponderance by creating institutions that impose self-restraint in exchange for the support of other states, thus 'locking in' its advantages.[10] This account goes beyond others that emphasize the need for a powerful state to assure weaker ones to prevent challenges to its power;[11] Ikenberry's 'binding' institutions are vital in establishing a bargain between strong and weak that makes the unequal hierarchical power relationship acceptable and sustainable. The fourth, normative-contractual category is closely related to the constitutional category, but it places more emphasis on the weaker states, which promote institutions as often the only means to constrain the powerful, using norms rather than power, to socialize restraint in great power behaviour. This variety of institutionalized order has been most thoroughly explored in the strategy and initiatives of Southeast Asian states towards regional great powers.[12]

What the existing literature makes clear is that institutions are not simply instruments or agreements that the powerful impose upon the weak. Precisely because they embody a bargain about self-restraint and hegemonic deference, institutions may be a vital component of the deliberate construction of a consensual hegemony. Indeed, institutions can be mooted by both powerful and weak states, which have different reasons for valuing them: the powerful to legitimize unequal power, and the weak to tame preponderant power. But do these different imperatives easily converge in the form of institutional bargains? Ikenberry's thesis, for instance, is that they are more likely to converge when there is one preponderant power and when the bargain is struck among states that share liberal ideology. In the East Asian case where neither of these conditions holds, analysing the evolving institutional bargain is necessarily an endeavour focused on the mediation of clashing priorities and beliefs. Furthermore, there are at least two levels of potential social contracting, mediating relations among multiple great powers on the one hand, and relations between great powers and 'the rest' on

---

[8] Mearsheimer 1994/5; Grieco 1988.
[9] Alagappa 2003, 76.
[10] Ikenberry 2001, 52–7.
[11] For a realist account of this assurance dynamic, see Mastanduno 1997.
[12] See Acharya 2003; Goh 2007/8.

The Struggle for Order

the other. Because of the intra-great power dynamics, it is difficult to draw a clear distinction between 'power' accounts such as balancing, and normative accounts that would have norms and socialization do the heavy lifting. Finally, institutions are the sites of contestation and negotiation—authors from the constitutional and normative-contractual schools make this point but do not pay sufficient attention to the often long-drawn-out renegotiation of the institutional bargain when systemic change occurs.

The relationship between institutions and order within the social compact framework adopted here draws most of all from Ikenberry's constitutional model, which arises from a similar application of the domestic analogy to the international realm. For Ikenberry, constitutional orders are recognized 'by the way in which agreed-upon and institutionalized rules, rights, protections, and commitments combine to shape and circumscribe the wielding of power within the order'.[13] At the heart of the constitutional settlement is the following bargain:

> ...the leading state gets a predictable and legitimate order based on agreed-upon rules and institutions. It obtains the acquiescence in this order by weaker states, which in turn allows it to conserve its power. In return, the leading state agrees to limits on its own actions and to open itself up to a political process in which the weaker states can actively press their interests...The...leading state agrees to forego some gains in the early postwar period in exchange for rules and institutions that allow it to have stable returns later, while weaker states are given favourable returns up front and limits on the exercise of power. Institutions...bind the leading state when it is initially stronger and the subordinate states later when they are stronger.[14]

While Ikenberry's conceptualization makes significant headway in explaining the convergent dynamics of taming as well as legitimizing and sustaining unequal power, it lacks a clear focus on reciprocity. Intent on explaining how the great power can 'lock in' its post-war victory, this account does not distinguish sufficiently between two separate aspects of the logic of institutional binding from the weaker states' point of view: the need to constrain and tame the potential excesses of the powerful, as opposed to the need to enmesh, bind, or otherwise commit the great power to the security and fate of the subordinate state. Ikenberry's main case study of post-Second World War US strategy in Western Europe emphasizes the latter imperative: the Western European states wanted above all to secure US defence commitments, to bind the United States into guaranteeing the region's security—vis-à-vis each

---

[13] Ikenberry 2001, 29.
[14] Ikenberry 2001, 57. This builds on the rationalist account that strong states may find institutions valuable because they lower transaction and enforcement costs and help deflect potential challengers—see Martin 1993.

other and against the Soviet Union—over the long term.[15] The other imperative of constraining US power would be achieved through self-restraint, legal processes, and by its partners having some shared decision-making influence. In general, as Hurrell points out, this is a fairly optimistic view when, in reality 'U.S. power is so great that it does not need to make concessions or to self-bind in order to prevent even major developing countries from shifting to more oppositional policies. Washington has many other forms of positive or negative sanctions with which to achieve this goal.' Indeed, because weaker states have a greater stake in sustaining institutions, they tolerate occasional hegemonic infringements on agreed norms in exchange for continued hegemonic engagement in these institutions.[16] Thus we cannot straightforwardly assume the ability of institutional arrangements to limit the excesses of power. Ikenberry and Tsuchiyama have more recently described the logic of 'tying down' a great power using norms and 'binding together' multiple great powers through institutionalized interdependence,[17] but power rather recedes into the background of this 'cosy' liberal institutionalist vision.[18] The taming of excessive power requires some power. This is clear in the case of the post-Napoleonic war settlement in Europe, which Ikenberry regards as a weak case precisely because of the stronger element of the great powers directly constraining each other.[19] Other authors have related the lack of institutional development in East Asia during the Cold War to the absence of multiple regional great powers intent on mutually constraining each other.[20] In the post-Cold War unipolar context, fears about the potential excesses of US power are more obvious, especially after Washington's military campaigns in Kuwait, Kosovo, and Iraq.

The social compact framework adopted in this book is able to account more consciously for the reciprocal, contested, and multilevel nature of institutional bargains involved in the renegotiation of order. The following analysis employs a conception of the institutional bargain with three elements:

(a) Restraint and commitment by the leading great power, which agrees to be bound by norms and formal-legal agreements on the scope of its authority. In return, it gains the support of other states for its leading role, their tacit agreement not to challenge its (bounded) authority or to exclude or

---

[15] See Ikenberry 2001, chapter 6.
[16] Hurrell 2005, 46–7.
[17] Ikenberry and Tsuchiyama 2002.
[18] Hurrell 2005, 33.
[19] Ikenberry 2001, chapter 4. In Clark's account, the Concert broke down precisely when stresses accumulated in the 'horizontal axis of legitimacy' when the great powers could not agree on collective restraint—Clark 2011, chapter 4.
[20] Duffield 2003.

undermine it in strategic affairs. The leading state agrees to this bargain for rational reasons as set out by institutionalists as well as for more ideological reasons, related to power projection and preservation.

(b) Mutual constraint of regional great powers, which agree to be bound by the same norms limiting their exercise of power. These great powers ensure mutual compliance by their ability to monitor and deter each other (what we may call institutionalized balancing behaviour).[21] In return, they gain a stable balance of power; voice, a special role and stake in the order; and recognition and non-exclusion from other states.

(c) Security binding of great powers by subordinate states, which defer to the authority of the leading state and facilitate the mutual constraint of the other great powers. In return, they seek the leading state's commitment to guarantee their security and autonomy; the great powers' rule-bound management of regional order; and some voice in the society of states. We may view the weaker states as mainly subcontracting the taming of power to the great powers, while concentrating themselves on enmeshing powerful states.

The Early Post-Cold War Period (1989–97)

During the Cold War, the non-communist part of East Asian order was underpinned by three strategic bargains centred on the United States. In dealing with the results of the Pacific War, the first bargain was the alliance between the United States and post-war Japan, by which Washington extended its security umbrella over and opened its markets to Japan. Aimed at rehabilitating defeated Japan, these came in exchange for the latter's disarmament, pacification, and guaranteed alignment with the 'free world'. The second bargain was struck between the United States and other newly independent states that chose non-communist forms of government—ASEAN and South Korea—exchanging the latter's strategic alignment and support for US aid, trade, and tolerance of non-liberal political-economic practices. The final bargain came during the second part of the Cold War, when communist China and the United States put aside their ideological differences from 1972 in return for an implicit coalition against the Soviet Union. By this bargain, Nixon and Mao extended each other bilateral security assurances in exchange for a tacit strategic alignment and division of labour to contain Soviet influence in East Asia.[22]

---

[21] See the related 'co-binding' concept in Ikenberry and Deudney 1999.
[22] See Goh 2005b.

All three bargains disintegrated towards the end of the 1980s. Japan's economic boom led to bilateral tensions with the United States over the rising trade deficit, with American charges of Japanese security free-riding jeopardizing their Cold War bargain. Sino-Soviet normalization and Soviet reforms also eased the strategic imperative before the collapse of the Soviet Union in 1990. The dissolution of the global superpower conflict generated two strategic uncertainties for the region: whether the United States would continue to uphold its economic openness, political support, and security commitments to the region; and the implications of China's rise after a decade of gradual economic liberalization and growth, now unfettered by the Cold War contest. At the regional level, the main strategic challenge was how to reckon with the unresolved Second World War legacy of reconciling a defeated Japan with regional society. As Clark points out, after 1989, US power and the United States–Japan alliance were the only things that stood between the changing status quo and the problem of Japan's power and role in the region. East Asia did not have, as Europe did, the institutional bargains encapsulated in NATO and the EU to mediate and manage the 'German problem' and to frame the post-Cold War settlement.[23] Furthermore, the Cold War-era conflicts in Indochina and the Korean peninsula persisted and required management and resolution.

These multiple challenges generated active debates and policies about redefining the region, and in institutional terms, disagreement centred on bilateral versus multilateral institutions, the inclusivity of the latter, the types of norms that ought to govern these new institutions, and the relative merits of alliances and wider security dialogues. During these early stages of regional negotiations, the key aspects of the evolving institutional bargain were: the mediating role of the 'middle powers' such as ASEAN, the tentative sectoral division between economic and security issues, the belief that time was on the region's side (in terms of confidence building and socialization), and the successful anchoring of the US security guarantee.

Economic Institutions: APEC and the EAEG

Accounts of the early post-Cold War period that privilege American foreign policy perspectives tend to reflect some of the triumphalism of those years. The George H. W. Bush administration's 'new world order' strategy stressed a 'one world' concept of 'indivisibility' after the Cold War divides had been demolished. This strategy was explicitly committed to an open world economy, managed by 'a series of interlocking multilateral institutions', centred on the United Nations and supplemented by regional institutions such as NATO, the North American Free Trade Area (NAFTA), and Asia-Pacific

[23] Clark 2001, 124–5.

Economic Cooperation (APEC).[24] This renewed emphasis on multilateralism picked up an enduring theme in post-Second World War US strategy, but this time, as Clark observed, victory was accompanied not by the forging of a new order but by a 'new round of accessions to the existing order'.[25] The idea of post-Cold War hegemonic consolidation and extension was encapsulated even more strongly by the Clinton administration's strategy of 'engagement and enlargement' to spread free markets and democracy around the world. In this context, it seemed that an important goal of Washington's foreign policy was to shape others' behaviour by both 'the implicit threat of exclusion' and 'the inducement of accession to the multilateral order' led by the victorious superpower.[26] As Robert Zoellick, then a staffer at the State Department's East Asia Bureau, explained, 'Our intention was to create institutions, habits, and inclinations that would bias policy in these countries in our direction.'[27]

Yet there was more troubled uncertainty in these early post-Cold War years than these accounts suggest. In Washington, the years between 1989 and 1993 saw intense uncertainty and worries about the potential decline of the United States in spite of the Cold War victory. The global economic balance of power and order appeared to be shifting: major US deficits in budget and exports were accompanied by exacerbated concerns about a protectionist 'fortress Europe' with the signing of the Single European Act in 1986 and the Maastricht Treaty in 1992, and heightening fears and anger about Japan's economic boom. American opinion was especially antagonistic towards the Japanese model of 'industrial policy, managed trade and mercantilism', which was seen as diametrically opposed to the US principles of open markets and free trade.[28] Such worries generated a mishmash of policies, including protectionism, a Western hemisphere trade bloc, proposals to entice some Asia-Pacific states into a free trade association (FTA) with the United States, ideas for building stronger economic ties with Southeast Asia and China instead of Japan, and linkage making US military commitments in East Asia conditional upon economic access. These reflected a growing American willingness to reconsider underwriting East Asian economic development and the whole Cold War economic bargain with East Asian states, starting with Japan. Now that Japan was no longer a front-line state, Washington's focus shifted towards containing its potential to challenge US leadership in the region.[29]

Within East Asia, therefore, Japan reeled from American pressure and criticism of its economic strategy, development model, and security free-riding.

---

[24] Cox 1997, 88; Haley 2006.
[25] Clark 2001, 183.
[26] Clark 2001, 183.
[27] Quoted in Ikenberry 2001, 246.
[28] Grieco 1999, 330; Ravenhill 1993.
[29] Bobrow 1999, 189.

China faced Western sanctions and cast the pall of its international pariah status over the region after the Tiananmen massacre of June 1989. Smaller countries feared that with the dismantling of the Iron Curtain, Western trade and investment would be increasingly redirected towards Eastern Europe, leaving them with an unhealthy dependence on Japan. At the same time, the formation of the European Union and the creation of NAFTA in 1991 in the face of the limping Uruguay Round of trade talks seemed to hail the shrinkage rather than enlargement of open markets in the global economy. There was significant resistance to American triumphalism in the region, but even more serious debates about how to manage the fallouts of the economic frictions and restructuring that had begun even before the Cold War ended. Indeed, the perception that the United States was reneging on the economic element of the Cold War bargain arguably generated the fundamental fear and momentum for negotiating new institutional bargains. Subsequently—and ironically—instead of the straightforward accession of new members into the existing global economic order, the United States found itself facing down the prospect of exclusion from a putative new institutional bargain in East Asia.

Across the Asia-Pacific, trade relations and liberalization were being reconsidered from the mid-1980s. While the United States explored bilateral and multilateral free trade agreements within and beyond North America, various East Asian states also began to make the case for high-level regional economic coordination and cooperation. Between 1986 and 1989, these impulses yielded the APEC forum, the region's first post-Cold War multilateral institution, in November 1989. While it was initiated by Japan's Ministry of International Trade and Industry in 1987–8 and Japanese officials worked behind the scenes to generate the necessary regional consensus, APEC was publicly promoted by Australia, with its less controversial role in a region traditionally wary of Japanese domination.[30] As one author notes, 'APEC was born out of fear—fear of a unilateralist or isolationist America, fear of [the] balkanisation of the world into competing economic blocs, and fear of the death of the GATT [General Agreement on Tariffs and Trade]-centred world trading system.'[31] The forum would be a loose institution promoting free trade, specifically the completion of the Uruguay Round and the buttressing of the GATT regime; supporting regional economic cooperation; and facilitating the management of United States–Japan trade frictions.

Japan's objectives in proposing the forum reflect these imperatives.[32] At the top of the Ministry of International Trade and Industry's agenda was the need to curb Washington's 'unilateralist tendencies' in foreign economic

---

[30] See Funabashi 1995, 55–65.
[31] Funabashi 1995, 105.
[32] For more details, see Funabashi 1995, chapter 10; Watanabe and Kikuchi 1997, 141–3.

policy.³³ A regional institution committed to shared principles would help to render US economic policies 'more predictable and available for regional multilateral scrutiny'.³⁴ At the same time, shifting economic bargaining into a multilateral arena would help to relieve the pressure on United States–Japan bilateral trade disputes. Second, APEC would buttress long-term US presence and commitment to East Asia by helping to sustain American satisfaction with its leading economic position. The APEC proposal was part of Japan's aim to shift from a US-dependent to a 'role-sharing cooperation' model of regional economic development in response to American pressures on perceived Japanese security free-riding in the 1980s, but without Japan seeming to take over US leadership. But APEC would also allow Japan to reassure its East Asian neighbours about its regional activism: the inclusion of other major economic powers (the United States and China), and the principle of equality in the multilateral institutions would prevent Japanese domination.³⁵

Yet the regional consensus on APEC was not so clear cut. For instance, the initial Australian proposal for the forum had omitted the United States and Canada, to the chagrin of the Japanese and the Americans.³⁶ But the more serious challenge came from then Malaysian Prime Minister Mahathir Mohamad's 1990 proposal of an East Asian Economic Group (EAEG) comprising the ASEAN and Indochinese countries, Japan, South Korea, China, Hong Kong, and Taiwan. While this initiative was unclear and contested, the idea was that it would be minimally a Uruguay Round lobbying group or 'caucus', with the potential for becoming a formal trade bloc.³⁷ While APEC did serve ASEAN countries' aims of encouraging Japanese and American commitment to the region and of stabilizing the inflow of trade and capital, Mahathir's proposal reflected two enduring concerns among them. The EAEG idea arose partly from the perceived lack of an Asian 'voice' in the global trade regime negotiations, and was designed to help counter the rise of US-led and European trading blocs. Essentially, ASEAN countries and Japan tried to contain how much the Cold War economic bargain with the United States would be undermined: they were worried that APEC and other Western-led institutions would increase the pressure on them to adopt formal negotiations, contractual commitments, and invasive regulations for freer trade. ASEAN states were additionally concerned about

---

[33] See e.g. Bhagwati and Patrick 1990.
[34] Ikenberry 2001, 242.
[35] Ashizawa 2008, 584–6; Drysdale 1991.
[36] Then Australian Prime Minister Bob Hawke subsequently asserted that he saw the necessity of including the United States eventually, suggesting that the initial omission was related to Australia's attempts to carve out a more independent role in East Asia—see Funabashi 1995, 62–4.
[37] Severino 2006, 265–6.

protecting their developing economies from the imposition of US conditions about intellectual property, human rights, and labour standards.[38] China was enthusiastic mainly because the regional grouping would help to end its diplomatic isolation in the face of Western embargo after the Tiananmen killings.[39]

Mahathir's failure to consult with his ASEAN peers beforehand and serious concerns about the economic and political viability of such an exclusively 'Asian' grouping ensured that the EAEG proposal did not bear fruit. The proposal was nevertheless extensively debated between 1990 and 1995, and subsequently revived after the 1997 Asian financial crisis. Meanwhile, the EAEG idea forced the issue of whether Japan or the United States should lead and be responsible for the health of the regional economy.[40] By virtue of excluding the United States, Mahathir's proposed alternative economic caucus was 'tailormade' for Japanese leadership and reflected the notion of a relative decline in US leadership in the regional political economy.[41] Certainly, Japan had overtaken the United States as the region's leading source of development aid and investment in the 1980s, but the United States still remained the main market for its manufactured goods.[42] Notably, Tokyo maintained a calculated ambivalence about the EAEG proposal for a number of years, as one author put it, 'striking a balance between getting the attention of the United States without imposing unwanted responsibility on itself as...the main alternative market for Asian exports'.[43] Ultimately, Japanese deference to the United States reflected its continued strategic dependency and priority of renewing bilateral American security commitments. Tokyo was reluctant to step up to the plate also because of the historical distrust in the region, worries that it might be seen as an Asian trade bloc, doubts about how viable a closed Asian economic grouping could be given dependence on US and European markets, and suspicion that Malaysia was trying to gain easier access to Japanese markets.

One other crucial reason was that two US administrations lobbied hard in Tokyo and other regional capitals to kill the proposal.[44] From Washington's point of view, the EAEG was problematic not only because it would exclude the United States, but also because it might promote the closure of Asian markets to the United States in favour of Japan. As a result, it paid more

---

[38] Rapkin 1995, 98–129.
[39] Chinese leaders responded repeatedly and positively to Mahathir's proposal, which was made while he was on a visit to Beijing—Liu 2008.
[40] Cronin 1992, 74.
[41] Rapkin 1995, 120.
[42] Rapkin 1995, 123.
[43] Cronin 1992, 132.
[44] Baker and DeFrank 1995, 609–11.

attention to developing APEC as the region's core economic institution.[45] Secretary of State James Baker explained US interests in APEC in three long-standing, fundamental objectives of American policy in the Asia-Pacific: 'to secure economic access to the region; to spread value systems preferred by Americans; and to prevent domination of the region by other powers'.[46] Yet the creation of APEC and the proposal for EAEG do not reflect particular proaction on the Bush administration's part to achieve these objectives using regional institutions: as discussed below, Washington possessed other unilateral or bilateral instruments and has never regarded an institutionalized bargain as a primary strategy tool in this region. Instead, institutional formation was driven by East Asian states, with Washington reacting to this process at a time when it was itself finding a new strategy in the region. Furthermore, the evolution of APEC up to 1997 did not suggest that the United States achieved its purposes of securing economic access and trade liberalization. APEC remains an institution for 'open regionalism' as opposed to preferential trade, but without substantive extensive formal trade agreements unlike NAFTA and the EU.[47] In spite of the annual leaders' summit since 1993 and the 1994 pledge to create an Asia-Pacific FTA by 2020, some critics charge that 'Japan, with support from some Asian countries, [has] succeeded in eviscerating virtually all traces of the type of liberalization program sought by the United States.'[48] Reflecting Southeast Asian states' insistence that APEC conform to the 'ASEAN way' of cooperation, the liberalization process that emerged by 1996 was voluntary, unilateral, consensus based, and non-binding.[49] It lacked common timetables and mechanisms to regulate the comprehensiveness and comparability of members' efforts.[50] The 1997 financial crisis and APEC's inability to respond further seriously undermined the institution.[51]

APEC's creation and the proposal for EAEG encapsulate the process of renegotiating the economic bargain in early post-Cold War East Asia. At its heart were two alternative bargains. On the one hand, the EAEG version would break with the US-oriented Cold War bargain in drawing a 'dividing

---

[45] Grieco 1999.
[46] Baker 1998, 165.
[47] Ravenhill 2001.
[48] Rapkin 2001, 389.
[49] For instance, key Malaysian adviser Nordin Sopiee set out publicly in 1989 ASEAN's conditions for agreeing to join APEC: the organization should not deal with security and political issues; should not lead to a trade bloc; and crucially, it should not undermine existing institutions; and specifically, ASEAN should remain at the centre of the APEC process—'Pan-Pacific Talks: ASEAN Is the Key', *International Herald Tribune*, 4–5 November 1989.
[50] See APEC 1995. Many ASEAN states especially remained defensive about the legalism of Western institutionalism within APEC, which might be used to force them into liberalization agendas—see e.g. Nesadurai 1996.
[51] On the lack of progress with liberalization, see Rapkin 2001.

line down the Pacific' and promoting a more autonomous regional economic order led by Japan. In exchange for Japanese leadership, the region would gain closer economic relations with the strongest regional economy. It would also be able to hedge between gaining a more cohesive Asian voice in global trade negotiations if GATT survived, and forming a defensive regional trade bloc if it did not.[52] The problem with this putative bargain was Japanese leadership and a general aversion to trade blocs. Reflecting their general resistance to replacing the favourable Cold War economic bargain with the United States, many East Asian states opted for the APEC version. This would create an 'inclusive, open regionalism' that would keep the United States in, increase Japan's regional economic role while reassuring its neighbours, and allow regional states to diversify their dependencies while opposing trade blocs. According to Ikenberry, East Asian states agreed to move towards freer trade in exchange for US commitment to more multilateral economic dispute settlement processes and a more predictable US presence in the region. In return, the United States gained political-economic access to these countries and locked them into political and market reforms.[53] But this interpretation is too cosy. A more accurate way to read the APEC institutional bargain in practice must recognize that the conditional side of the bargain is that East Asian states subscribed to the ideal regarding open economies, while holding at bay excessive demands on the formal liberalization of their own economic policies. This bargain has involved East Asian states trying to restore US confidence and attraction to trade and investment in Asia by 'incremental opening', and strengthening international regimes that uphold 'outward-oriented' growth strategies (such as the Uruguay Round and the World Trade Organization (WTO)). At the same time, they have tried to constrain US power by shifting the economic bargaining into an institution that has consensual decision-making procedures and no enforcement mechanism, and where other economically strong states wary of US unilateralism are members.[54] Hence, through to the mid-1990s, ASEAN countries continued to protest US efforts to link human rights issues with their labour practices, China fought most favoured nation–human rights linkage annually, and Australia's and Japan's trade tensions with the United States increased to the extent that Japan sought formal redress at the WTO.

Some authors interpret these dynamics as a clash of regional norms and identities,[55] but conceiving of them as the renegotiation of a regional institutional bargain that would recalibrate the means of constraining, binding,

---

[52] The seriousness of the latter option is reflected in the 1992 ASEAN agreement to establish an ASEAN FTA—see Nesadurai 2003.
[53] Ikenberry 2001, 244–5.
[54] Bobrow 1999, 192–3.
[55] E.g. see Acharya 2009a, 152–5.

and legitimizing unequal power better accounts for the mixed processes and outcomes. This is even better illustrated in the realm of post-Cold War East Asian security institutions.

Security Institutions: Revised US Alliances and the ARF

On the security front, the early post-Cold War period witnessed a more drawn-out process of change, in which three alternative institutional bargains were advanced and explored. Ultimately, though, there was more continuity in the core institutional bargain than on the economic front. The central security institution in the region was and remains the San Francisco system of post-Second World War US bilateral alliances, which also form the basis of Washington's regional strategy. As Baker reiterated in 1991, this system was the means by which the United States maintained a forward military presence 'to provide geopolitical balance, to be an honest broker, to reassure against uncertainty'.[56] This system of alliances was 'a balancing wheel of an informal, yet highly effective, security structure' that had the United States as the 'hub', the alliance with Japan as 'the key connection', and the other bilateral alliances with South Korea, Thailand, the Philippines, and Australia as the 'spokes'.[57] As an unashamedly US-centric, hegemonic strategy after the end of the Cold War, this aimed at sustaining the American preponderance of power, minimizing potential constraints on its exercise of power, and preventing the rise of challengers while keeping costs manageable and justifiable within the domestic context. Against this backdrop, Washington's post-Cold War imperative was then to adapt its Cold War alliance structure so as to manage effectively the contemporary security threats in the region, while ensuring that the United States still played the 'crucial and indispensable' role as 'the principal guarantor of regional order'.[58] This would be achieved by renegotiating the terms of the regional alliance bargains.[59]

In line with the George H. W. Bush administration's overall strategy for reducing and reconfiguring global US military deployments, Washington reduced its East Asian troop strength and sought greater allied contributions. Two East Asia Strategy Initiative reviews in 1990 and 1992 projected a

---

[56] A belief echoed repeatedly by key strategic partners in the region, especially Singapore, as they lobbied for Washington's continued defence commitments to East Asia in the 1990s. For a more sceptical view, see Acharya and Tan 2006.

[57] Baker 1991/2, 3–5.

[58] For a discussion of the post-Cold War US hegemonic order, see Mastanduno 2003, 151.

[59] As Tow (2001, 177) warns, we should avoid 'too broad an interpretation on defence guarantees in the bilateral security agreements' between Washington and its Asian allies, which do not offer 'necessarily automatic strategic commitment under all circumstances [but instead]...require constant re-evaluation' depending upon changing threat and cost assessments.

reduction in force levels from 135,000 to 100,000 by 1995, a target that was largely met.[60] In spite of Baker's attempts to convince regional leaders that '[t]he form of our presence may have changed, but the substance of our commitment is firm',[61] the uncertainties surrounding these changes, together with various domestic political changes and regional crises, led to two major alterations to the alliance bargains.

In Southeast Asia, where the San Francisco system was primarily pinned on air and naval bases in the Philippines archipelago, the US alliances came under serious domestic scrutiny following the overthrow of the Marcos regime in 1986. Filipino politicians initiated a regional debate, frustrated that the rest of the region was free-riding on the United States–Philippines alliance without having to deal with the domestic political costs. Until the Filipino Senate's decision not to renew the leases in September 1991, an unresolved regional tension prevailed, fuelling the uncertainty about the sustainability and mode of the US presence in the region with the end of the Cold War. Even as the Bush administration announced the planned troop reductions, the Southeast Asian countries were reaching a consensus about the need for new modes of supporting the US forward presence in the region outside the traditional basing structure.[62] In place of permanent bases, other countries such as Singapore provided facilities for maintenance, repair, and for the relocation of supporting infrastructure for the Seventh Fleet. By 1992, worsening United States–Japan trade conflicts, Japan's constitutional revision to allow the overseas deployment of peacekeepers, and the passage of a law in China making extensive claims to the South China Sea all prompted additional access agreements, as well as every ASEAN leader's public support for the US security role in the region.[63] While relatively peripheral 'spokes' in the alliance system, Southeast Asian strategic partners were front runners in agreeing on the need to maintain US forward presence and deterrence in the region even after the Cold War, and in renegotiating the form of the US alliance bargain so as to continue the security binding of Washington.[64]

The second set of renegotiations occurred in the alliance bargain between Japan and the United States. With the implosion of the Soviet Union, the United States was in a position to threaten credibly the abandonment of its Japanese ally because it no longer absolutely needed its bases on this front line.[65] In the early 1990s, Washington became more vociferous in linking

---

[60] U.S. Department of Defense 1990, 1992, 1993.

[61] Baker 1992.

[62] This was by no means a simple process: on the gradual renegotiation of the tension between ASEAN's non-intervention norm and the necessity for extra-regional security arrangements, and the compromise on modes of US presence apart from bases, see Ba 2009, 160–70.

[63] Ba 2009, 170.

[64] Goh 2007/8.

[65] Arase 2010, 40.

the resolution of bilateral trade conflicts with the continuation of US security relations with Japan.[66] At the same time, Japan faced two crises which prompted internal reviews of its defence strategy and military role: the first Gulf War in 1991 laid bare the limits of Tokyo's 'chequebook diplomacy' and reignited debates about moving towards being a 'normal' nation; and the 1993–4 North Korean nuclear crisis tested Japan's commitment to the US alliance even as it showed that the East Asian neighbourhood remained dangerous. It seemed that for Japan, 'security was not free, and it might not even be cheap any longer'.[67] These multiple pressures led to the first comprehensive defence reviews in twenty years in the new National Defense Program Outline in November 1995.[68] Revisions of the scope and burden-sharing terms of the United States–Japan alliance followed the April 1996 Clinton–Hashimoto Joint Declaration on Security, which committed the allies to reviewing the 1978 alliance guidelines to promote cooperation in 'situations that may emerge in the areas surrounding Japan'.[69] The Revised Guidelines that were adopted in September 1997 not only outlined the 'comprehensive planning mechanism' for allied military cooperation; the scope of the alliance now expanded beyond the defence of Japan to include enhancing regional security. Japan would take on a greater role in the alliance including non-combat rear support, search and rescue, relief and evacuation operations in regional contingencies not directly involving Japanese territory.[70]

Thus, by 1997, the United States–Japan alliance had evolved from being a component of the US Cold War global deterrence strategy to a more regionally focused partnership for crisis management and potential power balancing. The latter consideration grew more prominent as regional concerns about the rise of China gained traction throughout the 1990s, particularly after the 1996 Taiwan Straits crisis.[71] The terms of the alliance bargain also changed, towards a more symmetrical alliance with a more militarily capable Japan contributing more substantially, while still reaping the gains of a continued US forward presence deterring China and North Korea, access to US military technology, and a relatively low defence budget.[72] What the

---

[66] See Uriu 2009.
[67] Samuels 2007, 68.
[68] While these changes increased Japan's operational role in responding to regional crises, the NDPO also reduced the authorized Japanese force strength levels from 180,000 to 145,000, thus arguably increasing Japan's reliance on its American ally—see Hughes 2004a, 178; Tow 2001, 50–1.
[69] The Joint Declaration is available at <http://www.mofa.go.jp/region/n-america/us/security/security.html>. For details of the revisions to the United States–Japan alliance after 1994, see Funabashi 1999, chapter 12; Hughes 2004b.
[70] See Hosoya and Shinoda 1998.
[71] The 1994 National Defense Program Guidelines was the first Japanese security document to refer directly to the potential threat from China.
[72] Tow 2001, 53.

early post-Cold War crises demonstrated to Tokyo was that it needed to take on a greater role in order to revitalize the alliance with the United States, so that this linchpin of its national security and the regional order could be sustained.

For its part, the Clinton administration also decided in its 1995 East Asia Strategy Review to limit its force reduction by maintaining a troop level of 100,000 in the region. Adopting what its author Joseph Nye called 'the leadership strategy', based on revitalized regional alliances and forward deployments in the region, Washington wanted to assure its allies that it remained 'committed to lead in the Asia-Pacific region'.[73] In this context, the strengthening of the alliance with Japan was crucial also because it then prevented China from playing a 'Japan card' against the United States—that is, Japan would have forgone the option of 'switching sides' to ally with China against the United States. It also anchored the US presence and forestalled any attempt by the Chinese to expel the Americans from the region. 'From this position of strength', Washington would then 'encourage China to define its interests in ways that could be compatible with ours'.[74] In the wider regional context, Chinese strategists now read that, at a minimum, the alliance's main purpose was to allow Japan and the United States to share responsibility for regional order.[75] From the Chinese point of view, this entailed reneging on the Cold War bargain of restraining Japan, since the United States was now facilitating Japan's remilitarization within the alliance.[76]

The key to the alliance bargain is that it is a 'security guarantee' bargain, centred on the imperative of security binding of the United States by its allies and other partners in East Asia. The latter quickly prioritized the need to retain the US security commitments to the region in the wake of the Cold War because they continued to believe that Washington is a benign external power with no regional territorial ambitions and sufficient military capability and economic resources for the extended deterrence of potential aggressor states within the region. They would also prefer not to commit the significant resources otherwise necessary if they had to bear the burden of intra-regional power balancing by themselves. The US hegemonic assurance, then, takes the form of a recommitment to play the 'benign alliance leader' that would act to 'preclud[e] the rise of a hostile hegemon through selective crisis intervention and through deployments of superior military power in the region'.[77] It would also constrain the regional powers Japan and China and manage regional crises. But such hub-and-spoke bilateral alliances are hierarchical

---

[73] Nye 1995, 94, 102.
[74] A post hoc observation by Nye 2001, 98–9.
[75] Zhang 2003, 247–53.
[76] White 2008/9; Goh 2011a.
[77] Tow 2001, 198.

institutions with significant payoffs for the 'hub' power:[78] in return for its guarantees, Washington would brook little or no regional constraints on its own exercise of power and would act to minimize any such attempts.

One potential means of constraining US unipolar power after the Cold War would have been regional multilateral security institutions like the ones in Western Europe after the Second World War. Ironically, the regional security institutions created in the wake of the Cold War in East Asia were meant initially to reinforce the security binding of the United States rather than to constrain its power. They were, however, also aimed at addressing a negative consequence of the region's reliance on US dominance, its impediment to the intra-regional dialogue, rapprochement, and integration amongst the region's great powers that is essential to long-term regional stability.[79] From the uncertainties of US commitment, Japanese intentions, and Chinese political evolution thus arose a series of proposals and demands for supplementary multilateral security institutions, advanced between 1989 and 1993, and summarized in Table 2.1.

The different proposals advanced by the region's 'middle powers', Australia, Canada, Japan, and ASEAN, variously adapted the experience of the Conference on Security and Cooperation in Europe (CSCE), which had brought the superpowers and their allies from détente to the end of the Cold War.[80] As in the economic realm, an institutional bargain was not the George H. W. Bush administration's first preference for managing security relationships in East Asia. Senior State Department officials publicly insisted that the US bilateral alliance system was more than adequate to cope with the region's security challenges. Washington had preferred to pursue bilateral security relationships to maximize its power leverage in a region not viewed as vital or culturally similar enough to warrant a multilateral alliance system, and the Bush administration did not wish to try to fix what was not broken.[81] Furthermore, it opposed the idea of extending European-style common security approaches to East Asia in case it gave Moscow any leverage either to seek arms control or to re-establish a military presence in its Far East.[82]

Beyond US objections, there were three areas of divergence among the proposals. First, the proponents of multilateral security institutions differed on the question of membership and the degree of inclusivity. The 1990 proposal for a Conference on Security and Cooperation in Asia by Australian Foreign Minister Gareth Evans envisaged a new Asia-Pacific institution which, as in Europe,

---

[78] See Joffe 1995.
[79] Kupchan 1998, 62–3.
[80] On the CSCE as model for East Asia, see Findlay 1995.
[81] See Hemmer and Katzenstein 2002; Cha 2009/10. For an account that stresses regional wariness of multilateral alliances with the United States, see Acharya 2009a, 41–68.
[82] See Kerr, Mack, and Evans 1995, 236–8.

Table 2.1. Proposals for multilateral security institutions involving East Asia, 1989–93[83]

Proposer	Type of multilateralism	Scope	Institution	Process
United States (1990–2)	'flexible multilateralism'	Conventional threats; focus on some interstate conflicts	No new institutions; maintain bilateral alliances	Ad hoc, intergovernmental
Soviet Union/ Australia (1990)	CSCE model	Comprehensive; focus on CSBMs and arms control	New; Asia-Pacific wide (Conference on Security and Cooperation in Asia)	Government-led, institutionalized
Canada (1990)	'cooperative security'	Comprehensive; focus on non-traditional security threats	New; Northeast Asia only (North Pacific Cooperative Security Dialogue)	Two-track, evolutionary
Japan (1991)	'political dialogue for mutual reassurance'	Focus on CBMs, Japan's role in regional security and USA–Japan alliance	Building on existing institution, ASEAN Post-Ministerial Conference, but excluding socialist states	Intergovernmental, PMC as venue
ASEAN (1991–4)	'extended security dialogue', 'cooperative security'	Focus on CBMs among great powers, and between great powers and others	Using existing institution, ASEAN PMC to launch new security forum including other dialogue partners (ASEAN Regional Forum)	Intergovernmental, two-track, 'ASEAN style'

would bring together old adversaries in cooperation to address and resolve security issues.[84] The Australian proposal echoed Soviet leader Mikhail Gorbachev's various suggestions between 1986 and 1988 for a 'Pacific Ocean conference [like] the Helsinki conference' that would include all countries with a stake in regional peace and security.[85] The 1990 Canadian proposal, in contrast, bore a specific focus on the 'North Pacific', with dialogue involving only Canada, the United States, the Soviet Union, China, Japan, and the two Koreas.[86] Tokyo, on the other hand, shared firmly Washington's reluctance to include Moscow. Because of the concern that a CSCE-type process would necessitate addressing post-Second World War territorial disputes, Foreign Minister Nakayama Taro's 1991 proposal to ASEAN for a region-wide security dialogue left out all

---

[83] Adapted from Dewitt 1994, 2. I make a distinction between and provide more details of Japan's and ASEAN's proposals.
[84] See e.g. Evans 1990a, 1990b.
[85] See Menon 1989.
[86] Dewitt and Evans 1991.

the socialist countries in the region.[87] ASEAN, like Australia, preferred inclusive multilateralism: in the earliest versions, it was envisaged that ASEAN foreign ministers would hold an annual meeting with dialogue partners China, Russia, North Korea, Vietnam as well as other states with an interest in regional security.[88] When they eventually captured the institution-creation process that led in 1994 to the ASEAN Regional Forum (ARF), the Southeast Asians prevailed in their expansive definition of membership: they included China and Russia, and invited India in 1995 and Myanmar in 1996 against US objections.[89]

The second area of divergence related to the type of institutional process entailed in the new regional security institution: should it emulate the CSCE model, or adopt the more gradualist Canadian 'cooperative security' approach, or the even looser 'security dialogues' mooted by ASEAN and Japan? The various proposals derived from and agreed with the basic CSCE notion of seeking 'security with' partner states within a regional framework, rather than deterrence or balance of power-based strategies for 'security against' enemies. But the proposals differed on the need for a regular institutionalized interaction and legally binding agreements reflecting the CSCE assumption that it was possible to secure compliance with 'principles, rules and norms that permit nations to be restrained in their behaviour in the belief that others will reciprocate'.[90] Canadian ideas of 'cooperative security' stressed instead the development of a multilateral 'habit of dialogue', discussion, cooperation, and compromise in an evolutionary, pragmatic, informal, consultative, and consensual manner.[91] This came closer to the East Asian preference for looser and more consultative mechanisms to promote dialogue on broader regional security issues. Japan and the ASEAN states were reluctant to concede the relevance of the CSCE model in a region which did not share the rigid bipolar alliance system in Europe, but instead harboured numerous territorial conflicts, hosted critical alliances with the United States, and shared an aversion to formal and binding processes.[92] The Australians and Canadians reworked their proposals to take into account these sensitivities, moving towards the notion of security dialogues and 'softer' institutions and abandoning the CSCE reference.[93] As in APEC, ASEAN managed to prevail in insisting on an 'ASEAN style' of non-intrusive, non-legalistic, voluntary compliance process

---

[87] Soeya 1994.
[88] ASEAN-ISIS 1991.
[89] Ba 2009, 181–2.
[90] Dewitt 1994, 5; Acharya 2009a, 116, fn. 22.
[91] Wiseman 1992, 44; Dewitt 1994. An indication of how far apart US scholars and policy-makers were from their Asia-Pacific counterparts is the formers' totally different use of the term 'cooperative security' during this period—e.g. see Carter, Perry, and Steinbruner 1992, which referred rather to military cooperation to meet post-Cold War threats.
[92] For details of these objections, see Acharya 2001, 170; Acharya 2009a, 115–17.
[93] See Kerr, Mack, and Evans 1995, 239. Ba 2009, 175 notes, though, that the ASEAN states' continual rejection of Australian and Canadian proposals which had been modified to take into

for the ARF.[94] Further, they insisted that the ARF was not 'a multilateral security institution but a forum where Asia-Pacific countries can talk with one another so as to better understand each other's security concerns'.[95] This cautious and incremental approach to developing institutional processes was easy to adopt once the other countries had agreed to ASEAN's initiative of building upon the annual meeting between ASEAN foreign ministers and their counterparts from selected dialogue partner countries, called the ASEAN Post-Ministerial Conference (PMC).[96] The ASEAN PMC provided the model as well as the initial vehicle for deciding on an expanded version of these multilateral security dialogues.

The final and crucial source of disagreement centred on the scope of the new regional security institutions. Importing directly from the CSCE model would have meant a focus on broadening the scope of security issues to include not only military but also economic, social, and environmental questions; this was not in itself a problem for East Asian states already working with concepts of 'comprehensive security'.[97] However, the CSCE focus on disarmament and arms control in managing the superpower nuclear contest could not easily be transposed onto the Asia-Pacific, and the Asian states were also nervous about the Canadian proposal that focused specifically on non-traditional security issues including human rights, environment, and democracy.[98] This left the confidence- and security-building measures from the CSCE model as the remaining relevant process that the East Asian security institution might adopt.[99] Indeed, 'confidence-building measures' (CBMs) became the core focus of security cooperation within the ARF, as the first of three stages on the forum's agenda, preceding the development of preventive diplomacy and conflict resolution mechanisms in subsequent stages.[100] In the ARF process, CBMs were understood as creating trust and confidence through regular senior level consultations, exchanges among regional military establishments, and increasing transparency among members; for instance, the voluntary exchange of defence White Papers and the setting up of a regional arms register.[101]

---

account their concerns, and of Japanese proposals to build on ASEAN's own existing frameworks suggested that 'the primary problem...may have been...that...they came from outside ASEAN'.

[94] See Acharya 1997a.

[95] The Singaporean defence minister, quoted in *Jane's Defence Weekly*, 19 February 1994, 52.

[96] These had been taking place since the 1970s, and by 1990 included the United States, Australia, New Zealand, Canada, the EU, and Japan.

[97] Dewitt 1994, 2–4.

[98] See Satoh 1993, 5.

[99] On problems associated with applying European-style confidence- and security-building measures (CSBMs) to the Asia-Pacific, see Findlay 1989. A survey of contemporary regional attitudes towards CSBMs can also be found in Findlay 1990.

[100] ASEAN 1995.

[101] For contemporaneous assessments of the achievements and limitations of these CBMs, see Acharya 1997b; Simon 1998.

The Struggle for Order

Yet ARF CBMs also bear the hallmarks of a more explicitly great power political orientation, because of ASEAN's particular motivation for fostering the forum as a venue for the regional great powers to engage in regular multilateral dialogue. The Southeast Asian states have had fewer hang-ups about admitting the special role played by great powers: a fairly typical observation is that of the Singaporean Foreign Minister, who remarked at the 1993 ASEAN PMC that peace and stability in the region 'depend not only on whether the United States continues to lead... [They] also [depend] on how America settles her relationships with other major powers—Russia, China and Japan'.[102] From this point, the logic of the institutional bargain then runs along three parallel tracks. On the one hand, the ARF would reinforce ASEAN's (and Japan's) imperative of security binding the United States beyond the Cold War. First, it would help to lend legitimacy to the US role in regional security and justify its forward presence. Looking back upon the forum's achievements, one Southeast Asian leader observed in 2001 that through the ARF, ASEAN had 'changed the political context of U.S. engagement' because these countries had 'exercised their sovereign prerogative to invite the U.S. to join them in discussing the affairs of Southeast Asia'. As a result, 'no one can argue that the US presence in Southeast Asia is illegitimate or an intrusion into the region'.[103] This US security guarantee then acts as the touchstone upon which Japanese security moderation and Chinese socialization as a status quo great power would be achieved. The ARF would, by engaging the United States and the other great powers in dialogue and confidence building, help to regulate stable expectations among them, and thus perpetuate what is often referred to as the 'balance of power', but which in reality is the perceived stabilizing force of US preponderance.[104]

The second track of the ARF bargain was to develop self- and mutual constraint among regional great powers. ASEAN peddles the constructivist conviction that institutional membership would, over the medium term, create expectations and obligations on the part of the great powers, and over time, socialize them into embracing the principles and norms of the institution, such as those of sovereignty, non-interference, the non-use of force, and security cooperation.[105] As an omni-enmeshing forum, the ARF would

---

[102] Quoted in Emmers 2003, 116.

[103] Singaporean Prime Minister Goh Chok Tong, keynote address to the United States–ASEAN Business Council annual dinner, Washington DC, reprinted in *The Straits Times*, 15 June 2001.

[104] For the power-balancing motivations behind the ARF, see Emmers 2003, 115–16; Leifer 1996, 19. For an account of how this realist balancing logic interacts with the institutionalist enmeshment logic, see Goh 2007/8.

[105] Principles encapsulated in ASEAN's Treaty of Amity and Cooperation, which was endorsed by the ARF at its inaugural meeting in 1994. For constructivist accounts, see Acharya 2001; Johnston 2003; Busse 1999.

promote the mutual constraint of all the participating regional great powers, which agree to be bound by the same norms. This logic became more prominent in ASEAN thinking from 1993 onwards—when the Clinton administration seemed more supportive of a regional security institution, but China had made its worrying claims to the South China Sea. ASEAN's focus turned then to managing China's rise and 'the ARF was perceived...as a tool to encourage China to act with good international citizenship in mind...to be constrained through its participation in an embryonic security regime and respect for its norms and principles'.[106] For example, by endorsing the Treaty of Amity and Cooperation (TAC) principles, China would be socially and morally bound to some degree to pursuing a peaceful settlement of the South China Sea territorial disputes. This 'political engagement' of China was an attempt at its 'institutional entrapment' into the social fabric of regional society while it was still relatively weak and time seemed to be on ASEAN's side; by giving it a stake in regional stability, it might be socialized into a 'responsible regional power'.[107] This stood in contrast to the practice, when applying 'engagement' or 'enmeshment' to the United States, of stressing the security binding of the United States by retaining its military commitments in the region.

The third track of the ARF bargain was the mediating role of the 'middle powers'. Given the more limited power resources of smaller states and their preference for institutional constraints on unequal power, it was no surprise that the East Asian middle powers floated so many ideas for a regional security institution at the end of the Cold War. ASEAN managed to capture the new security institution-building process because of a combination of its pre-existing mechanisms for multilateral security consultations, and the acquiescence of the other key states. ASEAN leadership of the renegotiation of the regional security institutional bargain was established when the early alternative proposals ended up being channelled through ASEAN and debated and revised within its fora. This made for a different negotiation process than that for the economic institutions; one with more interactions and deep-seated problems of reconciliation with the indigenous subregional association's established norms.[108] ASEAN's concerns about its own centrality were key; given the activism of Australia especially, it risked being bypassed if did not take the initiative.[109] ASEAN gave up its long-held opposition to extra-regional multilateral military–security cooperation, but

---

[106] Emmers 2003, 117.
[107] Deng 1998, 35; Wanandi 1996, 121.
[108] Ba's account (2009, 171–92) is especially useful in highlighting the radical departures ASEAN had to make away from its original, hard-won norms against intra-regional military or security consultations (the principle of non-interference), and against extra-regional multilateral security relations.
[109] Ba 2009, 175.

in return, it insisted on maintaining leadership and using its own political priorities and diplomatic process to shape the institutional bargain. Informality implied equality and prevented agenda hogging by the Western states; inclusivity encouraged dialogue and forestalled balance of power politics among the great powers; while 'middle power' leadership further limited the 'power' agenda and facilitated dialogue amongst mutually mistrustful great powers.[110] Thus the establishment of the ARF in 1994 represented the triumph of 'ASEAN-style' institutionalism in East Asia. This institutional bargain also cemented the notion of smaller states as acceptable 'lowest common denominator' mediators in a regional security complex with mistrustful and distrusted indigenous great powers. Such 'counter-realpolitik' logic, though, applied in what was still regarded as a supplementary institutional bargain to the basic security guarantee bargain offered by the only benign external great power.[111] Hence, as one ASEAN foreign minister put it, the ARF 'is an important vehicle to supplement our bilateral relations with the major powers'.[112]

For Washington and Tokyo too, the ARF bargain was ultimately palatable and desirable respectively because it was clearly viewed as a supplement. By 1992, the Bush administration retracted its objection to the proposals for a multilateral security institution because it was useful as part of reassurance strategy accompanying its planned military reductions in the region.[113] The Clinton administration, with its pro-multilateralism rhetoric and decision to limit US troop withdrawals, saw the emerging regional security dialogue as 'a way to *supplement* our alliances and forward military presence, not to supplant them',[114] 'to surround the hard core of our security alliances with a softer exterior of dialogues and consultations'.[115] As for Japan, Nakayama's original emphasis in 1990 had anyway been to develop a multilateral forum that would first and foremost help ensure a continued US presence in the region. It would also support the United States–Japan alliance by providing a forum to discuss Asian fears about Japanese security strategy and to allow Japan to reassure its neighbours about its expanded burden sharing within the alliance.[116] This emphasis on 'reassurance' reflected an interest in using the evolving multilateral institutional bargain to legitimize Washington's incumbent unequal power under different circumstances, and to offer justifications for Tokyo's growing role in the regional order within the constraints of the US alliance.

China's willingness to participate in the ARF was crucial, given the institution's other main aim of socializing the rising power. Beijing's initial

---

[110] Almonte 1997/8.
[111] Johnston 2003, 123.
[112] Singapore Foreign Minister S. Jayakumar, 8 October 1999, quoted in Emmers 2003, 123.
[113] It was a reactive, low-cost, low-stakes American policy towards the ARF—Goh 2004.
[114] Clinton 1993.
[115] Joseph Nye, 1995, quoted in Tow 2001, 189.
[116] Midford 2000; Soeya 1994.

defensive response centred on concerns about the potential constraints to its sovereignty posed by the possibility of other states 'ganging up' within the institution to limit its power, or Western states using the institution to interfere in its domestic affairs. It was particularly insistent that the territorial disputes in the South China Sea should not be a subject for discussion. In spite of its reservations, Beijing signed up to avoid regional isolation.[117] Very quickly, however, Chinese officials began to appreciate the value of participating in the ARF for gradually demonstrating to their neighbours their status quo and cooperative intentions, and for countering the 'China threat' perception. But Beijing also used the forum and its CBM processes to question the utility of US alliances in the post-Cold War environment, and to promote its own alternative vision of multipolarity as the best guarantee of regional stability. China introduced its 'new security concept' that strongly reinforced the paradigm of cooperative security in the ARF, and lobbied for membership for other regional powers such as India.[118] These moves indicated that Beijing seemed primarily to value the multilateral security approach 'for its possible contribution to the weakening of US ties with its Asian allies',[119] and thus tried to steer the evolving institutional bargain more towards challenging, diluting, and constraining US power in the region.[120]

The formation of the ARF was the beginning of a semi-explicit process of renegotiating the great power social compact in post-Cold War East Asia, starting with the institutional bargain. Yet this multilateral security institution was supposed to boost the security binding of the guarantor power, while at the same time facilitating the mutual constraint of regional powers while developing their self-restraint. It was also a mechanism by which smaller regional states could enmesh the great powers deliberately to ensure their own continued autonomy and benefits. This new institutionalized security dialogue was thus made constitutive of the process of order negotiation, rather than simply regulative. It also signalled the beginning of an exploratory process of how to combine the three elements of the necessary institutional bargain.

Post Asian Financial Crisis (1997–2012)

The Asian financial crisis of 1997 was the critical post-Cold War watershed for the region. Perceived Western neglect and derision compounded the systemic economic shock to generate an imperative for self-help, which found expression

---

[117] Swaine and Tellis 2000.
[118] See Emmers 2003, 124–5; Goh and Acharya 2006, 98.
[119] Foot 1998, 435; Ma 2000.
[120] A more accurate interpretation, in my view, than simply reading Beijing's participation in the ARF as a tactical gambit for short-term gains in the South China Sea disputes, e.g. Lim 1998.

The Struggle for Order

in the first exclusively East Asian regional institution. But this turn to an exclusive regional bargain focused the spotlight on the difficulties of intramurally trying to constrain China's growing power and manage the resurfacing Sino-Japanese conflict. At the same time, the terrorist attacks of 11 September 2001 (9/11) and Washington's 'global war on terrorism' both renewed regional worries about shifting US commitments and managing the hegemonic strategic agenda and its potential excesses. The renewed nuclear crisis in North Korea also reinforced the need for sustaining the US security role in the region, even as the impetus grew for the creation of an explicit regional security community.

These conflicting imperatives exacerbated debates about institutional choice, remits—whether they ought to be functional or strategic—and, above all, membership. These were at base disagreements over different types of institutional bargains, rather than simply institutional design. They point to the ongoing renegotiation of the unresolved distributive peace (the distribution of authority and mutual constraint of unequal power), even though it appears on the surface like a debate about the regulative peace (the norms and rules that would sustain regional order).[121] The key aspect of this evolving negotiation is how to *layer* at least two different institutional bargains: an exclusive regional bargain focused on China–Japan and the dynamics of reconciliation and mutual constraint, versus an inclusive open regional bargain focused on US security binding and the dynamics of hegemonic deterrence and mutual constraint between the United States and China.

APT: Asian Crisis, Asian Response

The financial crisis which hit East Asia in 1997 critically dented regional self-confidence, but it also undermined the region's faith in the United States and international financial institutions. The deep disagreement about the causes of the crisis reflected the long-standing dispute over the merits of economic liberalization: the United States, Europe, and international financial institutions saw as the problem the insufficient liberalization of Asian financial markets and lax macroeconomic policies, while Asians generally blamed the unrestrained excesses of the global economy and transnational speculators.[122] East Asian leaders and business elite reacted bitterly to how they saw Washington constraining International Monetary Fund (IMF) and World Bank assistance to the region at the same time as it opposed Japan's proposal of the Asian Monetary Fund as a regional mechanism.[123] The ready

---

[121] This distinction is made usefully with respect to the wider post-Cold War settlement in Clark 2001.
[122] See Noble and Ravenhill 2000; MacIntyre, Pempel, and Ravenhill 2008.
[123] This is discussed in detail in Chapter 4.

American response to the Mexican crisis in 1993–4 and help for Brazil and Russia in their economic troubles in 1998 contrasted with its aloofness from Asia. The sense of betrayal blended with the suspicion that Washington was glad to see rising Asia get its 'comeuppance'.[124] Thus old fears of abandonment by the United States were exacerbated, more viscerally because it struck now at the heart of strategic economic overdependence on the United States and overturned prior assumptions that Washington felt sufficient economic stake in the region to intervene when necessary.

Out of this strong sense of inadequacy grew the 'ASEAN Plus Three' (APT) initiatives for regional economic cooperation, as a supplement to existing international economic and financial structures, to diversify the region's dependencies and to increase its collective bargaining leverage. With the inclusion of the Northeast Asian trio—China, Japan, and South Korea—the APT achieved the exclusive 'East Asian' grouping Mahathir wanted in his EAEG concept. APEC missed the chance of recapturing momentum by its inability to respond to the crisis, which hit the region in the midst of an ugly row in APEC about Early Voluntary Sectoral Liberalization (EVSL) that effectively stalled its central agenda of trade liberalization.[125] Further reflecting the tensions over trade liberalization, APEC's leading members fundamentally disagreed about the causes of the crisis.[126] Thus, the most important post-crisis regional financial arrangements grew outside APEC.[127]

ASEAN foreign ministers had already begun meeting with their Northeast Asian counterparts at the sidelines of the ARF from 1994, and Malaysia proposed in July 1996 to hold an informal leaders' summit with the full ASEAN complement of ten members plus the three Northeast Asian countries. While these interactions were influenced by the continuing economic and political frictions between East Asian states and 'the west'—for instance, in the 'Asian values' debate that peaked around 1996—the APT might not have gained the impetus it did without the exigency of the financial crisis.[128] The APT became gradually institutionalized after 1998 with the decision to make the summit an annual event, the establishment—at Seoul's suggestion—of a 'Vision Group' advisory panel for regional cooperation, and the strong emphasis on functional economic cooperation. APT summits are supplemented by separate meetings of the member states' finance, economic, and foreign ministers, senior officials, and senior economic officials; and the organization

---

[124] Higgott 1998; Milner 2003.
[125] On the ill-fated EVSL, see Krauss 2004.
[126] Nesadurai 2006.
[127] Ravenhill 2000, 329. Indeed, APEC exacerbated the wider tensions between Asian and Western members which could not find common ground, and it became less important to ASEAN especially because 'its politics and content mirror arrangements already in existence (and identified as the problem) at the global level'—Ba 2009, 220.
[128] See Terada 2003.

has developed cooperation and consultation on energy, agriculture, labour, health, tourism, and, most of all, financial issues.[129] The relatively concrete and operational APT agenda is encapsulated in the 2000 Chiang Mai Initiative (CMI), a regional surveillance and financing mechanism involving a regional network of bilateral swap agreements. With pooled resources and a clear policy agenda to enhance regional financial self-help, the APT was an 'embryonic' exclusive East Asian institution.[130]

The implications of these financial cooperation mechanisms for regionalism are analysed in Chapter 4, but from the outset, Tokyo stepped up to the plate and provided resources and financial expertise for combating the financial crisis and for setting up the CMI. Faced with a clear crisis in the relatively uncontroversial financial arena where it held a comparative advantage, Tokyo took the opportunity to exercise leadership in the region. The United States did not oppose the APT—indeed, as one author claims, the grouping 'institutionalised itself only while the United States did not pay particular attention to it'.[131] The Clinton administration was in any case more relaxed about regional institutions, but its failure to get Japan to open its agricultural market using APEC's EVSL process in 1997–8 had also led Washington's attention to focus on the WTO while Japan turned to the APT.[132]

The creation of an exclusive East Asian institution further aided Beijing's hope of diluting US power within the region as well as reassuring its neighbours. China was enthusiastic about the APT and Beijing had already gained appreciation in the region for refraining from depreciating the yuan during the financial crisis. The political momentum for exclusive regionalism notably moved from Japan and South Korea towards China when, in November 2000—while domestic political problems and leadership transitions distracted Tokyo and Seoul—Chinese Premier Zhu Rongji proposed the creation of a China–ASEAN FTA. While the economic viability and value of this trading area might be debated,[133] the political significance of the move lay in it being the first time that ASEAN had been recognized by a great power as one economic unit. In the 2001 Framework Agreement of Comprehensive Economic Cooperation, the two sides agreed to implement the FTA by 2010, and approved an 'Early Harvest programme' that immediately liberalized some sectors.

---

[129] Apart from annual summits, the APT process includes fifty-five other official bodies—fourteen ministerial and nineteen senior officials groups, two meetings of Directors-General, eighteen technical-level meetings, and two 'Track II' meetings—see ASEAN Secretariat 2009.
[130] Stubbs 2002, 442.
[131] Tanaka 2006, 69.
[132] See Ravenhill 2007a.
[133] For example, see 'ASEAN jittery about trade pact with China', *Straits Times*, 17 February 2010; Jiang 2010a.

The creation of the APT legitimized the pursuit of exclusionary institutions and expressed a consensus on 'East Asia' as a regional community. Within this climate, China's demonstrations of self-restraint in pursuing multilateral frameworks and in limiting its own interests especially in interactions with its small Southeast Asian neighbours gained in effectiveness. China's increasing use of multilateralism—and from our point of view, its pursuit of institutional engagement with the prospect of shaping the evolving institutional bargain—is sometimes inadequately portrayed as part of a strategy 'to balance against' the United States and Japan. Yet Beijing's thinking is more complex and has important implications for the evolving institutional bargain. China's key goals in its strategy of 'shaping neighbouring areas' [*suzao zhoubian*] through regional institutional activism are to avoid isolation, and to forestall containment or counterbalancing alliances. In an international order that Beijing strongly perceives as constituted by one superpower with many great powers [*yichao duoqiang*], it aims to prevent the superpower from being able to recruit containing partners from the great power ranks, and to prevent two or more peers among the great powers from trying to balance China. Beijing uses strong reassurance mechanisms and economic ties to persuade others that 'Cold War-style containment of China simply could not occur in this era of interdependence.'[134] In a defensive sense, Beijing thus uses the region as a 'shield from pressure exerted by other great powers'.[135] Instead of focusing on constraining US power directly, China aims to reshape the incentive structure and perceptions of its neighbours so that *they* would not agree to become complicit in a putative overt attempt by the United States to constrain China. This mode of thinking obviously ties in with China's traditional encirclement fears, but there is also strong recognition that the hegemon will need the support of other Asian states to justify and effect a policy of containment, and it is by turning off that air supply pre-emptively that China has the best defence or hedge.[136]

9/11: Global Crisis, Hegemonic Response

Beijing had reason to be concerned about US intentions, with the bombing of the Chinese embassy in Belgrade during the Kosovo campaign in 1999 and the EP-3 incident following the inauguration of George W. Bush in the spring of 2001, but Washington's entire strategic focus shifted resolutely

---

[134] Foot 2006, 88.
[135] Zhang and Tang 2005, 50–1.
[136] This deliberate shift of attention to other states is sometimes highlighted by Chinese scholars making the point that as long as they do not regard China as a danger, China's Asian neighbours may indeed take on greater importance in Beijing's policy attention than the United States—see Zhang and Tang 2005, 57.

after the 9/11 terrorist attacks. The 'global war on terrorism' had two major impacts on the developing institutional bargain in East Asia: it helped to level the negotiating field between the United States and East Asian states by creating more reciprocal strategic relations; but it also reinforced US strategic dominance in the region. At the outset, Washington's agenda-setting power was clear within global and regional institutions and relationships. A prime example was the 'APEC Leaders' Statement on Counter-terrorism', the organization's first ever political statement, issued at the October 2001 Summit, and the subsequent adoption and dominance of security issues in the hitherto economic institution's meetings.[137] Within East Asia, the United States has urged a focus on counter-terrorism in ASEAN, the ARF, and its bilateral alliances.

ASEAN has adopted various declarations, enhanced regional cooperation in intelligence sharing and coordinating anti-terrorism laws, and set up a regional anti-terrorism training centre with US funding. The ARF has adopted an agenda for implementing UN anti-terrorist measures including measures to block terrorist financing.[138] But reflecting the continued centrality of the San Francisco system, Washington's new strategic imperative had more profound impacts on its bilateral alliances. In Southeast Asia, US alliances with the Philippines and Thailand were revitalized as both were designated 'major non-NATO ally' status.[139] In Manila, where the decision to terminate the military bases agreement with the United States had been deeply regretted when the Filipinos discovered Chinese construction and naval patrols around the disputed Mischief Reef in the South China Sea in 1995, American combat forces were deployed in 2002 to train and support Filipino troops in fighting against Abu Sayyaf insurgents in Mindanao as part of the 'war on terror'.[140] A Joint Defense Agreement now gives the United States a long-term advisory role in the modernization of the Philippines Armed Forces and the reinvigorated alliance helps to entrench the American security presence in the region.[141] After 2001, Thailand has also facilitated US military reach in the region: US aircraft were allowed to fly combat missions from bases in Thailand during the Afghanistan and Iraq campaigns, and old Vietnam war-era US air and naval bases were reopened to allow the

---

[137] These focus on countering the terrorist threat to economic activities in the region and helped to reinvigorate APEC at a time when its members could not agree on its central trade liberalization agenda—see Ravenhill 2007b.

[138] These measures suffer from implementation problems; see Simon 2007.

[139] This status makes Thailand and the Philippines eligible for priority delivery of defence materiel and the purchase of certain controlled items like depleted-uranium tank rounds. They are allowed to stockpile US military hardware, participate in defence research and development programmes, and benefit from a US government loan-guarantee programme for arms exports.

[140] De Castro 2003; Banlaoi 2002.

[141] This point was not lost on Chinese analysts—see Zhai 2002.

Institutional Bargains: Taming and Legitimizing Unequal Power

United States to pre-position military equipment for forward deployment operations.[142] Recognizing Indonesia's importance as the largest Muslim nation in the region, Washington in 2005 restored military-to-military relations, which had been broken after Indonesian military involvement in the massacre of civilians in East Timor in 1991.[143] Also in 2005, Washington signed with Singapore a new Strategic Framework Agreement, which expanded bilateral cooperation in counter-terrorism, counter-proliferation of weapons of mass destruction, joint military exercises and training, policy dialogues, and defence technology. The Southeast Asian states were opportunistic in responding to Washington's post-9/11 security imperatives. There were indeed clear terrorist threats within the region as shown by the bombings in Bali and Jakarta in 2002–5, and the discovery of terrorist plots in Singapore and Malaysia, and transnational terrorist networks across the region. But these combined with medium-term uncertainties about China's rise, as well as regime security concerns, to turn regional leaders towards the small-state imperative once again of binding the United States more solidly as security guarantor.

The US counter-terrorism imperative wrought even more significant changes for the alliance with Japan and for Japanese 'normalization'. The new Koizumi government reacted quickly to support its American ally by passing the Anti-Terrorism Special Measures Law, which allowed the dispatch, in November 2001, of Japanese Self-Defence Forces (JSDF) to the Indian Ocean to provide logistic support to Coalition forces fighting in Afghanistan. When the Bush administration declared war on Iraq in 2003, the Japanese Diet passed another Law Concerning Special Measures on Humanitarian and Reconstruction Assistance to allow the JSDF to provide logistical support there.[144] Once again, Tokyo's rapid response was based on more broadly conceived needs to security bind its ally. Japan needed to boost the US alliance at a time when the threat from North Korea had escalated, with its Taepodong missile launch over Japan in 1998, Japanese sinking of a Korean spy ship in 2001, and the renewal of the nuclear crisis with Pyongyang's admission of a secret uranium enrichment programme in 2002. Together with the longer-term worries about China's rising power, these concerns have further driven the upgrading of the United States–Japan alliance alongside the strengthening of Japan's independent military capabilities since 2001. The Koizumi government committed to procuring a ballistic missile defence system in 2003, while the JSDF has been acquiring new military capabilities and technology in its own 'revolution in

---

[142] Goh 2005c, 32–4.
[143] See Foot 2004, 46–54.
[144] The Japanese Diet chose to enact these special legislative provisions instead of using the Revised Guidelines for the alliance partly to set limits on Japanese military involvement in US campaigns and to avoid future entrapment—for details, see Hughes 2004b, 126–37.

military affairs'.[145] Meanwhile, the 2004–6 United States–Japan Defence Policy Review Initiative identified common security objectives including the peaceful resolution of the Taiwan issue, and provided for the strengthening of US power projection from its bases in Japan and military interoperability between the allied forces. Since 2001, Japan has 'locked itself into' the US alliance even more firmly as it moves towards a 'global alliance'.[146]

US allies and security partners in East Asia, then, leapt at the opportunity presented by Washington's global war on terrorism (GWOT) to reinforce their security binding of the United States. They acted from regional threat perceptions and opportunistic regime boosting, but also from heightened concerns about potential hegemonic distraction and abandonment as the Bush administration's focus turned to the Middle East. Such thinking was based on a fundamental consensus on the security guarantee bargain that underpinned regional security.[147] At the same time, however, two considerations pulled in the opposite direction to fuel the urgency of constraining US hegemonic influence. First, the war on Iraq exacerbated the growing sense that US power had to be more actively tamed, not just channelled. East Asian states shared widespread international concerns about the Bush administration's willingness to flout key international norms in waging an illegitimate war, and the governments of countries with significant Muslim populations were increasingly wary of managing the domestic fallouts of such opposition. The Bush administration's penchant for 'ad hoc multilateralism' further fuelled worries that global and regional security institutions would be undermined.[148] China shared the growing desire to constrain the excesses of US power, especially since American deployments and bases in Southeast, South, and Central Asia as a result of GWOT now seemed to further China's encirclement.[149] These concerns reinforced the regional imperative to construct multilateral institutions that would supplement the security guarantee bargain with the United States.

Second, East Asian states saw a golden opportunity to seek a more reciprocal bargain with Washington, given the latter's urgent security imperatives. For the first time since the Cold War, the United States 'needs us more than we need them', and East Asian states in favour of 'open regionalism' worked to exchange their support for US counter-terrorism for vital improvements in economic access and political support for institutionalizing great power constraints, not just clearer security commitments from Washington. During the second Bush administration and onwards, the calls for Washington to pay more attention to the needs of the region in terms of economic recovery

---

[145] See Hughes 2009a; Samuels 2007/8.
[146] Hughes 2004b, 139; Cha 2007.
[147] See Chapter 3.
[148] Cossa 2009.
[149] E.g. Tang, Liu, and Chen 2003.

and long-term non-military strategic support grew.[150] The Bush and Obama administrations have reciprocated in this post-9/11 bargain. Notably, Washington has employed trade agreements and economic cooperation to signal its strategic commitment to the region. For their part, key East Asian states value these agreements as a means to diversify their potential overdependence on the Chinese economy.[151] For instance, the Bush administration launched the Enterprise for ASEAN Initiative to prepare Southeast Asian countries for negotiating bilateral FTAs, signed the first FTA with Singapore in 2004, and established a formal dialogue on trade and investment with ASEAN as a whole in the 2006 Trade and Investment Framework Agreement. Of greater economic significance is the United States–South Korea FTA, which came into effect in 2012. US recognition of the political symbolism of trade agreements culminated in the Trans-Pacific Partnership Agreement launched by US Trade Representative Susan Schwab in 2008, incorporating select APEC countries in a 'high quality, 21st century agreement'.[152] The other part of Washington's reciprocation for East Asian support of its counter-terrorism agenda was its support for the negotiation of a new institutional bargain for constraining regional power. American willingness to participate in regional negotiations now facilitates a fierce struggle over the nature of the associated institutional bargain.

'East Asian Community'? Sino-Japanese Mutual Constraints

While 'the greatest challenge in developing institutions is to strike a balance between US indifference and US dominance',[153] the same logic does not apply to the two regional great powers, China and Japan. While the dilemma of how to constrain their excesses of power is a constant preoccupation, isolation or abandonment is not a realistic option. Indeed, because of their indigenous status, China, Japan, and their bilateral relationship have come increasingly to be viewed as the key determinants of regional economic order, with the United States necessary only insofar as it provides a basic counterweight to Beijing's and Tokyo's strategic rivalry and potential ambitions.[154] This view is short-sighted, but it does highlight the growing

---

[150] See e.g. Goh 2005d.

[151] As one veteran Singapore leader counselled, 'There is still time for the U.S. to counter China's attraction by instituting a free-trade agreement with other countries in the region. This would prevent these countries from having an excessive dependence on China's market' (Lee 2010).

[152] Currently nine countries are TPP members: Australia, Brunei, Chile, Malaysia, New Zealand, Peru, Singapore, the United States, and Vietnam. Japan, Canada, and Mexico announced their desire to join in 2011. On the limitations to a significant agreement to ease trade restrictions for goods, see Elms 2012.

[153] Acharya 2009b, 181.

[154] See e.g. Funabashi 1996/7.

The Struggle for Order

salience of regionalist visions of the institutional bargain, as well as Chinese and Japanese activism in negotiating the new regional compact.

Regardless of its cumbersome name, APT members were well aware of the political significance and potential of this exclusive new grouping. By 2001, the East Asia Vision Group's report had articulated the aspiration of an 'East Asian community' (EAC) based on cooperation in all areas, including the medium-term aims of creating an East Asian Free Trade Area (EAFTA), regional facilities for financial cooperation, and establishing an 'East Asian summit'. Apart from integration and free trade, the group's 2002 report asserted the 'necessity and inevitability' of 'East Asia'.[155] In subsequent years, the EAC idea proved difficult to shake off—Japanese and Chinese leaders revived it in top-level proposals in 2002, 2004, and 2010, while ASEAN pursued its own tripartite economic, security, and sociocultural community-building project from 2003. The most concrete elements of negotiating this regional 'community' are explored in Chapter 4; but this increasingly explicit search for an East Asian society of states carried conflicting implications for the developing institutional bargain in terms of leadership and the mutual constraint of regional great powers.

Since 2000, Beijing had put its considerable diplomatic muscle behind the notion of creating a Sino-ASEAN FTA, but in the next few years it sent important signals that it was ready to undertake political agreements that would create voluntary restraints on its power through enmeshment in wider regional institutional structures. Adding to the 2002 Declaration on Conduct on the South China Sea disputes, in 2003 China became the first non-member state to accede formally to ASEAN's TAC,[156] thus binding itself to the norms of non-interference and non-use of force in settling conflicts. In the same year, the two sides signed the Joint Declaration on Strategic Partnership for Peace and Prosperity, addressing a wide variety of economic, political, social, and security issues. In 2004, Prime Minister Wen Jiabao explicitly linked the prospective EAC to expanded China–ASEAN cooperation, beginning with an EAFTA and the discussion of political and security issues.[157] Thus the Chinese vision of a regional community reinforced an exclusive East Asia, starting with a Sino-ASEAN-centred bargain concentrating on the great power reassurance of smaller states along the vertical axis. It remained silent on the horizontal axis of China's bargain with regional powers, particularly Japan, and the United States.

---

[155] ASEAN 2002; Tanaka 2006, 65–6.

[156] Drawn from the UN Charter and relatively innocuous, TAC norms include mutual sovereignty, territorial integrity, non-interference in domestic affairs, peaceful settlement of disputes, and the renunciation of the use of force.

[157] Shambaugh 2004/5, 75–6.

Institutional Bargains: Taming and Legitimizing Unequal Power

By comparison, the Japanese vision addressed the horizontal great power-to-great power axis, but only partially. In 2003, Japanese Foreign Ministry officials concerned about the growing momentum of the EAC idea counter-proposed a reciprocal bargain with the region: (a) Japan would support the ultimate goal of creating an EAC 'on condition that the rest of Asia accept the United States–Japan alliance as the bedrock of Japanese foreign policy; and (b) democracy, human rights, the rule of law, international law and norms, transparency, good governance, and other "universal values" would... [form] the basis for regional cooperation... as goals for evolutionary development'.[158] Thus, Japanese preferences for the EAC reiterated the more externally oriented 'Asia-Pacific' version of the bargain, starting with safeguarding Japan's particular strategic reliance on the United States. Furthermore, successful Japanese lobbying to include in the EAS Australia and India[159]—erstwhile US ally and security partner respectively, and fellow democracies—if not the United States itself, reflected what Noble calls the policy of 'watchful waiting to insure that any fledgling efforts at community-building... [in East Asia]... remain compatible with the United States–Japan alliance and with Japanese defined values and policy frameworks'.[160]

The East Asian Summit (EAS) that convened in December 2005 encompassed both visions and so was an odd creature. First, instead of a more formalized security-oriented summit of the APT members, the EAS consisted of APT, plus Australia, New Zealand, and India. As Breslin observed, the EAS thus abrogated the post-APT consensus on an exclusive East Asia by asserting what was in effect an 'anti-region'.[161] To accommodate Japanese concerns, and against Chinese preferences, all the EAS statements have stressed that the dialogue is 'complementary' to and does not challenge other existing security arrangements in the region, and the EAS meetings have been confined to discussions mainly about environmental, energy, and development issues.[162] Second, in spite of the renaming, ASEAN retained the director's chair:[163] ASEAN sets the EAS agenda and schedule, and established the criteria of membership—accession to TAC, formal recognition as an ASEAN 'dialogue partner', established record of substantive cooperation with ASEAN, and unanimous acceptance by ASEAN members.

---

[158] Noble 2008, 260.
[159] Koizumi fired the first figurative cannon in the great battle of East Asian membership when he conspicuously included Australia and New Zealand in discussing such a community—see Koizumi 2002.
[160] Noble 2008, 261. On Japanese lobbying of Australia, see Terada 2010.
[161] Breslin 2007.
[162] See chairman's statement of the First East Asia Summit, Kuala Lumpur, 14 December 2005, available at <http://www.asean.org/news/item/chairman-s-statement-of-the-first-east-asia-summit-kuala-lumpur-14-december-2005-2>. Accessed 30 November 2012.
[163] I deliberately eschew the more common term, 'driver's seat', as it is not yet clear whether the EAS vehicle is indeed being driven anywhere.

Even more than in the Asia-Pacific institutions, ASEAN's de facto leadership role was critical because of Sino-Japanese conflict and competition. The (limited) inclusivity of the EAS resulted from fears of China's potential dominance within the institution, particularly on the part of Indonesia and Singapore. Singapore wished not to exclude the United States, while Indonesia was reasserting its leadership role in Southeast Asia and did not want to be subordinated to China.[164] After a failed attempt to sideline the three additional members by suggesting a two-tiered, APT-centred structure, Beijing acquiesced to this expanded EAS. Apparently prioritizing the momentum of regional integration and confidence building, China compromised on this 'open regionalism' exercise.[165] Chinese acceptance of open as opposed to closed regionalism was also related to the pragmatic recognition that it could not realistically exclude US interests from the region, and that the principle of open regionalism might help to ensure that China itself could not be excluded from greater involvement in other regions.[166]

Since the inauguration of the EAS, however, the battle lines have been drawn between Japan and China. In what looks to be competitive institutionalism or 'institution-racing',[167] Japan has tried to check Chinese influence by pushing for inclusivity and open regionalism, functional cooperation, values of human rights, democracy, and conformity with global regimes.[168] Crucially, Tokyo launched a number of alternative economic initiatives intended to consolidate the EAS and 'drive a wedge' into the APT framework favoured by China.[169] In 2007, it proposed a Comprehensive Economic Partnership Agreement in East Asia (CEPEA) as an FTA to be pursued within the EAS. In 2008, Tokyo launched a Japan–ASEAN Comprehensive Economic Partnership Agreement involving free trade, investment, services, and other economic cooperation, and sold as 'the real thing' a full package of long-term, legally binding developmental benefits (as opposed to the partial packages that China offered). Japan's Ministry of Economy, Trade and Industry (METI) also proposed and funded an Economic Research Institute for ASEAN and East Asia, as a regional equivalent of the Organisation for Economic Co-operation and Development (OECD), to undertake policy research for regional economic integration, inaugurated in Jakarta in 2008. As Hughes

---

[164] Drysdale 2005, 5.
[165] See Qin and Wei 2008, 135–6.
[166] Su 2006.
[167] Goh and Acharya 2007, 7.
[168] See the Ministry of Foreign Affairs (MOFA) outline policy statement on the EAS, November 2005, at <http://www.mofa.go.jp/region/asia-paci/eas/outline.html>. Accessed 1 December 2012.
[169] On how METI and MOFA without coordination pursued similar strategies in response to the fear that China was beginning to dominate regional institutions, see Terada 2010.

rightly observes, Japan is trying to constrain Chinese power using institutions in novel ways:

> ...for Japan, regional frameworks have increasingly assumed the character of arenas for *channelling*, and if necessary *curbing*, the rising power of China. Japan has promoted its preferred format of the EAS to *counter* China's preference for the APT, to *dilute* that rising power and to *check* its perceived pretensions for regional leadership. Japan has similarly used regional EPAs and CEPs [Comprehensive Economic Partnerships] to *deflect* China's influence, and seems bent on *deliberately 'over-supplying' regionalism* so as to *diffuse* China's ability to concentrate its power in any one forum.[170]

China opposed Japan's plethora of regional economic initiatives, and Beijing 'steadfastly insists on relying on the [APT] as the main framework for regional economic cooperation, supports ASEAN's leadership role, and maintains a gradualist approach to East Asian multilateralism'.[171] Beijing had committed funds to the ASEAN secretariat for advancing the APT framework in 2004. Chinese officials are adamant that the EAS is too amorphous and ambitious and cannot replace the APT. Indeed, they managed to secure a chairman's statement to that effect at the inaugural EAS in 2005, which acknowledged that the APT was the main vehicle for achieving the vision of a regional community.[172] Chinese policy advisers now evince 'profound scepticism' about the prospects for a regional community in view of the 'apparently unnecessary geographical expansion of the region'; the continued regional dependence on US security ties and deference to US sensitivities; and Japan's 'oscillation' between boosting the US alliance and pushing for a leading role in regional integration.[173] Chinese analysts fully recognize Tokyo's attempts to 'contain' China's regional influence, and have warned over the last decade that Japan's misplaced priority on strengthening the US regional role is a key impediment to developing an East Asian community.[174]

In this regard, US policy changes in 2010 exacerbated the Sino-Japanese divide: the Obama administration signed up to ASEAN's TAC, facilitating its decision to join the EAS, while asserting US interest in maritime conflicts in the South and East China Seas.[175] Chinese analysts have read 'America's return to Asia' seriously and extrapolated it to expect US assertiveness in blocking East Asian regionalism and retrieving regional leadership for itself.[176] This has increased Chinese pressure on Japan to choose between 'an unequal, hegemonic/America-centred

---

[170] Hughes 2009b, 855 (emphases mine).
[171] Li 2009, 10.
[172] See article 10 in the 2005 EAS chairman's statement; Liu 2010.
[173] Li 2009, 3, 7.
[174] See e.g. Qin 2008.
[175] See Chapter 3.
[176] Song 2011; Song 2010.

The Struggle for Order

regional environment' and a 'commonly pursued East Asia community' that will allow China and Japan to 'build balanced and equal-footing-based relations with the U.S.'[177] One gauge of Japan's choice will be Tokyo's deliberations about whether to participate in the Trans-Pacific Partnership (TPP) talks, widely seen as a US-instigated alternative to an East Asian FTA.

Yet, in terms of the putative institutional bargain, both China's and Japan's initiatives on regionalism and institutions are relatively thin, primarily because they do not address the horizontal axis of great power-to-great power mutual constraints and understanding centred on a Sino-Japanese settlement. How are Chinese and Japanese power to be constrained, specifically vis-à-vis each other? What mutual assurances can the two countries offer, and what rights and duties can they expect towards each other? Within the evolving proposals, counterproposals, and political posturing, neither side is seeking to clarify any such bargain. Instead, they are offering stark alternatives of regionalism, and striving for symbolic leadership in the evolving regional mechanisms. Japan's notion of inclusive regionalism skirts the issue of mutual constraints and is aimed more at the pre-emption, deflection, or dilution of Chinese influence in the region, while ensuring US security binding. China is beginning to create institutional self-binding, but exclusively vis-à-vis its smaller neighbours in East Asia, while remaining opaque on how these agreements impact on its potential restraint vis-à-vis the other great powers.

For its part, the United States' role in negotiating the regional institutional bargain has been somewhat limited and reactive. Socialized during the Cold War into a hierarchical mode of interacting with East Asian partners within unequal alliances, Washington has been consistently unwilling to have its strategic options constrained by new regional norms. Until 2010, this allergy extended even to the minimalist norms encapsulated in ASEAN's TAC. The incipient East Asian multilateral security institutions are largely regarded as 'low-cost supplementary boosters' to US military strategy in the region, while the economic institutions are means to perpetuate an open economic system and to 'hold the line against potential Chinese efforts to close off the region'.[178] Clearly, as noted in Hurrell's observations at the beginning of this chapter and explored in the rest of this volume, US policy-makers find recourse to the other instruments of statecraft at their disposal. In terms of developing the institutional bargain in East Asia, the concessions that Washington has offered so far come mainly in terms of diplomatic attention and bureaucratic commitment to complex economic negotiations and processes. While these commitments are costly and symbolic coming from a superpower, the greatest importance of US

---

[177] Pang 2011, 61.
[178] Author interview with former Bush administration State Department official, January 2011.

participation in negotiating the institutional bargain comes in fact for its allies and partners in the region. American participation and signalling that it is willing to be constrained along with other regional powers help these partners to legitimize their continued dependence on greater US preponderance even after the Cold War, and their use of it to deter aggression and to countervail Chinese influence.

Ikenberry has drawn the United States–Japan and France–Germany post-Second World War parallel, arguing that their alliances formed the linchpins of regional reintegration. In the post-Cold War period, he further suggests that China should behave like post-unification Germany seeking enmeshment within European institutions.[179] Unfortunately, East Asia lacks the type of mature institutions that Western Europe has, with a distributive bargain at its heart. As will be explored in Chapters 3 and 5, because the United States interposed itself in Japan's place after the war, the necessary reconciliation has not yet occurred between the core regional powers, unlike in the case of France and Germany. Between China and Japan, there is no distributive settlement: the distribution of authority and mutual constraint of unequal power are unresolved, indeed unaddressed, between them. While the spotlight shines on the question of including or excluding the United States, the underlying driving force increasingly derives from China and Japan each trying to preclude options that may aggrandize the other. Regional observers are merely skirting around this fundamental problem when they lament China's unwillingness and Japan's inability to lead regional community building, or when they assert the imperative for China and Japan cooperatively to push forward regionalism beginning with a Northeast Asian FTA.[180]

Meanwhile, Japan, Singapore, and Indonesia's strenuous efforts to reassert an inclusive institutional model for the EAS highlight both the urgent need to address the Sino-Japanese bargain and the tendency to try to avoid precisely doing this by resort to 'diluting' institutions with other members. That the EAS 'solution' was deeply unsatisfactory is indicated by the renewed search for a regional security institution since 2008. The most prominent call was that of Australian Prime Minister Kevin Rudd for an 'Asia-Pacific Community' by 2020 that would encompass all issues, economic, security, and political. Rudd's initial, controversial proposal would have had an Asia-Pacific 'G8', a concert of great and medium powers: United States, China, Japan, Russia, South Korea, Australia, Indonesia, and India.[181] The attempt to shift the focus to the larger states in the region

---

[179] Ikenberry 2008.
[180] These calls are prominent in Chinese scholarship; see Zheng 2007; Liu 2010.
[181] 'Shape of the Future', *The Australian*, 20 December 2008; Woolcott 2009; Koh 2009.

reflects the great power lacuna (and the corresponding absence of an authoritative process of order negotiation) in the ongoing renegotiations of the institutional bargain.[182] Rudd's initiative failed because of ASEAN's opposition to being sidelined.[183] The Association demonstrated its political clout as regional institution builder by 'nesting' the APC idea within the ongoing evolution of its own existing institutional frameworks.[184] In 2010, ASEAN leaders announced plans to expand the EAS to include the United States and Russia—thus incorporating the Australian demand for inclusion of the two missing Asia-Pacific great powers, while retaining ASEAN's control of the agenda.[185] This new grouping first met in 2011, and it would appear that, after fifteen years, the process of renegotiating the regional institutional bargain has come back full circle to seeking the ARF-type of inclusive bargain, but with a more restricted, East Asia-focused membership.[186] There remains a significant degree of middle power activism on the institutions-building front still, and a very strong desire to entrench US security binding in spite of the growing discomfort with how to constrain US power. And yet there is still little recognition of the need explicitly to separate out the two levels of renegotiations needed: the vertical great powers-and-others level, and the great power-to-great power level. A number of occasional tri- and quadrilateral meetings among the great powers may seem to indicate some attention to the great power bargain, but these have yielded few results. For instance, the fledgling trilateral and quadrilateral security dialogues between the United States and its allies in the region are unlikely to develop into formal multilateral institutions because Japan, Australia, and South Korea are deeply unwilling to antagonize China by creating the impression of formal encirclement. On the other hand, the China, Japan, and South Korea trilateral summit meetings held since 1999 have operated mainly as CBMs rather than for the purpose of creating substantive strategic agreement and coordination.[187]

---

[182] See Goh 2009.

[183] Indeed, one veteran scholar of Southeast Asia senses that ASEAN leaders are sending a strong signal that 'the train of regionalism has left the station': ASEAN-led institutions are already firmly in place and cannot be reprogrammed; new ideas must simply adapt to them—Emmerson 2010, 8.

[184] Nair 2010, 30.

[185] The idea centres on an 'ASEAN+8' summit meeting when APEC meets in an Asian country, which will work out at two in every three years. The proposal also includes parallel meetings of the foreign and defence ministers.

[186] The ARF itself has stalled considerably due to members' inability to move beyond the CBM agenda or to have any impact on the management of key regional crises. Now the ARF is either ignored in the discourse about ways forward in regional institutions, or its potential disbandment is openly discussed.

[187] The meetings were held initially at the fringes of the APT, but since 2008 the three states have held independent summit meetings annually in Northeast Asia. In 2005 and 2006, China and South Korea cancelled the meetings to protest Japanese Prime Minister Koizumi's visits to the Yasukuni shrine.

Conclusion

The overgrown and competitive nature of the regional institutional landscape and the apparently vicious debate about inclusivity or exclusivity are manifestations of a confused reckoning with the post-Cold War resurgence of regional great powers as well as the reassertion of strategic dominance by the one remaining superpower. At the heart of the ongoing debates about regionalism and regional community is disagreement about two different models of what the institutional bargain ought to be. Ought it to be an inclusive institutional bargain that builds upon the US-led security order, to incorporate China into a condominium-type bargain of mutual constraint and enmeshment within institutional norms? In this bargain, the crucial dyad is United States–China, with Japan playing a supplementary role in supporting the United States as security guarantor. The norms that regulate this bargain will be liberal ones favoured by Washington, and Japan would be expected to play the role of post-Second World War West Germany to China's France. Or, alternatively, ought the bargain be an exclusive, 'East Asian' one centred on the negotiation and mediation of a new China-centred regional order? This regional community model must contain a core bargain between China and Japan on sharing power, as well as a bargain between China and Japan and the other East Asian states on how the formers' unequal power is to be restrained, under what reciprocal terms.

Which way one leans in this debate depends in large part on one's conception of the necessity for the security binding of the United States. In the inclusive model, the US security guarantee is crucial and so Washington must be bound to its regional commitments in order to prevent potential abandonment and to deter and ensure credible constraints on China. In the exclusive model, in contrast, the main mutual constraints that need to be built are those between Japan and China; the United States hinders and distracts from this task. And yet the foregoing analysis has shown that these two models are not necessarily considered as stark alternatives. Rather, the ebb and flow of the institutional debate over the last two decades have brought the central consideration to how to build in both these bargains together. Thus the regional institutional negotiation is now increasingly about how to *layer* these two bargains. The following chapters analysing negotiations about authority, community, and memory shed further light on which of these bargains has been accorded priority.

In this regard, how the widened EAS process evolves and interacts with the APT will be instructive. With its particular style and agenda, ASEAN may not be able to mediate productively the current process of layering. As Alice Ba has convincingly demonstrated, central to ASEAN's organizing bargain was the attempt to construct an anarchical 'Southeast Asian' society based on reciprocal sovereign equality and autonomy, while relegating hierarchical relations such as alliances and security guarantees to the 'extra-regional' or 'ad hoc' realm.[188] Yet, after the Cold War and especially with the legitimization of 'East Asia' and 'Asia-Pacific' as alternative societal constructs, this artificial separation is no longer feasible. Much of ASEAN's energy is thus expended upon the question of how to layer the previously extra-regional onto the Southeast Asian (the 'Plus' impulse). ASEAN's claim to brokering the institutional bargain is in agreeing not to take sides among the great powers but to facilitate their dialogue; this does not, however, substantively help in negotiating mutual constraints between them.[189]

Japan and the United States similarly work from pre-existing social structural and operational constraints, in having to wrestle with how to continue to privilege their alliance while negotiating new modes of power constraint and regulation with other powers. Since the end of the Cold War, Japan has faced the challenge of renegotiating two sets of bargains—that with its key ally as analysed here, but also that with its neighbours, which is examined in greater detail in Chapters 4 and 5. This chapter already makes clear, however, the constraints posed by Japan's role as the key hegemonic supporter state. The United States has been reticent about negotiating an institutional bargain with East Asia, but has participated in the process for three reasons. First, Washington's initial lack of interest regarding a regional (as opposed to bilateral) arrangement for the post-Cold War context left the initiative to activist Asia-Pacific states seeking to replicate the European institutional experience. Second, the growing convergence of Chinese and other East Asian preferences for conducting their new relationships within the norms of regional institutions obliged Washington to reciprocate so as not to risk losing an increasingly important means of legitimizing its power. Finally, American willingness to expend political energy on institutional development provides its allies and partners with a vital justification for their continuing support.

The only state starting with a relatively 'blank' slate is China, with its almost non-existent regional institutional profile since 1949. As scholars drawing from liberal institutionalist perspectives have pointed out, a 'complex patchwork' of somewhat 'fuzzy' regional institutions such as that in East Asia helps to mute the security dilemma by offering great powers multiple, flexible opportunities to cooperate with different groups of states without generating zero-sum games.[190] The hope, for example, is that China could have opportunities to allay its concerns about encirclement by the United

---

[188] Ba 2009.
[189] See Goh 2011b.
[190] Cha 2011; Wei 2010.

Institutional Bargains: Taming and Legitimizing Unequal Power

States–Japan alliance or the United States–Japan–Australia trilateral security dialogue through Chinese officials' interactions and cooperation with these counterparts in the many other regional meetings. Liberal Chinese scholars argue that East Asia is evolving peacefully towards a landscape of 'nested overlapping institutions' in which the US alliance system 'coexists' with the 'multilateral cooperation system'.[191] Among these, Su Hao's 'walnut' model notably suggests a vivid coexistence effect: the 'nut' or core of regional cooperation consists of exclusive East Asian institutions—the APT, ASEAN bilateral consultations with China and Japan, and China–Japan–South Korea trilateral cooperation—which nurture Sino-Japanese confidence and cooperation while mediating leadership competition between them and ASEAN. At the same time, cooperation with extra-regional powers such as in the EAS reduces suspicions and lowers US resistance, thus constituting the 'protective shell' around this process.[192]

On the one hand, these analyses are too optimistic about the fungibility of existing institutions—the plethora of arrangements span a wide range of functional and symbolic utility and efficacy, and member states do not easily find substitute channels for their strategic purposes. On the other hand, Chinese scholars especially tend to draw an artificial boundary between regional and 'external' powers (including the United States), implying that the type of institutional bargain sought is substantively different between them. Yet, as this chapter has shown, internal and external are not easily separated—there is implicitly a hierarchy in Su's two-layer system; the question is whether the China–Japan-centred regional institutional bargain or the China–US-centred inclusive bargain is more important. It is especially critical now for Beijing that it blends the two forms of institutional bargains that it must strike, first vis-à-vis the other great powers, and then with the other states in the region. In order to combine and layer these two sets of bargains, a regional social hierarchy must be forced, both in terms of privileging and ranking the great powers, and in terms of strategic priorities. Until member states are willing to act constructively to hammer out a layered bargain, the region's frenzied institution creating and racing will remain an epiphenomenon.

---

[191] Qi 2010. He draws from Oran Young's model of institutional change.
[192] Su 2008.

3

Authority and Public Goods: Managing Regional Conflicts

> ...in spite of a real and/or perceived reduction of the Soviet threat, what has previously been a traditional aspect of our military presence in [the Asia-Pacific]—the role of regional balancer, honest broker, and ultimate security guarantor—will assume greater relative importance to stability...as a new global order takes shape, our forward presence will continue to be the region's irreplaceable balancing wheel...While our presence cannot guarantee the absence of conflict in the region, it can work to localize and minimize hostilities while providing us diplomatic leverage for conflict resolution. In the regional milieu of the 1990s, this is a U.S. military role which will be understood, endorsed, and supported by virtually all the major regional players.[1]

Within East Asia, it is almost a truism that, using its system of bilateral alliances and policy of extended deterrence, the United States maintains order by deterring the use of force and keeping in check regional rivalries. Washington's claims to being an 'Asia-Pacific power' are hard to refute given its undeniably central position within the East Asian security complex, and its continuing unsurpassed ability to provide security public goods including freedom of navigation, deterrence of adventurism by both allies and enemies, and disaster relief. US public goods provision to non-communist East Asia was most obvious during the Cold War, when it extended the nuclear umbrella and often symmetrical containment to deter and fight communist aggression, and opened its market and investments to key developing allied economies. Washington dramatically demonstrated adaptive great power management in seeking rapprochement and strategic coordination with China in the 1970s, and by negotiating a three-way understanding with Beijing and Taipei regarding Taiwan's status and future that has held conflict at bay beyond the Cold War. The US defence document quoted above

---

[1] U.S. Department of Defense 1990, 5–6.

optimistically expected the belief in the United States as regional hegemon to endure, based on a relatively unproblematic transformation of club goods restricted to non-communist parts of East Asia into more genuine public goods for the whole region when the Cold War ended. It assumed regional agreement about legitimate use of force and modes of conflict resolution, as well as consensus on priorities regarding public goods. Yet these collective understandings—and the authority to shape and seek consensus around them—are rarely uncontested and come under particular question during periods of systemic transition.

US regional hegemony rests upon crucial assumptions about order provision and security guarantee. The end of the Cold War created the problem of how to re-justify Washington's predominance and role as regional security guarantor, conflict manager, and order provider. In the absence of a common foe and given the need peacefully to integrate rising China, as well as the sharpening focus on security challenges that were more obstinately regional in character, the terms of US hegemonic authority in East Asia had to be renegotiated. What would now constitute crucial security issues, legitimate behaviour, the parameters of interstate conflict and conflict management, as well as the terms for potential power sharing between the United States and regional powers? These strategic contestations found natural expression in the outstanding regional conflicts that did not track the Cold War's demise. By examining two major regional conflicts and their management since the end of the Cold War, this chapter reveals the intense contestation surrounding the prioritization of public goods and modes of conflict management, and analyses their impacts on Washington's authority in East Asia.

The next section presents the conceptual focus on public goods provision as a key basis of great power authority and marker of hegemonic legitimacy, in both material and normative terms. It relates public goods provision to classical ideas of the special role and responsibilities of great powers as creators and managers of international order, paying particular attention to great power management of conflicts. The empirical analysis that follows focuses on the evolution of the US role in regional conflict management after the Cold War, how this relates to the justification (and constitution) of its preponderant power, and the degree to which authority over conflict management has been shared or diffused or challenged. By analysing the two critical conflicts with systemic impacts on regional peace and stability—those on the Korean peninsula and in the South China Sea—this chapter evaluates the degree to which the United States has been able to renegotiate the bases for its hegemonic position pinned upon its authority to manage these conflicts. This authority has in turned hinged upon its ability to define and deter key threats to regional security, to lead in sustaining the status quo, and to provide for some renegotiation of its terms of management as strategic conditions change. Of special importance is the extent to which US authority has been renegotiated by co-opting China into its security agenda and goals and into playing a larger role to support them, but of equal or greater significance is the continued support of allies and consent of other states in the region to the United States drawing the figurative red lines using its preferred conflict-management mechanisms.

The two regional conflicts examined here are not easily subject to resolution, hence their management—how the contending parties are restrained within agreed parameters of conduct short of outright violence, how the disputed issues are contained to prevent overspill, and how cooperation in other areas may be pursued in spite of the outstanding conflict—remains the key to ensuring stability for the foreseeable future. The analysis in this chapter spotlights the central US role at the heart of the main regional conflicts, either as a direct party to unresolved post-war settlements, or by clear invitation from key contenders seeking American support. To a significant extent, the United States retains its hegemonic role in defining or resisting redefinitions of key public goods and in determining how these goods are to be provided and on what terms. China is party to the South China Sea territorial disputes and a co-manager, by US insistence, in the North Korean conflict. China's record in conflict management reflects its growing material resources and political clout, and its inherent position in East Asia, but is less indicative of Chinese authority as such. Insofar as authority is distinguishable from power by the consent and 'rightness' of obedience, deference, or demand for leadership, other East Asian states have by and large continued to grant Washington authority as the regional security guarantor in these test cases. They do not easily agree with the substance of what US authority demands in managing these conflicts, but there is consensus that no other actor is able, willing, or acceptable to shoulder the comprehensive burdens of security public goods provision.

Authority in Great Power Management

Within the sovereign state system, the privileged role and special rights of great powers to provide international order are acknowledged, and their managerial functions in promoting this order institutionalized, in ideas and practices of special privilege and responsibility.[2] As an institution of international society, great power management is inherently social. By Hedley Bull's definitive

---

[2] For an excellent account of the 'unique compromise between the principles of [sovereign] equality and [authority] differentiation' found through the negotiation and allocation of 'special responsibilities', see Bukovansky et al. 2012, 5.

account, this collaborative management is first aimed at preserving the society of states itself by regulating the boundaries within which great powers exercise their influence. Hence, great powers limit the systemic impacts of their conflicts through maintaining the balance of power and by crisis management and war limitation. Second, great powers manage international order by using their preponderance to impart 'central direction' to international affairs, either by imposing their will or by legitimate leadership.[3] Here, classical accounts tended to emphasize the unilateral exploitation of local preponderance, spheres of influence, or joint action in condominium or concert. By minding their own backyards, respecting each other's spheres, and sometimes jointly disciplining the recalcitrant, great powers regulate the social and physical boundaries where their interests and spheres meet.[4] But how do great powers actually provide leadership to other states? If, as Kindleberger notes, positive leadership is fundamentally 'the provision of the public good of responsibility', the interesting question then becomes how this process is rendered acceptable, and how this public goods provider role is justified and legitimized over time.[5] In other words, how unequal power is turned into authority.

Thinking about authority rather than power essentially turns the focus from the relative accumulation of resources towards the justification of power. Broadly, authority may be defined as rightful rule, by which the commands of the dominant actor are obeyed by others because they are seen as natural or legitimate.[6] The distribution of authority does not necessarily deviate from the distribution of power resources, but authority is conferred by the leading power's constituency, by demand or invitation, with this complicity entailing some process of negotiation about the reciprocal terms. Recent IR works marshal the concept of authority, but remain firmly lodged in material-instrumental approaches that emphasize rationalist bargains. For instance, in David Lake's prominent analysis of hierarchy as differential authority relationships, the leading state gains subordinate states' deference from its ability to provide 'social goods' to a tune 'sufficient to offset the latter's loss of freedom'.[7] But Lake only identifies power over outcomes—'the number of actions over which the dominant state can issue commands', such as military deployments and alliances—and pays no attention to the processes of negotiation of the bargains that underpinned these decisions.[8]

---

[3] Bull 1977, 200. For an update and upgrade of great power management above balance of power as a primary institution of international society, see Buzan 2004, 233.

[4] Compared to nineteenth-century Europe, contemporary international society arguably offers at once less and more scope for how great power management is derived—see Goh forthcoming/b.

[5] Kindleberger 1986, 304.

[6] See Bell 1975.

[7] Lake 2007, 54.

[8] Lake 2007, 56.

The latter type of analysis would reveal the tight interplay of material, ideational, and normative factors in socially negotiated categories that legitimize the privileges accompanying unequal power.[9] Such negotiations over authority occupy a formative role in creating new balances of power and are thus constitutive of order transitions.

As argued in Chapter 2, contemporary East Asia is precisely undergoing this transition of renegotiating the largely instrumental contractarian Cold War bargain towards a more complex, socially contested, institutionalized one. This chapter further explores the evolution of great power authority by focusing on the renegotiation of key security public goods and the hegemon's special responsibility for their provision. The various strands of hegemonic stability theory have established the strong association between hegemony and the stable provision of public goods, chiefly in the security and economic realms.[10] Because pure public goods such as peace or macroeconomic stability have non-excludable benefits and non-rivalrous use, a hegemon with sufficient capacity and will to bear the disproportionate costs is regarded as necessary to ensure their supply in the face of free-riding. The provision of public goods expresses hegemonic authority: in rationalist terms, it is one key element of establishing and maintaining the hegemon's special and indispensable role, and in normative terms, it involves defining what needs to be secured in relation to the common goals of regional society, and how.

In deliberately framing the analysis in terms of authority and security public goods, therefore, this chapter investigates the changing terms of US hegemony in East Asia by privileging questions about consent, negotiation, and power sharing. The cases that follow examine the renegotiation of US authority in East Asia expressed in its special responsibility for the management of key regional conflicts. On the basis of their wider regional or systemic impacts, four conflicts might have been suitable for this analysis: the divisions across the Taiwan Straits and Korean peninsula, and the maritime territorial conflicts in the East and South China Seas. In order better to analyse regional contestation over great power conflict management, I have narrowed my cases down to the two which are more obviously multilateral and have spawned a variety of conflict-management mechanisms. The United States–China dispute over the status of Taiwan has been widely regarded as the major potential trigger of great power war in the region since 1950, but conflict management across these Straits stabilized in the 1980s on terms that have not (yet) changed significantly since the end of the Cold War.

---

[9] E.g. Bukovansky et al. 2012, 13, 50.
[10] This is the emphasis of rationalist accounts of the United States' benign hegemony (Kindleberger 1986; Gilpin 1981; Snidal 1985), exploitative hegemony (Lake 1993), as well as unique, self-interested hegemony (Norrlof 2010).

Authority and Public Goods: Managing Regional Conflicts

I briefly discuss the application of this chapter's framework to the Taiwan problem below. At the same time, there is undeniably serious potential for armed conflict between China and Japan (with possible US backing) over the Senkaku Islands, but the development of conflict-management mechanisms here is too thin to date for the purposes of this study.[11]

In the realm of conflict management, great powers express their authority by their ability to do three things. First, to determine what is at stake: what needs to be defended or secured, to what ends? What is the broader principle or norm on the line, affecting the goals of international society and underpinnings of order? In the case of the Taiwan conflict, for instance, at stake is the basic principle of sovereignty but also the legitimate means of revising the status quo of national self-determination.[12] More specifically, what is the public good that needs to be provided? In discussing security particularly, it is useful to make a distinction between intermediate and final public goods. Here, regional peace and stability are the obvious outcome or final public good that is at stake for all parties. But contestation usually arises over the intermediate public goods, such as the international regimes governing the use of nuclear weapons or high seas, which contribute to the provision of the final public goods.[13] There is often dispute over the relative significance and content of such intermediate public goods. On Taiwan, the agreed intermediate public good is non-coercive resolution, but meanwhile the contestation centres on the extent to which the problem is even a public goods issue, with Washington asserting via its defence commitment to Taipei the issue's regional—indeed international—security character and Beijing insisting upon its domestic (and therefore private good) nature.

Second, a great power's authority is judged on the basis of its ability to organize and mobilize consent to provide the public good. In this case, how is the conflict in question to be contained or limited? What are the legitimate channels and modes of conflict management? Who or which actors are to be involved and how? For instance, the three United States–China communiqués that govern their management of the Taiwan issue acknowledge that it is a matter to be resolved by Taipei and Beijing alone, but their very existence legitimizes the central US role in the conflict.[14] The United States–China focus of conflict management is reinforced by Beijing's clear resistance to the potential involvement of other states, either US allies like

---

[11] See Emmers 2010a, 108–15.
[12] See Pan 2012.
[13] On this distinction and a more general discussion about public goods in the international realm, see Kaul et al. 1999.
[14] The communiqués and other major Chinese and American official statements on Taiwan are available at <http://www.taiwandocuments.org/doc_all.htm>. Accessed 1 December 2012.

Japan in the event of a conflict, or offers from states like Singapore to mediate. In substantive terms, what bargains can be made to limit or resolve the conflict; what acceptable norms and reciprocal understandings can be reached to establish agreed parameters of legitimate behaviour? Under what conditions and constraints is it acceptable for regional states to intervene or use force to resolve conflicts; and in what manner using what instruments can states seek to change the status quo? How are these reciprocal understandings codified? In the Taiwan case, China and the United States achieved consensus by 1979 on the principle of 'one China' by which Beijing was accorded diplomatic recognition and authority over all China, and Washington recognized that Taiwan is part of China and relinquished the right to encourage Taiwanese independence, though not its right to sell arms to Taiwan. While they agreed on the peaceful means of resolving the problem, they disagreed on the necessity of reunification as the eventual outcome. These understandings and divergences were codified not only in United States–China normalization communiqués but also in the US Taiwan Relations Act and a series of China–Taiwan official documents including the 2005 Anti-Secession Law which committed Beijing to negotiations for reunification.[15]

Finally, great powers exercise authority in conflict management through their ability to discipline dissenters. Such discipline is often coercive, either directly through sanctions and use of force, or indirectly through credible deterrence. Discipline also involves restraining allies in order to limit conflicts. As exercises of authority, this category of actions would be distinguished from the mere imposition of superior power by the complicity of other states, either through support for coordinating and applying sanctions, or by their invitation and facilitation of the great power's force projection. The Taiwan case best demonstrates the complex instruments of discipline on the US part: on the one hand, by building up mainly defensive capabilities, the United States and China effectively deter each other from escalating the conflict. At the same time, the United States deters Taiwan from seeking independence using a mix of assurance through arms sales but also the implicit threat of abandonment in its policy strategic ambiguity about the conditions under which it might intervene in a cross-Straits conflict.[16]

Table 3.1 summarizes this conceptual framework and its application to Taiwan as well as to the two case studies that follow.

---

[15] See Bush 2004; Tucker 2009.
[16] For the argument that a stable state of mutual deterrence exists across the Taiwan Straits, see Ross 2006a.

Table 3.1. Analysing authority over the management of key East Asian regional conflicts

	Defining the stakes		Mobilizing to provide public goods		Disciplining dissenters
	Principles	Public goods	Modes of conflict management	Codifications	
Taiwan	Sovereignty—right to independence; use of force to revise or maintain status quo	Domestic issue, private good (China) vs. regional issue impinging on public security good (US)	Mainly bilateral US–China; consensus re principles (one China, peaceful resolution); stable deterrence	Normalization formula; Taiwan Relations Act; Anti-Secession Law	Strategic ambiguity; coercive displays of force
Korean peninsula	Instruments of coercion—nuclear weapons, sanctions (and who gets to possess/use them); intervention (regime change)	Nuclear non-proliferation; settlement of Korean War; DPRK–ROK reconciliation	IAEA and KEDO subcontractors; power sharing in Six Party Talks; alliance management	1994 Framework Agreement; Six Party Talks (2005 & 2007 agreements); PSI	Sanctions (China); hegemonic reassertion (US)
South China Sea	Sovereignty; maritime jurisdiction	Freedom of navigation; peaceful conduct (conflict avoidance); constrained China	Global legal regime; regional conflict-avoidance frameworks	UNCLOS; 2002 ASEAN–China DoC	Unilateral assertions of authority; invited US military deterrence

The Korean Peninsula

The management of the post-Cold War Korean peninsula conflict, as the most volatile hotspot in East Asia, uniquely encapsulates the dynamics of authority renegotiation. This case is often unduly optimistically cited as indicative of some power sharing between the United States and China, with the Six Party Talks (6PT) forming an eventual base for a wider great power concert in East Asia. But widespread frustration with North Korea's behaviour and apparent disregard for others' assumptions about rational calculation also obscures the wider strategic implications of conflict management on the peninsula. The following analysis begins with the recognition that at stake in the conflict are legitimate instruments of coercion—specifically nuclear weapons and international sanctions—and who gets to possess and wield them. Moreover, it argues that the story of the Korean peninsula conflict since the Cold War ended revolves around two crucial interconnected plots. First is the struggle over what primary security public good is at stake in reintegrating North Korea into the regional and global order. Over the last two decades, US authority has been most starkly expressed through Washington's ability to resist the serious integration of the three key public goods at stake in negotiations with Pyongyang, in spite of the progress that was facilitated in the few instances when such a 'package deal' seemed to be available. This is interwoven into the second plot, which centres on the struggle of great powers individually and in concert to wield authority in managing the 'peninsula question'. Efficiency and legitimacy concerns prompted the United States to pursue multilateral negotiations with North Korea, but this hegemonic co-optation of the other regional powers has been limited by divergences regarding principles, participants, and modes of bargaining with Pyongyang. As a result, authority over conflict management here has been diffused, challenged, and instrumentally shared at times, but ultimately resides in the United States and its coercive, sanctioning focus.

Public Goods

THREE INTERMEDIATE PUBLIC GOODS

The contemporary phase of the Korean peninsula conflict is inextricably linked to the US hegemonic imperative to secure nuclear arsenals as one key means of ensuring peace and remaking world order towards the end of the Cold War. The consensus over superpower-led control of nuclear proliferation was embodied in the 1968 Treaty on the Non-Proliferation of Nuclear Weapons (NPT), one of the most comprehensive exercises in institutionalized great power restraint undertaken as part of the Soviet–American détente.[17] North Korea, with its Cold War-era nuclear programme supplied by Moscow, signed up to the NPT in 1985, but had not ratified the safeguards agreement with the International Atomic Energy Agency (IAEA) when US intelligence reported a nuclear processing facility at Yongbyon and indications of nuclear weapons-related tests in 1989. The US approach to counter-proliferation had been to use security assurances and economic inducements to persuade peripheral states to give up or freeze their nuclear weapons programmes.[18] The North Korean case was hampered by Pyongyang's intransigence, and Washington's response has been to resist perceived nuclear blackmail, and to sanction the North Korean regime until it complies with what it is obliged to do as a signatory to the NPT.

The North Korean leadership, on the other hand, faces an ontological and national security imperative. The unresolved peace settlement from the Second World War left Korea divided, and the absence of a formal peace process to end the subsequent Korean War leaves Pyongyang open to US animosity, operational targeting, and nuclear threats. Thus, Pyongyang pursues nuclear weapons because it feels threatened by the United States and these weapons are its best deterrent and bargaining chip. By this logic, the North Korean sense of security is the crucial intermediate security public good, which may be attained by tying the resolution of the nuclear issue to some sort of binding peace agreement.[19] The 1953 Armistice Agreement had called upon the four parties involved (South Korea, North Korea, the United States, and China) to continue peace talks, but standing in the way is a fundamental disagreement about the legitimate parties to such a process. For Pyongyang, the key is normalization of relations with the United States and the conclusion of a peace treaty that would codify mutual non-aggression and allow for the eventual withdrawal of US forces on the peninsula. North Korea wants bilateral peace talks with the United States on the basis that Seoul was not a signatory to the armistice agreement and that Washington bears ultimate authority in the South as it retains command of forces. But Washington has consistently deflected bilateral dealings with Pyongyang, and South Korea resists being sidelined in any peace talks.

To the extent that the post-1950 Korean conflict centres on the North–South divorce, inter-Korean relations are a pivotal part of the peninsula problem and its solution. As South Korea's economic development took off and particularly with the demise of its military governments in the late

---

[17] See Walker 2004.
[18] See Woolf 2012.
[19] See e.g. Drennan 2003; Atlantic Council Working Group on North Korea 2007; DiFilippo 2012.

1980s, inter-Korean reconciliation became an increasingly important element of the putative peace settlement. In 1972, the divided Koreas were shocked by the United States–China rapprochement into an initial détente of their own, with the first inter-Korean dialogue producing an agreement on the rudimentary principles of independent and peaceful reunification. But it was the end of the Cold War that galvanized their resumption of trade and pursuit of parallel UN membership, as well as two landmark agreements in December 1991. The 'Basic Agreement' codified a mutual non-aggression pact,[20] while by the Joint Declaration on the Denuclearization of the Korean peninsula (JDD) the two Koreas agreed not to develop or use nuclear weapons and to undertake mutual inspections. Seoul's changing threat perceptions regarding the North and the vagaries of South Korean domestic politics both constrained and facilitated conflict management on the Korean peninsula at critical junctures. Particularly influential was President Kim Dae-jung's 'sunshine policy' of sustained engagement towards North Korea, undertaken with the belief that ending inter-Korean confrontation could persuade Pyongyang to change its behaviour. This ensured that inter-Korean reconciliation became the third intermediate security public good from 1998 onwards, even facilitating a temporary parallel process of United States–DPRK (Democratic People's Republic of Korea) normalization talks.[21] In contrast, President Lee Myung Bak's greater prioritization of the North Korean nuclear and security threat significantly reinforced hardening US containment against Pyongyang after 2008.

'PACKAGE DEAL' PROGRESS

Conflict management on the Korean peninsula has been dominated by the US definition from the outset that the security public good at stake was preventing the spread of nuclear weapons technology and bolstering the international nuclear regime. The variable element has been the extent to which the concerned parties have been willing to relate nuclear non-proliferation to North Korean insecurity and the major missing pieces of the Korean War settlement. As the Cold War wound down, the George H. W. Bush administration's 'comprehensive engagement' approach towards North Korea came closest to reflecting the intertwined nature of these three public goods. While holding Pyongyang to its NPT obligations, the Bush administration

---

[20] See 'Agreement on Reconciliation, Nonaggression, and Exchanges and Cooperation between South and North Korea', 13 December 1991 (effective 19 February 1992), available at <http://www1.korea-np.co.jp/pk/011th_issue/97100101.htm>. Accessed 30 October 2012.

[21] The 'sunshine policy' was based on three principles: while South Korea would not tolerate armed provocation by the North, it also had no intention to undermine or absorb North Korea, and would actively pursue reconciliation and cooperation with it. Kim's policy separated economics from politics and emphasized flexible reciprocity.

extended three forms of strategic reassurance to Pyongyang: the unilateral withdrawal of US air-delivered nuclear weapons in South Korea, which crucially facilitated the rapprochement between two Koreas at the end of 1991; suspension of the annual large-scale Team Spirit military exercise with South Korea in 1992; and a high-level bilateral meeting with the North Koreans in 1992, after the latter agreed to receive IAEA inspectors. It also held out the prospect that denuclearization would bring the normalization of relations with the United States.[22]

However, Washington's stance narrowed and hardened in 1992–3 when IAEA inspectors discovered discrepancies between North Korea's reported inventory and facilities on the ground suggesting that plutonium had previously been extracted from spent fuel rods, and Pyongyang resisted 'special inspections' into its past nuclear activities. Over the rest of the 1990s, the Clinton administration would reiterate that it had no reason to bribe (rather than sanction) North Korea to do what it had agreed to do by ratifying the NPT; and that diplomatic relations with the United States were not a bargaining chip.[23] Washington regularly refused to wrap the issues of normalization and a peace treaty into a joint negotiation package with Pyongyang. US negotiators have asserted the primacy of the nuclear non-proliferation imperative by insisting that North Korea give up its nuclear weapons—the most extreme demand being 'complete, verifiable and irreversible dismantlement' (CVID)—as a precondition before delivering on agreed quid pro quos.

Notably, each of the few agreements reached during the prolonged staccato negotiations with North Korea were achieved when Washington deviated from this stance and dealt reciprocally with Pyongyang while addressing all three public goods. The October 1994 Geneva Agreed Framework codified the most comprehensive 'package deal' to date, involving parallel agreements on energy, security, and diplomatic relations. In return for Pyongyang's agreement to freeze and eventually dismantle its graphite reactors and plutonium reprocessing facilities under IAEA monitoring, the Clinton administration agreed to facilitate the construction of two light-water reactors (LWRs) and provide heavy oil as alternative fuel. Washington also agreed to provide formal assurances not to threaten or use nuclear weapons against the DPRK, in exchange for Pyongyang implementing the North–South JDD and engaging in North–South dialogue. In addition, the United States and DPRK would move towards the full normalization of relations. The Clinton administration took the imperative of reaching a long-term peace settlement seriously enough to start four-party negotiations for a peace treaty in August 1997.

---

[22] *National Security Review* 28, 'United States Policy Toward North Korean Nuclear Weapons Program', 6 February 1991, cited in Wit et al. 2004, 7.
[23] Wit et al. 2004, 7.

However, the Four Party Talks quickly floundered: American and South Korean emphasis on confidence-building measures and a multilateral peace regime clashed with Pyongyang's insistence on US troop withdrawal from South Korea and a bilateral peace treaty.[24] The Agreed Framework implementation was delayed when Congress withheld US financial contributions due to IAEA verification problems, North Korean attempts to extract maximum leverage, and coordination conflicts with South Korea and Japan.

The impasse was eventually broken in August 1998 when Pyongyang launched a three-stage rocket (the Taepodong-1) over Japan, dramatically reinforcing the nuclear problem.[25] North Korea's missile programme galvanized the Clinton administration towards bilateral talks in 1998–2000, during which Pyongyang agreed to open nuclear facilities to US inspections and to suspend missile tests, while Washington lifted some economic sanctions. In two high-level meetings in October 2000, President Clinton and Vice-Marshal Jo Myong-Rok agreed a joint communiqué affirming non-hostile intentions and a 'new direction' in United States–DPRK relations;[26] while President Kim Jong Il proposed during Secretary of State Madeline Albright's state visit to North Korea a commitment not to produce or proliferate long-range missiles in exchange for economic assistance and a commercial satellite programme from the United States.[27] But the Clinton administration did not take this new diplomacy further before the 2000 Presidential election results, and conditions for negotiating with North Korea turned decidedly less propitious with the George W. Bush administration's maximalist focus on US national security vis-à-vis nuclear-armed terrorists from 2001.

During the 6PT, North Korea continued to push for a 'package solution' that would trade in its nuclear programme for security assurances, diplomatic relations, and economic assistance.[28] Against the odds, the 6PT process produced a joint statement in 2005, followed by two subsequent implementation agreements in 2007. These developments were due in part to astute Chinese diplomacy, North Korea's increased bargaining power with its missile programme and first nuclear test in October 2006, and South Korean

---

[24] Lee 2006, 188–95.
[25] See the influential review of Korea policy by former Defense Secretary William J. Perry, which reiterated the urgency and primacy of the nuclear non-proliferation public good—'Review of United States Policy Toward North Korea: Findings and Recommendations', 12 October 1999, available at <http://www.state.gov/www/regions/eap/991012_northkorea_rpt.html>. Accessed 30 October 2012.
[26] United States–DPRK Joint Communiqué, 12 October 2000, available at <http://www.state.gov/www/regions/eap/001012_usdprk_jointcom.html>. Accessed 30 October 2012.
[27] 'N. Korean Leader Pledges to Scrap Missile Launches', *LA Times*, 25 October 2000; 'How Politics Sank Accord with North Korea', *New York Times*, 6 March 2001.
[28] 'Conclusion of non-aggression treaty between DPRK and U.S. called for', 25 October 2002, available at <http://www.kcna.co.jp/item/2002/200210/news10/25.htm>; 'Keynote speeches made at six-way talks', 29 August 2003, at <http://www.kcna.co.jp/item/2003/200308/news08/30.htm>. Accessed 30 October 2012.

pressure. The 19 September 2005 joint statement[29] explicitly wrapped in all three public goods: North Korea committed to abandoning all its nuclear weapons and existing nuclear programmes, and to returning to the NPT and IAEA safeguards.[30] In exchange, the United States reaffirmed that it had no intention to attack or invade the DPRK. The five parties declared their willingness to provide LWRs to North Korea, in exchange for the implementation of the North–South JDD. The statement also moved beyond nuclear proliferation as the six parties agreed to negotiate a permanent peace regime. The 13 February 2007 agreement on implementing the 2005 joint statement stipulated the phased programme of reciprocal actions linking the three public goods. North Korea would shut down and seal its plutonium reactor as the first step to 'disablement' in exchange for energy assistance, with more assistance to be delivered when it provided a detailed inventory of facilities to be dismantled. In parallel, the United States and Japan would open normalization talks with North Korea, and Washington would remove the DPRK from its list of state sponsors of terrorism as a prelude to lifting economic sanctions. These agreements amounted to reciprocal, step-by-step denuclearization in exchange for normalization. They also overcame US resistance to planning the 'peace regime' before the nuclear problem was totally resolved.

HEGEMONIC RESISTANCE

And yet the Bush administration remained ambivalent about the package deal approach and only reluctantly went along with these 6PT agreements. Pyongyang had crossed a line by its admission in October 2002 that it possessed a highly enriched uranium programme.[31] For many American policymakers, this was incontrovertible proof of North Korean duplicity and many previous advocates of engagement changed their minds about the feasibility of negotiating with Pyongyang.[32] Thus US negotiator James Kelly brought to the 6PT in August 2003 a huge agenda with demands spanning CVID, missile proliferation, human rights, money laundering, and drug smuggling;

---

[29] 'Full text of six-party talks joint statement', *China Daily*, 19 September 2005, available at <http://www.chinadaily.com.cn/english/doc/2005-09/19/content_479150_2.htm>. Accessed 30 October 2012.

[30] For a discussion of how the various parties tried to retain room for manoeuvre on constraining North Korea's plutonium as well as the uranium enrichment programme with more dual-use potential, see Funabashi 2007, 392–9.

[31] In his autobiography, former Pakistani President Pervez Musharraf 2006 stated that a proliferation network run by Pakistani nuclear official Abdul Qadeer Khan provided North Korea with about twenty centrifuges in the mid- to late-1990s. North Korea also bought about 150 tons of aluminium tubes from Russia in 2002.

[32] For instance, Victor Cha, who served as Bush's principal Korea adviser on the National Security Council in 2004–7, argued that this 'wholesale and secretive breakout' from the Agreed Framework now meant that any negotiations would constitute appeasement—Cha and Kang 2003, 156.

and thereafter Washington continued to demand that Pyongyang make the first moves to freeze its nuclear programme.[33] In this climate, the Bush administration apparently agreed to the 2005 joint statement mainly because advisers concluded that it was vague enough to remain open to further interpretation later.[34]

Unsurprisingly, therefore, Washington reasserted the nuclear imperative following both 6PT breakthrough agreements, and worked to render provision of the other public goods conditional upon it. In his closing statement after the 2005 joint statement, US negotiator Christopher Hill stated that the United States would reciprocate only when the DPRK had conducted verifiable denuclearization and complied with the NPT and IAEA safeguards, triggering a tit-for-tat reaction from Pyongyang that 'the LWR must come first'.[35] The agreement was hijacked just one day later when Washington announced that it was imposing financial sanctions on the DPRK for counterfeit money laundering through a small Macau bank. Highlighting the relatively small sum allegedly involved compared to much larger seizures of counterfeit US Treasury notes in South America and the Middle East that did not trigger sanctions, critics charged that the Bush administration was trying to scupper the joint statement.[36] North Korea's visceral reaction to this perceived 'act of war' would hold up the Six Party Talks for over a year, during which Pyongyang conducted a second missile test and its first nuclear test. Similarly, the 2007 implementation agreements were held up by Hill's renewed insistence that North Korea had not resolved the issue of uranium enrichment to US satisfaction. This insistence was intransigent, given that Hill himself had admitted that there were significant gaps in US intelligence about whether the DPRK's uranium enrichment programme (UEP) amounted to a weapons programme.[37] In any case, Pyongyang's heated denial led Washington to return to demands for CVID. Pyongyang in turn slowed the process of shutting down its facilities, and by the end of the Bush administration, the Six Party process was stalemated by hardening positions also in Tokyo and Seoul.

---

[33] 'U.S. Will Accept "Nothing Less" than Total Nuclear Dismantlement in North Korea, Kelly Says', *Washington File*, 15 July 2004.
[34] Kim 2006, 265–6.
[35] Funabashi 2007, 391, 403.
[36] McCormack 2007a.
[37] Hill acknowledged that it would need 'a lot more equipment than we know that they have actually purchased' to operate a uranium programme, and 'some considerable production techniques that we're not sure whether they have mastered'. He also conceded that the aluminium tubes that North Korea intended to use for an enrichment effort might have ended up 'somewhere else'—'Update on the Six-Party Talks', Brookings Institution, Washington DC, 22 February 2007. See also 'U.S. had doubts on North Korean uranium drive', *New York Times*, 1 March 2007.

Authority in Conflict Management

To the extent that Pyongyang has exercised nuclear leverage primarily to change the terms of its relationship with the United States, conflict management on the Korean peninsula depends fundamentally on these two players. As the superordinate state, the United States would be expected to dominate conflict management, in substance—such as resisting the expansion of core public goods at stake—but also in modality. Yet the significant range of modes of conflict management on the peninsula suggests some instability in Washington's ability to mobilize support for its preferred mechanism for providing the public good. Indeed, US authority in managing the Korean conflict has been constantly mediated through its preoccupation with national security priorities elsewhere, alliance politics with South Korea and Japan, and increasing pressure from China within multilateral channels of negotiation with North Korea.

SUBCONTRACTING

For much of the 1990s, authority over conflict management on the Korean peninsula was diffused because of Washington's distraction. The George H. W. Bush administration was fully occupied with transitions in Eastern Europe and the conflicts in the Middle East, Balkans, and former Soviet Union, while the Clinton administration was similarly engulfed while struggling to settle on a foreign policy strategy.[38] Thus, while retaining the ability to determine the goals, agenda, and parameters of these management efforts, Washington subcontracted the monitoring, inducements, and containment of the North Korean nuclear problem to various international organizations. The first of these was the IAEA, which together with the NPT embodied the international legal and institutional authority over nuclear non-proliferation. These were among the core liberal institutions that ex-Soviet sphere states would join and comply with as a key part of their accession into the new world order. The Bush and Clinton administrations used the NPT as the legal basis to demand that North Korea end its nuclear weapons programme and used IAEA procedures to kick-start sanctions. The first Korean nuclear crisis occurred in March 1993 when Pyongyang thumbed its nose at these authoritative norms and institutions by giving notice of its intention to withdraw from the NPT regime after defying IAEA demands for wide-ranging inspections.

In hailing nuclear non-proliferation as the unquestionable public good in this crisis, Washington drew on broad international support of the existing nuclear regime. For instance, 149 countries officially denounced

---

[38] E.g. Hyland 1999; Dumbrell 2008.

Pyongyang's threat to withdraw from the NPT. Notably, China did not oppose this nuclear priority, itself having acceded to the NPT in 1992.[39] But the task of obtaining Pyongyang's compliance to the NPT was subcontracted to the IAEA because of Washington's reluctance to deal bilaterally with North Korea. Critics charge that the agency was neither equipped nor mandated to negotiate and enforce NPT agreements, being a specialist monitoring agency. Moreover, the baggage of having been found lacking in the 1990–1 Iraq case seemed to drive the IAEA to prove the 'sanctity of its procedures' in North Korea.[40] The Clinton administration consistently insisted on the resumption of the IAEA's extensive monitoring process as a prerequisite for any deals with Pyongyang. During the crisis in 1993–4, by allowing the IAEA to determine the number and scope of inspections required, Washington delayed high-level talks with Pyongyang by a year. The IAEA also triggered the high point of the crisis in 1994 by threatening sanctions, prompting Pyongyang to quit the agency. That this crisis was eventually broken by former President Jimmy Carter's private démarche to Kim Il Sung in June 1994 only reiterated the diffused nature of US authority in managing the conflict.[41]

Defining North Korea's behaviour as non-compliance with international rules of non-proliferation left the United States and its allies with the classic dilemma of enforcement, and US unwillingness to bribe Pyongyang left only the avenue of sanctions. In this regard, authoritative management of the first crisis was shaky because it was based upon neither credible coercive power nor economic sanction. The superiority of US forces, including 'tripwire' deployments near the demilitarized zone in South Korea and nuclear weapons positioned offshore, deterred the DPRK. Yet, beyond avoiding outright war, that deterrence could not resolve the conflict caused by Pyongyang's coercive bargaining style.[42] Neither could it be used as the ultimate instrument for enforcement, since options for military action against North Korea were not reviewed feasibly by the defence establishment. For instance, the commander of US forces in Korea estimated 300,000–750,000 military casualties and countless civilian and economic losses in the South in the event of a war.[43]

---

[39] As Foot and Walter (2011, 159–60) observe, since then there has been 'a fairly lengthy but reasonably linear Chinese integration into the [international nuclear non-proliferation] normative framework from supportive rhetoric, domestic institutional creation, domestic legal development, and behavioural change'.
[40] Sigal 1998.
[41] For the split reaction of Clinton administration insiders to Carter's visit and the struggle to keep him on message in spite of Carter's well-known disapproval of the Clinton slide towards sanctioning North Korea, see Wit et al. 2004, 200–41; Brinkley 1998, 388–411.
[42] Cha and Kang 2003, 72.
[43] Wit et al. 2004, 102.

Authority and Public Goods: Managing Regional Conflicts

At the height of the crisis in June 1994, an Osirak-type pre-emptive strike option was discarded because of the lack of allied support, concerns about the international backlash, and doubts about the degree to which this would degrade North Korea's nuclear capacity.[44] This left the option of non-military sanctions, which had in any case been a constant feature of US policy towards North Korea during the Cold War.[45] Japan and South Korea delayed economic assistance and limited trade and investment with the DPRK at various junctures,[46] but the multilateral sanctions that would demonstrate key great power support of the US agenda and bestow authority and effectiveness to any proposed embargo remained elusive. The various UN Security Council (UNSC) statements were never backed up by sanctions in the first crisis, because of Chinese reservations and Russian opposition.

By the mid-1990s, it became clear that Washington's policy, regardless of whether it involved sanctions or a package deal, would require multilateral efforts for both efficiency and legitimacy considerations. Yet, until 2003, Washington largely retained authority over conflict management through its choice of partners and collaborative frameworks. To implement the complex and costly energy agreement in the 1994 Agreed Framework, the Clinton administration relied on a core group of US allies in the Korean Energy Development Organization (KEDO) for burden sharing. KEDO would distribute the costs of the heavy fuel and the two promised LWRs, with the latter borne largely by South Korea and Japan, the key Asian allies involved.[47] KEDO's main decision-making structure was initially confined to the three allies, and even when the European Union was admitted into the Executive Board in 1997 in recognition of its multimillion-dollar annual contribution, the implementation of the Agreed Framework remained within US allied hands. Even more significant was the George W. Bush administration's efforts to curb the proliferation of weapons of mass destruction (WMD) from the 'axis of evil' state sponsors of terrorism, which included North Korea.[48] Consistent with Bush's penchant for coalitions of the willing operating outside UN mandates was the Proliferation Security Initiative (PSI) announced in May 2003, after the attempted interdiction of a North Korean-flagged ship carrying missiles to the Yemen. PSI would be an ad hoc coalition for a global naval 'stop and search' campaign against nuclear material trafficking by US-designated 'rogue states', namely Iran, North Korea, Sudan, Syria, and

---

[44] Sigal 1998, 118.
[45] See Taylor 2010, 67–74.
[46] Hagström 2006, 391–2; Wit et al. 2004, 196.
[47] Armacost and Pyle 2001, 135; Sigal 1998, 253.
[48] 'Text of President Bush's State of the Union address', *Washington Post*, 29 January 2002; White House 2002.

Cuba.[49] Residing outside international maritime law, PSI allows Washington to retain authority over this joint global interdiction effort stressing independence, rapid response, and secret intelligence sharing.[50] Vis-à-vis North Korea, the PSI created an operational alliance that could potentially enforce a sanctions regime via sea blockades, independent to some extent of UN authority.[51]

POWER SHARING

From 2003 when the 6PT was convened, though, the United States appeared to co-opt China and the other regional powers into a form of shared negotiated authority in managing the Korean peninsula as a regional security conflict. As the most explicit instance of great power management in East Asia, the talks included all the key regional stakeholders to make North Korea accountable to international norms, negotiate an end to the civil war, and manage its regional strategic impacts. Far from being a coalition of the willing, the five stakeholders were not like-minded: there was agreement neither on the preferred outcome (Washington increasingly veered towards regime change, Beijing stressed regime survival and reform, and Seoul sought reunification) nor on the means to these ends (the United States and Japan were more inclined to use sanctions, while China and South Korea coordinated inducements). As such, any effective agreement reached in this process would be imbued with normative authority. While this outcome remains elusive, the 6PT helped to promote China's status as a regional great power and Beijing's preferred 'package deal' approach to eventually resolving the Korean conflict.

Beijing reluctantly adopted the role as mediator and facilitator of the 6PT in 2003, alarmed by the Bush administration's pre-emptive war doctrine, Pyongyang's withdrawal from the NPT, and the near-collision of North Korean interceptors and a US spy plane over the Sea of Japan.[52] Since then, Beijing has acted in classic great power management mode, disciplining its

---

[49] Nikitin 2008; Valencia 2005.

[50] An Operational Expert Group (OEG) of twenty-one states meets twice a year under the leadership of the Pentagon to share information and organize interdiction exercises. Members are Argentina, Australia, Canada, Denmark, France, Germany, Greece, Italy, Japan, the Netherlands, New Zealand, Norway, Poland, Portugal, Russia, Singapore, Spain, Turkey, the United Kingdom, and the United States. South Korea joined the OEG in November 2010, after North Korea allegedly sank the *Cheonan*. In addition, a diverse group of seventy-seven other countries have endorsed PSI and have observer status. See <http://www.state.gov/t/isn/c10390.htm>. Accessed 12 September 2012.

[51] Some see PSI as an integral part of a US strategy of regime change through economic pressure on Pyongyang—see Clegg 2011, 131.

[52] As one Chinese official observed when the talks started, '[W]e don't want another Iraq so near us. We don't want a war on our border.' Quoted in 'U.S. envoy opens talks with N. Korea; China included in discussions on crisis; no breakthrough expected', *Washington Post*, 24 April 2003.

awkward ally and mobilizing other stakeholders to address the three interrelated public goods. China repeatedly cajoled, threatened, and bribed Pyongyang to come to the 6PT table, engaged in shuttle diplomacy to set the agenda, set up a permanent working group of senior officials, issued written chairman's statements; and initiated the package denuclearization deal agreed in 2005–7. North Korea's 2006 nuclear test was a turning point, after which Beijing led by increasing the pressure on Pyongyang and aggressively persuading the other parties towards more intense negotiations. China overcame its opposition to sanctions as interference in internal affairs and supported two rounds of UNSC sanctions in 2006.[53] Bilaterally, it manipulated oil supplies to coerce Pyongyang to return to the negotiating table at the end of 2006, and to seal the Yongbyon reactor under IAEA inspection at the beginning of 2007.[54] The nuclear test forced the other parties to agree on the priority of curbing Pyongyang's WMD programme in the short term and cultivating a regional security framework to manage the Korean transition in the medium term.[55] But this renewed emphasis on the public good of regional security also entailed resistance against the hard-line elements of the US DPRK policy.[56] For instance, American discussions of a pre-emptive strike against DPRK nuclear capabilities and regime change in Pyongyang were criticized by China, Russia, and South Korea for unnecessarily risking war on the peninsula.[57]

China's innovation regarding the 'package deal' approach was to promote together with Russia, South Korea, and Japan a more ambitious multilateral framework for regional order. The September 2005 agreement committed the six parties to 'joint efforts for lasting peace and stability in Northeast Asia' by means of negotiating a 'permanent peace regime on the Korean peninsula at an appropriate separate forum' and to 'explore ways and means for promoting security cooperation in Northeast Asia'. The promise of a 6PT peace regime suggested a new regional order underpinned by multilateral great power management going beyond the United States–DPRK security assurances that had proven insufficient.[58] The February 2007 implementation agreement spawned an elaborate structure for division of labour in five working groups, and was an early codification of how authority would be shared

---

[53] 'Beijing "resolutely opposed" to DPRK nuclear test', *China Daily*, 10 October 2006.
[54] Twomey 2008, 417.
[55] Rozman 2007, 48.
[56] Their disparate national imperatives, or private goods, included for Seoul reunification without war; Beijing maximizing influence in both Koreas; Japan overcoming its history problem while blocking China's centrality; and Russia seeking the economic dividends of peace on the peninsula.
[57] Ashton Carter and William Perry, 'If necessary, strike and destroy', *Washington Post*, 22 June 2006; 'Bolton: Sanctions "help regime change"', *Financial Times*, 24 October 2006.
[58] For a list of verbal and written US security assurances to DPRK from 1989 to 2010, see Cha 2012, 307–14.

among the stakeholders in addressing the three public goods. China would lead on denuclearizing the Korean peninsula, spearheading—under close scrutiny by the United States—the most urgent task of persuading North Korea to declare and disable its nuclear assets. The United States would lead on DPRK–United States normalization, which would indicate how much and how fast Washington would accept Pyongyang into the international community—a critical factor for denuclearization to proceed. South Korea would oversee the energy and economic cooperation group, which, in tandem with North–South dialogue, would be critical for providing incentives for Pyongyang to deliver. It would require close coordination with China and would test Seoul's restraint in not allowing benefits to outstrip Pyongyang's denuclearization activities. Japan would meanwhile focus on bilateral normalization with the DPRK, working out other bilateral issues such as the abductees problem. Russia would lead the group on the Northeast Asian peace and security mechanism, the most long-term enterprise, with the four parties having first to agree a peace treaty to end the Korean War.

This approach went beyond subcontracting various aspects of conflict management because it held the prospect of institutionalizing the agreed shared responsibility, not just for the Korean conflict, but wider regional order. The September 2007 agreement generated such optimism that it seemed to some observers that 'the tectonic plates under East Asia are shifting...Japanese colonialism, the division of Korea...the long isolation of North Korea and its confrontation with the United States and with South Korea, and the bitter hostility between it and Japan: all these things suddenly seem to be negotiable'.[59] Certainly, the broad appeal of this model of multilateral stakeholder conflict management was reflected in the multiple calls for institutionalizing the 6PT beyond the nuclear crisis into a permanent Northeast Asian security institution.[60]

In terms of United States–China power sharing, the 6PT lends itself to at least two interpretations. The first credits the idea of China and the United States developing a joint responsible stakeholdership in East Asia. They would exercise concerted great power management by providing leadership, limiting the impact of conflicts, restraining allies, and ensuring that agreed rules are followed.[61] It is worth recalling that China's role in formally managing the Korean problem has come by repeated and widespread invitation—in the 1990s Seoul sought Chinese help to reach out to Pyongyang; the Clinton administration pressed China for help in the first nuclear crisis

[59] McCormack 2007a, 2.
[60] Moore 2008, 20.
[61] Robert Zoellick, 'Whither China: From Membership to Responsibility', speech to National Committee on United States–China Relations, Washington DC, 21 September 2005; Funabashi 2007, 314–18.

without success; the subsequent Perry process and sunshine policy efforts at engaging with North Korea went via China; and in the second nuclear crisis the United States sought mediation, South Korea sought help to oppose sanctions or a military response, while Russia looked to China to coordinate the great power response. By its 6PT role, China was explicitly recognized as the most important regional great power leading the joint provision of crucial security public goods. Official Chinese sources too acknowledged the boost to China's status as great power and responsible public goods provider through 'co-management' on an equal basis with the United States.[62] That China possessed a shared interest in counter-proliferation was without doubt, since DPRK nuclear posturing might trigger regional nuclearization in Japan, Taiwan, and South Korea. Another explosive conflict on the Korean peninsula would also jeopardize China's core imperative of resolving the Taiwan issue; while an eventual Korean reunification under Republic of Korea (ROK) leadership would adversely affect China's strategic landscape. The 6PT thus allowed Beijing to engage in defensive cooperation with the United States, to prevent potential encirclement, and even perhaps to shape outcomes such as the conditions under which Korean reunification would take place, and the promotion of alternative security frameworks to US alliances.[63]

These instrumental reasons for China's facilitation of the 6PT process belies a crucial difference between Chinese and American conceptions of stakeholdership: the Chinese notion is more dynamic, with the expectation that a recognized place at the table gains the stakeholder the right to negotiate the terms and conditions of the evolving order. The American notion, in contrast, stems from the post-Cold War triumphalist mindset that other great powers should prove themselves worthy of a stake in the US-led world order by acceding to the terms and conditions as they find them. This difference is reflected in the alternative interpretation of the 6PT as Washington subcontracting the diplomatic work of multilaterally managing the Korean nuclear problem to China. In this interpretation, the multilateral mechanism is aimed mainly at garnering sufficient legitimacy via UNSC support for a 'regime of discipline for the region to uphold the NPT through multilateral sanctions'. The associated US aim vis-à-vis China would be to forge a new multilateral order in which China's willingness to be incorporated as a 'responsible stakeholder' under US leadership is continually assessed, starting with the extent to which it is willing to align itself with US policy priorities on the Korean peninsula.[64]

---

[62] Chung 2006, 156; Zhao 2006.
[63] Shen 2009.
[64] Clegg 2011, 128–31.

Three factors mediate the extent of power sharing and support the sub-contracting narrative for the 6PT. First, the George W. Bush administration significantly reinforced nuclear proliferation as the key security public good at stake on the Korean peninsula, re-inscribing the problem onto its new national security imperative of counter-terrorism. The resulting *uber*-securitization of proliferation to/by terrorists found in Pyongyang an easy target; Bush's messianic style and visceral personal aversion to Kim Jong Il was as important as North Korean brinksmanship in stalling conflict management.[65] Crucially, the administration's March 2002 Nuclear Posture Review included the DPRK on a list of seven potential target states for pre-emptive nuclear attack, effectively reneging on the Clinton administration's negative security assurances to Pyongyang.[66] This threatening posture was reinforced by the relocation of the US 'tripwire' forces away from the demilitarized zone (DMZ);[67] the ballistic missile defence programme; and the strengthening of naval and air capabilities in Japan, South Korea, and the Pacific within striking distance of North Korea. The Pentagon also developed operational plans to foster regime change in Pyongyang.[68]

Second, the Bush administration's reasons for co-opting China reflected its continuing focus on sanctioning North Korea. As Cha put it, US engagement was 'an exit strategy that builds a coalition for punishment', rather than an open-ended policy seeking North Korean reform.[69] Great power coordination was geared towards improving the effectiveness of sanctions: the Bush administration needed China's participation to impose credible sanctions, since the United States 'could dangle carrots but could not wave big enough sticks' against Pyongyang.[70] The United States has very limited bilateral relations with the DPRK, but an estimated half of Chinese foreign aid went to North Korea and 80 per cent of the latter's fuel needs were met through imports from China.[71] Even neo-conservatives in the Bush administration admitted China's importance in the Korean problem due to its ability to turn the screws on Pyongyang. For them, the multilateral talks were important 'to prepare the way for synchronized pressure for China to take decisive measures'.[72] In other words, China was just as much a target of the 6PT process as the DPRK.

---

[65] Woodward 2002, 340; Moon and Bae 2004, 40.
[66] Kristensen 2002.
[67] A controversial decision that strained the United States–ROK alliance, and that South Korean President Roh agreed eventually to in a 'tactical...adaptation to the reality of America's hegemonic power'—Lee 2006, 238.
[68] 'Upping the ante for Kim Jong Il', *US News and World Report*, 13 July 2003.
[69] Cha and Kang 2003, 98.
[70] Victor Cha, pers. comm., June 2012
[71] Chung 2010, 90.
[72] Rozman 2007, 34.

Third, more than forging consensus on public goods and regional order, the 6PT process exacerbated divergence among the key players. Domestically, authority over US policy in Korea was snarled in distraction and discord; subcontracting China to manage multilateral pressure on Pyongyang was a way to park the North Korea problem while the global war on terrorism was being prosecuted. Antagonism towards North Korea, suspicions about allies, and even distrust of its own diplomats led to the Bush administration's rigid approach to Pyongyang. Liberals warned that North Korea must be given credible assurances to solve the nuclear problem,[73] but the US North Korea envoys were all constrained by neo-conservatives such as Vice-President Dick Cheney, Under-Secretary of Defense Douglas Feith, and Under-Secretary for Arms Control (and later UN ambassador) John Bolton, who regarded negotiation as incompatible with Washington's hopes for regime change in Pyongyang.[74] In the face of divergent priorities, alliance discipline proved difficult for Washington to maintain. Following the first inter-Korean summit in 2000, Seoul became increasingly unwilling to make North–South economic cooperation conditional upon the resolution of the nuclear problem, particularly given its opposition to Bush's inclusion of North Korea in the 'axis of evil'.[75] In the midst of the second nuclear crisis, Japanese Prime Minister Koizumi conducted normalization talks with the DPRK.[76] Moreover, South Korea's interests appeared increasingly aligned with China's, with their common approach favouring engagement, reforms, and eventual reunification. Beijing and Seoul coordinated closely in 2003–5 to persuade Washington to compromise and in 2006 to convince Pyongyang to return to the talks.[77] After 2004, they were united in opposing Japan's inclusion of the abductees issue on the 6PT agenda, and the two bilateral relationships broke down in 2004–5 over history disputes. In July 2005, Seoul split from Washington's opposition to energy assistance and publicly putting forward a Marshall Plan-like, front-loaded electricity-for-nuclear deal for Pyongyang.[78] Japan, in contrast, cleaved closer to the Bush administration's sanctions strategy from 2006, lobbying to invoke Article 7 of the UN Charter with potential for military action, as Abe Shinzo rode the tide of nationalist opinion against North Korea's nuclear test and abductees.[79]

---

[73] Kim and Kang 2009.
[74] On the broad division between the 'confrontation school' of counter-proliferationists and the 'pro-engagement school' of area specialists, see Funabashi 2007, ch. 4; Pritchard 2007.
[75] See Larson et al. 2004.
[76] More troubling for Washington were reports that Japanese officials were discussing an economic package in the region of $5–10 billion, worth a quarter to half of North Korea's GDP at the time—Manyin 2003.
[77] Shambaugh 2003, 49–50.
[78] 'South Korea offers a trade for North's disarmament', *New York Times*, 12 July 2005.
[79] Taylor 2010, 42–3.

United States–China divergences also heightened within the 6PT process. Temporarily subcontracting negotiations with Pyongyang to China did not entail a deeper desire for renegotiating regional order on Washington's part. China's hierarchy of priorities for the Korean peninsula diverged fundamentally from the Bush administration's; Beijing principally sought to prevent regime collapse in Pyongyang and to avoid a US attack on North Korea.[80] One obvious implication of creating a Northeast Asian security institution from the 6PT process would be to institutionalize China's co-leading role in East Asia more broadly. The way in which the Bush administration undermined the 2005 and 2007 agreements suggested not a division of labour over managing the counter-WMD public good so much as blocking of growing Chinese influence through the 6PT.[81] At the same time, China's support for UNSC sanctions against North Korea in 2006 came at the price of weakening these very sanctions. China agreed to vote in favour of Resolution 1695 against the DPRK's missile tests only after any reference to Chapter 7 of the UN Charter invoking the option of force was dropped; and supported Resolution 1718 against its nuclear test only after trade and travel sanctions were limited to luxury goods and WMD-related trade.[82] After Pyongyang's second nuclear test in May 2009, China again diluted UNSC sanctions, blocking in particular the US attempt to inscribe PSI principles of interdiction into Resolution 1874.[83] Beijing also continued allowing the DPRK to route trade and financial transactions through China.[84]

HEGEMONIC REASSERTION

By the time of North Korea's second nuclear test in 2009, the strategic climate had shifted away from the superficial great power concert to more intense Sino-American power competition. Reflecting the importance of allied complicity in hegemonic maintenance, the turning point came as a result of political transition in South Korea in 2008. Conservative President Lee Myung-bak's election ended a decade of sunshine policy with a return to linkage between denuclearization and economic cooperation. Criticized by detractors as reneging on the inter-Korean summit agreements, Lee's version of the 'grand bargain' with the North amounted to 'unilateral disarmament first, grand goodies later'.[85] This policy shift significantly altered the balance between inducement and coercion towards Pyongyang, since the ROK had overtaken China as the DPRK's top export partner by 2008.[86] With Seoul now

---

[80] Shambaugh 2003; Song 2011.
[81] Rozman 2007, 34.
[82] Snyder 2007, 36. These sanctions had 'no perceptible effect' on DPRK trade with China and the ROK—Noland 2009.
[83] Glaser 2009; Haggard and Noland 2010, 563–5.
[84] Congressional Research Service 2010.
[85] Kim 2011, 157.
[86] Kim 2011, 167.

ranged alongside Washington demanding CVID on top of Tokyo's insistence on the abductees issue being settled, heavy fuel shipments were suspended by December 2008 and the 6PT lay in tatters.

Lee's election also facilitated a significant tightening of the United States–ROK alliance. From April 2008, South Korea was given the same access to US military technologies as NATO allies.[87] In 2008–9, the two militaries developed joint contingency plans for North Korean emergencies that included invasion plans.[88] Pyongyang provoked this military encirclement: after launching a Taepodong-2 missile in April 2009, it announced that it was withdrawing from the NPT, nullifying the armistice agreement, and resuming its nuclear programme. Its second nuclear test in May caused Washington to issue the first written assurance of a nuclear umbrella for the ROK,[89] Seoul to upgrade its commitment to PSI, and Japan to impose a full trade embargo.

Even as Seoul and Washington announced evidence that the DPRK had resumed nuclear activities, North Korea allegedly sank the ROK navy corvette *Cheonan* in March 2010, killing forty-six crew. In the first artillery strike since the Korean War ended, North Korean forces fired 170 artillery shells and rockets at South Korea's Yeonpyeong Island, hitting civilian and military targets in November. While the first engendered intensified sanctions, the second led to a more militarized response in the form of large-scale US military exercises with Japan and South Korea in the Yellow Sea. North Korea's actions also fuelled increased alliance unity as Seoul delayed the planned transfer of US wartime command over South Korean forces back to the ROK. This coordinated response contrasted with China's apparent disregard for the security of DPRK neighbours in its slow response to the *Cheonan* incident and protests against the US-led military exercises.[90] Leaked diplomatic cables suggest that, exasperated with the North Korean regime acting like a 'spoiled child', Beijing was at something of a loose end about how to rein in its ally.[91] As a result, China lost the main source of its authority in great power management of the Korean conflict. North Korea's failed rocket launch in April 2012 destroyed a food-for-nuclear and missile moratorium deal between the Obama administration and the newly installed

---

[87] Kim 2009. Seoul's preference has been to develop an independent missile defence capability (unlike Japan's, which is integrated into the US alliance), but the operational implications of this are debatable given US command of ROK forces.

[88] 'NK regards OPLAN 5029 as declaration of warfare', *Korea Times*, 8 November 2009. The Roh administration had strenuously resisted such contingency planning.

[89] U.S. Department of Defense, '41st U.S.-RoK Security Consultative Meeting Joint Communiqué', 23 October 2009. Available at <http://www.defense.gov/releases/release.aspx?releaseid=13072>. Accessed 12 September 2012.

[90] Shreer and Taylor 2011; see also 'North Korea relies on China, but tends to resist its guidance', *New York Times*, 23 November 2010.

[91] 'Wikileaks cables reveal China "ready to abandon North Korea"', *Guardian*, 29 November 2010.

Kim Jong-un regime. It also encouraged an exclusive allied military response in the form of the first United States–Japan–South Korea trilateral military exercise in June 2012, and the formation of a trilateral security dialogue the following month.[92] By that autumn, the United States had agreed to develop a second missile defence system with Japan and to support South Korea in building its own, to counter the increased threat from the North.[93]

Since the end of the Cold War, the Korean conflict has been subjected to two contrasting modes of management: the US-led approach focused on stopping North Korea's nuclear weapons programme, and the China-led attempt to negotiate a multilateral package deal to resolve the nuclear issue alongside a wider peace settlement for the peninsula. China's contestation of US authority is most notable for Beijing's achievement in mobilizing the key stakeholder states in the 6PT, thereby defining the conflict as a regional issue through legitimate great power management. The various 6PT agreements also established the parameters of legitimate nuclear activity for North Korea, the reciprocal bargains its neighbours would extend, and began to codify the division of responsibility among the great powers acting in concert. Yet Washington has successfully reasserted the primacy of nuclear non-proliferation and its punitive approach at critical junctures, thereby undermining the tenuous progress made in the 6PT. Pyongyang's provocation and intransigence have provided crucial de facto complicity for these US endeavours, in spurring hardliners and threat perceptions in South Korea and Japan. Fundamentally, Washington's ability to mobilize support to provide this public good relies on its superior ability to discipline North Korea by applying military deterrence and strategic sanctions. China's authority stemmed in part from the perception of its good offices as mediator because of Beijing's wider understanding of the public goods at stake, but it fell short ultimately on limited Chinese capacity to restrain Pyongyang. As a result, while US authority has been distracted, diluted, subcontracted, contested, and even shared to various degrees, conflict management on the Korean peninsula remains defined by and dependent upon Washington's priorities and capabilities.

The South China Sea

In the South China Sea (SCS), China, Taiwan, and a number of Southeast Asian states stake rival claims to three groups of islands and atolls—the

---

[92] 'Korea, US, Japan kick off trilateral naval drills', *Korea Times*, 21 June 2012; 'S. Korea, U.S., Japan move closer to building trilateral alliance', *Korea Herald*, 12 July 2012.
[93] 'South Korea expands ballistic missile system range', *BBC*, 7 October 2012; 'S. Korea to develop missile defense system within years: defense chief', *Xinhua*, 13 April 2012; 'Seoul and Washington agree to Korean Air and Missile Defense', *The Hankyoreh*, 16 June 2012.

Paracel Islands, claimed by Vietnam and Taiwan and occupied since 1974 by China; the Spratly Islands, claimed in their entirety by China, Taiwan, and Vietnam, and in part by the Philippines and Malaysia; and Scarborough Reef and Macclesfield Bank, which the Philippines, China, and Taiwan dispute.[94] The wider regional order implications of these conflicting claims arise from their potential militarization and interruption of vital international sea lines of communication (SLOCs). As the United States is a non-claimant and neutral on the territorial disputes between China and its smaller Southeast Asian neighbours, this might be a good case for testing the limits of US authority and the extent of Chinese and ASEAN authority in conflict management. Yet key SLOCs in this area ensure US interest in the issue by way of the foundational public good, freedom of navigation. In this regard, US power will have functioned to limit the dispute to a largely bilateral one with China over the military uses of maritime zones. On the territorial disputes themselves, though, the limits of the evolving international maritime legal regime either to compel resolution or arbitrate amongst competing sovereignty claims, as well as the underdevelopment of regional conflict-avoidance frameworks, have exacerbated unilateral assertions of authority. This has in turn stimulated Southeast Asian demands for the United States to exert authoritative influence diplomatically and by military deterrence.

Public Goods

In East Asia's post-Cold War transition, the SCS has become a prime arena for negotiating the scope, domain, and modes of provision of two key security public goods. The first, freedom of navigation, is superficially uncontested—all parties to the disputes have repeatedly declared their commitment to the right of vessels engaged in peaceful activities to unimpeded passage in regional maritime routes. Yet, as various incidents demonstrated—most notably when Chinese ships harassed the US navy surveillance ship *Impeccable* in March 2009,[95] and cut the cables of Vietnamese and Filipino oil exploration vessels in March–June 2011[96]—there is significant contestation over what constitutes legitimate activity within the SCS. Washington regards freedom of navigation within maritime exclusive economic zones (EEZs) as an absolute public good that ought to be available to foreign commercial as well as military surveillance vessels. In contrast, Beijing holds that the passage of foreign military vessels within a nation's EEZ is detrimental to its national security—not a public good but a common pool resource, the use of which by one party diminishes its utility to another.

---

[94] Brunei also claims an exclusive economic zone extending to the south of the Spratly Islands, though not the islands themselves. For details of these disputes, see Smith 2010.
[95] Valencia 2009a.
[96] 'Vietnam and China oil clashes intensify', *Financial Times*, 29 May 2011.

Furthermore, US naval preponderance in the region exacerbates Chinese worries that Washington could exclude adversaries from their rights to maritime passage, in effect turning freedom of navigation into a club good.

Provision of regional peace in the SCS also turns on a second intermediate public good, the negotiation of acceptable parameters for the multiple disputes over territory and jurisdiction. That is, the agreed principles by which the disputes would be adjudicated, and the norms or rules that would guide conduct while the ultimate sovereignty questions remain unresolved. Given that the claimants' universal assertion of sovereignty creates a roadblock to actual conflict resolution, the challenge meanwhile is to find modes of managing the conflict that would minimize the potential use of force. This task has been shouldered by ASEAN rather than the great powers in measures mainly focused on conflict avoidance and joint development of resources in the disputed areas. In general, the role of great powers in providing these security public goods in the SCS is less clear cut than on the Korean peninsula. As the sole great power party to the intractable sovereignty disputes, China is directly engaged in a deeply asymmetrical contest with the weaker Southeast Asian claimants. This might create impetus for Beijing to impose its will, if not for Washington's capability and proven willingness to enforce the imperative of freedom of navigation. Not only do US leaders consider freedom of navigation a vital security public good, they also regard the possession and provision of it to be their hegemonic right. Yet Washington's neutrality in the territorial disputes and aloofness from regional multilateral efforts at conflict management impose a divide between the two public goods at stake.

The great power dynamic in dealing with the SCS disputes is not only potentially confrontational, but also mutually testing. Since its 1995 seizure of Mischief Reef in the Spratly Islands, China's behaviour in these sovereignty disputes has been regarded as a test of its intentions as a rising power. Yet, arguably more is required from China if it is to prove itself a responsible great power capable of *providing* regional order—it ought to be able to manage conflicts in a sustainable, institutionalized, mutually beneficial manner. The SCS disputes also test the basis of US regional hegemony, which is pinned on its commitment to providing critical public goods such as freedom of navigation. Washington's evolving approach to conflict management here will shed light on the extent to which it is able and willing to build further the normative and institutional elements of its hegemonic leadership, in contrast to relying primarily upon its preponderant coercive power.

Authority in Conflict Management

Conflict management in the SCS has occurred at three levels, at each of which is found an arena for contestation over the public goods at stake, the norms that ought to govern conduct and dispute resolution, and the means by which authority can be exerted.

INTERNATIONAL LEGAL FRAMEWORKS

At the broadest level, the SCS disputes are constituted but also exacerbated by the consolidation of the global maritime legal regime in a prolonged process that began in 1949. The resulting 1982 United Nations Convention on the Law of the Sea (UNCLOS) is the most comprehensive international treaty after the UN Charter. Dubbed the 'constitution for the oceans', UNCLOS is the 'seminal authority' in governing the control and use of maritime zones and resources.[97] It codifies three sets of agreements on (a) the principle that sovereignty over maritime zones would be claimed primarily from control of land territory; (b) definitions of baselines from which to measure these zones; and (c) limits on territorial waters (up to 12 nautical miles) as well as two resource zones—the EEZ of up to 200 nautical miles (within which the claimant state has rights to all economic resources, especially fisheries and seabed hydrocarbons), and the continental shelf, where coastal states might extend their claims to seabed resources to 350 nautical miles or more. UNCLOS also retained the freedom of navigation principle in protecting the right of all states to navigate freely within EEZ, and granting the universal right of 'innocent passage' through territorial waters.[98]

All parties to the SCS disputes have asserted their commitment to international law.[99] UNCLOS's relevance for conflict management here is reflected in the way even non-signatory states frame their disputes using divergent interpretations of its provisions, while its authoritativeness is indicated by the growing use of its associated procedures and channels by claimants to conduct their disputes. Notwithstanding its non-signatory status, Washington's disagreement with Beijing over military vessels and activities is a long-standing one within UNCLOS negotiations.[100] Washington's stance

---

[97] 'A Constitution for the Oceans', remarks by Tommy Koh of Singapore, President of the Third United Nations Conference on the Law of the Sea, 6–11 December 1982. Available at <http://www.un.org/Depts/los/convention_agreements/texts/koh_english.pdf>. Accessed 30 October 2012. Wilson and Kraska 2009, 269.

[98] For the sections of UNCLOS relevant to the discussion in this paragraph, see <http://www.un.org/Depts/los/convention_agreements/texts/unclos/part2.htm>.

[99] For instance, Chinese leaders repeatedly state China's commitment to freedom of navigation 'according to international law'—e.g. Foreign Minister Qian Qichen quoted in 'ASEAN-China: Southeast Asia hopes on Spratlys row raised', *Inter-Press Service*, 31 July 1995. The most recent assurance came from FM Yang Jiechi—see 'China says South China Sea freedom of navigation "assured"', *Channel News Asia*, 5 September 2012.

[100] The United States remains outside the regime because of opposition from right-wing Republicans within the Senate and a coalition of interest groups who regard the Convention as inimical to US sovereignty and national security interests—Browne 2004; Schachte 2008; Wright 2012.

is that 'innocent passage' is a right granted by international law, and that warships should not be discriminated against. The Chinese, in contrast, cite UNCLOS Article 19(2), which includes in activities considered to be non-innocent weapons practice, launching or taking on board military devices, and 'any act aimed at collecting information to the prejudice of the defence or security of the coastal State'.[101] China extends a similarly explicit security character to navigational rights in the EEZ, specifically objecting to US military surveillance activities within its resource zone as infringing on its 'security interests and sovereign rights'.[102] For the United States, the UNCLOS provision for universal rights to freedom of navigation and overflight in EEZ includes non-aggressive military activities such as surveillance, as long as they give due regard to the coastal state's rights concerning resource exploitation. Chinese interlocutors frequently cite the April 2001 collision of a Chinese military aircraft with a US EP-3 spy plane off the coast of Hainan to highlight the dangers arising from such foreign surveillance activities. The harassment of the *Impeccable* in the same area eight years later served to reinforce the Chinese point that US spying on its naval installations flouts UNCLOS provisions.

China reflects a wider resistance to US definitions of the freedom of navigation public good. For instance, Chinese scholars draw support from a set of guidelines drawn up by a 'Track II' group of senior officials, legal experts, and maritime specialists from the Asia-Pacific in 2005. Aimed at clarifying the rights and obligations of coastal and user states within EEZ after the EP-3 incident, these guidelines stipulate that 'ships and aircraft of a State undertaking military activities in the EEZ of another State have the obligation to use the ocean for peaceful purposes only; and to refrain from the threat or use of force, or provocative acts, such as stimulating or exciting the defensive system of the coastal State; collecting information to support the use of force against the coastal State; or establishing a "sea base" within another State's EEZ without its consent'.[103] While these guidelines are exhortatory and non-binding, their codification adds to US concerns about emerging customary law giving coastal states the right to regulate navigation through their EEZ. This is particularly pertinent to the United States, which as a non-signatory to UNCLOS remains subject to evolving customary law of the sea.[104]

---

[101] As the parties were unable to reach consensus on this issue, it was left vague in the Convention—see Oxman 1981, 235.

[102] Beckman 2012, 7; Yang 2012, 56.

[103] EEZ Group 21 2005. Funded mainly by the OPRF, the Group consisted of five representatives from Japan, and one each from Australia, Indonesia, the Philippines, China, South Korea, Vietnam, India, Russia, the United States, and the International Tribunal for the Law of the Sea.

[104] See, for instance, Van Dyke 2005.

Authority and Public Goods: Managing Regional Conflicts

Regarding the SCS territorial disputes, claimant states have utilized the international legal channels associated with UNCLOS to air and legitimize their conflicting claims, and to block each other's attempts to formalize their maritime regimes. The prime example is the process by which states submitted information to the Commission on the Limits on the Continental Shelf (CLCS) to support claims for extended continental shelves in 2009. In introducing domestic legislation to clarify its baselines according to UNCLOS's archipelagic definition, the Philippines included the disputed features in the SCS as a 'regime of islands'. Malaysia and Vietnam lodged a joint submission to CLCS to extend their continental shelf claims beyond 200 nautical miles into the SCS as measured from their baselines.[105] China formally objected to all these submissions on the grounds that they infringed on its 'indisputable' sovereign rights and jurisdiction in the SCS, leading to an exchange of diplomatic Notes Verbale to the UN Secretary-General among the disputants. This airing of the legal dispute included China's circulation to UN members of the infamous 1949 'nine-dashed lines map' on which its claims are based. Through this exchange, Beijing appeared to clarify that it claimed the islands in the SCS and their associated maritime zones, rather than sovereignty over all the waters within the lines.[106] By their CLCS submissions, Malaysia, Vietnam, and the Philippines also seemed to limit their sovereignty claims to 12 nautical miles' territorial waters off SCS islands. Some legal scholars are thus optimistic that various claimants are gradually clarifying their sovereignty claims in line with UNCLOS provisions, and that this ascription to a 'common framework...should make it easier to explore possible solutions'.[107]

Yet, even though there may be growing recognition of the authority of the UNCLOS legal frameworks in legitimizing sovereignty claims, the territorial disputes themselves remain outside the governance of this maritime regime. UNCLOS has no provisions to adjudicate on territorial disputes. Even if the sovereignty claims were agreed, by UNCLOS definitions only a small number of the disputed features in the SCS potentially qualify as 'islands', the only offshore features from which maritime zones may be claimed.[108] Furthermore, while the content and extent of China's claims to the offshore features and waters of the SCS remain unclear, discussion of the

---

[105] China as well as the Philippines invoked the rules of procedure of the CLCS successfully to prevent the Commission from considering Vietnam's and Malaysia's submissions on the grounds that they referred to an area in which maritime disputes exist.

[106] Examining Chinese laws and official statements, Fravel 2011 draws the more general conclusion that the only possible interpretation of the nine-dashed lines is that they delineate ownership of the Paracels and Spratlys.

[107] Beckman and Davenport 2010; Beckman 2010, 2.

[108] The interpretation of these provisions is still debated—see Van Dyke and Brooks 1983; Song 2010.

interpretation of UNCLOS provisions is premature.[109] Because of Beijing's deliberate ambiguity, the Southeast Asian claimants fear the potentially extensive and illegal Chinese claim on territorial waters covering over 80 per cent of the SCS.[110] While UNCLOS has a compulsory dispute settlement system, there is nevertheless an 'opt out' clause for certain categories of disputes, and China has exercised its right to exclude from this system issues of boundary delimitations, military activities, and fisheries and research activities in overlapping EEZs.[111]

REGIONAL CONFLICT-AVOIDANCE FRAMEWORKS

The main mode of conflict management regarding the SCS territorial disputes is conflict avoidance, chiefly through diplomatic and non-binding regional mechanisms led by ASEAN and involving China. ASEAN's conflict-management role began at the non-official 'Track II' level in 1990, when an Indonesian diplomat and maritime legal expert convened annual workshops on managing potential conflicts in the SCS involving ASEAN and non-member claimant states Vietnam, China, and Taiwan.[112] These exercises set the tone for subsequent ASEAN efforts to set aside sovereignty disputes in favour of confidence building through cooperation in scientific research, environmental protection, and resource management; and promote preventive diplomacy through regular official dialogue.[113] ASEAN's first official step at managing the conflict came in response to the passage of China's 1992 Law on Territorial Waters and Contiguous Areas by which it formally claimed the Paracels, Spratlys, and over 80 per cent of the SCS. In a July 1992 Declaration, members invoked ASEAN's TAC and called for all parties to 'exercise restraint with the view to creating a positive climate for the eventual resolution of all disputes...by peaceful means, without resort to the use of force'.[114]

China's surprise occupation during the 1994 monsoon season of Mischief Reef in the Spratlys, claimed by the Philippines, triggered sufficient ASEAN protest to persuade Chinese leaders to agree to multilateral discussions about the dispute. At the time, the simultaneous souring of relations with the United States and Japan had caused the Chinese foreign policy establishment to conclude that their twin imperatives, of preventing encirclement by the United States and ensuring economic development, would best be achieved through positive diplomacy to de-securitize China's rise.[115]

---

[109] Zou 1999; Beckman 2011.
[110] On China's sovereignty claims, see Valencia et al. 1997, 20–4; Tonnesson 2002.
[111] Beckman 2011, 25–7.
[112] Vietnam joined ASEAN in 1995. These workshops remain the only SCS multilateral forum that includes Taiwan.
[113] Djalal 2002.
[114] ASEAN Secretariat 1992.
[115] See Johnston 2008, chapter 4.

Southeast Asia was a premier demonstration precinct for Beijing to cultivate benign perceptions to mediate 'China threat' perceptions.[116] After four years of wrangling, ASEAN and China produced the first multilateral agreement on conflict management in a Declaration on the Conduct of Parties in the SCS (DoC) in November 2002. The agreement hails every relevant existing normative framework—the UN Charter, UNCLOS, ASEAN's TAC, and China's Five Principles of Peaceful Coexistence—to commit the parties to peaceful dispute resolution 'without resorting to the threat or use of force...in accordance with universally recognized principles of international law'; to self-restraint, including not further occupying uninhabited features; and to enhancing exchanges and cooperation including providing voluntary advance notice of military exercises in the area.

Insofar as China has signed its only multilateral agreement regarding the SCS with ASEAN and has formally ascribed to the Association's norms, ASEAN has claimed for itself an authoritative role in mobilizing support from the key stakeholders to provide the public good of conflict avoidance. ASEAN's authority in leading these frameworks stems from China's ascription to its approach based on exhortation and volunteerism rather than regulation and enforcement. The SCS conflict-management mechanisms represented the high point of ASEAN engagement policies towards China, discussed in Chapter 2. China appeared to be responding to ASEAN's attempts to bind it socially and morally to peaceful conduct: Beijing became the first external party to subscribe formally to TAC in 2003, proposed bilateral SCS joint development schemes with Brunei and the Philippines in 2005, and began joint patrols with Vietnam in the Gulf of Tonkin in 2006.[117]

To the extent that authority rests upon efficacy in regulating the parameters of agreed legitimate conduct, however, there are significant limitations to ASEAN's leadership role. The DoC was only a political statement by the parties agreeing to work towards a formal code of conduct (CoC); considerable scepticism surrounds ASEAN's ability ultimately to deliver a binding code that would sustainably restrain the conflicting claimants or help to clarify and resolve the territorial disputes.[118] In negotiating the DoC, ASEAN's inability to reach internal consensus left it vulnerable to Chinese pressure to compromise on key issues, including the complete avoidance of the sovereignty claims, the exclusion of Taiwan, the non-binding and non-geographically specific nature of the agreement,[119] and the failure to ban further construction on occupied features.[120]

[116] See Wang 2004; Ba 2003.
[117] See Goh 2007; Shambaugh 2004/5.
[118] For a flavour of the debate, see Buszynski 2003; Wu and Ren 2003.
[119] Malaysia and China objected to the Philippines' and Vietnam's insistence on a binding code; while China resisted Vietnam's desire to include the Paracels explicitly in the agreement.
[120] Emmers 2010a, 73–4, 119–20.

ASEAN and China failed to agree a CoC in the decade after the DoC was signed, a period during which China's strong preference for bilateral means of conflict management remained evident. For instance, Beijing and Manila signed a confidential three-year agreement for joint commercial surveys of oil and gas resources around the Spratlys in 2004, in spite of DoC obligations that all signatories have to agree upon the modalities, scope, and locations for any such cooperation.[121] China also dealt bilaterally with Vietnam to manage their conflict: after tensions in 2007–8 over skirmishes in the disputed area, the mutual raising of the administrative status of disputed islands and China's reported pressure on ExxonMobil to drop out of an exploration deal with Vietnam in the SCS, the two sides agreed to joint exploration of energy resources, collaboration in research, and information exchange between armed forces.[122] After the dispute flared again in 2011, they negotiated a six-point agreement on principles for solving maritime disputes, including the establishment of a hotline and bi-annual border discussions.[123]

China's basic opposition to negotiating with ASEAN as a block on the SCS did not dissipate with the signing of the DoC. Beijing effectively blocked progress towards implementing the declaration by rejecting ASEAN's practice of consulting with each other to formulate a common position ahead of negotiations with China. By 2009, frustrated Southeast Asian officials complained publicly about Chinese backtracking on the commitment to multilateral conflict management. In 2010, their disquiet intensified with reports that Chinese officials labelled the SCS one of China's 'core national sovereignty interests'—a term which it had previously only applied to Taiwan, Tibet, and Xinjiang.[124] Indirectly acknowledging the limits of ASEAN's authority, Vietnam used its position as the rotating chair of the Association to 'internationalize' the SCS disputes. To increase the pressure for a CoC, Hanoi ensured that the issue was discussed in wider Asia-Pacific fora at the ASEAN Regional Forum ministerial meeting and the ASEAN Defence Ministers Plus Eight inaugural meeting in 2010. It also successfully lobbied Washington to make strong public statements on the dispute at both events.[125] Those in favour of moving towards a binding code triumphed with the July 2011 China–ASEAN Agreement on Guidelines for the Implementation of the DoC. The legitimacy of ASEAN's collective role in the negotiations was also asserted when the Association's Senior Officials Meeting was tasked with drafting the

---

[121] Vietnam joined the renamed Joint Marine Seismic Undertaking agreement in 2005, but domestic opposition within the Philippines stymied any progress before its expiration in 2008. See Valencia 2008; Baviera 2012, 11–18.

[122] Emmers 2010, 80.

[123] 'China and Vietnam sign agreement to cool sea dispute', *Reuters*, 12 October 2011.

[124] 'Changing tides to watch in the South China Sea', *Straits Times*, 14 June 2010; Swaine 2011.

[125] Swaine and Fravel 2011.

Authority and Public Goods: Managing Regional Conflicts

legally binding CoC.[126] Be that as it may, ASEAN authority suffered a body blow when the Association's foreign ministers failed to agree a joint statement during its 2012 meeting because Cambodia, as the rotating chair, was reluctant to put pressure on China.[127]

Essentially, ASEAN–China SCS conflict-avoidance frameworks aim to maintain the status quo until the sovereignty disputes are resolved. Like the international legal frameworks, they do not address directly these sovereignty issues. Rather, the hope is that the disputants can be persuaded to freeze and shelve their competing claims for the time being, and (a) mutually abide by norms to constrain their conduct to peaceful means; while they (b) pursue joint development schemes that would cultivate 'win–win' cooperation without prejudicing their territorial claims. However, the small number of joint development schemes in the SCS 'has so far not constituted a feasible strategy to de-escalate maritime sovereignty disputes' since claimant states have not been able to shelve sovereignty questions.[128] Moreover, China and some ASEAN states continue to resist developing formal norms constraining behaviour. As argued in the previous chapter, a stable regional order rests upon the constrainment of unequal power within institutional bargains, but ASEAN's multilateral dialogue process 'is not embedding Chinese power nor is it convincingly addressing the lingering uncertainty over Beijing's territorial intentions'.[129]

UNILATERAL AND COERCIVE AUTHORITY

As long as the rival parties cleave to their sovereignty claims in the SCS, regional stability cannot be achieved via international legal frameworks, and regional conflict-avoidance measures remain partial and unstable. These limitations justify self-help from claimant states, in terms of asserting unilateral authority and by harnessing US deterrence as the ultimate guarantor of stability. Assertions of unilateral authority take three forms: occupation, administration, and enforcement of disputed areas. In the Spratlys, for instance, Taiwan occupies the largest island in Itu Aba, China occupies seven features, Malaysia five, the Philippines nine, and Vietnam twenty-one.[130] But China stands out for its use of force and assertiveness. Chinese forces expelled Vietnam from the Paracels in 1974 and seized new territory in the Spratlys in another naval confrontation in 1988. After occupying Mischief Reef in 1994, China built defence structures on it, triggering similar actions by other claimants.[131] Unimpeded by the 2002 DoC, the various claimants

---

[126] 'South China Sea guidelines agreed', *Jakarta Post*, 21 July 2011; Thayer 2011a, 7–8.
[127] 'SE Asia meeting in disarray over sea dispute with China', *Reuters*, 13 July 2012.
[128] Emmers 2013.
[129] Emmers 2010b, 130.
[130] Schofield and Storey 2009.
[131] Emmers 2010a, 67–72.

continued to station troops, build military and administrative infrastructure, settle populations, and develop tourism on occupied features. China also planted markers on unoccupied reefs in the Paracels in 2006.

China, Vietnam, and the Philippines have reinforced their occupation activities with unilateral assertions of formal authority. Each has passed domestic legislation—China's 1992 Territorial Waters Law, the Philippines' 2009 Baselines Law, and Vietnam's national Law of the Sea adopted in 2012—to lay formal claims to the disputed territory.[132] Philippine President Beningno Aquino formally renamed parts of the disputed area the West Philippine Sea in 2012.[133] Others boosted the status of the administrative bodies responsible for the disputed territories: after Vietnam upgraded Spratly Island to a 'township' in April 2007, Beijing created a prefecture-level city based in Sansha in the Paracels, complete with its own garrison command.[134] In addition, both sides have conducted large military manoeuvres and live firing exercises within disputed areas during periods of tension in 2007, after criticism of China's assertiveness during the ARF meeting in 2010, and in June 2011 after the cable-cutting episodes.

More significantly, these three states have asserted unilateral authority in the SCS by increasing their surveillance and enforcement activities vis-à-vis each other's resource claims and exploitation. China has imposed and enforced an annual unilateral fishing ban in parts of the Sea. From 2005, Chinese maritime security patrols have detained Vietnamese fishermen, confiscated their catches,[135] and at times rammed and shot at Vietnamese and Filipino boats. In 2011, China tried to deny the Philippines and Vietnam access to hydrocarbon exploration within their own EEZ: the cable-cutting incidents suggest that Chinese agencies retain a policy of enforcing their perceived sovereign rights within China's nine-dashed lines, regardless of the nuances of Beijing's diplomatic communiqués. The two-month stand-off between Chinese and Filipino vessels after the former tried to chase Filipino fishermen away from Scarborough Shoal in April 2012 reinforced regional worries about increasingly assertive Chinese claims in waters within other claimants' EEZs far away from the key disputed islands.[136]

While China has not been alone in these assertions of authority, its actions have been stronger than others' to support claims which are 'both unusually extensive and intentionally vague'.[137] Furthermore, China's coercive actions are undertaken by a mixture of naval, paramilitary, and other

---

[132] 'China lawmakers slam claim to islands by Hanoi', *China Daily*, 1 October 2012.
[133] 'Aquino signs order on West Philippine Sea', *Philippine Star*, 12 September 2012.
[134] 'China establishes Sansha city', *Xinhua*, 24 July 2012; 'China approves military garrison', *BBC News*, 23 July 2012.
[135] 2010 saw a peak of these Sino-Vietnamese incidents, coinciding with Vietnam's attempts to internationalize the dispute as ASEAN chair that year—see Thayer 2011b, 357–61.
[136] Swaine and Fravel 2011, 5–6.
[137] Roy 2012.

vessels from multiple agencies empowered with surveillance and denial duties. Chief amongst these are two paramilitary law enforcement agencies: the China Marine Surveillance, charged with maritime law enforcement under the auspices of the State Oceanic Administration; and the Fisheries Law Enforcement Command—both well equipped with patrol vessels and undergoing upgrading and expansion.[138] These competing law enforcement agencies, along with the People's Liberation Army Navy (PLAN), local government, the Foreign Ministry, and energy companies diffuse domestic authority for policing China's SCS claims, piling coordination problems and competitive bureaucratic dynamics on top of the pressures of rising mass nationalism.[139] China's use of paramilitary forces presents an unarmed, non-military approach while holding its superior naval power in reserve.[140] This pushes the militarily inferior Southeast Asian claimants in a no-win situation: not reacting risks allowing China to create de facto authority over disputed areas, while reacting forcibly risks being accused of belligerence against unarmed ships, and deploying warships risks asymmetrical military confrontation.[141]

Since 2010, Vietnam and the Philippines have tried to ease this game of 'chicken' by turning to the United States for strategic reassurance regarding the SCS. Their advances coincided with rising US concerns about Chinese maritime assertiveness after the 2009 *Impeccable* incident, China's reluctance to condemn North Korea after the sinking of the *Cheonan* in March 2010, and Chinese officials' reference to the SCS as a 'core national interest'. Longer-term US worries about China's growing military power and corresponding demands for spheres of influence were also fuelled by the discovery of a new Chinese underground nuclear submarine base on Hainan Island that can be used as a staging post for pursuing its maritime claims in the SCS.[142] This critical naval base will raise China's stakes in protecting its maritime access in the area and tip the balance of military forces among the rival claimants even more in China's favour.[143]

Since 2010, the Obama administration has extended strategic assurance to the Southeast Asian states in the form of diplomatic support and military deterrence. More important has been Washington's intervention in SCS conflict

[138] 'China increases its surveillance fleet capabilities', *Taipei Times*, 14 May 2012; 'China to promote drones for marine surveillance', *Xinhua*, 23 September 2012.
[139] See International Crisis Group 2012.
[140] 'Small wars loom large on China's horizon', *Asia Times*, 6 April 2012.
[141] Holmes 2012.
[142] Valencia 2009b; Emmers 2010a, 74–6.
[143] For instance, Vietnam, the most militarily powerful of the Southeast Asian claimants, only procured its first six Kilo-class diesel–electric submarines in 2009, a year in which PLAN reportedly possessed fifty-eight diesel–electric and eight nuclear-powered submarines in addition to the largest fleet of combat aircraft amongst the claimant states. 'Vietnam takes on Russia with Russian submarine deal', *The Telegraph*, 17 December 2009; 'China's interest is guarding subs', *Canberra Times*, 10 September 2012.

management through the definition of the key public goods at stake and how to provide them. As discussed above, in 2010 Vietnam sought diplomatic support from Washington for ASEAN's floundering efforts to avoid an SCS conflict with China. In the first extensive articulation of US policy on the SCS since the Mischief Reef incident in 1995, Secretary of State Hillary Clinton issued a statement at the ARF meeting in July 2010. Clinton asserted US 'national interest in the freedom of navigation, open access to Asia's maritime commons, and respect for international law' in the SCS. Inasmuch as these were universal principles shared by 'the broader international community', resolving the SCS disputes was 'pivotal to regional stability'. That is, since these disputes involved public goods, they could not be managed purely bilaterally, and the United States had a legitimate reason to be concerned. Some of the Southeast Asian states had urged clear US support of ASEAN's agenda for multilateral negotiations with China and an 'authoritative reiteration of the wider international principles and interests at stake'.[144] Clinton delivered, but went further in stamping US authority over conflict management: she held out the prospect of sustained US involvement in the process of negotiating a CoC in extending US help to 'facilitate initiatives and confidence building measures'.[145] This antagonized the Chinese foreign minister into warning ASEAN that 'China is a big country and other countries are small countries, and that is just a fact.'[146]

President Obama highlighted the three key public goods at stake in the SCS as freedom of navigation, peaceful dispute resolution, and respect for international maritime laws,[147] while Secretary of Defense Robert Gates put similar items forward as 'principles for regional peace and stability' at the inaugural ASEAN Defence Ministers '+ 8' meeting in October 2010. Gates reminded his counterparts of Washington's long-standing commitment to providing both club and public security goods in the region: 'The United States has always exercised our rights and supported the rights of others to transit through, and operate in, international waters. This will not change, nor will our commitment to engage in activities and exercises together with our allies and partners. These activities are a routine and critical component of demonstrating our commitment to the region, maintaining peace and stability, and promoting freedom of navigation.'[148]

---

[144] Author interview with Filipino Foreign Ministry official, June 2011.
[145] Clinton 2010.
[146] 'Clinton wades into South China Sea territorial dispute', *Washington Post*, 23 July 2010. On the limitations to Southeast Asian willingness to push the United States–China divide too far, though, see 'ASEAN caught in a tight spot', *The Straits Times*, 16 September 2010.
[147] 'Obama and ASEAN leaders call for peaceful resolution of maritime disputes', *LA Times*, 25 September 2010; 'Sino-U.S. ties falter over South China Sea', *China Daily*, 27 September 2010.
[148] 'Remarks by Secretary Gates at ASEAN Defense Ministers Meeting Plus', 12 October 2010, available at <http://www.defense.gov/transcripts/transcript.aspx?transcriptid=4700>. Accessed 12 September 2012.

Authority and Public Goods: Managing Regional Conflicts

Washington's definition of peaceful dispute resolution was also fleshed out by Clinton at the ARF in supporting 'a collaborative, diplomatic process by all claimants for resolving the various territorial disputes without coercion', a formula that went beyond previous injunctions against 'the threat or use of force'.[149] After the stand-off at Scarborough Reef in 2012, an official State Department statement on US policy towards the SCS raised the bar by comprehensively urging the resolution of disputes 'without coercion, without intimidation, without threats, and without the use of force'. It singled out the unilateral assertions short of military force that China undertook, including coercive economic actions[150] and China's upgrading of Sansha City. Following ASEAN's diplomatic failure at the July 2012 foreign ministers' meeting, the US statement also endorsed the ASEAN-led conflict-avoidance frameworks as the key mode of regional conflict management and stressed active support for 'ASEAN unity and leadership in regional forums'.[151]

The Obama administration also hailed international legal frameworks as a key mode of conflict management, with Clinton explicitly backing the UNCLOS principle that 'legitimate claims to maritime space in the SCS should be derived solely from legitimate claims to land features'.[152] The State Department also specifically recommended 'the use of arbitration or other international legal mechanisms' to resolve these territorial disputes.[153] From 2010, therefore, the Obama administration appeared to shift beyond its traditional narrow focus on ensuring freedom of navigation towards wider attention to modes of managing the territorial disputes in the SCS. There was regional appreciation for the Obama administration's efforts to provide leadership and bring dissenters in line through authoritative support for ASEAN's institutional processes and international legal redress. As regional concerns grew after the Sino-Japanese stand-off in September–October 2010 when Japan detained a Chinese trawler near the Senkaku islands,[154] Singapore Prime Minister Lee Hsien Loong publicly hailed the United States' role as regional security guarantor and manager. He emphasized the need for Washington to maintain an active presence in Asia to show that it was

---

[149] Clinton 2010.
[150] China suspended banana imports from the Philippines.
[151] Department of State press statement, 'South China Sea', Washington DC, 3 August 2012, available at <http://www.state.gov/r/pa/prs/ps/2012/08/196022.htm>. Accessed 12 September 2012. For Beijing's defensive reactions, see 'Statement by Spokesperson Qin Gang of the Ministry of Foreign Affairs of China on the U.S. State Department Issuing a So-called Press Statement On the South China Sea', 4 August 2012; 'South China Sea should only be resolved by concerned parties, FM says', *Xinhua*, 5 August 2012.
[152] Clinton 2010.
[153] DoS press statement.
[154] 'Obama: U.S.-Japan alliance a security "cornerstone"', *Seattle Times*, 23 September 2010; 'Japan, U.S. affirm cooperation on disputed Senkaku islands', *Japan Today*, 12 October 2010.

'here to stay', since 'America plays a role in Asia that China cannot replace', including 'maintaining peace in the region'.[155]

This US role as regional security guarantor stems critically from its superior coercive authority in providing credible extended deterrence, and the regional demand for it appeared to be met vigorously in the Obama administration's 'return', 'pivot', or 'rebalance' towards Asia at the end of 2011. Militarily, this translated into a plan for modernizing basing arrangements, strengthening and connecting its security partnerships, and enhancing its military presence across the Asia-Pacific.[156] As part of the redistribution of US forces after the drawdown from Afghanistan and Iraq, and occurring at a time of fiscal austerity, this 'rebalancing' arguably held more symbolic than operational significance. The rebalance will involve a modest projected increase in US Asia-Pacific military deployment, from 50 per cent to 60 per cent of its total air and naval forces.[157] But some new arrangements, while modest, targeted the SCS: the rotational deployment of 2,500 US marines in northern Australia within projecting distance of the SCS, and four new US Navy littoral combat ships—vessels developed for rapid reaction in coastal waters—in Singapore.[158] The SCS focus was also reinforced when Clinton affirmed the United States–Philippines alliance from the deck of a US warship in Manila Bay and referred to the seas around Scarborough Shoal as the 'West Philippine Sea'.[159] The nuclear attack submarine USS *Carolina* spent a week in Subic Bay during the Sino-Filipino stand-off over Scarborough Shoal. Making hay in the 'pivot' sun, the Benigno Aquino government requested advanced aircraft and other equipment assistance from its ally.[160] In July 2012, the two sides agreed that American troops and aircraft would reuse facilities at the former US bases in Subic and Clarke Field.[161] United States–Vietnam military interactions have also increased since 2010, when the two countries conducted their first bilateral defence dialogue and joint military exercise.[162]

Yet Southeast Asian complicity with US hegemonic reassertion in the SCS has clearer limits than that of US allies in Northeast Asia. The desire for US strategic support aims to harness its superior coercive authority to pressure China into negotiating and abiding by binding conflict-avoidance norms

---

[155] 'U.S., ASEAN to push back against China', *Wall Street Journal*, 22 September 2010.
[156] Clinton 2011; U.S. Department of Defense 2012.
[157] Panetta 2012.
[158] 'U.S. Marine base for Darwin', *Sydney Morning Herald*, 11 November 2011; 'Singapore agrees to U.S. deployment of littoral combat ships', *Channel News Asia*, 2 June 2012.
[159] 'Clinton reaffirms military ties with the Philippines', *New York Times*, 16 November 2011.
[160] 'Obama, Aquino hail growing U.S.-Philippine alliance', *Washington Post*, 9 June 2012; 'U.S. helps the Philippines improve its military capability', *Guardian*, 6 August 2012.
[161] 'U.S. can use Clark, Subic bases', *Philippine Star*, 6 June 2012.
[162] 'U.S. and Vietnam stage joint naval activities', *BBC News*, 10 August 2010; 'U.S., Vietnam explore enhanced defense cooperation', *American Forces Press Service*, 18 August 2010.

with ASEAN, not to boost US hegemony per se. American diplomatic pressure in 2010 had helped to push China towards agreeing the guidelines to implement the DoC with ASEAN in 2011, but the military elements of the subsequent US 'pivot' engendered more resistance from Beijing. Indeed, Washington's SCS focus appeared in 2012 to intensify the security dilemma by both emboldening the Philippines and antagonizing China into adopting stronger stances on their territorial dispute. This in turn reignited ASEAN's strategic ambivalence. The Indonesian foreign minister cautioned that new US basing arrangements in Australia might provoke a 'vicious cycle of tensions and mistrust', while his Singaporean counterpart warned against a zero-sum, anti-China attitude in a region that is 'big enough to accommodate a rising China and a reinvigorated U.S.'[163] Even as Manila hailed US alliance support and stepped up antagonistic rhetoric against China, Cambodia as Chair refused to put pressure on China regarding its conduct in July 2012, thus jeopardizing ASEAN's diplomatic convention and reputation. Exercising their traditional leadership role in promoting ASEAN autonomy, Indonesian leaders stepped in to negotiate a six-point ASEAN agreement on principles guiding the CoC discussions.[164] Their approach to the SCS disputes reflects most ASEAN states' imperative of autonomy: to restrain China without making it impossible to live with, to borrow US deterrence without becoming entirely dependent upon it, and to safeguard ASEAN's relevance and role in regional conflict management. With its more viable independent military means and chequered history of conflict with China, Vietnam even more amply demonstrates this strategic caution. In 2010, even while it sought US authority to pressure China over the SCS disputes, Hanoi maintained close strategic ties and even deference to Beijing. The Vietnamese deputy defence minister assured China that Vietnam would not form an alliance with another country, allow foreign bases in its territory, or develop relations with another country targeted at a third party. The two sides also held five confidential meetings to discuss principles for settling maritime disputes, and inaugurated a bilateral Strategic Defence and Security Dialogue.[165] Unlike Manila's recent focus on harnessing US deterrence capability behind itself, Vietnam's strategy of self-help stressed developing some military ties with the United States to express its autonomy rather than to balance Chinese power.[166]

While the US military pivot towards Southeast Asia is fairly limited, the Obama administration's wider political rebalancing towards Asia reinforces

---

[163] 'China, Indonesia wary of U.S. troops in Darwin', *ABC News*, 17 November 2011; 'Singapore warns U.S. against anti-China election rhetoric', *BBC News*, 8 February 2012.
[164] Sebastian 2012.
[165] Li 2012, 9–10; Thayer 2011b, 362.
[166] See Thayer 2011b, 364.

its strategic reassertion in Northeast Asia since 2008. This increases both the deterrence of and antagonism in China. In the SCS, Beijing has a greater impetus for conflict avoidance, but also to retain manoeuvrability by entrenching its strategic ambiguity and indirect coercion in the territorial disputes, be these paramilitary actions or exerting influence over weaker ASEAN states to stymie efforts towards a CoC. China has exhibited less voluntary or demanded leadership in conflict management. Beijing wants to resolve the issue with as much advantage to itself as possible. It has shown a calculated openness to multilateral negotiations, but ultimately China has been reactive to and limiting of ASEAN attempts to negotiate a binding framework for conflict avoidance. Moreover, China's assertions of unilateral authority suggest an incremental entrenching of its sovereignty claims, rather than managing the dispute either by shelving them in favour of cooperation, or institutionalizing rules of the road. While ASEAN states differ on the extent to which they wish to rely upon the United States as regional security guarantor, China's reticence will perpetuate their demand that the United States maintains its expanded role in conflict management. This boosts US authority as the sole great power manager of regional order.

Conclusion

The expectation that hegemons or great powers lead by providing security public goods and managing systemic conflicts is an intuitive one, undergirded by a number of assumptions about the ease with which great powers are able to impose or gain support for these tasks. The foregoing analysis demonstrates the significant contestation, negotiation, and variability inherent in the development of post-Cold War ideas, norms, and architecture to manage conflicts and adjust the terms of great power authority in East Asia. The Korean peninsula conflict is dogged by disagreements over the prioritization of and relationship between three intermediate public goods, and subject to two competing modes of conflict management led by the United States and China. But the conflict with North Korea has spawned a clear trajectory of great power management, efforts at power sharing, and incipient notions of how the core great powers might divide and share responsibility for wider regional order. The South China Sea disputes, on the other hand, retain the separation between the freedom of navigation public good mainly concerning the United States and China, and the management of the territorial disputes between China and Southeast Asian claimants. The deep asymmetry in China–Southeast Asia relations forestalls wider aspirations regarding regional order in their attempts at conflict avoidance. Moreover, the inadequacy of international legal frameworks and of unilateral assertions of authority in restraining the continuing territorial disputes has prompted various Southeast Asian disputants to turn back to the United States for diplomatic and military guarantees.

Given the exigencies of re-justifying US preponderance, shifting alliance politics, rising powers, and more complex security issues, legitimacy and efficiency concerns have prompted Washington towards sharing responsibilities and even delegating authority to selected partners in conflict management. These dynamics highlight the negotiated nature of great power authority, and the contingent nature of consent to that authority. And yet this contingency exists within clear parameters. Like the conflicts studied here, this contested negotiation process remains unresolved, and the failure to reach agreement in both cases to institutionalize conflict management has led to a partial reversion to the old, instrumental bargain of exchanging US military deterrence and guarantees for complicity with US strategic leadership in East Asia. If actions are anything to go by, East Asian states prefer US great power management in terms of maintaining military preponderance and a security umbrella upon which they may call in times of crisis. Since 2010, South Korea, Japan, and ASEAN have all turned to the United States for reassurance in the face of threats from North Korea and China's harder line on maritime disputes. Some authors argue that as the unipolar power, the United States has disproportionate ability to manipulate the terms of its own legitimacy and by implication to perpetuate its hegemonic authority.[167] Yet this chapter suggests that East Asia has not required Washington to exert itself on this front—judging from regional security public goods provision, its legitimacy appears to rest still upon its military preponderance and the belief in its benignity relative to other threatening actors.

China, in contrast, is a confounding case for the 'Spider-Man' thesis that growing power begets greater responsibilities. Beijing has been generally reticent about providing leadership in managing regional conflicts, apparently ambivalent about the potential impacts on justifying its growing power. The limits to China's strategy of professed benignity and mutual benefit are clear in the South China Sea, where it has been reluctant to negotiate conflict limitation with its weaker neighbours in Southeast Asia. In Northeast Asia, China suffers the latecomer's dilemma of staking out a place in a strategic landscape defined by US hegemonic imperatives and institutions. Here, Beijing has not been able to leverage on its invitation to co-manage the Korean peninsula conflict either to mediate US strategic priorities sufficiently to ensure its support for the 6PT agreements or to discipline its North Korean ally. If there is indeed a 'crisis of authority' brought about by an increasingly contested distribution of roles, rights, and responsibilities in the current international

---

[167] Brooks and Wohlforth 2008, chapter 6.

The Struggle for Order

order,[168] East Asia is late in coming to this struggle. This chapter shows that, through its continued authority in conflict management, the US hegemonic role remains robust, with US-defined security public goods and US-preferred modes of management prevailing. There has been some division of labour in security public goods provision, either with allies and partners or sub-contracted where necessary—but without the expectation that Washington's right to determine the hierarchy of priorities will be changed. At the same time, the various US administrations have been responsive to invitations and demands from East Asian allies for involvement and coordination, thus garnering significant complicity.

In East Asia thus far, US authority as conflict manager and regional security provider appears sustainable—not merely because of US military might or the attraction of US ideals, but mainly because Washington is not required to *solve* these conflicts. It has only to manage them by containing the conflicts within agreed boundaries so as not to affect unduly regional stability. This is best illustrated on the Korean peninsula, where the key stakeholders do not necessarily yearn for resolution, because a resolution in any form would create serious strategic implications for all. South Korea would have to absorb the daunting costs of reunification; China the strategic worries about a unified Korea with US military support; and Japan the competition of a powerful neighbour. Most of all, the United States would lose a vital justification for its forward deployment, bilateral alliances, and security guarantor role in East Asia. Trying to sustain this US role beyond peaceful Korean reunification would require renegotiating the strategic bargain with a clear anti-China focus that none of its allies would find comfortable. Thus Washington—and often Tokyo—focuses on the nuclear proliferation public good, engendering the charge that the United States either wants to perpetuate the North Korean problem or cause regime change in order to sustain its regional hegemony.[169] By the same token, China's facilitation of an ambitious and complex bargaining process tying together the three public goods was aimed more at creating medium- to long-term negotiation and institutional change in North Korea and in the region, than at bringing about a clear resolution of the Korean problem. In this climate, the unresolved territorial disputes with China in the SCS support an important supplementary demand for US deterrence in the Southeast Asian maritime theatre. Perpetuating these conflicts helps to justify US military preponderance and to fuel the imperative for the US role as regional security guarantor.

Each of these conflicts could reach indigenous tipping points as a result of radical strategic decisions on the part of East Asian states—North–South

---

[168] Ikenberry 2011; Bukovansky et al. 2012.
[169] E.g. Yu 1997; Xia 2006; Zhebin 2004, 145.

reconciliation on the Korean peninsula, or a radical Sino-Southeast Asian SCS settlement. Short of such breakthroughs—which themselves may prompt another round of order renegotiation in the region—US authority remains. In Northeast Asia, US allies' (particularly Japan's) threat perception of the DPRK and US resistance of China's greater management role or vision of a multilateral package deal; and in Southeast Asia the inability to effect conflict avoidance through joint development, all reinforce Washington's continuing prerogative in defining the nature, stakes, and terms of these conflicts in such a way as to require US management.

4

Regionalism and Community: Renegotiating Regional and Global Economic Order

East Asian states share a sense of ontological security that is deeply entrenched in the imperatives of economic viability and success. Economic developmentalism was regarded as essential for post-Second World War reconstruction in Northeast Asia and for nation building in Southeast Asian post-colonial states. US strategy for rehabilitating post-war Japan centred on the latter's economic reconstruction and interdependence with the Southeast Asian hinterland, while China's post-Cold War economic boom was fed by regional investments and know-how and has in turn reoriented regional production networks and galvanized economic regionalism in East Asia. In this context, the economic realm has witnessed significant contestation between rival ideologies and claims, and in the post-Cold War era, more intense regional dynamics that may be construed as resistance to US-dominated global economic ideologies and institutions.

This chapter studies the functional development and political construction of a regional 'community' or international society, which accompanied economic development and recent attempts at economic integration in East Asia. It analyses the notion of an 'East Asian Community'—the discourse about which was introduced in Chapter 2—by focusing on its substantive manifestation. Distinctive practices of economic development and integration are some of the most obvious ways in which regional identity and a regional 'community' can be asserted. Unsurprisingly, against the background of China's spectacular economic ascendance, East Asian states have concentrated on recreating an economic compact in the process of renegotiating regional order. The Asian financial crisis (AFC) of 1997 imparted greater urgency and salience to this enterprise, and strengthened the political appeal of resisting hegemonic economic ideology and institutions by forging distinctive regional alternatives. More than in the political realm, the negotiation of a particularly East Asian social compact in the economic realm crucially depends upon leadership from regional great powers. Regional economic interdependence and integration must be built on the basis of the strongest and largest economies providing to the others market access, investment, lending, and short-term liquidity, as well as developing mechanisms for economic governance. Thus the question of China's and Japan's regional leadership resurfaces with a vengeance in this chapter.

East Asia's 'Frustrated' Regionalism

While the existence of regional order is not necessarily premised upon a strictly distinct and integrated regional community, the renegotiation of regional order in East Asia since the end of the Cold War has been enmeshed in a growing web of regionalization and regionalism. On the one hand, the volume and significance of intra-regional interactions has increased markedly, especially in terms of transborder flows of people, money, and goods, driven by advances in communications, technology, and other aspects of globalization. This 'bottom-up' or spontaneous process of functional regionalization has been gradually supplemented by a more 'top-down' state-driven agenda of regionalism, manifested in various forms of regional cooperation and institutionalization analysed in Chapter 2.[1] Together these processes promise to give flesh, form, and blood to the 'geopsychological'[2] notion of East Asia—but in so doing, they have created tensions that feed back into the dialectics of negotiating regional order.

The focus here is on the nexus between regionalization and regionalism: the part of the story where the fruits of functional regionalization are exploited by state actors and harnessed towards more overtly political goals based on some collective vision of community. The first part of the empirical discussion below analyses the transition from the economic regionalization engendered by the 'overspill' from Japanese economic growth in the 1970s and 1980s, towards a more variegated mode of regionalization spurred by competing transborder production networks from the 1990s. These developments constituted the functional core of East Asia as an economic region, but they also encapsulated the key limitations of economic regionalization that would hamper more ambitious aspirations for regionalism. The late 1990s saw the rise of state discourses and projects of regionalism. Within the subsequent transition forced by Japan's faltering economy and China's rapid growth, these competing projects became log-rolled into the wider geopolitical contest as these two regional powers engaged in legitimation through regionalism.

[1] Pempel 2005; Frost 2008, 14–17.
[2] Pempel 2005, 3.

East Asian regionalism is by now a rich field, encompassing not only economic and financial issues, but also sociopolitical elements of state and non-state interactions and community building in a neighbourhood in which the 'blurring of public and private power is a given'.[3] Economic regionalism here has two aspects, both politically driven: trade-based regionalism, seen in the proliferation of FTAs; and financial regionalism, reflected in the active process of regional financial cooperation and governance building since 1997. The second part of this chapter focuses on financial regionalism because the greater activism and more substantive advances made here present a stronger case for studying the renegotiation of regional order, often presented as directly challenging the US-led international order.[4] The analysis highlights that the political feat of creating 'East Asia' has been dogged by two fractious questions: regional leadership and the extent to which the region should remain tied into, or resist, the changing global normative order. East Asian regionalism remains a 'frustrated' enterprise,[5] and two struggles come to the fore in the negotiation of regionalism.

First is the struggle over the internal hierarchy of the putative East Asian community. As the 'new regionalism' literature usefully highlights, there is a fundamentally ideological content to social relations within a defined geographical area, which can lead to either cohesion or fragmentation.[6] On the one hand, the region can be a discursive vehicle for the collective articulation of space, engendered by shared norms and identity, and cooperative action. The region is also an essential site for the projection of power by leading states, which can play important roles in galvanizing a sense of regional identity and cohesion. On the other hand, the region can also become an instrument of great power competition, as it is 'a locus for the very (re)definition of leadership in the collective management of [social] space'.[7] In the recent history of East Asia, Japan has been crucial in driving regionalism, be it through the Co-Prosperity Sphere that it attempted to forge by force in the 1940s, the regionalization of its developmental model in the 1980s, or its regional economic cooperation initiatives after the Cold War and the 1997 AFC. The current renegotiation of East Asian order is accompanied by

---

[3] Higgott 1997, 166. See Curley 2006; Nesadurai 2009.

[4] Trade-based regionalism is arguably less well developed, with many of the major multilateral free trade agreements either still under negotiation (e.g. the Trans-Pacific Partnership, the East Asia FTA, or the Regional Comprehensive Economic Partnership), or very new (e.g. the ASEAN–China FTA).

[5] Nair 2009.

[6] See, for instance, the publications from the United Nations WIDER project on new regionalism, e.g. Hettne, Inotai, and Sunkel 1999; Hettne, Inotai, and Sunkel 2000. The ascribed 'new regionalism' literature has since become a broad church, but started out as studies seeking analyses of regionalism beyond the Western European case—see Hurrell 1995.

[7] Gilson 2007, 149.

competition between Japan and China to lead the most promising round of regionalism thus far, fuelled by China's entry into the capitalist world economy. The analysis below asks how this ongoing renegotiation of the regional political-economic leadership hierarchy is developing. Are China and Japan finding cooperative mechanisms that take into account their different capacities and economic strengths? Or is the mutual competition leading to potential stalemate or fragmentation in the regional political economy?

The second struggle is over the policing of the boundaries between the putative regional community and the global economic order. The region is a mediating level of international life, in between national and global structures, and regionalist enterprises can act as 'filter[s] for globalisation'.[8] But again, the relationship between regional and global can lead either to homogenization or to resistance. On the one hand, regions are important conduits for the spread of global norms and ideologies. Some argue, for instance, that the economic regionalism drive in East Asia is spurred by state leaders who want to join regional groupings to gain access to large external markets, even if this comes at the price of domestic economic liberalization.[9] Regionalism then becomes 'a tool in the internationalisation of the state', which seeks legitimation from external norms and institutions.[10] Even more notably, East Asia is indelibly tied into the US-led global economic order because of the underdevelopment of a relatively autonomous regional order during the Cold War and by the external orientation of its regional economic production structures. Thus, as discussed in Chapter 2, early post-Cold War economic regionalism in East Asia was aimed at supporting global liberalization. The analysis in this chapter further shows East Asian states returning to partial support of the neoliberal economic orthodoxy and of international financial institutions shortly after the 1997 crisis.

Yet the region can at the same time challenge global norms.[11] Without adopting the starkly combative narrative of resistance favoured by some 'new regionalism' scholars, there is often nevertheless an element of partial resistance in regionalist enterprises. For instance, Helen Nesadurai usefully highlights two key variants in ASEAN practices of economic regionalism: 'open' regionalism that is driven by the desire to attract foreign direct investment (FDI) but exclude the neoliberal, deregulatory agenda assumed by Western models; and 'developmental regionalism', in which 'regionalism is employed as a means to nurture domestic-owned capital through temporary and partial resistance to global market forces'.[12] In spite of the 'decoupling'

[8] Wallace 2002, 149; Katzenstein 2005.
[9] Bowles 1997, 225.
[10] Bull 1999, 959.
[11] Breslin 2006.
[12] Nesadurai 2003, 21.

thesis that was prominent in Asian policy-making circles in the 2000s,[13] broader East Asian regionalism since 1997 has been aimed mainly at mediating the adverse effects of globalization, rather than undermining or replacing the global economic order. Indeed, as the following discussion highlights, the story of East Asian financial regionalism after 1997 largely consists of a reformist, not revolutionary, interaction with the changing global neoliberal regime.

The upshot of these complex dynamics is that East Asian regionalism is constituted not only by intensifying regional interdependence, but also by a growing leadership and legitimation struggle between the two regional economic great powers, Japan and China. At the same time, the contest over different visions of 'region' encompasses also the evolving negotiation between the nascent regional community and the international society defined by US hegemony. In this sense, the debate about 'closed' or 'East Asian' versus 'open' or 'Asia-Pacific' regionalism is a red herring. The real questions reside in the relationship between the normative structure of the regionalist enterprise and that premised upon the US-led neoliberal economic order. Can regionalism provide for an alternative normative structure that resists the global orthodoxy? Or, does the regional structure support the global, and for what ends? What does the ongoing negotiation of this relationship tell us about the viability of an East Asian economic and political community? It is on this issue that we gauge the significance of the regional leadership contest between China and Japan, and in turn the significance of East Asian regionalism.

The analysis in this chapter presents three key findings. First, the stark juxtaposition of regionalism against globalism is unhelpful in East Asia, where economic regionalization has been remarkably open and externally oriented. This functional characteristic fundamentally limits the prospects for the 'closed' regionalism project. It also means that the regional renegotiation of economic order is deeply interwoven with that at the global level. Second, the realm of macroeconomic and financial governance has been undergoing dynamic change and renegotiation since the 1980s. At the global level, the provision of the financial public goods that has long been regarded as a hegemonic imperative does remain dominated by the United States—for example, it continues to provide the world's reserve currency—but there has been gradual burden sharing in terms of contributions to and disbursement of capital liquidity, for instance. These ongoing global renegotiations impact on the major East Asian economic

---

[13] The idea that East Asia was a sufficiently self-contained economic entity that had the potential to sustain its dynamic economic growth independently of the performance of the other developed market economies.

powers. Japan and China are both unwilling or unable to monopolize the supply of regional financial public goods, not just because of capacity considerations, but also because they have multiple aims at the global level—to limit exposure to different types of risk commensurate with their financial profiles, to block each other's potential gains in status, and to preserve certain beneficial aspects of the existing order while reforming less desirable aspects. Third, therefore, the point is not that the US-led global liberal ideology and institutions cannot be challenged, but rather that *hegemonic* institutions are extremely costly to replace. Thus change is more likely to happen in terms of the actors who constitute the hegemonic core and its functional norms, rather than in the basic institution of hegemony and its constitutive norms.

The Functional Basis of East Asian 'Community': Economic Regionalization since the 1980s

Economic regionalization is understood here as the spread of production networks spanning and knitting together East Asia, rather than the quantitative accumulation of intra-regional trade and investment flows. While intra-regional trade in East Asia did expand significantly from the 1980s onwards,[14] standard trade statistics which assume that goods are produced from start to finish within one country provide an incomplete picture of patterns of dependency. Intra-East Asian trade is asymmetrical, dominated by imports rather than exports, because of component trading—that is, separate parts of a particular product are produced in different country locations, and then sold on to a final assembly point within the region before being exported.[15] Thus regionalization in East Asia turns on this pattern of regionalized production, by which firms operating across national economies incorporate them within transborder production networks.

The asymmetry in East Asian intra-regional trade stems from the particular nature of the involvement first of Japan and then of China in regional production networks. Economic regionalization was the result of Japanese firms deliberately spreading production processes into the region in the 1980s, when Japan's massive trade surplus prompted the United States to erect barriers to trade, while land and labour costs soared in Northeast Asia. To circumvent these restrictions, Japanese corporations searched for export platforms further afield. The key factor for increased regionalization turned out to be the 1985 Plaza Accord, which oversaw the appreciation of the

---

[14] Drysdale and Garnaut 1997; Park and Shin 2009.
[15] Athurokala and Hill 2010.

Japanese yen (along with the currencies of the two other newly industrialized economies (NIEs), Taiwan and South Korea) against the US dollar in order to moderate Japan's trade surpluses. The strengthening of these currencies rendered Southeast Asian economies more competitive in export terms, boosting the latter's efforts to attract overseas investment. Together, these factors fuelled a surge of Japanese and NIE investment in the region. Japanese manufacturers accounted for the largest share by subcontracting out the lower-technology stages of their production processes to manufacturing affiliates in less-developed regional economies. Retaining the highest value-added high-technology processes (research and development, design, and precision manufacturing) within Japan, these firms increasingly used East Asia as an assembly base for supplying local markets and exporting to the rest of the world.[16] In the process, they increased intra-regional economic activity and interdependence. For instance, from 1986 to 1992, the share of East Asian exports to other countries in the region rose from 32 per cent to 44 per cent, while those to the United States fell from 37 per cent to 24 per cent.[17]

Japanese-driven economic regionalization in the 1980s evinced two key characteristics. First, it created a hierarchical order because of technology dependence on Japan. In their assertive account of how Japanese corporations undertook 'strategic distribution' and forged a 'regional production alliance', Hatch and Yamamura argue that East Asia experienced a form of 'embraced' development. Regional economies were pulled into a vertical network dominated by large Japanese manufacturers which replicated their close-knit domestic production chains (*keiretsu*) on a regional scale.[18] Affiliated firms in the region imported the majority of parts from Japan while supplying small proportions of low-technology parts themselves, creating significant host country trade deficits with Japan. While regional economies benefited from guaranteed markets for their products and access to technology and capital, this system inevitably created concerns about asymmetrical dependence or even dependent development that would lock regional economies into a relatively unskilled position in the regional division of labour.[19] As others have noted, the analogy of Japan as the 'lead goose' in a 'flying geese' regional development trajectory is mistaken. By establishing regional export platforms, Japanese firms did not help less-developed economies to

---

[16] Good accounts include Hatch and Yamamura 1996; Athukorala and Yamashita 2008.
[17] Selden 1997, 321.
[18] Hatch and Yamamura 1996—the authors identify three stages of development in these networks, each of which increases the degree of local production and joint ventures, but they emphasize the continuing technological and organizational control and standardization exerted by Japanese parent firms.
[19] Bernard and Ravenhill 1995b; Hatch and Yamamura 1996; Ravenhill 1999.

catch up but instead protected their own technological comparative advantage and upgraded their domestic productivity, thus increasing Japan's competitiveness and technological leadership in the region.[20]

This was made possible by the second key characteristic of these regional production networks, their external export orientation. Instead of import substitution for regional economies, these networks form trade triangles, whereby inputs are bought from Japan, processed in the NIEs and increasingly in Southeast Asia and China, and exported to third-country markets. This form of regionalization was open and did not lay the foundation for a regional trading bloc; it also bolstered the importance of the United States and Europe as the traditional external markets. Indeed, East Asian regionalization in the 1980s and 1990s was made possible by the United States absorbing the costs of the 'Asianisation of the Japanese economy' by being the market for the increased manufacturing output.[21] Ironically, therefore, the Plaza Accord hailed a worsening of US trade deficits with East Asia as a whole, since Japan extended its unbalanced trade relations by regionalizing production.[22]

The pattern of East Asian economic regionalization became more complex in the late 1980s and 1990s for two reasons: China opened up, and the Japanese economic bubble burst. As domestic economic liberalization gained pace, China rejoined the international political economy as a major industrializing country receiving capital and investment. This crucially restructured the regional economic order as so-called 'Chinese' or 'Greater China' networks developed when very significant overseas Chinese capital flows accompanied industrial relocation into coastal and hinterland China from Hong Kong and Taiwan to take advantage of lower costs of production.[23] These Chinese networks are similar to Japanese ones in the sense that they perpetuate the export-oriented regional production system. However, Chinese networks tend to be entrepreneurial and commercial rather than technological, and open in that they incorporate outside suppliers. This openness has allowed the renewed activism of American multinational corporations, which, in order to counter dependence on Japanese production networks, decided in the 1990s to extend underlying technologies to firms in Hong Kong, Taiwan, Korea, and Singapore, thus turning these assembly affiliates into competitors for Japanese firms.[24] The dominance of

---

[20] Hatch and Yamamura 1996; Bernard and Ravenhill 1995a.
[21] Bernard and Ravenhill 1995a; Tokunaga 1992. Thus some argue that the United States was in fact the real 'lead goose' in East Asian development in this period—see the important qualification in Cumings 1997.
[22] Katzenstein 2005, 111–12.
[23] Selden 1997, 324–32.
[24] Borrus 1997. As Borrus notes, US networks had located significant assembly plants in Southeast Asia from the late 1960s, but had become almost totally dependent on technology from Japanese competitors by the end of the 1970s.

Japanese networks has been diluted significantly by these US-led networks that produce sophisticated industrial electronics and are concentrated in the NIEs and increasingly China. Hitching Chinese production networks to American research and technology, these rely on competitive supply systems in which regional firms provide significant value-added inputs. US firms maintain control mainly by domestic standard setting in defining the product and technology trajectory, while working with regional affiliates in a relatively decentralized manner.[25] At the same time, NIEs, especially Taiwan and Singapore, have also generated their own, more limited regional production networks in selected electronic goods, which operate in the middle ground between the US and Japanese models.[26] Thus the current regional economic landscape is dominated not by rival national economies but by multiple networks competing on an often non-national basis. Some of the most complex networks, such as those manufacturing for Apple, even incorporate partners from the United States, China, Japan, South Korea, as well as Taiwan.

As the Japanese recession persisted in the 1990s, Japanese firms slowed their production relocation and investment in the region. This allowed the other economic networks to compete more actively and to outpace Japan, for instance in investing in China. As such, while Japan remains the most developed regional economy, 'the weakness of the pulse of the Japanese economy at the "heart" of the system [means that] the circulation of capital and technology through the system is too weak to organize the system around it'.[27] The current regional economic order is less clearly hierarchical because Japan no longer dominates in terms of capital generation and technological sophistication; Taiwan and South Korea produce similar types of goods. Each production network also leverages on different national economies, developing distinct comparative advantages in different sectors, creating a complex division of labour within which East Asian economies manoeuvre in and out of different production networks.[28] State actors are less able to exercise direct control over industrial policy or national firms in a landscape containing other key players like ethnic business groups and cross-border economic zones.[29] In this sense, East Asia has become more regionalized in terms of the volume of regional economic interactions and complexity of interdependence.

The past three decades of regional production sharing and the forging of economic networks highlight three characteristics about the East Asian

---

[25] Borrus 2000.
[26] Ernst 2000b; Wong 2000.
[27] McIntyre and Naughton 2005, 90.
[28] McIntyre and Naughton 2005, 90; Katzenstein 2005, 116.
[29] Peng 2002; Yeung 2009.

economic order. First, it contains hierarchies of dependency. While the hierarchy based on Japanese techno-nationalism has been diluted, the often competitive positions of Japan and China within regional production networks adversely affect the potential for substantive cooperative regional leadership, especially in the realm of trade-based integration. Second, both Japan's and China's regional economic leadership positions are based on production rather than consumption—until China especially can develop a significant consumer base, the regional economy must remain dependent upon external markets, as well as external technology and standard setting. This seriously limits the possibility of 'closed' forms of economic regionalism.[30] Third, competing cross-border production and financial networks within and beyond the region undermine notions of a neat 'regional' category, further weakening assumptions of the confluence of region and community that the proponents of 'closed' regionalism wish to promote.[31]

The openness and dependencies of the regional economy were clearly manifested in the financial realm and helped to create and constitute the AFC of 1997. To begin with, Japan's long recession and growing economic and financial weakness contributed conditions for the crisis. Tokyo's policies to stimulate the Japanese economy in 1990s included a 'cheap money' policy of low interest rates that created a huge flow of Japanese capital into East Asia at a time of loosening capital controls in regional economies. The bursting of Japan's speculative bubble and deflation also caused the yen to depreciate relative to the US dollar, in turn creating a debt crisis for regional economies that had 'heated up' on the back of cheap US dollar loans that now became more expensive with the appreciation of the dollar.[32] The region's dependence on the US dollar and vulnerability to dollar–yen fluctuations and global market volatility were partly a result of Japan's traditional unwillingness to internationalize the yen and to exercise monetary leadership in the region in spite of its leading role as investor, creditor, and donor. If regional currencies had been pegged partly to the yen rather than solely to the US dollar, the currency crisis that began with the collapse of the Thai baht in July 1997 might have been less severe.[33]

---

[30] This argument is made most clearly in Katzenstein 1997, 40–1.
[31] Breslin 2007 notes, for instance, that intra-East Asian financial flows are often created by regional investors acting as middlemen between Western companies and Asian producers.
[32] Asian borrowers had banked on the continued depreciation of the US dollar since the Plaza Accord to boost their competitiveness in the US market.
[33] Katzenstein 2005, 33–4. Others, e.g. Radelet and Sachs 1998, suggest that the yen–dollar depreciation was less significant a factor than investor actions and structural weaknesses within the haphazardly liberalized financial markets in key East Asian economies in creating the crisis.

The Struggle for 'Community': Financial Regionalism since 1997

The 1997 regional financial crisis marked a watershed for Japan in terms of moving from a functional, corporation-led regionalization of production to Tokyo's deliberate activism in regional financial leadership and the development of a political agenda of regionalism. In the decade that followed, the regional and global financial crises provided a critical stimulus for economic considerations to prevail in pushing forward 'integrative logics and strategies' at the regional level.[34] This did not mean, however, that geopolitical imperatives were ignored; rather, great power competition was evident throughout each stage of negotiating financial regionalism and in the recalibrations of the relationship between regional and global economic order. If it is true that financial power tends to become critically important during periods of hegemonic transition,[35] then Japan's picking up of this mantle seemed to be a harbinger of regional self-help and resistance to global financial orthodoxy and institutions. Indeed, it is difficult to read subsequent East Asian financial regionalism simply as an outgrowth of hegemonic globalization.

Japan's Opening Bid: The Asian Monetary Fund

Faced with a rapidly spreading 'contagion' of currency crises in its neighbourhood, Tokyo reacted quickly with a $100 billion Asian Monetary Fund (AMF) proposal at the September 1997 meeting of the World Bank and IMF. To be financed, run, and aimed at East Asian countries, it would provide emergency short-term financing for the crisis-hit Asian economies without the conditionalities imposed by the international financial institutions (IFI). Japan would contribute half of the reserves, with the remaining half coming from other major regional economies such as Hong Kong, Singapore, China, and Taiwan.[36] The AMF proposal was somewhat out of character for a Japan that was widely perceived as being self-interested, averse to formal regional economic governance, and reactive in foreign policy.[37] Given the severity of the crisis and resentful regional perceptions that the IMF's conditional bailouts were slow, inadequate, and wrong, Tokyo's proposal could be read as a timely self-help mechanism to provide a more appropriate regional alternative, led by East Asia's strongest economy. The exclusive and self-sufficient

---

[34] Breslin 2010, 709.
[35] Arrighi quoted in Selden 1997, 339.
[36] The notion was that East Asia, with an estimated collective foreign exchange reserve of $800 billion, had sufficient surplus to finance the debt of the crisis-affected countries (about $300 billion)—Altbach, 1997.
[37] See, for instance, Katzenstein 1997; Calder 1988.

East Asian focus of the AMF, however, suggested a challenge to the US-led global neoliberal financial regime.

Japan's leadership and initiative on regional financial crisis management after 1997 have led some authors to suggest that in this arena, 'Japan proposes and other states (including the United States) react'.[38] Whether Japan's activism arose in 1997 primarily from Tokyo's desire to grasp the mantle of regional political leadership is less clear than the fact of a widely felt leadership vacuum in East Asia during the financial meltdown. Japan stepped readily into this breach, which was defined more ideologically than materially. The alienation between East Asian states and the United States, the 'West', and IFI arose from divergent interpretations of the causes of the AFC. The US Treasury and the IMF worked broadly out of the existing neoliberal orthodoxy, diagnosing the 1997 crash as an insolvency crisis. Critics charged that the IMF's previous bailouts of debtor countries without sufficient conditionality had encouraged risky lending and created 'moral hazard'.[39] Also, Asia's state-led economic development practices were prone to so-called 'crony capitalism', whereby domestic firms were favoured with access to state-subsidized capital and encouraged into excess overseas borrowing and bad investments, the effects of which were exacerbated by poorly regulated banking systems.[40] Thus the solution to such a crisis would be a bailout, but with stricter conditionalities involving deregulation, privatization, and liberalization under 'structural adjustment' packages.

In contrast, the Japanese diagnosis was of a currency crisis caused by excessive capital liberalization—developing countries had opened their capital accounts too much and too quickly, allowing unmanageable flows of capital that disrupted their exchange rates and monetary policies. These countries—such as Thailand and Indonesia—tended to be small economies with thinly traded currencies, which then had insufficient foreign exchange reserves to defend themselves against a sudden loss of market confidence that saw the rapid flight of capital. This was thus a liquidity crisis that required rapid and short-term injection of large amounts of money.[41] The proposed AMF would provide a large pool of reserves to the countries that needed it. By functioning independently of the IMF and the United States, it would also help to insulate East Asia from the very agenda of rapid liberalization pushed by the United States and IFI that had led to the crisis in the first place. This disagreement was overtly political and reflected the

---

[38] Grimes 2009a, 72.
[39] A situation in which the decision-maker makes risky decisions with the knowledge that the costs of failure will be borne by someone else—bailouts of banks by external financial institutions being a classic case. For critiques, see, for instance, Stiglitz 2002; U.S. Congress 2000.
[40] Wade 1998; Kang 2002.
[41] Hayashi 2006, 66–70.

growing tensions between IMF conditionality and statist models of development.[42] Some authors trace Tokyo's assertive stance to its gradual disenchantment with Japan's perceived marginalization in the IFI from the 1980s, feeding into the Ministry of Finance's subsequent interpretation of the disagreement over the 1997 crisis as a contest between Washington's neoliberal economic agenda and Tokyo's defence of the Asian developmental state model.[43]

Unsurprisingly, the United States opposed the proposal. A Japan-financed AMF would challenge both the authority of the IMF and US hegemony in the Asia-Pacific.[44] Deputy Treasury Secretary Larry Summers allegedly accused Japan's top currency official Sakakibara Eisuke of betrayal in leading Asia in a challenge against the United States.[45] The US Treasury then applied bilateral and multilateral pressure on Japan and other Asian states to drop the proposal.[46] It also initiated some short-term provisions for slightly greater and faster IMF responses to the crisis. The AMF idea failed also because of Chinese opposition. Until the mid-1990s, China was reticent regarding regional multilateral cooperation, worried about its weak potential bargaining position in such settings, and suspicious of Japan's desire for regional leadership.[47] The Japanese Finance Ministry's neglect in not consulting with its Chinese counterpart fuelled Beijing's doubts about Japan, which trumped Chinese scepticism about the willingness of Western IFI to help Asia.[48] But, even though it undertook self-restraint in not devaluing the yuan, Beijing did not counter-propose any better ideas for collective action at the regional level. Instead, the US Treasury advanced a counterproposal to create a regional surveillance system.[49] By November 1997, the Americans managed to persuade a gathering of Asia-Pacific finance ministers and central bankers to agree to the so-called Manila Framework, by which the United States, Japan, China, Australia, and the crisis economies committed to a system of mutual financial surveillance run out of a new IMF regional office in Tokyo. The crisis economies would have access to expanded IMF funds through a financing

---

[42] Some have suggested that the United States and the IMF took the opportunity of the Asian financial crisis to 'roll back' the Japanese developmental state model—e.g. Cumings 1999; Hughes 2000.

[43] This constructivist explanation is relatively persuasive, given that most Japanese firms were opposed to the AMF proposal because they favoured the liberalization of Asian markets, and the Japanese Foreign Ministry was also opposed to the idea because it would strain relations with the United States—Lee 2006, 358–60. See also Wade 1996.

[44] Johnstone 1999; Higgott 1998.

[45] Quoted in Lee 2006, 357.

[46] See Lee 2006, 357–8; Rapkin 2001, 396–8.

[47] See Johnston 2004; Deng 1997.

[48] On the widespread cynicism about IFI among Chinese observers, see e.g. Dong 1998; Wang 1999.

[49] Lee 2006, 357.

'window', though at $20 billion, this pot was considerably smaller than that proposed for the AMF.[50]

To some observers, the Manila Framework illustrates the way in which US hegemony was reasserted and Japan's deference to the United States and neoliberal economic ideology reinforced.[51] Yet Tokyo gave up neither its proactive search for East Asian financial mechanisms nor its material and normative leadership in regional financial governance. In 1998, Japan introduced the New Miyazawa Initiative, committing $30 billion in loans to East Asian crisis economies. The Initiative extended credit guarantees that helped crisis economies to borrow in international markets—a scheme that Malaysia, for instance, benefited from after Kuala Lumpur imposed capital controls and burnt its bridges with the IMF in 1997.[52] The Initiative also created currency swap lines from Japan to South Korea and Malaysia—these lines allowed the latter's central banks to exchange agreed amounts of their local currencies for US dollars from the Bank of Japan, thus supplementing their foreign currency reserves without having to borrow.[53] Tokyo consciously used and developed regional financial mechanisms: some of the Miyazawa Initiative money was channelled through the Asian Development Bank's (ADB) Asian Currency Crisis Support Facility, and the ADB Institute was set up in Tokyo as a research centre for alternative monetary and development policies. Also, the notion of an AMF did not die—the APT finance ministers continued to discuss the idea after 1997, and the subsequent cooperative financial mechanisms in the APT have laid the foundations for a future AMF.

The Chiang Mai Initiative: Financial Regionalism?

In spite of the divergences in 1997, the AFC provided a critical impetus for East Asian states to push for greater regional cooperation and self-help in preventing and managing financial crises. This discourse gained momentum within multiple regional fora, but really took off within the newly formed APT framework, the first summit of which took place shortly after the outbreak of the 1997 crisis. Crucially at this time, China came round to supporting Japan's push for a regional currency crisis mechanism, and East Asian leaders agreed at the 1999 APT summit to establish such a mechanism. At the May 2000 APT finance ministers' meeting, the Chiang Mai Initiative (CMI) was unveiled. The CMI consisted of two components, the

---

[50] This was sketched out as a 'standby' mechanism—members were not formally committed to specific provisions, while affected members would still be subject to some IMF conditions—Grimes 2009a, 79. Conceived as a temporary supplement to the IMF, the Framework was dissolved in 2004.
[51] See Gill 2003, 151.
[52] On Malaysia's policies and recovery from the AFC, see Beeson 2000; Kaplan and Rodrik 2001.
[53] Grimes 2009a, 79–80; Hayashi 2006, 99–102.

first being a monitoring system consisting of economic review and policy dialogue among a network of 'contact persons' to facilitate regional multilateral surveillance. This was itself unusual, given the potential of intrusion into member states' domestic financial policies, and was an indication of the degree to which the imperative for 'regulatory regionalism' had been recognized in East Asia.[54] The second component was a regional system of bilateral currency swap arrangements that would inject liquidity in times of crisis. At the outset, these swap arrangements were limited and cautious. Starting out at $38 billion in 2000, the total pool was remarkably small compared to the massive foreign reserve holdings of Japan and China.[55] The largest available reserve pools for Indonesia and South Korea only amounted to $13 billion each. This pot was subsequently doubled to $80 billion in 2005. However, the crucial IMF link remained: members wishing to draw substantively—more than 20 per cent—from their available CMI funds were obliged to apply to the IMF and thus be subject to IMF conditionality. The bilateral nature of these swaps also translated into variations in the parties involved, currencies denominated, and directions of swapping. As such, the CMI did not amount to a truly 'regional' arrangement in the sense of being multilateral and institutionalized.[56]

Nevertheless, the CMI was a 'milestone' that marked East Asian financial cooperation, and by 2009 the volume of swap arrangements had grown to $90 billion.[57] Yet, as Pempel observed in 2007, these arrangements did not amount to a comprehensive regional alternative financial system. What the CMI provided was 'an interim firebreak that enhance[d] Asia's capacity to cope collectively with any future monetary crises and to limit unbridled dependence on the IMF and its policy prescriptions'.[58] It was tested in the global financial crisis in 2008–9 (GFC), when the South Korean won notably came under speculative attack, creating precisely the type of condition that the CMI swaps were designed to help dampen. Yet Seoul chose to negotiate a $50 billion bilateral swap with the US Federal Reserve and subsequently augmented its pre-existing bilateral swap lines with the central banks of Japan (with a three-year $30 billion swap) and China (with a two-year $26 billion swap).[59] Acting as the fast lender of first resort in the 2008–9 crisis—in contrast to the Treasury's reaction in 1997—the US Federal Reserve also offered

---

[54] For discussions on regionalism created by a complex of private and public regulatory regimes in the financial, health, and other realms, see Jayasuriya 2004.
[55] Japan's holdings were $1 trillion as of May 2010, and China's $2.45 trillion as of August 2010. Figures available at <http://www.japaneconomynews.com/category/foreign-reserves/>; 'China Favors Euro Over Dollar as Bernanke Alters Path', *Bloomberg*, 17 August 2010.
[56] Good accounts of the CMI include Amyx 2004; Grimes 2006; Henning 2002.
[57] Emmers and Ravenhill 2011, 140; Chey 2009, 452.
[58] Pempel 2007, 51.
[59] Grimes 2009b, 47.

Singapore a similar arrangement. East Asian states were unwilling to use the CMI mechanisms because of their allergy to the IMF after 1997. The 20 per cent rule meant that in such a major crisis, APT members would have to deal not only with IMF conditionality but also the domestic political fallouts of going cap in hand to the Fund again—and for amounts that did not come close to what the US Federal Reserve could offer.[60] In addition, though, China particularly used a series of bilateral currency swaps with its trading partners as a crisis prevention measure: by providing for bilateral trade in their respective currencies rather than dollars, these swaps provided a measure of insulation from the global currency crisis.[61]

To address these drawbacks, the APT pushed to multilateralize the CMI in May 2009, creating a $120 billion reserve pool, with Japan and China co-leading the contributions at 32 per cent each, South Korea contributing 16 per cent, and ASEAN 20 per cent. Each country is eligible for drawing on an amount that is a ratio of their contribution, with the Northeast Asian countries able to draw up to $19.2 billion and Indonesia, Thailand, Malaysia, and Singapore up to $11.9 billion.[62] The increased resources and regionalization of the Chiang Mai Initiative Multilateralization (CMIM) were accompanied by some institutionalization, such as weighted voting on procedures. Nevertheless, critical limitations and questions remain, the most crucial of which relate to disbursement, which initially remained tied to the 20 per cent IMF rule, and was subsequently raised to 30 per cent in 2012.[63] The APT membership is divided on this issue, with Singapore and—surprisingly, perhaps, given the claims about a 'Beijing consensus'—China most vocally in favour of retaining it.[64] Additionally, the reserve pool is not a centralized fund, but rather a collection of 'self-managed' reserve assets remaining under the care of the committing countries until called upon. The question of financial monitoring mechanisms becomes more urgent as the CMIM reserve pool grows, but the APT Macroeconomic and Research Office (AMRO) launched in May 2011 is still a long way from discharging its twin responsibilities of providing macroeconomic surveillance and central implementation of the CMIM.[65]

---

[60] Emmers and Ravenhill 2011, 141.
[61] Major swaps included RMB200 billion ($29 billion) with Hong Kong, RMB100 billion ($14.5 billion) with Indonesia, and RMB40–80 billion with Malaysia. Chin 2010, 707.
[62] Emmers and Ravenhill 2011, 141.
[63] 'The case for an Asian Monetary Fund', *Asia Times*, 12 July 2002; 'ASEAN's AMRO may "replace" IMF financial role', *Jakarta Post*, 8 April 2011.
[64] Ravenhill 2010, fn.54.
[65] 'ASEAN+3 countries deepen financial cooperation', *People's Daily*, 6 May 2011. At their May 2011 meeting, APT finance ministers also initiated studies on strengthening the legal status of AMRO and creating a crisis prevention facility, and agreed that central bank governors would participate in subsequent meetings.

The Struggle for Order

To what extent then, does the CMI encapsulate East Asian struggles to forge a regional community? The type of regionalism that this financial regime represents is regulatory beyond the financial monitoring sense: it is also regulatory in the political sense of key states attempting to mediate the financial excesses of the hegemonic global economic order and to manage economic competition within the region. Developed largely in response to crises, financial regionalism in East Asia is primarily targeted at shoring up the weakest regional economies in the event of another contagious crisis. The collateral effects on abetting China and Japan's divergent aspirations and imperatives at the global level do not amount to a coherent challenge to existing global financial governance arrangements. Moreover, for the purposes of this book, the politics of the CMI shed light on the shifting dynamics of resistance, deference, and contestation between Japan, the United States, and China during the broader process of renegotiating regional order. As already noted, Japan has been the key 'mover and shaker' in the East Asian financial realm. In spite of the failure of its initial AMF proposal, Tokyo was able to develop important credit lines to its needy neighbours and to spearhead the growth of a regional liquidity facility. The CMI succeeded where the AMF failed because China supported it and the United States did not oppose it.[66]

The major reason for US acquiescence to the CMI was Japan's decision not to confront the United States and IFI with an independent alternative regional financial regime. Instead, the CMI was created explicitly as a regional subsidiary and complement to the existing global regime through the 20 per cent link to the IMF, and also through the implicit reliance on IMF standards of financial surveillance.[67] Tokyo's revised approach suggests significant limits to its willingness (if not its capacity) seriously to challenge US hegemony and the neoliberal economic order. Indeed, Japan's apparent resistance has always been tempered by pragmatic caution, and in the years immediately following the AFC, two changes occurred which urged Japan more towards reform than resistance or revolution. First, Japanese policy-makers began to reassess the causes of the 1997 crisis and the willingness of leaders of neighbouring affected economies to undertake necessary economic reforms. Particularly in light of Japan's expenditures to support regional financial stability through the Miyazawa Initiative, Tokyo began to re-appreciate the dangers of moral hazard in a region slow to commit to serious financial regulatory reforms.[68] Thus Japan sought ways to limit its

---

[66] Chey 2009.
[67] Grimes 2009b, fn.19.
[68] On the significant domestic political obstacles to financial regulation beyond 'mock compliance', see Walter 2008.

exposure, both financial and political.[69] Financially, Tokyo had no desire to carry the entire burden of being the lender of first resort for all of East Asia. On the political side, Japanese leaders were faced with the classic dilemma of putative Japanese regional leadership in considering how to make funding provision decisions without stepping on American, Chinese, and other neighbours' sensitivities.[70] The CMI helped to ease Japan's discomfort because it allowed Tokyo to subcontract a large proportion of liquidity reserve provision, decision-making about disbursement, as well as monitoring and certification, to a third party, the IMF. As Grimes put it, this provided a way that would be 'simultaneously effective in avoiding...rivalries between Japan and China, credible in addressing moral hazard, and reassuring to the U.S.'[71] Put differently, Japan shifted its regulatory focus from seeking a regional buffer against the crises of the hegemonic global economic system, towards managing the moral hazards of its own putative regional role as financial leader.

Tokyo was willing to give up what could have been a direct challenge to the United States and turn instead to boosting the IMF and the existing global financial regime also because of changes to the Fund after 1997. Part of Washington's campaign to kill the AMF proposal in 1997 had included increased quotas for some East Asian states within the IMF; and the quota adjustments in 1998 had allowed Japan to rise above Germany into second place within the Fund. Also, partly in response to the AFC, the AMF proposal, and Japanese activism in the IMF, other key quota holders began to reconsider the strict conditionality and austerity requirements tied to its crisis rescue packages.[72] During the 2008–9 global economic crisis, the G20 countries further increased the IMF's emergency lending capacity, and supported counter-cyclical lending for emerging and low-income economies from multilateral banks.[73] These alterations made it easier for Japan to defend the CMI's linkage to the Fund, and to help boost the IMF's capacity and legitimacy by increasing its national contribution.[74]

Some authors suggest that the CMI and CMIM create an institutional basis for a more credible potential challenge to the IMF in future crises through regional insulation and the credible threat of East Asia's (at least partial) exit from the global regime.[75] At the very least, the CMIM places East Asia in a

---

[69] This reluctance to contribute to a regional mechanism without conditions is shared among the region's creditor states that would be the additional sources of reserve financing, particularly China and Singapore.
[70] The discussion in this paragraph draws from Grimes 2009a, 80–1; Amyx 2004.
[71] Grimes 2009a, 81.
[72] Grimes 2009b, 48.
[73] See G20 2009a.
[74] Grimes 2009b.
[75] See Katada 2004; Lipscy 2009.

better position to apply pressure for IMF reforms.[76] Implicitly, this is a potential regional challenge that would be led by Japan. Yet the prospect of this happening is unclear. Tokyo's serious reservations about underwriting the region are amply reflected in the official characterization of the CMIM as a 'complementary liquidity funding mechanism within the framework of the IMF'.[77] Sino-Japanese rivalry further limits the CMI mechanisms' potential challenge. On the one hand, the agreement between China and Japan about the CMI helped to raise the costs of US objection in 2000, since the latter would fuel the challenge from and attraction of China. But to suggest that the CMI captures their 'joint leadership' of regional financial cooperation takes it too far.[78] Tokyo's aim, with the CMI–IMF link, is partly after all to avoid having to cooperate more concretely with China to manage regional financial stability.[79] Both sides also retain a strong competitive streak in spite of their joint largest contributions to the reserve pool: Japanese observers frequently point out that Japan is the largest single contributor since China's portion includes a significant input from Hong Kong; while Chinese observers argue that Beijing's contribution should be raised to reflect the country's elevation to the world's second largest economy.[80] The subsequent tussle over the AMRO directorship was settled with a one-year term for a Chinese inaugural director, and a two-year term for his Japanese successor.

Further, we may expect continuing limits to their leadership at both the global and regional levels because the Asian economic powers' interests are still too divergent and regional states do not want to shoulder the massive economic and political costs of the required reforms. Hence, in the CMI, the APT took a remarkable ten years to move 'from a loosely coordinated swap network to a slightly more coordinated pooling arrangement'.[81] For its part, China supported the CMI because of its 'flexible and symbolic' nature, with no binding obligations or central decision-making function—indeed, Beijing had favoured a 100 per cent linkage of CMI funds to IMF conditionality.[82] China's aim was to try to help mediate its own and the region's exposure to the excesses of the global economic system, while retaining freedom of action and not having to commit to high regulatory costs. Moreover, supporting the continuation of IMF conditionality helped Beijing to signal its non-revolutionary approach to IFI reforms, and to leverage on its regional

---

[76] Lipscy 2009, 37.
[77] See Katada 2009.
[78] Chey 2009, 455.
[79] Grimes 2009a, 81–2. Further cooperation would entail negotiating details of a regional mechanism for information exchange and financial monitoring, and a system for decision-making, disbursement, and supervision of loans.
[80] Field interviews, Beijing, May 2011, Tokyo, October 2011.
[81] Ciorciari 2011, 950.
[82] Jiang 2010b, 611; Amyx 2008.

clout in its search for a greater voice in the existing structures of global economic governance.

China's support for CMI was log-rolled into its changing international diplomatic strategy and altered stance towards regional institutions after 1997, a growing realization of the need for collective action to ensure economic security,[83] and the desire to bolster exclusive regionalism in the APT. In particular, the very positive regional reception both to Japan for the Miyazawa Initiative and to China's restraint in not devaluing its currency, the renminbi (RMB), persuaded Chinese policy-makers that supporting the CMI would lend credence to its claim of being a responsible regional power. Beijing subsequently proposed new dialogue channels for APT finance ministers, supported and led studies on regional financial cooperation and reserve pooling, and campaigned for regional support for the CMIM.[84] Financial regionalism helped Beijing to demonstrate reassurance towards its neighbours and its co-leadership position with Japan in CMIM helped it to project regional leadership to counter perceived US hegemony. But China's status gains belie continued limitations to its technical and financial capacity and transparency, which set its interests apart from Japan's. For instance, even as the APT undertakes the urgent task of developing a regional financial surveillance mechanism, the degree to which Beijing will be able to participate in more intensive regulatory regionalism is in doubt, given the sensitivities of Chinese officials to sharing detailed information about their domestic financial system.[85] Beijing's participation in deeper regional financial and monetary cooperation (which require relatively free financial flows) will be limited by the high level of state control over exchange rates and capital account, and the fragile state of its banking and financial system. Yet its rhetoric at times outstrips these underlying structural constraints—for instance, Chinese academics' criticisms of initial Japanese proposals for CMIM as not going far enough in providing for regional monitoring disbursement mechanisms.[86] This exacerbates worries in Japan of, for instance, potential Chinese pressures to abandon the CMIM–IMF link. China may be tempted to make political hay by supporting such a move, but it would leave Japan, with its more open and well-developed financial capabilities, to carry the can in terms of moral hazard in underwriting a resurrected AMF, and to run the political hazard of thus jeopardizing its relationship with the United States.[87]

---

[83] See Zha 1999.
[84] See Jiang 2010b, 612–14.
[85] See Jiang 2010b, 614.
[86] Gao 2004, 21–6.
[87] Grimes 2009a, 105–6.

Limits to East Asian Financial Regionalism

East Asia has experienced a significant regionalism drive in the wake of the 1997 financial crisis. As shown here and in Chapter 2, the economic upheaval created sufficient impetus to bring together in formal frameworks the ASEAN states, Japan, China, and South Korea. The discursive and institutional conditions following the formation of the APT consolidated the notion of 'East Asia' as the conjoining of Southeast and Northeast Asia, even if the problematic entities of North Korea and Taiwan are excluded for now. The regionalist momentum subsequently helped, along with the GFC, to create the strong sense that a global shift in balance of power was under way and that international institutions ought to be reformed and regional institutions strengthened. And yet, as the preceding analysis shows, there remain serious limits to East Asian regionalism, even in the financial realm that has seen so much apparent cooperative action and progress.[88] These limitations arise from (a) clashing Japanese and Chinese priorities and motivations for promoting and leading regionalism; (b) the shallow economic basis for the overtly political regionalism project; and (c) the enduring porous and dependent nature of the region in relation to the global economic order.

JAPAN–CHINA COMPETITION

The tensions between Japan and China over regional economic leadership stem from the transitional problem of how to move East Asia from multiple production network regionalization to a more coherent regionalism based on a combination of China as manufacturing hub, Japan as technological hub, and Japan and China as leading regional markets and financial guarantors. The challenge is to create an economic region with political vision, under the shared leadership of Tokyo and Beijing. Yet the widespread worry is that long-standing Sino-Japanese geopolitical rivalry, exacerbated by intensified nationalism, has now found new expression in competitive regionalism.[89]

Japan has found itself increasingly having to balance between two sets of competitive impulses: on the one hand, promoting and defending the 'Asian model' of economic development in the international and global institutional realm, and on the other hand, countering growing Chinese economic influence within East Asia. As discussed in Chapter 2, Tokyo was caught off guard by Beijing's regional economic cooperation initiatives from 2000, and began seriously to regard China as a rival for regional leadership. This

---

[88] Two other initiatives that East Asian states have pursued in parallel to develop a regional bond market are not discussed here because of their relatively limited progress, impact, and prospects to date. For details on the Asian Bond Market Initiative and the Asian Bond Fund, see Grimes 2009a, 160–203.

[89] See, for instance, Pang 2003; Terada 2006.

was as important a reason as Tokyo's changing assessment of the practical burdens of sponsoring regional economic bailouts in shifting its focus from the ideological battle over the 'Asian developmental state' model towards keeping Chinese economic influence at bay. Alongside Japan's critical role in turning the Chiang Mai Initiative in a direction compatible with IMF macroeconomic regulations, rather than as a replacement of or competitor to them, has been a broader shift under recent conservative prime ministers Koizumi and Abe towards promoting 'universal values' (such as democracy and human rights) consonant with US goals.[90] Yet, as discussed in the following section, this is by no means a straightforward shift from one strategic goal to the other; Tokyo remains ambivalent about its interaction with the global economic order and IFI, which in turn necessitates some economic leadership sharing with China in order to achieve a measure of national and regional self-insurance.

China faces a similar set of dilemmas: as its economic power and profile grow, it gains capability and leverage over international economics and politics at the same time as it is rendered more vulnerable to external crises and pressures that often require collective management. For Beijing, the key priority is economic growth and development; it is less eager even than Japan to promote any alternative vision or order, but rather is focused on integrating into the world economy on terms as favourable to itself as it can manage to obtain. China's main aims are to avoid isolation, manage conflicts with the United States, and head off Japanese competition—in that order.[91] Thus, while Beijing would prefer to create East Asian economic institutions that it can lead and exclude the United States, Chinese policy-makers prioritize achieving economic regionalism in ways that advance their interests without 'overly complicating' their relations with Washington.[92] At the same time, Chinese policy-makers profess themselves relatively relaxed about the competition with Japan for regional economic leadership. For example, the former regard Japan's prospects for negotiating a regional FTA as dim, given domestic agricultural protectionism.[93] In interviews in 2010–11 with this author, mid-level Chinese officials consistently professed that Chinese and Japanese schemes for regionalism are not mutually exclusive, and admitted that they tend to regard China's competitive prospects as improving with time vis-à-vis Japan's.

---

[90] See, for instance, Sohn 2010. I have argued that this shift reflects Tokyo's long-standing strategic deference to US hegemony in East Asia—see Goh forthcoming/a.
[91] Author interviews with Chinese scholars and policy advisers, Beijing, March 2011 and November 2011.
[92] Wan 2010, 529.
[93] Potential Japanese membership in the Trans-Pacific Partnership—though the prospect seems unlikely in the foreseeable future—would change this.

For China, the contest with Japan is limited by its credibility concerns vis-à-vis its benignity claims in the region, and capacity considerations. The latter are seen clearly in China's limitations in projecting power while still integrating into the global economic order. For instance, claims that China is exercising soft power by extending unconditional aid and loans to developing countries and changing the rules of the international aid regime have to be balanced by the realization that Beijing profits particularly from recipient countries' disillusionment with existing donors not meeting their pledges, and picks low-hanging fruit in terms of extending high-profile aid to regimes that have few other options.[94] In international finance, China faces serious obstacles to increasing its capacity and influence. In spite of Beijing's use of its massive foreign currency reserves for international development financing, and the characterization of these as strategic national reserves for emergencies such as large-scale natural disasters, the United States especially continues to view Chinese currency policy in terms of neo-mercantilist manipulation. Furthermore, as China tries to internationalize its currency as a means of insuring itself against dollar crises, it runs into significant limits posed by its underdeveloped domestic financial regulatory structure, uncertainties facing its political system, and its huge current account surplus.[95]

On the financial front, therefore, China's focus is on autonomy and insulation to protect its developmental imperative. Over the last decade, this priority has motivated Beijing's willingness to work with Tokyo and to share some leadership of regional financial arrangements. Yet underdeveloped capacity and transparency, dissatisfaction with the global economic order, and mutual competition for regional leadership act as fundamental brakes to what such cooperation can amount to. Given Japan's significantly more robust financial strength measured by openness and integration into the global economy, Beijing is unlikely to want to lock in the existing disparity in their capabilities by agreeing to a financial and monetary governance mechanism at this time.[96]

ECONOMIC INTERDEPENDENCE VERSUS POLITICAL SYMBOLISM

In a related vein, the second limitation of East Asian economic regionalism is that it remains more politically than functionally driven. While regionalism is, by definition, a political project, the conventional understanding

---

[94] Woods 2008; Goh 2011c.
[95] A significant reserve currency needs to be bought by others, and so the country must tend to be a net debtor rather than saver so foreign investors can buy its debt securities. On the difficulties with internationalizing the RMB, see Kelly 2009.
[96] Katada 2008.

Regionalism and Community

is that economic expressions of regional cooperation are built on dense regional interaction arising from socio-economic logic.[97] Yet, in East Asia, the regionalism train has far outstripped the regionalization platform. In the most detailed analysis to date, Ravenhill shows that measured by the conventional indicators of trade and financial interdependence—regional trade intensity, intra-regional FDI, and actualized preferential trade agreements—post-1997 regionalism in East Asia bears either no relation to or an inverse correlation with interdependence. For instance, less than a third of ASEAN's FDI inflows originated in APT countries between 1995 and 2006, with the percentage actually declining after 2002. Further, the region as a whole has retained its dependence on external markets, which account for up to two-thirds of the value of its exports.[98]

Understanding economic regionalism initiatives as deriving from a basically political 'domino effect' helps to explain the limited economic effects and minimal practical use of financial and trade agreements such as the CMI. The glaring primacy of the political is also evident in the tightrope that Japan especially constantly perceives itself walking, between the need to exercise regional financial leadership and the imperative of safeguarding its national competitiveness and high stakes in the global economic order. In the realm of regional trading agreements, the limitations of the fundamentally political drivers of initiatives are even starker. For instance, the economic substance of the ASEAN–Japan Comprehensive Economic Partnership Agreement is remarkably thin—it does not address crucial issues in cooperation such as labour mobility, and it retains restrictive product-specific rules which are in some cases more limited than stipulated in existing bilateral agreements.[99] The China–ASEAN FTA, with a similarly politically driven purpose, has been subject to policy fluctuations: the Foreign Ministry led in the initial framework agreement, but the subsequent substantive negotiations were carried out by the Commerce Ministry, which toed a more cautious line since it was motivated by economic interest and constrained by more protectionist elements within the domestic political system.[100] The irony is that there is evidence that many East Asian countries routinely apply lower tariffs in trading with each other than the legal ceilings they discuss in formal trade negotiations, because of the component trading within regional production networks.[101] If some observers are

---

[97] There are, of course, explicitly political regionalist projects, such as the Visegrád group (the Czech Republic, Hungary, Poland, and Slovakia), which generate subsequent economic regionalism.

[98] These figures are from sources that adjust for the double-counting arising from the significant components trade within East Asia. See Ravenhill 2010.

[99] Corning 2009.

[100] Jiang 2010a.

[101] Hale 2011.

correct that this forms a de facto preferential trading area, then the problem is not only the political motivation behind formal trade agreements but also the failure of the political endeavour to hitch itself onto an existing economically motivated trend.

REGIONALISM AND INTERNATIONALIZATION

If regionalism connotes community building or integration as a form of implicit resistance to the global order, then East Asian economic regionalism continues to be hampered by the region's close interlinkages with the global economy. One might read this as structural dependency between the developing periphery and the variegated 'Western developed' core (including Japan), or as the legacy of post-Second World War American imperium manifested in highly porous regional orders. In either case, even though the 'new' regionalism in East Asia could pose a challenge to the global economic order, this has either not been at the top of the agenda for the key drivers of regionalism, or only sporadically and indeterminately. As the foregoing analysis made clear, overall, post-1997 attempts to strengthen financial ties across the region 'avoided any direct challenges to existing global monetary arrangements such as those posed by the AMF'.[102]

Instead, regionalism developed more as a hedge, an insurance policy against the possible failure of the global system. Indeed, the post-1997 regionalism drive may be read as a continuation of East Asia's wider hedging reaction to the disruptions of the post-Cold War period—regionalism, whether in the form of regional security dialogues, regional trade agreements, or regional financial mechanisms, is an attempt to secure 'inclusive club goods' in the face of the uncertainties about US-led provision of 'public goods' in terms of free trade, financial stability, and collective security.[103] Yet, as shown in the CMI case, regional alternatives to securing preferential access and to diversifying export markets and financial resources are very much a fall-back option, since leading East Asian economies are unwilling to bear the risks of providing regional club goods with the region's limited regulatory capacity. The latter, especially Japan and China, are also global economic players who have the additional option of increasing their leverage within global financial regimes, or of implementing international currency policies, in order to manage the uncertainties of the existing global economic order. They do not necessarily have to seek the regionalism-as-resistance option. Indeed, given their global economic profiles, Japan and China also harbour status and gains ambitions at the global level, which at times take precedence over their regional aims.

[102] Pempel 2007, 50.
[103] Aggarwal and Koo 2008.

East Asian Financial Regionalism and the Changing Neoliberal Economic Order

East Asian states have been building the road to economic regionalism across a rapidly evolving global landscape with emerging large economies in the traditional periphery and a series of financial crises. Even as they have explored the outlines of new, subsidiary regional structures of financial governance since 1997, leading East Asian states have been increasingly involved in the ongoing renegotiation of the global economic order. The relationship between these two levels of order transition is not straightforward, but the hegemonic global economic order is remarkably resilient, not least because of support from the East Asian economic powers—a state of affairs which necessarily constrains regionalism as a putative form of resisting globalization and global norms.

Over the last two decades, the international order has altered most significantly in terms of the nature and distribution of economic influence. Economic power has diffused away from the core of the United States, Western Europe, and Japan with the dramatic shift in global manufacturing capacity and capital accumulation towards emerging economies, especially China. The hegemon is now the world's largest debtor: for instance, US external borrowing had risen steadily from below 2 per cent to a peak of 6 per cent of GDP by 2005–6, driven by high inflows of capital from the post-crisis Asian economies and commodities exporters experiencing improving terms of trade, and low external savings rates.[104] Meanwhile, China and Japan, major buyers of US debt, are the world's largest holders of foreign exchange reserves.[105] In 2007 alone, emerging economies accumulated about thirty times the currency reserves that the IMF lent during the AFC.[106] High-level debates about the systemic risks of such large global imbalances intensified after the 2003 G7 and IMF meetings where Western officials pressured Japan and China to lower their intervention purchases of US dollars. During the 2008–9 global financial meltdown, then Treasury Secretary Hank Paulson led the charge that China and other surplus countries had depressed real global

---

[104] The leading proponent of this 'global saving glut' theory is the Chair of the US Federal Reserve Board, Ben Bernanke—see e.g. 'Remarks by Governor Ben S. Bernanke: The Global Saving Glut and the U.S. Current Account Deficit', Sandridge Lecture, Virginia Association of Economists, Richmond, VA, 10 March 2009. Available at <http://www.federalreserve.gov/boarddocs/speeches/2005/20050414/default.htm>. Accessed 30 October 2012.

[105] China's foreign reserves holding hit $3 trillion in March 2011, nearly triple that of second-placed Japan ($1.1 trillion), and dwarfing that of Russia, India, and Brazil (also ranked among the top ten largest holders), which have between $3 and $5 billion each—'China should cap forex reserves at 1.3 trillion', *Xinhua*, 23 April 2011; 'Taiwan's foreign reserves 4th largest in the world', *The China Post*, 4 June 2011.

[106] Setser 2008, 13.

interest rates and caused investors to underprice risk and the market to overheat.[107] The GFC itself exacerbated global imbalances, as emerging markets took advantage of the US government financial bailout and stimulus plans to step up their purchases of US debt. China became the largest holder of US debt: its holdings of official US debt stood at 46 per cent in 2008, and peaked at $1.175 trillion in October 2010.[108] China also edged out the World Bank as the largest lender to developing countries in 2009–10.[109]

Thus some see the global economic order evolving into one with multiple 'poles' possessing exceptional capability to control significant capital flows.[110] For our purposes, how does this apparent 'power shift' affect the relationship between the normative structure of the East Asian regionalist enterprise and that premised upon the US-led neoliberal global economic order? To begin with, it is worth reiterating the difficulties inherent in translating this diffusion of control over surplus capital into direct power, or the ability to bring about favoured outcomes. In theory, foreign creditors could coerce a dependent borrower state by threatening to withdraw or cut their purchases of new debts, rebalance their foreign exchange reserves portfolios, or otherwise undermine market confidence in the debtor currency.[111] Yet, during the 2008–9 crisis, China's attempts to exert financial leverage over Washington did not yield much fruit. In spite of the Chinese government adjusting the components of its US debt holdings, selling off US debt, and publicly suggesting an alternative international reserve currency, Beijing failed to pressure the US government either to guarantee the debts of troubled US government-sponsored enterprises, or to offer special protection to Chinese holdings in US assets.[112] Above all, China's ability to convert its control over capital into direct political influence is limited by its strong economic interdependence with the United States; its threats to diversify away from the US dollar or dump US debt are short on credibility because of the lack of other options.

At the same time, existing financial and economic structures and institutions which express US hegemony are resilient and adept at refracting opposition and redirecting challenges in ways that bolster its legitimacy. Domestically, in spite of exposing the limits of US institutional capacity to

---

[107] 'Paulson says crisis sown by imbalance', *Financial Times*, 1 January 2009.

[108] Cited in Drezner 2009, 13; 'China's move to reduce US debt holdings normal', *People's Daily*, 21 March 2011; 'China trimmed holdings of US debt again', *China Daily*, 18 May 2011. As the second largest holder of US debt, Japan held $900 billion as of April 2011.

[109] China lent about $110 billion to governments and businesses in developing countries, against the World Bank's $100.3 billion—'China's lending hits new heights', *Financial Times*, 17 January 2011.

[110] Subacchi 2008. See also Chin 2011.

[111] For a discussion of a range of such leverage, see Kirshner 1995; Setser 2008; Drezner 2003.

[112] Drezner 2009, 33–42.

regulate and ensure benefits to its own citizens, the 2008–9 'credit crunch' did not delegitimize key financial institutions. Few counter-hegemonic discourses or institutions have arisen with the United States; instead, the discourse has been focused on largely technical issues of crisis management, and dominated by the concerns of banks and hedge funds.[113] At the global level, this hegemonic resilience is manifested in two ways: the tendency for core problems with the global economic system (and thus their resolution) to be defined almost exclusively in reference to US national interests or imperatives; and the adaptability of existing economic institutions and norms in co-opting challengers.

Global Imbalances and the 'Regions Gap'

The GFC discourse has been dominated by the continuing focus on the US deficit vis-à-vis China and pressures on Beijing to allow the undervalued RMB to appreciate. This focus on 'currency wars' may suggest that multilateral institutions like the IMF and G20 are less relevant.[114] These sentiments would find resonance in India, Russia, Brazil, and other countries also experiencing adverse economic effects of China's undervalued currency. At the other end of the scale, economists and political observers have also raised increasingly shrill warnings about the deep domestic sources of global imbalances: remarkable levels of domestic debt and the American model of growth through consumption require a structural shift akin to a fiscal revolution, while China's skewed model of growth through production and promoting national champions requires domestic market development that entails painful internal market liberalization.[115]

Yet global imbalances are not just a United States–China issue—the Bretton Woods global economic system enabled many economies to make externalities out of their current account imbalances. As the main global issuer of reserve assets, the United States could finance a growing current account deficit during the 2000s since there was growing demand for buying US debt. China, along with other emerging economies in Asia, has resisted the upward pressure on its currency by intervening in markets to sell its own currency to stabilize the exchange rate; and through domestic monetary intervention to manage the inflationary impacts of such currency sales ('sterilization'), all to delay having to adjust its balance of payments. Japan and the developed European economies took advantage of the depreciationary impacts of the shift to a system of floating exchange rates to shelter their

---

[113] Konings 2009, 94.
[114] James 2011, 535.
[115] See e.g. Holslag 2011.

domestic economies from trade liberalization and external competition—they financed economic growth through exports to the United States, but delaying structural reforms in their labour and product markets exacerbated current account imbalances once the euro began to appreciate in the 2000s. Thus the savings glut both in emerging economies and Western developed economies contributed to the scramble for high-yield low-risk assets, a bubble that eventually burst in 2008.[116] The putative solutions to the ongoing global structural adjustment require not only domestic financial policies, but rethinking of the ideological assumptions, institutional design, and distribution of benefits within the existing global economic order.

In the post-GFC negotiations, on the one hand, are those who treat the issue primarily as one of reformulating financial regulation and creating economic stimulus for growth. On the other hand, others argue for a more radical renegotiation of the 'global compact' to tackle global imbalances and reassess the ways in which multiple economies can seek macroeconomic 'adjustment with growth'.[117] For both schools of thought, developing regional financial regimes play potentially important roles. In terms of financial and especially currency regulation, regional coordination on exchange rate policies may be helpful. For instance, on the issue of currency intervention, the major intervening countries, China, Japan, and South Korea, experience significant functional interdependence—given China's role in the regional production network, its current account surplus is in fact a 'regional' trade surplus with the United States and Europe, and regional economies share an interest in intra-regional exchange rate stability while allowing more flexibility against other currencies. Thus coordinated currency appreciation among China, Japan, and South Korea, for example, would help to maintain their relative competitiveness to each other at least.[118] Ongoing debates about strengthening regulatory regimes also privilege regional–global cooperation. The UN Stiglitz Commission suggests that the reformed global financial architecture might be made up of a network of regional monetary funds, working in tandem with a scaled-down IMF.[119] In East Asia, others have pushed for cooperation between CMIM and the IMF to avoid duplication and to enhance a division of labour—for instance, AMRO can add more frequent surveillance of East Asian economies to the IMF's annual cycle; while the IMF can provide technical advice and involve AMRO in IMF surveillance missions.[120]

---

[116] See Dunaway 2009.
[117] Brown 2010.
[118] Volz, 2010.
[119] United Nations 2009.
[120] Henning 2010. Grimes 2011 warns against overestimating AMRO's potential for surveillance given the lack of technical capacity, and argues for the continued necessity of third-party surveillance in the CMIM.

Creating cooperation between global and regional regimes is a way to manage potential resistance and challenges posed by regional frameworks. For those looking to renegotiate a new global 'deal', it is the universal attempt to increase exports to ensure growth that makes the currency imbalance and realignment issue so intense. But this can only lead to competitive quantitative easing to depreciate currencies (a 'currency war') and the creation of another low-interest-rate bubble. Structural reforms are needed in key economies like China and Germany to move towards a more domestic demand-led growth model—a point acknowledged by G20 finance ministers in February 2011, when they discussed indicators of evaluating imbalances that place exchange rates in the wider context of global trade balance and investment flows.[121]

These global-level coordination plans, though, beg the question of which economies exactly will be allowed to grow by how much. Ultimately, this global compact entails the renegotiation of the distribution of benefits as well as costs, and the process cross-cuts with the higher-profile struggles for voice and representation of emerging and developing economies in global economic governance. On key issues ranging from trade negotiations to regulatory and institutional reform, East Asia is expected to deliver. Yet there is a gap—in terms of agenda, aspiration, and connection—between evolving financial regionalism and East Asian states' relative lack of activism within changing global economic governance structures that give them a greater role.[122] The reasons for this disconnect may be technical, political, or related to a time lag; however, one insufficiently studied element is that the tensions between regionalism and global reformism for China and Japan are exacerbated by hegemonic resilience, both in terms of the adaptability of the dominant economic ideology and the potential for sharing authority in global economic governance.

Ideology, Authority, and Co-optation in Global Governance

Financial regionalism in East Asia is one of the key manifestations of global power diffusion with the end of the Cold War and the rise of emerging powers. Regionalist impulses and innovations may in turn affect the nature of the global economic order currently being renegotiated, particularly in terms of ideology and authority.

Ideologically, as the earlier analysis about the AMF demonstrates, East Asian financial regionalism has at times been framed within the search for

---

[121] G20 2011. On the opposition of emerging economies to the relatively intrusive regulation entailed in this US-proposed Mutual Assessment Process, see Dunaway 2011.
[122] Drysdale and Armstrong 2010.

alternatives to the neoliberal orthodoxy, by building on the statist 'Asian model' of development. Neoliberal economic ideology is often understood as the so-called 'Washington consensus' around a monetarist neoliberal model stressing market forces while 'rolling back' the state, which characterized the 1980s 'counter-revolution' against Keynesian economics.[123] And yet, by the time of the AFC, the Washington consensus was already being reformulated. In the 1990s, Washington itself rediscovered an interest in state regulation: multinationalization and globalization necessitated transnational coordination in managing labour, banking, and investment flows, and while the norms of this new financial architecture were negotiated in international institutions like the WTO, implementation devolved to individual states, which entailed augmenting states' regulatory capacities.[124] Further, criticisms of the neoliberal model's social costs led IFI to seek re-legitimation by addressing issues of good governance: poverty reduction, social safety nets, consultations with civil society.[125] Thus, by the 2000s, there was no longer a Washington consensus as such, if by that we mean the categorical free market neoliberalism that flourished briefly in the 1980s. Indeed, the AFC and its initial mishandling by the IFI added to the momentum of renegotiating the neoliberal economic model. Resisting the prevailing global economic ideology, therefore, would have involved shooting at a moving target. Furthermore, as discussed earlier, even in the most credible attempt by an East Asian state to create a partial alternative regional financial mechanism based on a divergent developmental ideology, Japan eventually changed its mind about the AMF plan.

There was no clear connection between East Asian financial regionalism and the changing neoliberal orthodoxy. On the one hand, some charged that the rehabilitation of crisis-affected Asian economies offered 'an experiment in reinventing neo-liberalism in the region', resulting in the imposition of what Beeson and Islam call the 'augmented Washington consensus' on the region.[126] On the other hand, unlike Latin America for instance, East Asia 'simply has not had a history of failed neo-liberalism to react against'.[127] For East Asia, the baseline was special access to US and Western markets during the Cold War, and always a higher degree of state intervention than

---

[123] Williamson 1999; Toye 1987. In contrast to the Bretton Woods system that allowed states to maintain capital controls in the belief that unregulated capital flows were destabilizing and could undermine state autonomy and social stability, in a monetarist system, the state's role was limited to exercising strict control over inflation, maintaining budgetary discipline to stabilize prices, and adopting market-friendly policies of deregulation, privatization, and trade and capital account liberalization to attract foreign capital. For an alternative interpretation of the neoliberal turn as bolstering US state capacity for control of credit, see Konings 2009.
[124] Best 2003.
[125] Thirkell-White 2005; Pincus and Winters 1999.
[126] Beeson and Islam 2005, 204.
[127] Grugel, Riggirozzi, and Thirkell-White 2008, 513.

the Washington consensus entailed. Also, alongside resentment against the neoliberal international establishment, there was recognition of the causal contribution of crony capitalism within East Asia itself. Thus there was an openness to the idea that liberal reforms might create growth and jobs, and democratic reforms might bring socio-economic redistribution. This was seen most dramatically in Indonesia, where the AFC triggered the downfall of the Suharto regime and a troubled democratic transition. But effects of the AFC were diverse and included the backlash in Thailand against the IMF's neoliberal reforms, which helped to power Thaksin Shinawatra's populist Thai Rak Thai party. Hence, there was no regional agreement on the relationship between the Asian and Washington consensus models of development and the financial crises, and little basis for an ideological challenge to the evolving neoliberal ideology. Further, the developmental state model might have recovered somewhat from the 1997 attack by the resilience of East Asian economies during the 2008–9 crisis, but this crisis did not legitimize any specific alternative ideology apart from boosting statist approaches to economic management.[128]

The Washington consensus has been internally and externally challenged and the tensions between sociopolitical authority and market forces are being renegotiated at different levels, but there is not a wholesale rejection of the macroeconomic focus at its core. Closely related to this ideological resilience is another set of renegotiations about authority within the global economic order, centred on the divergences between the 'old establishment' at the heart of the most recent economic crises, and the emerging powers. But this reform of global economic governance structures, especially in the IMF and the creation of the G20, also reveals the adaptability of the existing hegemonic order in co-opting potential dissenting challengers.

The limits of the G7/8[129] and the IMF- and World Bank-centred global economic order were dramatically highlighted by the AFC and the multiple current account crises across the world in the 1990s and 2000s.[130] Globalization had so exacerbated interdependence that the G8 could not continue to exclude the major emerging economies from global economic governance if it wanted to be able to respond effectively to crises that affected global markets. But to persuade these growing economies to undertake necessary reforms, and to feel a larger stake in the existing order, they had first to be persuaded of its legitimacy through expanded representation. The G20

---

[128] Breslin 2011, 114–15.
[129] The G7 forum—consisting of the United States, UK, France, Germany, Italy, Japan, and Canada—expanded to include Russia in 1997.
[130] Mexico (February 1995), Argentina (April 1995; March 2000–January 2003), Thailand (August 1997), Indonesia (November 1997), South Korea (December 1997), Russia (August 1998), Brazil (December 1998), Turkey (December 1999–February 2002), and Uruguay (2002).

grouping, established in 1999 for finance ministers and central bank governors, was expanded in 2008 to the summit level.[131] Since 2007, the G8 summits have also included Brazil, China, India, Mexico, and South Africa in G8+5 discussions, while the so-called BRICS leading emerging economies have exerted collective pressure on these new groupings to undertake greater regulatory and representational reforms.

The G20 has seen some progress so far in terms of economic cooperation and reform, such as its peer review system of members' macroeconomic and financial policies, the first such exercise to include both developed and developing economies.[132] BRIC and G20 finance ministers also succeeded in expanding membership of the G7's Financial Stability Forum (FSF) for cooperation in market supervision and surveillance, to include G20 countries when the Forum was re-established as the Financial Stability Board (FSB) in 2009. The more ambitious agenda, though, has been the reform of IFI, particularly the IMF's mandate and governance structure. G20 states have exerted pressure on the IMF to increase emergency lending to emerging economies and developing countries, and important changes have occurred: the expansion of the New Arrangements to Borrow for crisis-hit economies, as well as the establishment of the Flexible Credit Line and Precautionary Credit Line to help vulnerable economies prevent crisis.[133] The G20 also successfully lobbied the World Bank to support counter-cyclical lending to developing economies, and the IMF to devolve to regional development banks some of the new resources for rapid crisis assistance—the ADB, for instance, was able to introduce a counter-cyclical support facility to disburse up to $3 billion to crisis-affected developing economies in Asia.[134]

G20 members also reportedly linked significant increases in their IMF contributions during the GFC to voting reform.[135] At the 2009 London summit, the G20 countries trebled the resources available to the IMF to $750 billion—with Japan committing an additional $100 billion and China pledging $40 billion—and agreed to a variety of additional trade finance and concessional lending to the tune of $350 billion.[136] In return, they agreed on the FSF

---

[131] Argentina, Australia, Brazil, China, India, Indonesia, Mexico, Saudi Arabia, South Africa, South Korea, Turkey, the G8 countries, and representatives from the EU, IMF, and World Bank.
[132] Rana 2010.
[133] What the IMF director called 'modernizing conditionality'—'International Policy Cooperation: Essential for Securing the Global Economic Recovery and Modernizing the Global Financial Architecture', Address by Dominique Strauss-Kahn, Managing Director of the IMF to the European Parliament, Strasbourg, 17 March 2010.
[134] Chin 2010, 708.
[135] 'BRIC nations say no IMF cash without representation', *Reuters*, 14 March 2009.
[136] G20 2009b. The president of the World Bank stated that the $1.1 trillion G20 package 'broke the fall' of the world economy—'Pittsburgh should be a turning point for the poor', *Financial Times*, 29 September 2009. In 2012, the G20 again pledged further resources under a scheme to double the IMF's fighting fund.

expansion and early implementation of IMF voting shares reforms—agreed since April 2008 but delayed in the ratification process—by January 2011. In November 2010, the IMF board agreed a shift of 6 per cent of quota shares to emerging and developing economies, bringing all the BRIC countries into the Fund's group of ten most powerful members by 2012 (mainly at the expense of Britain, France, and Saudi Arabia).[137] This 'rebalancing' will also affect the composition of the Fund's Executive Board, which will see two European members replaced by two emerging countries, as well as the introduction of elections for all Executive Directors. The extent to which these reforms fully address legitimacy and efficiency concerns may be debated, especially since Washington has ceded no portion of its preponderant voting shares.[138]

The reform of global economic governance is an ongoing process in which China expects its growing interests and rising clout increasingly to be taken into account. The Chinese discourse centres on two aspects: fairer representation in the IMF, and diversification of reserve currencies away from US dollar dominance.[139] In July 2011, China gained representation at the top of the Fund's hierarchy, when Zhu Min was appointed to a newly created post of deputy managing director, and Beijing expects its voting share within the Fund to rise beyond the 3.65 per cent agreed to in November 2010.[140] Meanwhile, China is attempting to diversify its global financial dependencies. In March 2009, the governor of the Bank of China proposed that the IMF's international reserve asset, the Special Drawing Right (SDR), be strengthened to act as an alternative reserve asset option over the long term.[141] The G20 agreed the following month to increase their allocation of SDRs to $250 billion, but the impacts of this agreement are debatable given the reluctance of the G7 to contemplate more fundamental reforms.[142] By the end of 2009, China had sold off about $34 billion worth of US bonds, dropping to second place behind Japan as the largest holder of US bonds.[143] While some observers see this as part of the agenda to undermine Washington's central

---

[137] The ten largest members of the Fund will then consist of: (1) the United States, (2) Japan, (3) China, (4) Germany, (5) France, (6) the UK, (7) Italy, (8) India, (9) Russia, and (10) Brazil.
[138] See e.g. Takagi 2010; 'China C. Bank adviser says US should cut IMF voting share', *Reuters*, 24 May 2011.
[139] A good detailed discussion of Chinese official and academic thinking on this subject is found in Tianda yanjiu keti zu 2010.
[140] 'China urges Lagarde to deepen IMF reforms', *China Daily*, 29 June 2011.
[141] 'China eyes SDR as global currency', *China Daily*, 23 March 2009; 'China's subtle moves ahead of G-20 summit', *The Nation*, 30 March 2009.
[142] France had declared as priority further discussions about the wider use of SDRs as a reserve currency when it took over the presidency of the G20 in 2011—'Lagarde says French G20 to discuss wider use of SDR', *Reuters*, 1 September 2010—but the issue was overshadowed by the Strauss-Kahn resignation and then the Eurozone crisis.
[143] 'China sells $34.2 billion of U.S. Treasury bonds', *Guardian*, 17 February 2010.

role, it could also be read as defensive diversification by a country in a weak position because of overdependence upon the United States.[144] Beijing's willingness to push for more serious alterations to the existing global financial order, or alternatives to it, is constrained by its reluctance to appear radical on the global stage, but also fundamentally by the risk that trying to shift rapidly out of its own deep dependence on the US dollar as its key reserve currency would diminish the value of remaining dollar assets.[145]

Of course, China's financial reform strategy contains a strong national dimension. As one Chinese analyst put it, the time is ripe for China to 'widen its economic-resource space', by deepening its role in East Asian economic cooperation to develop a regional base from which to expand its leverage. This ought to be accompanied by strategies to 'raise China's ability to dictate prices in the international financial market', which would entail building up an international financial centre and internationalizing the Chinese currency.[146] Beijing has been promoting international use of the tightly controlled RMB through bilateral currency swaps and trade agreements to start reducing dependence on the US dollar. Hence the attempted 'regionalization' of the RMB through its use for trade with Hong Kong, Macau, and some ASEAN countries, and negotiations with BRICS to denominate bilateral trade in local currencies.[147] Singapore was designated the second international hub (after Hong Kong) for clearing RMB trade in mid-2011.[148] More significantly, China began direct currency trading with its largest trading partner, Japan, in June 2012, ending the practice of denominating most of their bilateral trade (worth $300 billion in 2010) in US dollars.[149] Internationalization of the RMB would eventually allow China to seek a larger and more formal role in global economic governance, and eventually to promote the RMB as an alternative reserve currency.

Yet it is difficult to interpret these moves as revolutionary attempts to replace the existing global economic order. In many respects China and Japan have acted to reform but boost the existing order. Even Beijing seems

---

[144] Kirshner 2008. China returned as the top lender to the United States by 2011, though with a slight reduction in the value of its bond holdings—'China's holdings of Treasuries decline for first time', *Bloomberg News*, 1 March 2012.

[145] Hence the Chinese government did not press the suggestion at subsequent summits and denied that it was government position to replace the dollar—'China reassures on dollar debate before G8', *China Daily*, 6 July 2009.

[146] Wang 2011.

[147] Since the GFC, China has signed currency swap agreements with South Korea, Hong Kong, Malaysia, Indonesia, Singapore, and New Zealand, amongst others. Most recently, China agreed to US$30 billion currency swap deals each with Australia and Brazil to support trade transactions in RMB—'China and Brazil in $30bn currency swap agreement', *BBC*, 22 June 2012. Beijing is also in talks with Tokyo to allow direct trading between the yen and the RMB.

[148] 'Singapore aims to be renminbi hub', *Financial Times*, 11 April 2011.

[149] 'Japan, China to begin direct currency trading on June 1', *China Daily*, 29 May 2012.

to have few delusions about alternatives to US leadership in the global economy. While calling for the diversification of the world's reserve currencies, Chinese leaders were at the same time repeatedly urging Washington to intervene to maintain the value of the dollar. China's vice-foreign minister publicly acknowledges 'the reality' that the dollar is 'the most important major international reserve currency of the day, and for years to come'.[150] In the recent financial crises, Japan and China showed themselves willing to play the role of back-up lenders of last resort, both in Asia and in Europe. After 1997, Japan's Miyazawa Initiative was followed by cooperation with China and other East Asian states in the CMIM currency swap agreements. When the GFC hit in 2008, Chinese leaders initially focused on looking after China first, since 'China's sound economic growth is in itself a major contribution to global financial stability and economic growth.'[151] But by 2009, China and other emerging economies not only joined the G7 in helping the IMF to increase credit to crisis-hit countries, but also ensured that industrial economies with large export sectors could rely on emerging market demand to recover. Noting that over 70 per cent of China's trade surplus with the United States in 2003–9 was accounted for by Chinese purchases of American Treasury Bonds, one observer characterized it as 'the largest economic aid package since the Marshall Plan'.[152] During the 'euro panic' in the spring of 2011, China and other major holders of reserve currencies turned the tide by declaring their interest in euro holdings.[153] Since then, China has bought EU government bonds and assets on official buying missions in Europe, including bond purchases in the troubled economies of Greece, Spain, and Portugal, and billion-dollar business contracts with the larger economies, Germany and the UK.[154] Beijing has acted out of self-interest—whether in search of bargain-basement-priced assets or to expand access to key European markets—but such measures reaffirm neoliberal economic ideology and do not present alternative ideas for more radical change.

At the institutional level, the expanded structures of governance are even more pronounced in boosting the traditional hegemonic role of the IFI. The G20, for instance, has not departed significantly from the agenda of the

[150] 'Vice FM: US should maintain stability of dollar', *China Daily*, 6 July 2009.
[151] 'China's sound growth major contribution to global financial stability: Hu', *Xinhua*, 24 October 2008; Wen Jianbao, 'How China is winning the fight against inflation', *Financial Times*, 24 June 2011.
[152] Holslag 2011, 82.
[153] James 2011, 532.
[154] 'Enter the dragon to save the euro', *Telegraph*, 30 June 2011; 'Wen Jiabao goes shopping and vows to help the euro', *Spiegel Online International*, 28 June 2011; 'China pledges continued support for European debt', *Wall Street Journal*, 26 June 2011. Figures for the composition of Chinese reserve holdings are not available, but some economists suggest that Beijing is likely to be channelling its new foreign exchange reserves more into Eurozone debt than US assets—'Beijing's moves point to Europe aid', *Wall Street Journal*, 24 June 2011.

G7: the emphasis remains macroeconomic imbalances and exchange rates, and the IMF has not undergone significant governance reform (such as a significant increase in Asian shares of quotas, or the removal of the executive board from day-to-day operations to try to depoliticize the Fund's decision-making). In its key 'recession buster' role, the G20 has challenged neither the Bretton Woods institutions nor US global economic dominance,[155] but rather bolstered the IFI by generating new resources for the IMF, the World Bank, and regional development banks. The G20 has also bolstered the IMF's monitoring role by adopting the FSB in its core action plan for macroeconomic and financial monitoring.[156] The group has also declared high-level support for the WTO's free trade agenda.[157]

As the leading East Asian economic powers, China and Japan come under frequent scrutiny for potentially challenging the existing order, to the extent that some observers are almost disappointed with the lack of tangible leadership they have shown in global governance reforms so far.[158] Yet, for Beijing, the priority has been to increase China's voice and representation while gradually altering undesirable elements of the existing global order from within.[159] Leading Chinese analysts identify a serious 'global governance deficit' that China as a self-proclaimed 'builder' of international order can fill within existing arrangements.[160] Having recognized that it benefits from the existing system, China has turned into a key proponent of it—Beijing does complain about aspects of it but these are voiced 'from within the system and matched by a desire to protect and reform it'.[161] Chinese analysts are reluctant to call for the outright replacement of the existing order. Rather, the aim is to seek some sort of 'power sharing' with the United States and other 'responsible stakeholders', as opposed to a 'destabilizing' power transition that would entail 'political and perhaps military conflict if we try to overthrow the current system'.[162]

Japan works from the different position of being part of the established set of great powers within the existing global economic order: it is essentially conformist and pro-status quo. Thus, while engaging actively in the G20 process, Tokyo has resisted supplanting and diluting the G7/8 as the core group of leading states. MOFA officials have reiterated the lasting importance of the G8 as a steering committee determining the agenda

---

[155] Zhu 2011.
[156] Cooper 2010, 741.
[157] G20 2009b.
[158] E.g. see Acharya 2011.
[159] Wang 2008.
[160] Wang 2009, 13; Ruan 2005, 28.
[161] Glosny 2010, 118.
[162] Author interview with Chinese economic analyst, Beijing, May 2011.

for the G20, while liberal Japanese policy thinkers advocate the retention of the G7 as a 'core caucus' of leading democracies and market economies working efficiently within the G20 to 'support global order'.[163] Even though China and Japan have different priorities in negotiating the ongoing reforms, they do converge on the need to advance their positions at the global level and to maintain and strengthen the existing order. The upshot is an ongoing 'process of negotiation and mutual accommodation over the existing order from countries firmly entrenched in that order'.[164] The establishment of the G20, BRICS, and other emerging power groupings is primarily the means by which the latter seek to expand the membership of the elite group of global great powers that manage global order—the aim is to share power, and by sharing, increase the authority of this group; it is not to resist or replace the ideological or structural foundations of this order.[165]

It is too soon to assess the G20 and BRICS contributions to reforming the global economic order, but they have clearly generated momentum for the reform agenda, and stimulated competing initiatives at the international and transnational levels, such as Secretary-General Ban Ki Moon's UN Conference on the Global Economic Crisis, and the World Economic Forum's Global Redesign Initiative. This ferment has generated a corresponding demand for regional-level governance structures—the Stiglitz Commission's suggestion for a network of regional monetary funds has already been alluded to. Without resurrecting the AMF idea, China's central bank governor criticized the IMF's inadequate crisis prevention role in 2009, asserting that 'regional institutions such as the ADB could also alleviate the impact of financial crisis through increasing spending and boosting regional activities'.[166] Yet such ideas are, as Breslin observes, basically order maintaining, since they aim to resist not the neoliberal project per se, but 'unfettered liberalisation', not by creating regional-level alternatives, but rather a 'mediating layer of governance between national and global economies'.[167] In this regard, the emerging economies are particularly focused on building up a form of defensive autonomy, in the sense of reducing their developing financial markets' reliance on US and European markets and boosting their potential for creating supplementary regulatory paths.[168]

---

[163] Dobson 2010, 40.
[164] Glosny 2010, 125.
[165] This expanded representation of leading states necessarily only goes part way towards addressing legitimacy concerns: while it may address the major power-to-major power level of inequalities, it perpetuates the divide between a (now slightly bigger) group of major economic powers and the 'marginal majority' of other states. See Payne 2010.
[166] Chin 2010, 708–9.
[167] Breslin 2006, 35.
[168] Helleiner and Pagliari 2011, 177.

The overall picture at the global level, therefore, is characterized by hegemonic resilience. In terms of both ideology and authority, the existing neoliberal, US-led global economic order has been rescued and reinforced in the face of recent crises. Emerging powers such as China have been co-opted into an adaptable order with prospects of power sharing, while incumbent economic leaders such as Japan concentrate on retaining as much leverage as possible within existing governance structures. In this context, modes of financial regionalism in East Asia have been boosted as a means of spreading and devolving this global hegemony, thus fundamentally constraining their potential challenge. And yet this state of affairs does not arise from the structural imposition by global forces, but rather from active choices made by the key East Asian great powers. China and Japan are playing multiple games and often privileging domestic economic growth and the global order maintenance regarded as essential to it—so they negotiate a certain type of regional community that can sustain, or at least not interfere with, these priorities.

Conclusion

This chapter has discussed the political project of financial regionalism since the Asian financial crisis, against the context of the type of economic regionalization experienced in East Asia since the 1980s, as well as the intensifying renegotiation of the global economic order since the global financial crisis in 2008–9. It finds that East Asian regionalism's significance lies mainly in the political marshalling of a regional community in recognition of the growing functional and ontological interdependence fuelled by China's rise. But this is not an autonomous community capable of mounting a challenge against the existing global economic order. It functions more as a means for East Asian states to apply pressure for and to strengthen ongoing regulatory development and governance reforms; and only in the long term might regional financial arrangements be pursued as potential alternatives to global ones.

The potential of regional financial arrangements for tackling the adverse effects of financial crises and contagion is limited and debatable within East Asia—because of Sino-Japanese competition and conflicting interests, the emphasis on political symbolism, and precisely the pursuit of regionalism merely as a fall-back hedge against global failures. At its core, the East Asian financial regionalism project is conservative vis-à-vis the global order, and the analysis in this chapter highlights three key reasons.

First, East Asian economies' traditional structural interdependence with external—especially European and American—markets renders them more sensitive to global economic conditions and regulations than regional ones.

Thus the stark juxtaposition of regionalism against globalism is unhelpful in East Asia, where economic regionalization has been remarkably open and externally oriented. This functional characteristic fundamentally limits prospects for the 'closed' regionalism project. It also means that the regional renegotiation of economic order is deeply interwoven with that at the global level, leading to the second reason centred on poor regional leadership.

China and Japan face complex and at times conflicting demands and interests at the global level, where the stakes are higher than at the regional level in terms of status, markets, and profits, particularly at a time of active renegotiation and reform. Globally, the provision of the financial public goods that has long been regarded as a hegemonic imperative does remain dominated by the United States—for example, it continues to provide the world's reserve currency—but there has been gradual burden sharing in terms of contributions to and disbursement of capital liquidity. These ongoing global renegotiations impact on the major East Asian economic powers' ability to concentrate their resources at the regional level. Japan and China are both unwilling to monopolize the supply of regional financial public goods, not just because of capacity considerations, but also because they have multiple aims at the global level—to limit exposure to different types of risk commensurate with their financial profiles, to block each other's potential gains in status, and to preserve certain beneficial aspects of the existing order while reforming less desirable ones.

The third reason for conservative East Asian regionalism is perhaps the most significant, as it bears on the costs of hegemonic transition. The point is not that the US-led global neoliberal ideology and institutions cannot be challenged, but rather that hegemonic institutions are extremely costly to replace. Particularly in light of the demonstrated adaptability of the existing ideological and authority structures in reforming and sharing some power, rising powers like China are led towards policies to integrate into the global order rather than to decouple from it, while incumbent members of the great power club like Japan are incentivized into greater engagement within the existing order to protect their interests in the face of new members. Thus change is more likely to happen in terms of the expanded membership of actors who constitute the hegemonic core and its functional norms, rather than in the basic institution of hegemony and its constitutive norms.

At the regional level, China and Japan seek some differentiation and insulation from global market failures through diversification. Their regionalist policies tend to be heavy on political symbolism but lighter on economic substance, and so they ultimately support global norms and institutions. Emerging and regional powers have greater capacity to resist global economic hegemony or orthodoxy, especially because of their control of capital, and they are helping to create an international financial order that is 'more

The Struggle for Order

fragmented, in which power is more diffused and non-global arrangements play a more prominent role'.[169] This fragmentation heralds increasing decentralization in the financial regulatory order, and disaggregation into multi-layered arrangements in critical functions such as financial safety nets.[170] Yet the most that might be argued to come out of such fragmentation thus far is that China and Japan are leaning towards facilitating a multi-tiered, rather than multipolar, global economic order.

---

[169] Chin 2010, 694.
[170] Helleiner and Pagliari 2011; Rana 2012.

5

Order and Justice: Contesting the Collective Memory Regime

One nagging theme emerges from the preceding analyses of institutional bargains, authority in conflict management, and regionalist endeavours in East Asia: the constraints posed by the Sino-Japanese relationship. The parameters of the ongoing order transition are staked out by what China and Japan will or will not seek and tolerate from the other, and US hegemony attains de facto sustainability as a result. Within analyses of Sino-Japanese discord and alienation, the 'history problem' invariably occupies a prominent position. Centred most controversially on Japan's apparent reluctance to admit responsibility for Second World War atrocities, the East Asian 'history problem' surfaced in the 1980s when Japanese domestic discord over war guilt spilled over into political contestation between the region's major powers.[1] Contemporaneous analyses of these tensions tend to focus on clashing memory cultures and the dynamics of domestic politics. Yet the most significant element of these memory conflicts is strategic and relates to the interrupted and partial transitions in East Asian regional order.

First, these contemporary history disputes are best understood against a longer process of resistance and conflict reaching back to the late sixteenth century, when Japan challenged the Sino-centric regional order by launching the Imjin War against Korea and China. Japan subsequently resigned altogether from this Sinic order by consciously adopting the norms and practices of Western international society after the mid-nineteenth-century Meiji Restoration. Tokugawa Japan's distancing from the Sinic order culminated in the First Sino-Japanese war of 1894–5, which dramatically exposed Qing

[1] This chapter might have drawn on a range of disputes over history across East Asia, including the conflicts between Thailand and Cambodia, Korea and China, and the Philippines and the United States. I have chosen to focus on the Japan-centred Second World War disputes in Northeast Asia because of their relative salience for the wider contemporary regional security order.

China's decline in the face of domestic dissent, Western technological competition, and imperial encroachment. This rupture also culminated in Japanese imperialism: the annexation of Korea in 1910, invasion of Manchuria in 1931, and then all-out war with China in 1937–45, during which the China-centred tributary order finally disappeared.[2] Contemporary reckonings with this shared past therefore involve coming to terms not only with the Second Sino-Japanese war but also with Korea's subjugation under Japanese colonialism, and the wider regional dynamics of resistance, challenge, and decline entwined in the transition away from the older Sinic order.

Second, an early and crucial dimension of US hegemony in East Asia was its role in determining the terms of the peace after Japan's surrender in 1945. This peace settlement alienated Japan not only from China but also from its other East Asian neighbours, notably Korea. Strategically, the United States emasculated Japan through a 'peace' constitution and security dependence. Through its subsequent alliance, Washington extended a security umbrella over Tokyo in exchange for Japan's disarmament, pacification, and guaranteed alignment with the 'free world' in the Cold War. In effect, this compact saw the United States stepping into the breach between Japan and China as an 'outside arbiter play[ing] a policing role'—by making Japanese defence dependent on itself, the United States extended a 'dual reassurance', simultaneously guaranteeing China and Japan their security against each other, obviating the need for them to engage in direct security competition.[3] By its hub-and-spokes alliances with South Korea and Japan, the United States also encouraged some strategic alignment between them while precluding the need for urgent reconciliation. This great power bargain disintegrated with the end of the Cold War. In particular, the revitalization of the United States–Japan alliance based on a more active military role for Japan undermined Washington's ring-holding role between Japan and China, as Beijing began to regard the alliance as a means less to constrain than to facilitate Japan's militarization. In sum, there was a partial power and order transition between China and Japan in the sixteenth to nineteenth centuries that reached an impasse with Japan's defeat in the Second World War and subordination to the United States. China, Japan, and to a lesser extent South Korea, have now to face each other directly at the heart of this unfinished and delayed transition in East Asia.

This face-off is made more traumatic because the post-Second World War impasse not only interrupted mutual reckoning between China and Japan; the war settlement also left out China, Korea, and other regional actors. Japan's ultimate defeat by the United States in the Pacific theatre and the

[2] See Suzuki 2009; Phillips 2010, 200–58.
[3] Christensen 1999, 50; White 2009.

nationalist/communist split in the Chinese camp precluded peace settlements between Japan and its Asian neighbours. Instead, Washington leveraged on its role as liberator of the Pacific theatre and occupier of Japan to design a limited, Western-oriented post-war settlement, which excluded China and Korea from the San Francisco Peace Treaty (SFPT) and reparations agreements. The American occupation authorities also defined early war history by limiting the prosecution of war crimes at the Tokyo Tribunal, facilitating the rehabilitation of Japanese conservative political forces, and contributing to the 'myth of the military clique' in assigning responsibility for the war.[4] Alongside relatively limited reparations and US aid in rebuilding Japanese industry, these terms were viewed by many war victims as constituting a remarkably soft peace for Japan. Thus between Japan and China and Korea yawns a gulf of unresolved conflict, power transition, and moral claims, circumscribed by US hegemonic power after 1945. The resurfacing of history conflicts from the 1980s reflected growing resistance against these fences of memory in East Asia.

Understanding this interaction between memory, domestic politics, and strategic transition drives us towards the inescapable normative dimension of regional order. Historical disputes or contested memories are competing justice claims to do with accurate representation of events and experiences, reparation, apology and remorse, and meaningful commemoration. They spotlight the moral conflict accompanying order transition, which has to be mediated within the new social compact. At the heart of this challenge is the relationship between order and justice, which remains relatively under-theorized in the International Relations literature.[5] Often, the implicit assumption is that there is a trade-off between order and justice, or that order is prior to justice. More optimistic about the prospects of reconciling the two, liberals are apt to suggest that even though justice can be pursued only within the parameters of order, order is best provided in meeting demands for justice. Yet moves towards justice tend to be constrained 'because they bump up against a global political order that remains heavily structured around inherited pluralist mechanisms that are deformed by various sets of inequalities—of capacity, leadership, and advantage'.[6] Post-Second World War East Asia inherited a deformed mechanism, a partial collective memory regime forged by external victors with the complicity of regional states due to Cold War exigencies, which foreclosed regional justice claims for decades. But the following analysis demonstrates that, in practice, there is a negotiated bargain between the demands for order and justice within any social compact, which is unlikely to represent a balanced

---

[4] He 2009.
[5] See Hurrell 2003.
[6] Foot 2003, 17.

reconciliation between the two. Yet the inequalities that cause these 'deformities' are contingent, and their shifting results in renewed demands for justice and the renegotiation of the bargain.

Thus at the heart of the East Asian history disputes are two core issues of order and justice: Japan's challenge of and subsequent alienation from the East Asian order; and the pending war settlements between Japan and its neighbours. A major sticking point in the ongoing order transition is the renegotiation of the great power compact between China, Japan, and the United States. But this depends upon a mutual reckoning between China and Japan about the terms of Japan's reintegration into contemporary regional society, for which a better reconciliation of demands for justice is crucial. This chapter explicitly unpacks the key content and modes of these conflicts over history, delivering an account of hegemonic power over the region's collective memory, resistance to the established Second World War memory regime, and attempts to renegotiate the balance of justice and order in this vital moral realm. This process is an integral part of the ongoing order transition; more starkly than the themes addressed in previous chapters, it highlights the contingent and the deeply normative nature of the regional social compact.

The following section discusses the conceptual connections between history, memory, and international order, and sets up the framework of collective memory regimes for analysing how collective memory interacts with power and justice claims in the East Asian order transition. The subsequent analysis is in three parts. The first begins by describing the post-1945 memory regime created around East Asia's Second World War history. The second part analyses the challenges to this memory regime and rival claims to representational justice in the face of unequal material and discursive power. The crucial contestation has occurred within Japan, where conservative nationalist interest groups have pushed to revise the memory regime centred on Japan's defeat. These forces are examined through the long-running controversies over history textbooks and the Yasukuni shrine. But regional challenges to the collective memory regime also intensified in the post-Cold War period, wrought by changing political contexts within China and South Korea. The state-driven Chinese challenge focused on Japanese atrocities and Chinese resistance, while in South Korea non-governmental activist groups ignited a regional campaign for restitution for Asian victims of Japanese aggression, especially former comfort women. Together, these cases highlight four key elements destabilizing the pre-existing memory regime: the role of sub-state and transnational groups; challenges to the master narrative about causes of Japanese aggression; resistance against the exclusions and occlusions of the post-war settlements; and, ultimately, resistance against the hegemonic memory regime. The third part analyses the implications of this increasingly explicit public sphere of contestation over collective memory, including the significance of attempts to negotiate 'joint' versions of regional history. The final section relates these findings to the broader regional order transition. Contestation and renegotiation of the collective memory regime of the Second World War clearly impact on, and are affected by, normative beliefs about the proper social compact between the states involved. These rival claims carry strong prescriptive implications for the United States', China's, and Japan's roles in the hierarchical order being negotiated. Because the difficulties inherent in mediating these justice claims hamper the negotiation of a social compact that would tame Sino-Japanese discord in particular, they also impede a significant transition away from US hegemony.

History, Memory, and International Order

The literature on East Asian politics and security readily identifies the 'history problem' as a major stumbling block for regional cooperation. Historical memory is widely recognized as playing a key part in nationalism and other negative identity dynamics in post-Cold War Northeast Asia, which in turn generates distrust and a strong undercurrent of regional instability.[7] Much of this literature focuses on 'history wars' or the 'memory problem' as an explanation for tensions between Japan and China and Korea particularly, and is primarily concerned with the conditions for their possible reconciliation.[8] Yet disputes over history and memory tend to be presented as an intermediate variable affecting bilateral relationships, subject to geopolitical disputes, changing power distribution, and regime type. Analyses focusing on rising nationalism and intractable cultural clashes also tend towards hand-wringing conclusions that the problem is insoluble.[9] This chapter focuses on two areas that have received less sustained analytical attention: the substantive normative content of these memory conflicts and their effect on renegotiating new boundaries and understandings of shared history; and the relationship between these vital normative contests and the evolving regional order.

Offering better analytical traction for understanding the relationship between historical disputes and order transition is the concept of 'collective memory'. Understood as 'inter-subjectively shared interpretations of a poignant common past with a high degree of affect', collective memory is a vital part of political culture.[10] It manifests in the form of communications

---

[7] See e.g. Hasegawa and Togo 2008.
[8] Key works include Rose 2005; Lind 2008; He 2009.
[9] One exception is Dudden 2008.
[10] Langenbacher 2010, 26.

(textbooks, political rhetoric), symbols (flags, national anthems), and symbolic interactions (commemorative ceremonies).[11] Far from being a comfortable consensual interpretation of past events, collective memory is negotiated, contingent, and liable to contestation. Constituting 'the memories of the collectivity as a (necessarily fictitious) whole', collective memory is necessarily 'the inter-subjective outcome of a series of ongoing intellectual and political negotiations'.[12] Focusing on collective memory highlights the historical contingency of political orders more generally: the social compacts that underlie them are products of a particular set of forces at a specific juncture, and therefore subject to renegotiation when conditions change. Collective memories of the Second World War in East Asia were forged as discourses and practices associated with the political and strategic imperatives of nation building, alliance, and security during the Cold War, and these regimes of remembering and forgetting were vitally constituted by US hegemony. Under renegotiation since the end of the Cold War are new norms of collective memory, including whether and how to establish an agreed record of shared history, to make restitution for historical wrongs, to mourn and learn from history, and in doing so to 'move on'. This renegotiation takes place at multiple levels, for collective memories, particularly those about war and colonialism, are national creations and are contested within the domestic political sphere and by non-state actors.

To analyse the dynamics of contestation over collective memories about the Second World War in East Asia, this chapter employs the notion of 'collective memory regime', defined as a structure of social meaning that surrounds collective memory, constituted by discursive and power relationships, and which develops over time institutionalized practices.[13] We may conceive of a collective memory regime as an interlocking normative framework with two elements (Figure 5.1). The first element is the 'historical script', which centres on the dominant collective memory (e.g. of invasion or defeat in war), and includes the values and lessons drawn from the experience (e.g. what ought to be done, what cannot be tolerated), and the supportive ethical discourses (e.g. 'never again'). In this chapter, the historical script element is used to describe the existing set of collective beliefs about the war experience. The second element is composed of 'master narratives' about (a) the causes of the crucial events of the collective memory; and (b) the evolution of the memory itself. This element is used here to analyse primary avenues of contesting and renegotiating the collective memory. A collective memory

---

[11] Berger 2002, 80. Symbolic interactions are more the focus of political sociologists—see e.g. Schwartz and Kim 2010.
[12] Berger 2002, 83.
[13] I adapt this framework from Langenbacher's (2010, 30–1) elaboration of 'memory regimes'.

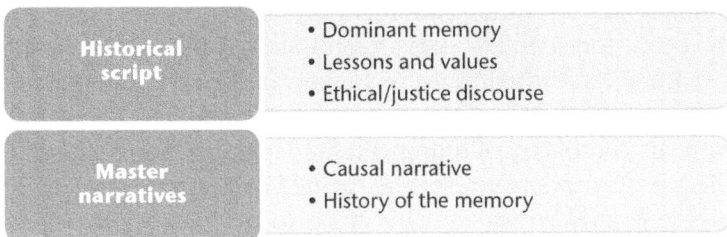

Figure 5.1. The collective memory regime

regime is negotiated by political actors and translated into public scripts, but it is also a contingent bargain about historical experience, narratives, and baggage.[14] Existing collective memory regimes are destabilized when master narratives are contested and/or when key elements constituting the dominant collective memory itself are challenged.

This analytical framework allows us explicitly to explore the interactions between collective memory and power in three ways. Most obviously, it is a vehicle to study the power of memory as a cultural or instrumental form of influence over contemporary politics, and the impact of the associated competing justice claims on the order transition. But the collective memory regime framework also foregrounds contests to wield power over memory as part of the broader struggle for regional order. These dynamics include the creation of collective memory regimes to serve strategic imperatives, but also resistance to the hegemonic memory regime, and contests between state and non-state actors to determine the content of collective memory. Finally, this analytical framework allows us to grapple with memories of power, and the contingent normative bargains by which East Asian states and peoples live with histories of victory or defeat, dominance or oppression, prior structures of authority and unfinished transitions.[15]

The Post-Second World War Collective Memory Regime

The noted Asianist Lucian Pye observed in 1996 that '[f]or more than 50 years the Japanese people have acted as though they had no recollection of having started a major war and then of losing it'.[16] While Pye reflected palpable Chinese and Korean frustrations with Japanese conservative views,

---

[14] For good examples, see the chapters on European war memories in Langenbacher and Shain 2010.
[15] The basic tripartite relationship between memory and power is highlighted in Müller 2002.
[16] Pye 1996, 28.

the sentiment fails to capture two important characteristics of the collective memory regime forged in East Asia after the Second World War: (1) the determining hand of the United States, as the sole post-war occupation authority in Japan, in creating the official history of the war; and (2) that this was done with the complicity of ruling elites in Japan and key East Asian states. The collective memory regime of the Pacific War created between 1943 and 1952 was constituted by complicity in a selective process of remembering and forgetting and a balance of order and justice heavily weighted in favour of order. The feasibility and legitimacy of this bargain stemmed from the combined force of Cold War exigencies, authoritarian states, and outward-oriented Cold War structures in Northeast Asia.[17]

Outlined in Table 5.1 (p. 173), this post-1945 collective memory regime was based on the *dominant memory* of Japan's defeat in the Pacific theatre. This script concentrated on Japanese expansionism in the 1930s: even though the Allied Powers dated Japanese aggression back to 1895 in the 1943 Cairo Declaration and the 1951 SFPT, US occupation authorities deliberately shrank the temporal frame of the war memory. The Japanese term 'the Greater East Asian War' was banned in favour of the American term 'the Pacific War', and the Supreme Commander of the Allied Powers (SCAP) conducted a national education campaign on the official history of the Pacific War focused solely on Japanese imperial history after the invasion of Manchuria in 1931 and emphasizing US military and technological supremacy that wrought Japan's complete surrender.[18]

These occupation histories lay the blame for Japan's defeat on a small clique of military men who conspired to wage wars of aggression to dominate Asia.[19] The *causal narrative* associated with the collective memory regime, therefore, was a relatively circumscribed one. It notably exonerated the Japanese people. In the 1945 Potsdam Declaration, the Allied Powers already identified 'irresponsible militarism' as the key enemy and stated that '[t]here must be eliminated for all time the authority and influence of those who have deceived and misled the people of Japan into embarking on world conquest'. The particular blame on militarists was strengthened by the Principle 10 provision that '[w]e do not intend that the Japanese people shall be enslaved as a race or destroyed as a nation, but stern justice shall be meted out to all war criminals'. The war crimes tribunal in Tokyo also identified as the source of Japanese aggression a 'criminal militaristic clique', which 'systematically poisoned with harmful ideas of the alleged racial superiority

---

[17] Berger 2008.
[18] Leading national newspapers published the ten-part series 'Taiheiyo Sensōshi' [A History of the Pacific War] 8–17 December 1945, and the series 'Shinsō wa kouda' [This is the Truth] was broadcast on national radio for ten weeks from 9 December 1945.
[19] See Dower 1999, 456; Mayo 1984.

of Japan' the minds of the Japanese people, and conspired with the other Axis Powers to dominate the world.[20] Prominent among the 'Japan crowd' at the State Department, this view also exonerated the Emperor, arguing that the 'military clique and cult' in fact 'succeeded in gaining control over the Emperor himself and rendered powerless the Emperor's advisers'.[21] This liberal American view, rooted in admiration for the Japanese aesthetic and progress, regarded the 1930s expansionism as a 'mis-step' in its trajectory of modernization and liberalization. Like Japanese conservatives, the 'Japan crowd' conceded that the 1930s war was an ill-considered response to the United States and Chinese nationalists, but not necessarily that Japanese imperialism itself was bad.[22] Taken to its logical conclusion, this 'military clique mis-step' narrative would have entailed the massive reformation of feudal Japanese society. But the long and deeply interventionist American occupation that such reforms would require was rendered unfeasible by the exigencies of domestic politics and the onset of the Cold War.[23]

Nevertheless, the 'Pacific War' memory and the 'military mis-step' causal narrative resulted in limited liability for Japan. The war crimes trials conducted under the International Military Tribunals for the Far East (IMTFE) delivered only a partial settlement, because of the American decision not to prosecute Emperor Hirohito in spite of the fact that he was head of state throughout the war and was the ultimate authority for the Japanese campaign; and because of the exclusion from the indictments of Class B and C war crimes conducted against Asians.[24] There was little appetite within American official circles for prosecuting Emperor Hirohito because of the perception that trying him would create turmoil in Japan and likely lead to an even longer occupation. SCAP was convinced too that the Emperor's authority was crucial to post-war reform; for instance, the first critical step of enacting the new Japanese constitution would not have received the Japanese government's cooperation if the Emperor had been subpoenaed.

---

[20] 'Indictment from the International Military Tribunal for the Far East', n.d., World War II File, Bontecou Papers, Harry S. Truman Presidential Library, p. 1. Available at <http://www.trumanlibrary.org/whistlestop/study_collections/nuremberg/documents/index.php?documentdate=0000-00-00&documentid=18-2&pagenumber=1>. Accessed 30 September 2012.

[21] Memorandum of Conversation by the Acting Secretary of State 28 May 1945, in *Foreign Relations of the United States 1945*, 6: 545–7. The acting secretary was Joseph Grew, who had been Ambassador in Japan at the time of the Pearl Harbor attack.

[22] For a useful discussion about contending schools of thought on Japan among American occupation officials, see Schonberger 1989.

[23] For a brief analysis of contesting American views, see Ninkovich 2007.

[24] Significant controversy surrounds the 1946–8 Tokyo Trial particularly, at which twenty-eight Japanese war leaders were tried for Class A 'crimes against peace'—for critical views, see Minear 2001; Hosoya 1986; Dower 1999, 442–84; more balanced assessments are found in Boister and Cryer 2008; Totani 2008. Military tribunals were also convened throughout Asia to try Class B (conventional war crimes) and C (crimes against humanity) war criminals—see Piccigallo 1979.

In relation to war crimes against Asian victims, two Japanese were found guilty at the Tokyo Trial in connection with atrocities committed in Nanjing, but no charges were brought in any tribunals against those responsible for the enslavement of Chinese forced labourers and 'comfort women' from Korea, China, and other Asian countries.[25] Neither was any charge brought against experimentation on mainly Asian victims at Japanese chemical and biological warfare facilities, including the infamous Unit 731.[26] Indeed, major Asian countries were excluded from the formal peace settlement at San Francisco in 1951: China was left out because Britain and the United States could not agree on whether the People's Republic of China (PRC) or the Republic of China (ROC) would represent it, and Korea because of the ongoing war. Japan signed a Treaty of Peace with the ROC in 1952 by which the latter followed the SFPT convention of waiving reparation claims against Tokyo, but it was not until normalization of relations in 1972 that Japan and the PRC issued a joint statement affirming the same terms of peace. There is no treaty to acknowledge the end of Japanese colonial rule in Korea, although Japan signed a treaty of basic relations with the ROK during normalization in 1965, and agreed to work towards normalization with the DPRK in 2002. As Carol Gluck observes, 'by casting the war in domestic terms, whose causes lay at home and could therefore be addressed by postwar reforms for a "Japan reborn", the Occupation contributed to a nearly total amnesia of empire'.[27]

By implication, the *lessons and values* drawn within this collective memory regime were threefold. First, to overcome the missteps of its imperial and feudal past, Japan should continue to modernize; and as the Cold War set in, the imperative of modernization through capitalist industrialization and democratization strengthened. Second, Japan would demilitarize—depending upon the United States for external security needs, subjecting Japan's Self-Defence Forces to civilian control and limiting it to the defence of the main Japanese islands—to avoid the resurgence of a military cult and expansionism. By Article 9 of its post-war constitution, Japan denounced its sovereign right to make war or to use force to settle international disputes; and by the 1951 US–Japan Security Treaty, 1954 Mutual Security Assistance Pact, and 1960 Treaty of Mutual Security and Cooperation, Japan submitted to US military protection in return for providing basing facilities for US forces. Third and finally, Japan would be rehabilitated and would join international society on the

---

[25] On the collusion of US occupation forces in marginalizing Japan's war atrocities in China and Korea, see Conrad 2003.

[26] Some charge that a US cover-up was the major reason—see Harris 2002. But thus far there is no conclusive documentary evidence to support Harris's circumstantial claim that US officials offered immunity to Japanese officials and scientists in exchange for access to their experimentation results.

[27] Gluck 2007, 51.

terms of the SFPT, its new constitutional constraints—and as a 'free world' ally of the United States.[28] In the United States–Japan-focused Pacific War memory regime, the Japanese elite collaborated with the American occupation authorities to construct a 'foundation narrative' in which Japan's defeat was portrayed as a drama of its rescue by the United States from the militarist clique and conversion into a 'pacifist' and 'democratic' nation.[29] Japanese leaders forged a domestic consensus that privileged Japan's economic reconstruction and its reinvention as a global trading state that hinged on the cheap security ride provided by the US treaty. Brokered with difficulty by Prime Minister (1948–54) Yoshida Shigeru, who faced opposition from right-wing conservatives and industrial interests opposing such stringent constraints on Japanese rebuilding, the Yoshida doctrine nevertheless persisted during the Cold War with only minor adjustments.[30] Therefore Japan could once again return to its previous trajectory of distancing itself from Asia, now aided by the post-war settlement and strategic orientation towards the United States.

The resulting *ethical discourse* in this post-1945 collective memory regime might be described as 'withholding judgement about a historical misadventure'. This stems in part from Japan's dual identity as victimizer of Asian neighbours and victim of American atomic bombings: there is a sense that punishment was dealt in Japan's total defeat and massive destruction, and in its demilitarization thereafter. Critically, the partial nature of the peace settlement with Asia was masked because the Cold War put on hold China's, Korea's, and other Asian countries' willingness to excoriate or settle accounts with Japan. As the popular sociological dichotomy between 'honour' and 'dignity' cultures suggests, in Japan's culture of honour, much turns on the shame felt by the perpetrator when others perceive him to have transgressed.[31] Conversely, an honour-bound transgressor may be more likely to feel that he has 'gotten away with it' if others do not take him to task.[32] Thus, because Japan's neighbours did not consistently shame it before the 1980s, this facilitated a tendency to withhold judgement within the collective memory regime. It allowed many Japanese to 'blank out' the traumas of war and defeat, to disassociate from the 'militarists' of the war era, and to expect that the past ought to be laid to rest.[33]

The *history of this collective memory* is marked by a coincidence of sentiment and expediency between Japan's ruling conservatives and SCAP, reinforced

---

[28] See Samuels 2007, 39.
[29] Igarashi 2000. See also Dower 1999.
[30] Samuels 2007, 39–62; Edström 1999.
[31] This distinction was popularized in the United States in Benedict 1946.
[32] In a culture of guilt, the expectation is that he would feel guilty anyway.
[33] Kim 2008, 102.

The Struggle for Order

by the strategic complicity of China and Korea particularly. As discussed in the following section, domestic liberal dissent was present throughout the post-war period within Japan, but until China and Korea's public challenges in the 1980s, the Pacific War regime held. Indeed, this was not only official history, but also legal collective memory, since Japan was compelled by the SFPT to accept this representation of history embodied in the IMTFE verdicts and other terms of peace. He Yinan has written persuasively about the active complicity of the Japanese conservative elite in post-war 'myth-making', initially in pressing SCAP to focus on blaming the 'military clique' and not the Emperor, and then in downplaying Japan's victimization of Asia, and in honouring former imperial soldiers.[34] Her analysis suggests that acquiescing to the American Pacific War memory parameters allowed Japan to draw social and geographical blinds over its colonial and war culpability and liability.

Even more vital was the complicity of China's Asian neighbours in accepting the boundaries of this collective memory regime, which was amply illustrated by the issue of reparations. The Potsdam Declaration and the initial post-surrender plan for Japan included obligations for Japan to pay reparations in kind to the Allies, including China.[35] However, with the hardening of US strategy towards the Soviet Union after 1947, the Japanese reparations programme was cancelled at the drafting of the San Francisco treaty, when the reparations waiver agreement was forged at American insistence. Justice claims receded in urgency once Washington's priority turned to the strategic task of rebuilding Japan quickly as an ally in the anti-communist struggle, for which resources could not be spared for massive war indemnities. The ROC continued to insist on reparations up to the negotiations in February 1952 for a bilateral peace treaty with Japan,[36] whereupon it agreed to waive its claims because of Chiang Kai-shek's desire to secure US military support and to gain international recognition for the ROC. The PRC honoured this waiver in its 1972 normalization with Japan also for strategic reasons, to achieve international recognition and quasi-alignment with the US camp against the Soviet Union.[37] Before the 1980s, Beijing suppressed investigations of Japanese war crimes and Premier Zhou Enlai even explicitly reiterated the distinction between the 'militarists' and the majority of Japanese people in normalization talks with Prime Minister Tanaka Kakuei.[38] The mainland's reluctance to contest the memory regime stemmed from the even deeper domestic fracture

---

[34] He 2009, 123–33.

[35] As an ex-Japanese colony, Korea did not qualify for war reparations.

[36] The Treaty left open the possibility of bilateral negotiations for reparations. In the event, only four Asian countries received indemnities in separate bilateral agreements with Japan in the 1950s and 1960s (Burma, Indonesia, the Philippines, and Vietnam); others were offered economic and development assistance in return for waiving their claims.

[37] Ito 2003; Ogata 1988.

[38] Tian 1997, 103–4.

between the two Chinas. The Chinese communist government's official history of the 'war of resistance against Japan' too was partial and preoccupied with portraying the Chinese Communist Party (CCP) as nationalist liberators and the Chinese Nationalist Party (Kuomintang, or KMT) as reactionary collaborators. Separating out Japanese leaders from Japanese people for blame also conformed to class-based ideology. Ultimately, the mainland Chinese discourse about the war of resistance against Japan has been enveloped into the wider narrative about the origins of the CCP, and Beijing avoided close examination of Chinese victimization at Japanese hands to boost the CCP's post-civil war triumphant nationalist narrative.[39]

Koreans by and large feel fewer constraints in expressing their historical resentment towards Japan, with which they have endured an explicitly hierarchical relationship. While historically subordinated within Sinic order, Korean national memory particularly marks the trauma of Japanese invasions during the sixteenth century and Japan's 1910 annexation and subjugation. Further, Japan's aggression in the Pacific War directly contributed to the division of Korea. Unsurprisingly, the Korean discourse emphasizes how the Japanese memory regime 'erases' or 'forgets' Korea. The Pacific War collective memory regime similarly sidelines Korea in its exclusion as imperial territory from the peace treaties and issues of compensation. The longer history of Japanese colonialism in East Asia is also excluded from this regime. Yet both Koreas maintained a de facto complicity with the Pacific War memory regime in not challenging it at the official level during the Cold War. For South Korea, upon which the following analysis touches, significant economic and strategic exigencies also caused leaders to push through unpopular rapprochement policies with Japan, which entailed a more active subscription to the Pacific War memory regime. President Park Chung-hee's authoritarian regime normalized relations with Japan in spite of public opinion in 1965, motivated by the economic assistance that Tokyo could offer the South to industrialize in competition with the North, and to help legitimize the regime that had taken power through a coup. But in signing the Basic Treaty and accepting Japan's $800 million in grants and soft loans as compensation for its colonial rule, the Park government effectively followed other Asian states in waiving the country's further rights to compensation.[40] Both Park and President Roh Tae-Woo, who upgraded diplomatic relations

---

[39] He 2009, 133–40; Mitter and Moore 2011.

[40] But the disbursement of these funds was kept secret and when disclosed in 2005 revealed that Seoul had spent over $350 million of compensation money meant for individual victims on infrastructure projects—'Declassified documents could trigger avalanche of lawsuits', *Chosun Ilbo*, 17 January 2005. In 2002, Kim Jong-Il followed suit by agreeing to waive reparations claims and accepting instead various forms of economic aid and cooperation when the DPRK and Japan would eventually hold normalization talks.

with Japan in 1983, also acted upon the strategic imperative of gaining United States–Japan alliance support for South Korea's security.[41]

Contesting the Collective Memory Regime

Within a few years of the Cold War ending, resurgent nationalism threatened the implicit regional consensus embodied in the East Asian post-war collective memory regime. In Japan, conservative forces vocally challenged the perceived slide into 'self-flagellating' national memory making, with some right-wing groups going so far as to insist that 'a historical perspective [that] accommodate[s] the views of Asian neighbours would be tantamount to surrendering Japan's own, legitimate, history'.[42] Chinese leaders in turn began to play the 'history card': for instance, Premier Li Peng warned Tokyo against suspending bilateral grant aid after China's nuclear test in 1995, since 'Japanese militarist aggression inflicted such gigantic damage upon China as to dwarf the Japanese government credits so far extended.'[43] At the same time, South Korean activist groups galvanized embarrassing civil campaigns and lawsuits against the Japanese government for compensation for Asian war victims.

Despite their regional spread, these overt challenges were fundamentally driven by the dissolving tenuous domestic consensus underpinning Japan's acceptance of the post-1945 collective memory regime, and Japanese domestic contestation fuelled regional attention and indignation at the inadequacies of the existing collective memory regime in addressing justice claims. Political, ideological, and ethical divisions within Japan rendered the memory regime negotiated between the occupation authorities and the ruling conservative elite unstable. This unresolved Japanese domestic bargain on war responsibility played out in cycles of memory revisionism and counter-revisionism, tracking the relative political fortunes of conservatives versus progressives. This struggle mirrored the clear right–left divide in post-war Japanese politics since the 1955 merger of the conservative Japan Democratic Party and Liberal Party created the Liberal Democratic Party (LDP) which dominated the political establishment for over forty years, with the regrouped Japan Socialist Party (JSP) in opposition.[44] From the 1960s,

---

[41] For instance, Park turned to Prime Minister Fukuda to help dissuade President Carter from withdrawing US troops from South Korea in the 1970s—Rozman 2008, 181–2.

[42] *Akarui Nippon giin-renmei* [Parliamentary League for a Bright Japan] founding declaration, June 1996; Association for the Creation of a New Textbook, December 1996—both cited in Tamaki 2010, 122.

[43] Cited in Mochizuki 2003, 103.

[44] In line with the Cold War anti-communist agenda, Washington provided funding and political support for the LDP—Pempel 1998, 101.

Table 5.1. The collective memory regime and its challenges

	Post-1945 'Pacific War' collective memory regime	Challenges to the 'Pacific War' collective memory regime			
		Conservative Japanese textbooks	Campaign to renationalize Yasukuni shrine	China's patriotic education campaign	Korean comfort women
Historical script					
Dominant memory	Japan's defeat in the Pacific War	Great East Asia War; Japan's historical achievements (including imperialism)	Japanese war casualties/victims ('fallen heroes')	Japan's atrocities; China's war of resistance against Japan	Asian victims of Japanese aggression and colonialism (women)
Lessons and values	Rehabilitation through modernization, demilitarization, orientation towards the United States	Pride in country; recognition of ancestors; 'history is not a trial'	Mourning and commemoration of sacrifices and loyalty to nation	National unity and strong state to avoid humiliation; vigilance against resurgence of Japanese militarism	Restitution for atrocities: acknowledgement and apology, compensation, commemoration
Ethical/justice discourse	Withholding judgement about a historical misadventure	More 'balanced', 'objective' history—victors' justice imposing guilt on Japanese	Japan is entitled to national mourning and commemoration using appropriate cultural and religious rituals	Immoral whitewashing and denial	Violation of human rights, war crimes, search for justice
Master narratives					
Causes	Military clique misstep	Inevitable, 'world history' context of colonialism and war; liberation of Asia; atrocities because of war chaos	Legitimate national commemoration prevented by unjust 'victors' peace' and neighbours' bullying	Japanese militarist aggression	Military practice and crime, state culpability, societal complicity
History of the memory	Domestic and regional complicity: domestic politics & strategic imperatives	Pendulum struggle: pegged to conservative political fortunes, changing strategic context, neighbouring countries', and civil society pressure	Important role of right-wing groups within domestic politics; Japanese leaders willing to harness issue for political purposes	Regime security/domestic politics public → over-mobilization → official reining back and partial reversal	'Coming into memory': transnational activists, Japanese state's resistance to legal restitution, complicity of other states

The Struggle for Order

war memory increasingly became a site for domestic contestation as Japan's growing international status, participation in the Vietnam War, and establishment of diplomatic relations with South Korea and Communist China generated controversy about its national identity and war responsibility. Popular books about the Nanjing massacre and Korean 'comfort women' forced into sexual slavery for the Japanese army during the Second World War further stirred public consciousness.[45] By the end of the 1970s, Japanese politics of war memory were being played out within an 'immensely broadened discursive and activist landscape', and the negotiation of collective memory had become 'a public issue in its own right'.[46] When regional controversies broke out over Japanese history textbooks in 1982, therefore, they internationalized an already vibrant Japanese debate about war memories, responsibility, and nationalism.

The 1990s saw resurgent contestation over Japanese war memory because of internal and external changes. Emperor Hirohito's death in 1989 and the fiftieth anniversary of Japan's Second World War defeat in 1995 catalysed emotions in an increasingly socially diverse country. Crucially, the LDP lost nearly four decades' stranglehold on government at the 1993 elections, and was forced into cross-bench coalitions to retain power. This dissolution of the '1955 system' created opposing pressures, on the one hand to compromise across party lines, and on the other hand to dig more deeply into fundamental political positions in order to appeal to key political constituencies. The result was a 'more complex, defused and fragmented' foreign policy-making process in Tokyo.[47] China policy was particularly affected by the relative decline of 'China hands' in the Ministry of Foreign Affairs, negative public sentiment, and frustration with Japan's extended economic recession. By this time, Japan's ability to 'escape' the region was eroded by economic imperative as Japanese corporations expanded their interests within East Asia, and the need for strategic legitimacy as Japan's role in regional security increased with the revitalized US alliance. Japanese politicians were forced to tend to relations with neighbouring states, including addressing the history disputes.

However, the easing of Cold War strategic imperatives, the rise of the other East Asian economies, and liberalization of civil society also left Japan's neighbours more willing to challenge the boundaries of the existing collective memory regime. The lifting of martial law and democratization in South Korea, and resurgent patriotism with greater social autonomy in

---

[45] Most notable were Honda Katsuichi's 'Chūgoku no Tabi' [Travels in China] series of articles in *Asahi Shimbun* throughout the 1970s; Senda 1973; Kim 1976.
[46] Seraphim 2007, 18, 27.
[47] Murata 2006, 37.

China further created mutually reinforcing effects. The Japanese right fired up Chinese and Korean sentiment, adding to the latter's intransigence on Japan's need to 'face up to its past'; and Korean activists set an example vis-à-vis pressure on Japan which Chinese activists felt compelled to match or exceed. Together, these multiple struggles for justice generated a powerful undercurrent that impeded the negotiation of a new social compact among the Northeast Asian states, and placed limits on their strategic relationships. Divisions on war memory also became increasingly fraught as nationalist factions in Japan became more vocal and better organized in favour of revising war history; and more local and transnational rights-based groups became actively involved in issues such as war restitution.[48] As the following analysis reveals, the power of memory has been very much in evidence in post-Cold War East Asian politics, but power over memory remains contested and incoherent, as states struggle to sustain their previous privileged position in memory making against challenges from non-state groups and neighbours.

The Textbook Controversies: Disputing the Content and Lessons of History

Within Japan, domestic dissent over the post-war collective memory regime centred very early on history textbooks. Contestation over history textbooks is essentially struggles over the content and lessons of memory. Textbooks pronounce the contingent bargain first on the historiographical question of 'what really happened', and second on the socio-ethical issue of 'whether this ought to be included in educational material'. As 'weapons of mass instruction', they embody 'outcomes of negotiations between various social actors over what counts as legitimate knowledge'.[49] In Japan, the practice of the Ministry of Education (commonly known by its Japanese abbreviation Monbushō)[50] vetting textbooks creates a prime site for discursive and textual struggles over the inscription of collective memory.[51] Attributing the success of Japanese militarism partly to the educational system which had 'created a nation of passive citizens who blindly followed the policies of their government and military', the US post-war occupation authority issued new textbooks that delegitimized earlier Japanese cultural and political systems.[52] However, the tenuous Japanese acquiescence to the Pacific

---

[48] See Seraphim 2007.
[49] Ingrao 2009; Schneider 2008, 113.
[50] The Ministry of Education, Sport, Science, and Technology; *Monbu-kagaku-shō* in Japanese.
[51] In contrast to China and South Korea, where textbooks are written and published by the state, in Japan commercial publishers develop textbooks according to state-issued guidelines and submit drafts to the Ministry of Education for approval as school texts; the Ministry's screening process often entails required revisions to these drafts before approval, and schools may choose from a list of approved texts. See Nozaki and Inokuchi 2000.
[52] Nelson 2002, 130.

War memory regime was soon exposed when the responsibility for textbook screening passed to Monbushō after 1950 and nationalist conservatives in the Democratic and Liberal parties manoeuvred to replace liberals on textbook examining boards.[53]

The conservative and nationalist Japanese critique of the Pacific War memory regime centres on its narrow focus on the *dominant memory* of Japan's defeat in 1945: using the prime arena of history textbooks, these critics have worked to broaden the scope of national memory to encompass Japan's significant achievements in modernization, liberation, and development. At the heart of this struggle has been the search for a more 'balanced' and just memory regime to replace the one perceived to have been imposed via 'victors' justice' at the end of the Second World War. Particularly intense because it was an integral part of post-war national rehabilitation for Japan, this normative contest reflected an alternative philosophy of nationalist history education, which stressed the importance of cultivating in the younger generation national identity and pride, rather than teaching the lessons and shame of the past as though history were a trial. The textbook controversies span over four decades, in three 'textbook offensives' when conservatives tried to reform history texts for lower and middle schools. Each offensive generated domestic resistance from progressives, who would subsequently make some headway in returning history textbooks to more critical accounts of Japan's imperial past and war actions, but which would trigger backlash and greater agitation on the part of growing conservative lobby groups. The *history of this memory contest* followed a pendulum trajectory, pegged to conservative versus progressive political fortunes within Japan and exacerbated by the growing participation of non-state interest groups and China and South Korea. By the last decade of the Cold War, the simultaneous conservative attempts to erase Asian victims and play down Japanese culpability also managed to provoke resistance and contestation from China and South Korea in spite of their strategic imperatives. Yet each round resulted in efforts by successive Japanese governments to recognize and accommodate neighbours' sensitivities to some degree, beginning the process of negotiating a shared memory regime.

In the first 'textbook offensive' in the late 1950s and 1960s, conservatives on textbook screening boards set the tone by attacking the dominant mnemonic of the national memory regime: the 'Pacific War' was deemed 'not a historical term' and publishers were told to revert to the imperial Japanese term, the 'Great East Asian War', which broadened the account to include the successes of Japan's earlier campaign. They also challenged the memory regime's *causal narrative*, specifically pushing authors to adopt a 'world

---

[53] Indeed, the textbook campaign provided ideological glue for the LDP merger in 1955.

history perspective' suggesting that Japanese imperialism and invasion were not unusual in the context of widespread Western colonial practice at the time. On the basis that 'a view even exists that [Japan's war] presented the chance of independence for Asian nations' from the Western colonial powers, textbook authors were asked to excise details about the Nanjing massacre, Unit 731, comfort women, and the 'immeasurable suffering and damage' Japan inflicted on Asian nations.[54] During the second textbook 'offensive' in 1980–2, authors were asked to highlight the extenuating circumstances of 'war chaos' behind Japanese war atrocities, and to remove references to the responsibility of the military chain of command for the Nanjing massacre.[55] In exhorting textbook authors not to 'write bad things' about Japan in the war, these conservative textbook screeners helped to reinforce the 'blank' in the *ethical discourse*. Working from a nationalist pedagogy, they denigrated 'excessive fervour to encourage soul-searching' in providing *lessons* of the past, instead asserting that the purpose of teaching history was 'to recognise the efforts of ancestors, to heighten one's consciousness of being Japanese, to instil a rich love of the race'.[56] This trend was revived after the Cold War: the 1998 Monbushō guidelines for middle-school civics and history textbooks prioritized the need to 'deepen our love for the history of our country in order for its citizens to nurture self-consciousness as Japanese'.[57]

There has been a constant strain of domestic resistance to such conservative revisionism, encapsulated in a series of high-profile lawsuits from 1965 to 1997, by which one Japanese historian, Ienaga Saburō, led a campaign to challenge such nationalist history education based on ethical evasion.[58] By the mid-1970s, the screening criteria for history textbooks relaxed, influenced by the publicity surrounding Ienaga's partially successful court ruling, as well as a period of relative 'equality' in the Diet between the LDP and the JSP.[59] This was followed by a conservative backlash in the late 1970s and early 1980s when party disarray in the LDP caused right-wing politicians again to resurrect the Great East Asia War discourse, aided by a widening base of nationalist intellectuals and business interests.

---

[54] Cited in Nozaki 2008, 22.
[55] Ienaga 1993/4. Domestically, the most controversial element of the 1982 textbook screening process was the removal of references to Japanese military atrocities in Okinawa—see Allen 2002, 27–52.
[56] Ienaga 2001, 158.
[57] Cited in Nelson 2002, 130–1.
[58] In three lawsuits spanning three decades, Ienaga sued the state for unconstitutional censorship of his texts through the textbook authorization system that violated his freedom of expression. In 1974, a Tokyo District Court ruled that the textbook authorization system was a form of censorship. Ienaga succeeded in his third lawsuit, culminating in a 1997 Supreme Court ruling that upheld the constitutionality of the textbook authorization system, but identified the abuse of discretion by Mombushō and ordered that Ienaga be compensated. See Nozaki and Inokuchi 2000; Thakur 1995.
[59] See Ienaga 1993/4.

The 1981–2 textbook screening round constituted a watershed at which the textbook controversy became internationalized. Against the heated domestic political debate, the Japanese media reported that the required changes to history textbooks included the replacement of the word 'invasion' (*shinryaku*) with the more neutral 'advance' (*shinshutsu*) for the Japanese campaign against China. This sparked high-level diplomatic complaints and intense media and civil protests in China, South Korea, and Vietnam.[60] Against this regional resistance, the LDP government chose to stand down. It introduced a new 'neighbouring countries' clause in Monbushō's criteria for textbook approval, thus institutionalizing the requirement for 'necessary consideration, in the interest of international friendship and cooperation' to neighbours' sensitivities.[61] By this clause, the Japanese state formally acknowledged that the educational imperative of instilling national pride could not come at the expense of upsetting Japan's neighbours or denying their experiences.

The end of the Cold War and the easing of strategic imperatives intensified this contestation and accommodation as China and South Korea participated more vigorously in the regional memory struggle. August 1993 was the next turning point, both in Japan's domestic political history and in the contest over the national memory regime. That year, Korean ex-comfort women testified before a Japanese government inquiry, leading to the chief cabinet secretary's landmark admission that Japanese forces were involved in these 'comfort' facilities. His statement of 'firm determination' to remember this 'through historical research and education' entered the issue into the realm of legitimate memory, including through the medium of textbooks.[62] At the same time, the end of the LDP's single-party rule facilitated high-level revisions to the memory regime. The landmark LDP–JSP coalition in 1994 included a bargain to co-sponsor a Diet resolution apologizing to Asian victims on the fiftieth anniversary of Japan's surrender. This was accompanied by Prime Minister Murayama Tomiichi's 15 August 1995 cabinet statement, then the fullest apology ever issued for Japanese colonialism and aggression. Against significant Diet opposition, Murayama explicitly named Japan's 'colonial rule and aggression', called it 'mistaken national policy', acknowledged and apologized for the 'tremendous damage and suffering' especially to Asian peoples, and declared the main lesson that 'Japan must eliminate

---

[60] For a detailed discussion of the 1982 textbook controversy, see Rose 1998, chapters 4 and 5. Media reports about the 'invasion/advance' change turned out to be wrong, since the replacement had already been made in the 1960s and 1970s and no such request for revision had been made in the 1981–2 screening round.

[61] Nozaki 2008, 81; Ienaga 1993/4.

[62] Statement by the Chief Cabinet Secretary Yohei Kono on the result of the study on 'comfort women', 4 August 1993, available at <http://www.mofa.go.jp/policy/women/fund/state9308.html>. Accessed 20 August 2012. By 1994 references to comfort women could be found in all junior high school textbooks.

self-righteous nationalism [and] promote international coordination as a responsible member of the international community.'[63]

These official revisions fuelled a 'neo-nationalist crusade' from right-wing politicians and a strengthened coalition of activist interest groups, conservative media, and publishing houses.[64] Notable amongst the latter was the Japanese Society for History Textbook Reform (JSHTR, *Atarashii Rekishi Kyōkasho o Tsukuru kai*), established in 1996 with a two-front campaign. The first involved putting pressure on the government and textbook writers to shrink the boundaries of the national memory regime in terms of content and lessons. In the governmental realm, the campaign succeeded in marshalling Diet-level support from right-wingers in the LDP and other parties, who lobbied for removing references to Japanese war atrocities and dropping the 'neighbouring countries' clause from textbook screening criteria.[65] The local level saw well-organized public campaigns uniting different interest groups, such as the Council for Correcting Textbooks which was formed by members of the associations of war-bereaved families and Shinto shrines. By the late 1990s, with the LDP's return to dominance, a 'patriotic education campaign' was in full swing.[66]

In the 2000 screening round, Monbushō openly sought 'more balanced' textbooks that downplayed Japanese war atrocities: references to the Nanjing massacre were changed to 'incident', while mentions of Unit 731 were removed and those of comfort women almost wiped out.[67] JSHTR's second aim of introducing a new, conservative history textbook was achieved when its *New History Textbook* was approved in 2001 and again in 2005. This text provides the ultimate overview of the extreme right-wing justice claims for revising the memory regime. It asserts the dominant memory of the Great East Asia War, while suggesting that Japan cannot be blamed directly because the war was inevitable: the causal narrative is that it was a form of self-defence by Japan forced into aggression by other colonial powers and aimed at liberating Asian colonies. It argues that Japan's 'southward advance...served to spur on nascent independence movements in Asia', and describes Japanese colonial rule in Korea as legal and beneficial to the Korean people. The text

---

[63] Statement by Prime Minister Murayama on the occasion of the 50th anniversary of the war's end, 15 August 1995, available at <http://www.mofa.go.jp/announce/press/pm/murayama/9508.html>. Accessed 20 August 2012. Murayama failed to gain Diet approval for this statement, so it was presented as a personal statement. The Diet resolution preceding this statement was watered down and endorsed only by a minority because of conservative boycotts—see Mukae 1996. A petition campaign garnered over 5 million signatures and endorsement from 70% of LDP Diet members.

[64] Nozaki and Selden 2009.

[65] Hein and Selden 1998; Kitazawa 2001.

[66] Rose 2005, 60.

[67] Nozaki 2005 suggests that these changes arose partly from self-censorship by textbook writers within the increasingly nationalistic climate.

highlights the unjust 'victors' justice' that forced a disproportionate sense of guilt onto the Japanese people. Indeed, it begins by advising students, 'let's stop applying judgements of right and wrong to history as if in a court of law based on today's morality'.[68]

Although this text has not been widely adopted for school use and does not reflect the mainstream history syllabus in Japan, its approval does represent the contingency of the 'neighbouring countries' clause and the salience of the right-wing revisionist justice claims within the Japanese establishment. The JSHTR textbook has acted as the lightning rod for the regional memory conflict. The official approval of this textbook met with massive public protests and cancellation of various intergovernmental exchanges by China. Seoul's official response was stronger: it recalled the South Korean ambassador in Tokyo, cancelled joint naval exercises, withdrew support for Japan's campaign for a permanent seat on the UN Security Council, and banned imports of Japanese cultural products.[69] In response to official lists that Seoul and Beijing submitted with specific objections to the textbook's contents, the Koizumi government insisted that it could not control the content of textbooks, the neighbouring countries clause notwithstanding. As an indication of prevalent order concerns vis-à-vis the United States, in contrast, American concerns about the anti-American elements of the revisionist trend were met by JSHTR's voluntary removal of these elements from the 2005 version.[70] The textbook controversy will remain a significant element of the regional memory struggle for the foreseeable future, since the conservative demand for a more complete account of Japanese history in education cannot be met without also addressing more adequately the omissions and obfuscations in the memory regime about Japanese colonization and aggression in Asia. Yet the textbook saga also bears constructive potential in renegotiating a collective memory regime. As discussed below, this third textbook offensive also generated landmark attempts at official and non-official negotiations of joint history texts between Japan and South Korea, and Japan and China.

Yasukuni Shrine: Revisionism through Commemoration

The revisionist challenge within Japan is even more starkly manifested in the contest over reinstating the Yasukuni shrine as the national site for

---

[68] References to the approved version of the 2001 JSHTR textbook are from Nelson 2002. An English translation of the two key chapters of the 2005 textbook is available on the JSHTR website: <http://www.tsukurukai.com/05_rekisi_text/rekishi_English/English.pdf>. Accessed 6 March 2013.

[69] Su 2001; Chung 2011, 214–15.

[70] This move contributed to the divisions between traditional and pragmatic conservatives within the Society and the eventual break-up of the JSHTR—Takayama 2009, 583.

commemorating Japan's war dead. Between 2001 and 2006, as far-right LDP politicians repeatedly attacked progressive gains in the domestic memory struggle, Prime Minister Koizumi Jun'ichirō himself added fuel to the fire by his annual visits to the Yasukuni shrine, significantly escalating regional public mobilization against Japanese revisionism. More than that over textbooks, the Yasukuni struggle centres on the instrumental mobilization of memory for political purposes. It embodies the Japanese right-wing challenge to the legal post-war settlement as set out in the IMTFE and SFPT, and highlights the entrenched role of right-wing groups in the process of Japanese memory making, since they are a vital power base for the LDP establishment. Yet war commemoration in Japan remains circumscribed by the legal terms of its peace settlement, and by deep-seated domestic ambivalence about the justice demands of the far right.

Commemoration takes on a particular justificatory hue when applied to the war dead, since it tends to be accompanied by a narrative that allows survivors to relate these deaths to a greater cause and enduring purpose. In Japan's case, however, the total defeat of its imperial enterprise, international denunciation of its aggression and expansionism, and the criminalization of its purposes and some of its perpetrators called into question the validity of the cause for which over two million soldiers died between 1931 and 1945.[71] In defeat, Japanese society has been obliged to work out its own terms of redemption, of how to include and honour in the *dominant memory* Japanese servicemen and their sacrifices regardless of the outcome of the war. There is broad agreement on the *value* of remembering the sacrifices and loyalty of the fallen to the Japanese nation, even if national policy of the time turned out to be wrong.[72] *Ethically*, more moderate Japanese views claim the nation's right to its own practices of mourning, including the use of a Shinto shrine associated with its militarist past and containing indicted war criminals.[73] But in this unresolved debate, the right-wing answer takes the *justice* discourse further by challenging the very terms of peace imposed upon Japan at the end of the last war. The leading right-wing pressure groups in this issue are the powerful Japan Association of Bereaved Families (*Nihon izoku kai*, JABF) and the smaller Association of Shinto Shrines (*Jinja honcho*), Military Pension Federation (*Gunjin onkyu renmei*), and Association to Commemorate the Spirits of Fallen Heroes (*Eirei ni kotaeru*), all with close links to the LDP.[74] In their view, Japan enjoys sovereign entitlement to its

---

[71] The numbers enshrined in Yasukuni are 17,176 from the Manchurian invasion, 191,250 from the Sino-Japanese war, and 2,133,915 from the Pacific War. These constitute the vast majority of those enshrined, which totals 2.47 million—figures cited in Tanaka 2008, 121.
[72] Nelson 2003, 454.
[73] Takashima 2006.
[74] See Wakamiya 1999; Shibuichi 2005.

own means of national commemoration, and the heart of the problem lies in the 'victors' justice' of the peace settlement which outlawed official commemorative rituals associated with the cultural-political system that was arraigned for aggression. Rather than redemptive mourning, therefore, right-wing groups seek justice in the form of release from the defeat, dishonour, and judgements about Japan's war actions. In pushing for the reinstatement of national Shinto commemorative practices, they aim to resurrect national identity and pride, and to resist perceived bullying from neighbouring countries for apology and restitution.[75] These efforts have concentrated on reinstating the Yasukuni shrine as the national site for commemorating Japan's war dead.

The Yasukuni shrine 'resonates with talismanic symbolism'[76] because it was critical in the recreation of the Japanese nation state during the Meiji restoration. Established in the 1860s in the practice of the new Shinto state religion to enshrine the souls of men who died defending the new nation, Yasukuni played an increasingly important role as Meiji Japan accumulated war experience. Upon the outbreak of full-scale war in the 1930s, it epitomized the spiritual reward in store for soldiers who would prove their loyalty to emperor and nation.[77] In the post-war constitutional separation of religion, emperor, and state,[78] Yasukuni was redesignated as a private institution, but reverted to semi-national status after occupation when in 1956 the Ministry of Health and Welfare began procedures to enshrine Second World War war dead there. Conservative attempts to reclaim Yasukuni formally began with an LDP-tabled Diet bill in 1969 to return the shrine to state patronage. In an indication of the strong opposition from other Diet members, the bill was defeated five times in five years.[79] Thwarted right-wing groups then turned to putting pressure on politicians and leaders to pay official visits to the shrine to commemorate the end of the war, thus refuting by practice rather than legislation the constitutional ban on state-sponsored religion.

This campaign to centre official commemoration of Japan's war victims on Yasukuni challenges the justice claims and legal institutions of the post-war memory regime. The shrine's origins bind it to the glorification of war, and to honouring not only the war dead but also the ideology of militarism and

---

[75] Nelson 2003.

[76] Kingston 2007, 295.

[77] 'See you at Yasukuni' was the ritual farewell of Kamikaze pilots towards the end of the Pacific War, for instance.

[78] Article 20 states: 'Freedom of religion is guaranteed to all. No religious organization shall receive any privileges from the State, nor exercise any political authority. No person shall be compelled to take part in any religious acts, celebration, rite, or practice. The State and its organs shall refrain from religious education or any other religious activity.'

[79] On the close cooperation between LDP members and right-wing groups in promoting the rehabilitation of ties between Shinto and the state, see Nelson 2003, 461–3.

emperor worship that sent them to war. More recently, its strong association with revisionist narratives is encapsulated in the shrine museum, which echoes the conservative script of the Great East Asia War while casting Japan as the primary victim of atomic bombings and an unjust peace settlement. The museum's displays include clear repudiations of the IMTFE and SFPT.[80] As such, contemporary Yasukuni is associated with the nationalist right wing, which wants to 'reclaim Japanese history from the verdicts imposed upon Japan following its defeat in 1945' and idealizes the pre-existing imperial and spiritual Japanese nation.[81]

This campaign also challenges the legal foundations of the peace settlement because convicted war criminals lie among those venerated at Yasukuni. After 1959, a change in Japanese law allowing Class B and C war criminals and their families to receive war pensions meant that they were also included for enshrinement. In October 1978, fourteen Class A criminals were enshrined by an ultra-nationalist chief priest, who reportedly stated that 'overturning the verdicts of the Tokyo Tribunal is essential to achiev[ing] Japan's spiritual renaissance'.[82] The depth of discomfort with this development within Japan is indicated by periodic—thus far unsuccessful—proposals within the government to de-shrine war criminals. More significantly, an imperial palace memorandum made public in July 2006 linked the cessation of Emperor Hirohito's visits to the shrine to the interring of Class A criminals.[83]

Article 20 of the constitution bans state organs and officials from undertaking religious activities, including paying tribute at a religious institution such as the Yasukuni shrine. By its strictest definition, this principle has been violated by successive Japanese prime ministers since 1951.[84] Indeed, the cause of nationalizing Yasukuni has been taken up at the highest political level, with various prime ministers seeking to brandish their nationalist credentials. The first overt revisionist challenge over Yasukuni was mounted by Prime Minister Nakasone Yasuhiro, who conducted an explicitly official visit as prime minister on the anniversary of Japan's defeat in 1985. While he responded to pressure from right-wing groups like JABF,[85] Nakasone had come to power with an avowedly revisionist agenda, pledging a 'complete resettlement of post-war politics'.[86] He publicly criticized the Tokyo Trials

---

[80] The museum underwent some revisions in 2002 and 2007, but the twentieth-century narrative underwent few changes except for the eradication of references critical of the United States, akin to JSHTR's textbook amendments discussed earlier—see O'Dwyer 2010, 151–4.

[81] Deans 2007, 283. For an analysis and refutation of these revisionist claims, see Goto 2003.

[82] Cited by Tanaka 2008, 123.

[83] 'Hirohito visits to Yasukuni stopped over war criminals', *Japan Times*, 21 July 2006.

[84] Until 1985, these visits were undertaken privately rather than officially, and tended to avoid the anniversary of the end of the war on 15 August 1975.

[85] Nakasone 2001.

[86] Tanaka 2008, 124.

version of history and the 'self-torturing belief that our country was to blame for everything', and tried to end the 1 per cent GNP cap on defence spending.[87] China launched unprecedented diplomatic protests against the visit, incensed by the perception that Nakasone was not only sanctifying the memory of imperial expansion but also officially denying the culpability of war criminals. Demonstrating the mutually reinforcing effects of the expanded public sphere of memory contestation, Chinese protests helped to publicize within Japan the enshrinement of war criminals that had changed the nature of Yasukuni's symbolism.[88]

In the face of Chinese condemnation, Nakasone ceased to visit Yasukuni while in power.[89] Yet his politicization of the issue created nationalist backlashes both in Japan and in China. By backing down, Nakasone implicitly accepted China's interpretation of these prime ministerial visits to Yasukuni as glorifying Japanese aggression and rejecting the verdicts of the Tokyo tribunals. He also exacerbated Japanese nationalist irritation and reinforced right-wing groups' determination to revise Japan's memory regime.[90] After 1985, Chinese leaders began to portray Yasukuni as a litmus test of Japanese leaders' attitudes towards history and relations with China. By the time Koizumi reignited the issue in 2001, Beijing had adopted a stance by which it 'makes no distinction between official or private visits, pays little attention to whether the prime minister makes one bow or two, or how he signs his name in the visitor's book, and makes no reference to the constitutionality of such acts... a prime ministerial visit [simply] represents an attempt to justify the war and glorify war criminals'.[91]

For Koizumi, an extraordinarily successful politician who managed to stay in power for five years juggling very divisive domestic and foreign policies, Yasukuni was a more calculated political exercise targeted at the small but important right-wing nationalist core constituency for the LDP. The significant funding and vote mobilization capabilities of this support base were critical for Koizumi because his ambitious domestic reform agenda alienated significant portions of conservatives and liberals alike. While his foreign policy stance of strengthening the security relationship with the United States and expanding the Self-Defence Forces' role overseas bought support from pro-US conservatives, his intransigence on Yasukuni appealed to the nationalist conservatives who prefer greater security autonomy for Japan.[92] He was

---

[87] Wakamiya 1999, 171–2.
[88] Kushner 2007.
[89] Nakasone 2001.
[90] Tanaka 2008, 128–30.
[91] Rose 2005, 116.
[92] The argument that Koizumi needed such theatrical nationalistic performances in order to make Japan's continuing and growing strategic subordination to the United States more acceptable is made in McCormack 2007b.

careful to qualify his performance, explaining that his visits were for mourning the war dead rather than glorifying war criminals, and he only visited on 15 August once.[93] But the visits fulfilled the political purpose of reinforcing Koizumi's image as the maverick reformer, and showing that Japan could not be pushed around by its neighbours.

Essentially, Koizumi tried to redraw the parameters of the regional contest over collective memory by resisting China's blanket opposition to Japanese leaders' public mourning of the war dead at Yasukuni. But he was met with full-scale resistance from China, including Beijing's boycott of summits with Koizumi during his time in office, leading to a stalemate in bilateral relations that one scholar likened to the Berlin Crisis.[94] South Korea also opposed the visits, including suspending the first China–ROK–Japan trilateral summit meeting in 2005.[95] Domestically, Koizumi faced increasing opposition, including from the ten-million circulation conservative newspaper *Yomiuri Shimbun*; by 2006, even the head of the War Bereaved Families Association had asked Koizumi to stop his visits and suggested that Class A war criminals be reinterred somewhere else.[96] Subsequent prime ministers, even those associated with right-wing politics, such as Aso Taro and Noda Yoshihiko, have avoided visiting either the shrine or the issue.

Unlike the textbooks or comfort women issues, the Yasukuni controversy has involved contestation with little prospect of renegotiating the boundaries of the collective memory regime. The intense politicization of shrine visits has been ultimately polarizing: it is no longer possible to distinguish between national mourning of the war dead on the one hand and state intervention in religion, glorification of an aggressive past, and rejection of Japan's peace settlement on the other. If the concern is chiefly about state commemoration, an alternative national site does exist in the form of the Chidorigafuchi cemetery for unknown soldiers, a secular war monument that contains the remains of 350,000 war dead, and where the official state remembrance ceremony is held on 15 August each year with the Emperor and government leaders in attendance. Yet the instrumental harnessing of Yasukuni's political symbolism has entrenched the revisionist nationalist fixation on Yasukuni as the only legitimate national shrine, and transformed the debate into a more expansive conflict over the terms of Japan's post-war peace.[97]

---

[93] The government was forced to stipulate this stance formally—see Japan MOFA 2005.
[94] Shi 2010.
[95] Shibuichi 2005, 210–12.
[96] Kingston 2007, 305, 310.
[97] For a flavour of the partisan debates, see Breen 2008.

China's Challenge: Patriotic Education and the War of Resistance

Politically, regional contestation of the collective memory regime is marked by the growing convergence of nationalist conservative challenges within the unstable Japanese domestic memory regime, and changes in patriotic education, civic participation, and technologies of public mobilization in neighbouring states, especially China and South Korea. Normatively, the nationalist Japanese search for greater justice in more balanced accounts of history and legitimate national commemoration are pitted against external challengers claiming justice for Asian war victims who have been neglected in the dominant memory.

China's memory challenge fundamentally stems from the central government's imperative of reifying the state and Party in the face of socio-structural changes, and initially arose because of Beijing's shifting priority in regimenting national war memories. As noted above, after 1949, Beijing had been relatively restrained towards Japan and complicit with the 'military clique' causal narrative for the Pacific War, facilitating 'an illusion of Sino-Japanese friendship in the 1970s without first settling the historical account'.[98] In promoting their economic reform agenda in the 1980s, though, reformist CCP leaders tried to harness Chinese patriotism to their cause by rallying around the unresolved partial war settlement with Japan. Sparked by conservative textbook revisionism in Japan, China's subsequent patriotic education campaign vilified Japanese atrocities and fuelled resistance against the historical script and master narratives of the war.

Honouring the KMT's role in the war of resistance against Japan had been problematic after the communist victory, but in the 1980s, the context for Communist China's politics of memory changed in two important ways. The pressure to align with the West was greatly reduced after normalization with the Soviet Union in 1982; and in conjunction with Deng Xiaoping's reassessment of China's Maoist history, officially sanctioned Chinese historiography began to rehabilitate the nationalists. In publications and films, the KMT's war role was portrayed in a more positive light compared to previous versions in which it was blamed for the fall of Nanjing and for collaborating with the Japanese army.[99] This coincided with growing history scholarship outside China recognizing KMT agency in the war.[100] Just as the recognition of the KMT's role intensified a narrative of the Chinese people's resistance, it drove attention towards the causes of this suffering: Japan's war aggression and atrocities.[101] Thus, throughout the 1980s, new history museums,

---

[98] Reilly 2011a, 469.
[99] Barmé 1993.
[100] See, for instance, Yang 2007; Wakeman and Edmonds 2000.
[101] Waldron 1996.

textbooks, state-backed television dramas, and commemorative events were created to mark key episodes of the war of resistance against Japan.

Within this shifting mnemonic context, Deng and other Party reformists intensified their instrumental politicization of war memory to manage the pressures from conservative factions opposed to the ambitious economic reforms and domestic unrest resulting from the economic redistributions and adjustments necessitated by them. Thus, in response to the textbook controversy and other bilateral frictions with Japan, Deng likely chose to make concessions to the conservatives by adopting a relatively hard line.[102] After the Tiananmen killings in June 1989, the CCP launched a concerted patriotic education campaign to bolster the Party's legitimacy and public support of its developmentalist agenda. This effort entailed reifying the aspects of national memory that emphasized the suffering of the Chinese nation and the Party's role in its liberation. The war of resistance provided an obvious hook on which to hang this narrative, sharpened by details of Japanese culpability and war atrocities.[103] In the CCP's 1990s patriotic education campaign, the *dominant memory* now centred on the Japanese 'imperialist invasion and the Chinese people's heroic resistance'.[104] One key *lesson* then was that 'China must increase its national strength to avoid the backwardness which leads to bullying and humiliation.'[105] Party propaganda, textbooks, and museums on Japanese atrocities also undermined the distinction in the prior *causal narrative* between a few Japanese militarists and the Japanese people—fuelling a second lesson, that China must be vigilant against a tendency towards militarism and aggression in the Japanese people as a whole. Against this background, the Chinese public's sensitivity and vigilance—and at times vigilante behaviour—intensified against perceived Japanese whitewashing, denial, and failure to make restitution for war deeds.

Thus a nationalist trend developed concurrently within China after 1989, when patriotism gradually became the 'consensual national ideology', facilitating a diverse political agenda including the incitement of mass movements against imperialism. Chinese public intellectuals pushing this envelope[106] gradually edged out moderate views, and as mobilized public opinion began to play a greater role in memory politics, the central government in Beijing increasingly had to balance between regime legitimation through marshalling patriotism, and taming the excesses of mass patriotic fervour targeted

---

[102] He 2007, 51–6.
[103] See for instance, Mitter 2000; Wang 2008.
[104] This was the exhortation of the State Education Commission to school teachers in 1994—quoted in He 2007, 57.
[105] Rendered upon a plague at the 18 September History Museum in Shenyang, China—cited in Reilly 2011a, 471.
[106] The most prominent examples of anti-Japanese literature were Song 1996; Xiao 1998.

at Japan. By the 2000s, when Japanese nationalist revisionism seemed to reach new heights over conservative textbooks and the Yasukuni shrine, the problems associated with whipping up Chinese nationalist sentiment against Japan became clear. The 2000s witnessed a surge of history activism, facilitated by a marked shift towards Internet-based mobilization. Large-scale and at times violent anti-Japanese protests occurred repeatedly in many major Chinese cities in response to the JSHTR textbook, Koizumi's shrine visits, and escalations in the territorial dispute over the Senkaku/Diaoyutai islands. Geopolitical factors—Japan's campaign for UN Security Council permanent representation, and the LDP's overt push for constitutional revision that would remove Article 9 restrictions on Japan's ability to employ military force—reinforced the strategic impacts of the history problem. Indeed, the *lessons* of the patriotic education campaign's emphases of the Sino-Japanese war create in many Chinese minds only a very small step between conservative revisionism within Japan and regional insecurity. As one Chinese scholar pointed out, 'Japan's failure to provide a balanced portrayal of its role in [the Second World War] to its younger generations...is a dangerous signal that the right-wing groups are gaining power, which will lead to a remilitarization of Japan and eventually jeopardise regional peace.'[107]

From 2005, the central government attempted to modify its patriotic education discourse by playing down Japanese atrocities, but the effects of patriotic education and new media proved resilient.[108] The depth of sentiment is indicated by the vitriolic public denunciations of those arguing for differentiating between Japan's past imperialist behaviour and present identity. In 2002–3 a political commentator and a prominent realist scholar suggested that Beijing should move beyond the history issue and seek common strategic interests with Japan,[109] but they were roundly denounced as 'traitors' by patriotic netizens on thousands of Chinese websites.[110] The central government's intolerance of public criticism was demonstrated in 2006, when another scholar wrote critically about China's own distorted history textbooks that promoted a narrative of victimhood and fuelled xenophobia against Japan. The journal in which the article appeared was temporarily closed down and its editorial team sacked.[111]

While the substance of China's justice claims vis-à-vis the acknowledgement of Japan's war atrocities is relatively less contentious, China's challenge to the collective memory regime is not essentially about these atrocities. Rather, the patriotic war of resistance script and its lessons about vigilance

---

[107] Jin 2006, 38.
[108] See the analysis in Reilly 2011b.
[109] Ma 2002; Shi 2003.
[110] Gries 2005.
[111] Yuan 2006; 'Leading publication shut down in China', *Washington Post*, 25 January 2006.

against Japanese militarism serve domestic political purposes and thus pose two significant obstacles to renegotiating a new collective memory regime. First, Beijing's fuelling of nationalism against Japan creates an ontological security dilemma, since the narrative of Chinese victimization necessarily requires the vilification of a perpetrator, Japan.[112] Second, the Chinese state's struggle to retain power over national memory and policy vis-à-vis Japan is increasingly compromised in the wider public realm with its potent mixture of technology-hyped transnational Chinese history activists, and an increasingly commercialized media eager to produce and sell patriotic anti-Japanese products to a receptive market.[113]

Korean 'Comfort Women': Victimization and Restitution

The most substantive regional challenge to the Pacific War collective memory regime has come from the international campaign for recognition and restitution for ex-comfort women. The euphemistic term refers to young women forced to offer sexual services to the Japanese Imperial Army in the theatres of conflict across Asia and the Pacific. Estimates range from 40,000 to over 400,000 women, though 200,000 appears to be the commonly accepted figure amongst activists.[114] The majority were recruited from Japan and the Japanese empire (Korea and Taiwan), while others (of Chinese, Filipina, Indonesian, and Dutch origin) were forcibly abducted or appropriated in occupied areas.[115] Aided by a vocal coalition of human rights, feminist, legal, and other activists spanning Asia and the United States, the survivors who came forward posed an explicitly moral and legal challenge to the Japanese state as well as other governments, establishments, and judiciaries complicit in upholding the Pacific War memory regime.

The justice claims of the comfort women were particularly compelling because they targeted multiple exclusions of the Pacific War collective memory regime. First, this challenge came not only from individuals but specifically from disgraced women who were amongst the most lowly ranked in the hierarchy of war victims. In seeking a rightful place for these women as

---

[112] As Suzuki (2008, 1) suggests, to overcome its own history of aggression in the region, China's identity construction entails partly creating 'a "moral" national identity by positing the PRC as an unjust "victim"' of Japan, the 'bullying Other'.

[113] Reilly 2011a.

[114] The 200,000 figure comes from Yoshimi 1995, the first to work from Japanese documentary sources. The 400,000 figure comes from Chinese scholar Su 2000, who accepted that most of these women were Korean and added his estimate of 200,000 Chinese women on top of that figure.

[115] In the only instance of legal redress, some cases of Dutch women prisoners of war forced to be comfort women in the Japanese-occupied Dutch East Indies (present-day Indonesia) were tried in a B/C-level war crimes tribunal in Batavia in 1948, at which twelve Japanese military officials were convicted and one sentenced to death.

war victims, campaigners tried to overcome simultaneously the barriers of race, gender, and empire which had rendered the issue 'morally invisible' before.[116] Second, the Korean comfort women's cause was especially resonant because it is yoked to Japan's colonial subjugation and imperial past, which were excluded from the Pacific War memory regime and for which Japanese nationalists are unapologetic. By assiduously keeping the issue on the international and national agendas in Japan and South Korea, the campaign lent significant weight and ignominious detail to the revision of the *dominant memory* of the war to include Japan's chequered history in Asia. This need for recognition within the dominant memory was perhaps most vividly captured in the December 2000 Women's International War Crimes Tribunal on Japan's Military Sexual Slavery organized by various non-governmental activist groups, at which sixty former comfort women testified to an unofficial court.[117] Held in Tokyo, the event was a poignant counterpoint to the IMTFE tribunals.

The *history* of the comfort women's 'coming into memory'[118] was marked by one old Korean woman, Kim Hak-sun, who publicly recounted her personal experience in August 1991. In addition to leading other ex-comfort women in filing a lawsuit for compensation from the Japanese government, Kim also galvanized researchers and activists, and wrested formal acknowledgement and apologies from Tokyo. When Japanese scholar Yoshimi Yoshiaki presented Japanese archival evidence of the military's involvement in setting up 'comfort stations' during the war in 1992, official apologies to Korea followed from the government and Prime Minister Miyazawa Kiichi. The Japanese government subsequently conducted its own inquiry, including hearing the testimonies of sixteen ex-comfort women in Seoul. Chief Cabinet Secretary Kōnō's 1993 definitive statement came in response, acknowledging that the Japanese military was 'directly or indirectly involved' in establishing the comfort women system, that 'in many cases [comfort women] were recruited against their own will', and 'they lived in misery at comfort stations under a coercive atmosphere'. He extended the government of Japan's 'sincere apologies and remorse', and noted its responsibility to consider how best to 'express this sentiment'.[119] This swift response came in part because of the irrefutable evidence, but also because of a window of opportunity provided by the dissolution of the LDP grip

---

[116] Gluck 2007, 67.
[117] See Dudden 2001; Chinkin 2001.
[118] Gluck 2007, 65.
[119] 'Statement by Chief Cabinet Secretary Yohei Kōnō on the Result of the Study on the Issue of "Comfort Women"', 4 August 1993, available at <http://www.awf.or.jp/e6/statement-02.html>. Accessed 20 August 2012. As noted above, acknowledging this history in textbooks was specifically mentioned and carried out.

on power within Japan, allowing progressive parties to share power after 1993. And yet there remained broad cross-party consensus about the limits to culpability to which the Japanese state could admit, as revealed in the subsequent struggle for restitution.

The coincidence of easing strategic imperatives and democratization in South Korea facilitated media coverage and activism of groups such as the Korean Council for the Women Drafted for Sexual Slavery by Japan.[120] The comfort women campaign launched a stinging *ethical* assault centred on the Japanese military's gross violations of human rights, war crimes against these sex slaves, and the aged survivors' urgent search for justice. This transnational campaign built on significant developments in international law that began to recognize the rights of individuals—a process in which the post-Second World War war crimes tribunals, including the Tokyo Trials, were crucial. Critical to the comfort women campaign were two UN reports on the issue in 1996 and 1998 which unequivocally labelled the practice 'military sexual slavery' and argued that it constituted a crime against humanity.[121] The 1998 report charged that the Japanese Imperial Army maintained 'rape centres'.[122] These legal arguments are controversial, but they gained salience during the 1990s with the rise of feminist causes worldwide and international media coverage of the systematic abuse of women in ongoing conflicts in Rwanda and the former Yugoslavia. Further, when the state of California enacted a law in 1999 extending the period within which Second World War-related claims could be made to 2010—as opposed to twenty years after the event in Japan—a number of former comfort women brought their cases to US courts.[123]

The ethical content of war atrocity claims tends to be straightforward; it is the credibility of the claims that requires political and memory work. The case for the comfort women met with resistance based on evidence, contextual practice, and the legal fences built around state culpability as a result of Japan's post-war treaties. There is no substantial documentary record of the numbers or origins of the women involved, and the estimated numbers are derived using a chilling matrix involving the servicing rate and the replacement rate of these women.[124] Also disputed is the extent to which women were coerced into providing sexual services. Critics in Japan, ranging from

---

[120] See <http://en.womenandwar.net/contents/home/home.asp>. Two other prominent groups are the Global Alliance for Preserving the History of World War II in Asia (an international federation of more than forty organizations) and the Center for Research and Documentation on Japan's War Responsibility.

[121] Coomaraswamy 1996; McDougall 1998. They cited, amongst other legal grounds, the 1949 Geneva Conventions and Nuremberg and Tokyo tribunals' definitions of crimes against humanity.

[122] McDougall 1998, 84.

[123] Rose 2005, 80–1.

[124] See information from the Asian Women's Fund, available at <http://www.awf.or.jp/e1/facts-07.html>. Accessed 20 August 2012.

The Struggle for Order

historians to conservative politicians, point to the lack of documentary evidence that these women were taken by force, rather than their being professional prostitutes.[125] In line with other militaries' practices, the Japanese military established brothels during the war. As distinct from rape and abduction in occupied territories—which activities critics maintain were limited in number—recruitment for these comfort stations took place mainly within Korea and Taiwan using pre-existing prostitution brokers and networks. The ethical issues here then are wider socio-economic ones to do with deprivation and deception in recruitment, rather than war crimes. These considerations of coercion and context impact upon the *causal narrative* for this Japanese war atrocity in highlighting the wider societal complicity in patriarchal Asian societies that not only condoned such sexual exploitation of women but also kept these victims shamed and silent for decades, posing innumerable obstacles in turning these women's shame into men's crimes.[126]

The Japanese military's culpability has been accepted by the Japanese government—the Miyazawa apology and the Kōno statement did not split hairs over how these comfort women were recruited. But the crucial part of the comfort women's search for justice is the moral *value* placed on restitution for these grievous wrongs that were previously unaccounted for. In the various campaigns, lawsuits, and at the 2000 Women's Tribunal, these women demanded from the Japanese government formal acknowledgement and apology, compensation, and commemoration. Legal redress in particular is a key means of controlling memory content; lawsuits, for instance, are both 'a form of witness to the past and a means of preventing its recurrence'.[127] The government apologies and history textbook coverage ensured that the comfort women entered the national discourse on war memory. In substance, though, successive Japanese governments have taken pains to distinguish between Japan's moral responsibility and the Japanese state's legal liability. Harking to the Pacific War memory regime's fences, they have maintained that the SFPT and Japan's various bilateral agreements with Asian countries preclude further individual claims against Japan for its war actions. This stance has been supported by the Japanese judicial system, which has rejected all the ten lawsuits filed by comfort women in Japanese courts.[128] The Japanese government has also drawn a cautious line on compensating surviving victims.[129]

---

[125] See Togo 2008; Nozaki 2003.
[126] Ueno 1999, 137; Chong 2004; Soh 2008.
[127] Hein 2003, 130.
[128] Based on the last point alone, the landmark Supreme Court ruling on 27 April 2007 against a suit brought by former forced labourers and comfort women set a precedent that would quash other cases in the system—'Japan court rules against sex slaves and labourers', *New York Times*, 28 April 2007.
[129] See Yamazaki 2006, 57–70.

When the LDP lost power in 1993, new JSP Prime Minister Murayama's coalition government was unable to overturn the Japanese establishment's opposition to fulfil his party's promise to compensate the comfort women. In 1995 Murayama settled for creating the semi-official Asian Women's Fund (AWF) to disburse 'atonement money', apology letters, and welfare programmes to former surviving comfort women.[130] By the time the AWF ceased its activities in 2007, it had paid compensation and support to 285 women, only a handful of whom were South Korean.[131] The Korean Council opposed the non-governmental nature of the AWF, and the South Korean government disbursed its own compensation funds to survivors.[132]

Yet the comfort women challenge to the collective memory regime reveals a wider pattern of reticence and resistance from political leaders and communities across the region. For instance, despite the intensity of the campaign, successive South Korean governments have refrained from fanning the flames of this issue. Even President Kim Dae-jung, a declared human rights champion, declined to table the comfort women issue at the UN. The Korean Council's campaign to erect a comfort women memorial in the national independence memorial site was vigorously opposed by interest groups offended by the potential elevation of these women alongside other war heroes.[133] In Taiwan, the initial government campaign to offer state compensation to former comfort women has flagged partly because of the need to maintain the support of the pro-Taiwan lobby in Japan—largely made up of conservatives.[134] The Chinese government's reticence is equally notable— in spite of documentary evidence that the largest concentration of Japanese military comfort stations was in mainland China, and despite Chinese scholars' claims that up to 200,000 Chinese comfort women existed,[135] Beijing has not intervened directly in the issue in the way other governments have. This lack of state-level pressure helps to explain why Chinese comfort women have not received any apologies from Japanese leaders and were not included in the AWF's work.[136] The United States proved to be an important arena for the active campaign for redress for the comfort women when a lawsuit was

---

[130] The compensation money distributed by the AWF was raised privately, while the Fund's operational costs and funding for medical welfare support were borne by the Japanese government.
[131] See the AWF's closing report at <http://www.awf.or.jp/e3/dissolution.html>. Accessed 20 August 2012.
[132] The 1998 round of these Korean compensation payments was made on the condition that recipients did not sign up for AWF disbursements. For details about regional responses, see Soh 2003.
[133] Soh 2008, 230–1. The Korean Council set up a museum for war and women's human rights in a different district in Seoul and erected a memorial statue in front of the Japanese embassy in Seoul in December 2011.
[134] Suzuki 2011.
[135] Chen and Su 2000.
[136] Rose 2005, 90; author interview with Chinese scholar working on history conflicts between China and Japan, Beijing, November 2011.

filed in a US court in 2000, and when Californian congressman Mike Honda successfully ushered through a House resolution in July 2007 asking that Japan 'formally acknowledge, apologize, and accept historical responsibility in a clear and unequivocal manner' for the comfort women system. But the George W. Bush administration set an important precedent by issuing a statement of interest in May 2001, arguing that these lawsuits would affect negatively United States–Japan treaty relations.[137] The District of Columbia court and appeal judges subsequently dismissed the case on the grounds that it was a 'nonjusticiable political question' and 'inimical to the foreign policy interests of the United States'.[138]

The ex-comfort women arguably have the strongest justice claims vis-à-vis revising the East Asian collective memory regime, and their activism over two decades has pushed the boundaries of the moral debate about Japan's past interactions with its neighbours. The history of their campaign, however, also exposes the limitations of this justice imperative pushed by individuals and activists in the face of regional states' order concerns. Beyond the political recognition of their existence and the 1993 apologies, political complicity and enduring social hierarchies constrain the prospect of formal restitution for these women.

Renegotiating Collective Memory and Regional Order

The hegemonic nature of the Pacific War collective memory regime was short-lived because its centre could not hold. Within Japan itself, the memory regime was increasingly challenged by entrenched right-wing nationalists aiming to revise its causal narrative and ethical content. Regional complicity might have held for longer because of continuing economic and strategic exigencies, if moral and nationalist sentiment had not been stoked by Japanese right-wing revisionism. Regional challenges have in turn focused on the exclusions of Japan's moral responsibility to remember 'correctly' and atone for its war actions in Asia. State and non-state actors' challenges to the partial collective memory regime and the internationalization of struggles over lessons, commemoration, and restitution have created a public sphere of memory contestation in East Asia. Conceptually, this is a shared discursive and policy space in which memory disputes are conducted, renegotiations of memory can take place, and a new collective memory regime might be created out of separate, parallel national scripts.

---

[137] See 'Summary of *Hwang Geum-Joo et al v Japan*', available at <http://www.gwu.edu/~memory/data/judicial/comfortwomen_us/comfort_women_us.html>. Accessed 20 August 2012.

[138] Dudden 2008, 92. Similar rulings were passed for related Asian forced labour cases.

Order and Justice: Contesting the Collective Memory Regime

An optimistic view suggests that the search for such convergence, while contentious, is essentially dialogical and can help to clarify mutual intentions and create focal points for 'normal diplomatic negotiations' between the states concerned. Indeed, the Japanese government's record of responding to regional protest and new evidence about contentious history issues suggests that such dialogical contestation can help to foster moderation and accommodation.[139]

In practice, within East Asia, a range of joint history projects among Japan, South Korea, and China indicate early attempts at the scholarly and elite levels to construct such bases for a new collective memory regime out of these disparate discursive struggles. To date, the most advanced result emerged from a non-governmental project of trilateral history writing involving fifty Chinese, Japanese, and Korean historians, teachers, and activists, which took three years to craft a joint history reader, *The Modern and Contemporary History of Three East Asian Countries*, published in May 2005.[140] Undertaken in direct response to JSHTR's 2001 textbook campaign, this unofficial and supplementary textbook presents a liberal, reflective version of shared history bridging major gaps in each country's dominant narratives of the war.[141] For instance, it overcomes Japanese disagreement with the Chinese insistence that the Nanjing massacre's death toll was 300,000 in the following way:

> According to the investigation of the Nanjing War Crimes Tribunal in 1946, some 190,000 people were executed on a massive scale at various execution sites and their bodies were disposed of by the Japanese military. There were also 150,000 corpses that were individually executed. These corpses were found and buried by the charitable organizations in Nanjing. The judgement of the Tokyo tribunal stated the following: 'during the first six weeks of the Japanese occupation, over 200,000 civilians and POWs were executed. This number did not include those victims whose bodies were dumped into the Yangzi River or executed by other means.'[142]

The ambiguity was judged acceptable, because the sum of the first two figures exceeded the Chinese official toll, while the Japanese could still claim

---

[139] Suh 2007, 386–7. Suh goes further in arguing that dialogical disputes over history provide a buffer for power disputes, since the former can be negotiated without resorting to war.

[140] *Mirai o hiraku rekishi: Higashi Ajia sankoku no kingendaishi* [A History that Opens the Future: Modern and Contemporary History of Three East Asian Countries] (Tokyo: Kôbunken, 2005); *Dongya sanguo de jinxiandaishi* [The Modern and Contemporary History of Three East Asian Countries] (Beijing: Shehui kexue chubanshe, 2005). For an informal English translation of the contents page, see <http://www.gwu.edu/~memory/issues/textbooks/jointeastasia.html>. Accessed 20 August 2012.

[141] See Wang 2009.

[142] *Dongya sanguo*, 131.

significant overlap between the two numbers.[143] In contrast, the relevant discussion in the JSHTR textbook, relegated to a note, reads:[144]

> At this time, many Chinese soldiers and civilians were killed or wounded by Japanese troops (the Nanking Incident). Documentary evidence has raised doubts about the actual number of victims claimed by the incident. The debate continues even today.

Potentially more influential, though, are the state-sponsored joint history commissions, precisely because they do not involve like-minded liberals and thus must bridge the ends of the spectrum of the public sphere. In this regard, Japan and South Korea have made some progress. Inspired by European examples, the Korea–Japan Joint Committee for Promoting History Studies was established in 1997 and was elevated to a Joint History Research Committee following the 2001 textbook controversy, spawning a second version after the 2005 textbook controversy.[145] These historians' main achievement was dialogical. Organized as a series of separate—sometimes parallel—essays, followed by commentary and reactions from other authors, these studies provided unprecedented textual dialogue among a large group of historians engaging each other over disputed historiography. For instance, the latest report issued in March 2010 provided a historiographically grounded outlet for the well-aired disputes over the content and tenor of references in Japanese texts to Japan's colonial rule in Korea,[146] and the existence of systematic and deceptive recruitment of comfort women. Japanese scholars countered with criticisms of Korean textbooks that neglected to mention Japan's renunciation of war in its post-war constitution and the 1995 Murayama statement.[147] This Committee made some progress on the colonial issue by agreeing based on documentary evidence some of the circumstances of Korea's annexation.[148]

Media reactions to these efforts predictably focus on the failure to agree on a single version of history, but more important in such a dialogical process is the clear expression of divergent national memory narratives such that at key junctures of disagreement, the separate streams are forced to engage through argument and clarification of sources, beliefs, and analysis. This is an essential

---

[143] Wang 2009, 113.

[144] JSHTR, 'New History Textbook 2005', English trans., 49, http://www.tsukurukai.com/05_rekisi_text/rekishi_English/English.pdf. Accessed 6 March 2013.

[145] Japan Center for International Exchange 2008; Babicz 2009, 116.

[146] For instance, the South Korean historians argued against the procedural legality of Korea's forced acceptance of the Second Japan–Korea Agreement in 1905 (which made Korea a Japanese protectorate) and the 1910 Annexation Treaty, while Japanese scholars continued to assert that the treaties were valid under contemporary law—'Japan, S. Korea researchers at odds over forced labour, "comfort women"', *Japan Times*, 24 March 2010.

[147] 'Panel still bickers over history issues', *Asahi Shimbun (English)*, 25 March 2010.

[148] 'Japan office never existed in 4th century', *Korea JoongAng Daily*, 24 March 2010.

Order and Justice: Contesting the Collective Memory Regime

step for regionalizing the renegotiation of national memory regimes and for laying the foundations for negotiating a regional collective memory regime further down the line. In theory, this joint history commission approach offers significant potential for renegotiating the shared memory regime in a process whereby each side clarifies and subjects to research and scrutiny national narratives. This critical questioning of other and self may lead to the revision of each side's own narrative in repeated cycles, such that narratives come closer without needing to merge. In this way, 'truth turns out to be a communication process', and the participants recognize not just multiple narratives but also that each group is the legitimate bearer of a possibly contending narrative.[149] Such a process contrasts with the predominant modes of contesting the Pacific War memory regime analysed in the previous section, which are asymmetrical in communicative style. Only one side is expected to change in response to demands from the other, because one side is wrong or evil while the other is sacrosanct.[150] However, the joint history approach requires sustained interaction and commitment to the dialogue process, which can only yield results over the medium term. Even the most acclaimed case of the German–Polish School Textbook Commission established in 1972 under United Nations Educational, Scientific and Cultural Organization (UNESCO) auspices took five years to issue its recommendations and a further twenty-four years to publish its formal guidelines for the teaching of history.[151]

South Korea and Japan have embarked with relative progress on such a sustained dialogue, and while the resulting discursive convergence is limited, this is not debilitating.

China and Japan, in contrast, are at the more rudimentary stage of setting up such a dialogical process. Joint history projects with China have been more difficult, given the level of state control and Beijing's concerns about public opinion. In 2006 President Hu Jintao and Prime Minister Abe Shinzo agreed to set up a Joint History Research Committee made up of prominent Japanese and Chinese historians. The work plan mirrored that of the first Korea–Japan Joint Committee, but the result was very different: when released in January 2010, the Sino-Japanese report provided only parallel country chapters without the vital commentary and exchange, and omitted post-war history altogether. The head of the Japanese team has publicly attributed these omissions to severe Chinese government pressure for fear of negative public reaction within China.[152] Yet deeper epistemological

---

[149] Pingel 2008, 189.
[150] Pingel 2008, 196.
[151] Borodziej 2003, 35–8.
[152] See Kitaoka 2010. The Chinese team leader's account highlighted the differences in temporal and normative focus, but was more sanguine about the achievements of the exercise in distinguishing between 'misunderstanding' and historiographical divergences—Bu 2011.

and methodological concerns divided the two teams from the outset: the Chinese historians resented the close empirical focus the Japanese historians gave to explaining the contingent processes and context of particular events, which seemed to lend excessive objectivity and moral ambiguity to their accounts. The Japanese historians, on the other hand, disliked the national and nationalist focus of their Chinese counterparts and distrusted their scholarly objectivity.[153] The Committee made modest progress: there was no contention about Japanese aggression and, by implication, 'a common recognition... [on] the issue of who bears responsibility for the war'.[154] They also agreed that a massacre occurred in Nanjing in 1937–8, and presented the evidence for their divergent estimates of the numbers killed.[155] The constraints to this exercise were significant, be they Chinese state intervention or the influence of Japanese conservatives in each national committee. The China–Japan bilateral commission is set to continue its work, and there are plans to establish an official trilateral commission for joint history. At this juncture, the potentially limiting factor is the cynical use of these joint commissions as a semi-official arena to park the history problem, freeing the respective governments from the political burden of renegotiating the balance between justice and order in the collective memory regime.

Conclusion

The contested and porous nature of East Asia as a region or community has been unpacked in previous chapters. Ironically, Japan's early twentieth-century expansion provided the most compelling framework for 'narrating' East Asia—its invasion of China, colonial control over Korea and Taiwan, and advance deep into Southeast Asia wove a web of connected history for this disparate region. In practice, though, the 'brutal "adhesive force"' of this shared experience proved fleeting: the collective memory regime of the war was a partial one from the start, crucially contested within Japan and increasingly resisted by its neighbours.[156] In turn, these overlapping processes of contestation have forced a collective reckoning in the empty heart of Northeast Asia, an essential step in renegotiating a new regional order.

---

[153] These differences are alluded to in the Japanese report (see Japan MOFA 2011, 4) and Bu 2011, and also confirmed in more explicit terms in the author's conversations with two Committee members in Oxford, January 2012 and Tokyo, November 2011.

[154] Bu Ping, the CASS historian leading the Chinese team, quoted in 'Japan–China history report to break new ground', *Japan Times*, 21 January 2010.

[155] For the English translation of the Japanese chapters for the modern period, see Japan MOFA 2011, 136–40.

[156] Sun 2011, 12.

These memory contests essentially push for changing the balance between order and justice in the regional social compact.

The states and peoples of Japan, China, and Korea demonstrated significant willingness to live with the Pacific War collective memory regime for part of the Cold War period because of strategic and political exigencies. Order concerns prevailed because of systemic inequalities and security imperatives, but shifts in these inequalities after 1989 ignited disparate demands for justice. Regional contestation came to the fore for two different reasons: on the one hand, China's rise and the changing Sino-Japanese balance of power in favour of China created pressure for a more satisfactory collective recounting of and accounting for their shared history. The desire to integrate China and construct an East Asian regional community also necessitated some means of writing Chinese, Korean, and Asian victims back into the memory regime of a shared history.[157] Yet the more entrenched dynamics are found at the domestic and societal level. The crucial dissatisfied constituency resides within Japan itself, in a small group of right-wing nationalist conservatives who wield influence as the power base of the dominant post-war political party. China and South Korea's contestations of the memory regime were triggered by reaction against this Japanese conservative revisionism, and have been subsequently fuelled by rising patriotic sentiment and civic activism coinciding with the strategic shifts of the dying Cold War.

These memory contestations impact upon the wider renegotiation of the social compact in East Asian regional society. Collective memory regimes are underpinned by contingent bargains that balance between order and justice, and the domestic and regional contests over textbooks, the Yasukuni shrine, and comfort women were aimed at renegotiating this normative bargain. Particularly since the mid-1990s, they have caused the balance of order and justice to shift perceptibly in three ways. First, the Asian war victims and their justice claims have been explicitly recognized, not only by the Japanese state and public, but also by the various Asian states that had been complicit with the previous amnesia in favour of order and security concerns. Moreover, the content and fences of national and collective memory have been challenged as Japan's neighbours dispute what in their shared experience to remember and what to forget, and what are acceptable boundaries of contention and divergence. This process has been fractious, but has gone some way towards foregrounding the Asian war and its victims within the collective memory regime through political and educational narratives, Japanese apologies, semi-official restitution, and interactive research. This trend begins to address the partiality of the post-war settlement.

---

[157] Jager and Mitter 2007, 9.

Second, the main effect of these multiple contestations has been to create a vibrant regional public sphere of legitimate resistance based on deep-seated struggles for justice. Most explicitly since the war crimes tribunals, moral and justice claims have gained salience vis-à-vis strategic imperatives, even in the realm of high politics. For instance, the three Northeast Asian countries have interrupted significant plans for bilateral and trilateral strategic cooperation for overt reasons of historical disputes. While observers often despair at these nationalistic displays, over the longer term, these legitimate contestations in the public sphere lay the groundwork to stimulate deeper reconciliation. The expectation is that repeated rounds of discursive and political contests and dialogue would help to narrow the boundaries of remaining divergences— so much so that a stable shared joint memory regime might be achieved within agreed parameters. Such a process would not dissolve the trauma or ruptures in regional memory, but would pacify the 'history problem' within renegotiations of the regional social compact. Currently, the prospects for such pacification appear relatively dim because the channels and incentives for such normative renegotiation are limited, but this is necessarily a longer-term prospect.

Finally, the post-Cold War regional memory contests have indelibly forged the connections between order and justice in East Asia. Essentially, the challenges to the Pacific War memory regime analysed in this chapter are deep-seated contests about Japan's role in the regional order. By surfacing the normative content of this struggle, this chapter has unpacked the multiple layers of visceral resistance, only part of which arises from political machinations. The instrumental and presentist use of history detracts from neither the normative, emotive, and moral dimensions of memory nor its constitutive power. While Japanese nationalists want to break free of the peace treaties' wholesale condemnation of Japan's post-Meiji Restoration transformation, Japan's neighbours cannot relinquish their focus on Japan's role as revolutionary against the Sinic order, spoiler of their nation-building and modernization trajectories, and violator of their peoples in war. Japanese imperialism directly hindered modern state building in both Korea and China, but China additionally bears the shame of having had not just its hierarchical position but the whole political order it led usurped by Japan. As China recovers its regional prominence, the imperative of accounting for this shared past has intensified and grown rigid within the soil of state-induced patriotism and popular nationalism. As long as Chinese patriotism and memory resistance mark Japan out as the region's unrepentant pariah, any social compact between them will be elusive. Similarly, for as long as memory distrust and mutually denying nationalism prevail between South Korea and Japan, Seoul will evince more comfort in strategic interactions conducted via Washington as the alliance 'hub', or in coordination even with Beijing, than in significantly altering its strategic relationship with Japan.[158]

The US position in East Asia after the Second World War was built upon Japan's traumatic divorce from the Sinic order, and the terms of US hegemony negotiated after 1990 remained rooted in the continued estrangement between Japan and China. By holding apart these two adversaries, the US-led order provides few channels and opportunities for addressing their conflicting justice claims in a strategically salient way. Moreover, Washington has proved by selective intervention its power to maintain vital fences of memory in East Asia. Substantively, US governmental intervention has stymied legal processes to challenge Japan's liability to Asian war victims; while American political clout with key conservative interest groups in Japan has helped to insulate the United States–Japan strategic relationship from potential negative repercussions of history disputes. The resulting instability and resistance over the collective memory regime intensify in intractability, in turn reinforcing Japan's, China's, and Korea's reliance on the United States as ring-holder. In other words, the limits to the ongoing renegotiating of the moral order in East Asia stoke the tendency to choose imperatives of order over those of justice, by reinforcing the conviction that the conflicting justice claims cannot be either renegotiated prior to, or reconciled with the demands of, achieving order.

---

[158] For instance, Seoul postponed an agreement for military intelligence sharing with Tokyo in 2012, citing domestic disquiet over their unresolved history—'South Korea and Japan put military intelligence pact on hold after outcry', *CNN*, 29 June 2012.

6

Conclusion: The Hierarchical East Asian Order

> ...the rise of others...does not, by itself, amount to any decisive objection to the development of a U.S.-centred hegemony in the near future.[1]

This book began with the question of how to explain the post-Cold War East Asian strategic landscape that seems to accommodate both the rise of China and the continuing preponderance of the United States, and to allow significant activism on the part of non-great power states. What kind of change has the region been undergoing? Can this transition be captured in a useful framework? What interactions and implications do trends in this vital region have for global order? Developing an English School approach emphasizing the social dimensions of power and its inequalities, the conceptual framework proposed in Chapter 1 takes as its starting point international order, conceived as norm-governed interaction produced by a social compact among members of the regional society of states. This social compact serves to mediate between contending interests, beliefs, and values held about authority, security, and community. It is contingent and negotiated among states with differential power attributes, and comes under contestation and renegotiation in times of systemic disruptions such as the end of the Cold War. I further proposed that this drawn-out process of renegotiation is most appropriately considered an order transition, as opposed to a power transition that turns mainly on the relative distribution of material power and the theory of which is preoccupied with the incidence of war. In developing order transition as an analytical framework, I identified the essential elements of the status quo order that come under negotiation during transition, focusing on the normative structure of regional society. For East Asia, the four core elements of this normative structure are institutional

---

[1] Clark 2011, 4.

bargains, security public goods provision, regionalism and community, and collective memory revision. Each was analysed in the four preceding chapters. The analysis stressed processes, highlighting the multiple actors and constituencies, contestation, and non-linear nature of this serial negotiation of order, which cannot be captured within parsimonious characterizations such as balancing and bandwagoning. The analysis also paid particular attention to the complex dynamics of consent and resistance accompanying unequal power, within both the vertical dimension (between great powers and others) and the horizontal dimension (among great powers).

Renegotiating the Normative Structure

Two threads weave together the complex East Asian renegotiations of the core collective strategic understandings vital to the region: legitimate power, and resistance. First, the intense negotiations about new institutional bargains to constrain as well as legitimize unequal power, and about great power authority in providing the public good of conflict management, reflected two imperatives: to tame the excesses of US super power and the rising influence of China, but also to harness US preponderance. Chapter 2 showed that, very soon after the Cold War ended, regional institutions became the prime site for negotiating and constituting the new regional social compact centred on different degrees of taming and justifying the unequal power of the United States, China, Japan, and ASEAN in particular. Because they were spearheaded by the smaller states of Southeast Asia, the institutional bargains sought not only to induce the great powers to exercise self-restraint, but also to subcontract the monitoring and countervailing of multiple great powers within agreed rules and norms to these great powers themselves. Most notable, though, were the reinvigorated or new bargains to bind the United States to guaranteeing the security and autonomy of its allies and partners and to managing regional order in a rule-bound way. The spate of institutional rivalry is essentially a face-off between two different models of what the institutional bargain ought to be: an 'inclusive' bargain perpetuating the US-led security order but incorporating China into a condominium, and retaining Japan's supplementary role as supporter state; or an 'exclusive' new China-centred 'East Asian' order that would require a core bargain between China and Japan on their respective status as well as a wider regional bargain on how China's power will be restrained. The analysis suggests that the apparent stalemate in institutional development reflects regional attempts to ensure that both bargains can coexist. The yet unresolved question is of course how this might be achieved.

Meanwhile, Chapter 3 revealed the strong and widespread East Asian preference for the United States as regional security guarantor—a vital basis of

US hegemony. There has been intense contestation surrounding the prioritization of public goods and modes of conflict management in post-Cold War East Asia because of divergent interests, domestic politics, and attention spans. For reasons of efficiency and legitimacy, Washington has sought to share the burdens as well as some authority in conflict management with China, international institutions, and its allies. But to a significant extent, the United States retains the right to define the nature and hierarchy of public goods and to determine how these goods are to be provided and on what terms. Insofar as authority is marked by deference and demand for leadership, other East Asian states have largely continued to grant Washington authority for three reasons. Most importantly, Washington has shown itself to be responsive to allied security concerns and requests for strategic support from other states. Secondly, American deterrence capabilities have not yet been disproven, unlike China's demonstrated inability to restrain North Korea or commit to serious conflict resolution in the South China Sea. Finally, in neither of these two key cases is there widespread political appetite for the difficult process of actually solving the conflicts, thus reinforcing the US role as ultimate deterrent and guarantor.

The second theme that threads through renegotiations of the normative structure of East Asian regional society is resistance. Indeed, much of post-Cold War renegotiations has been about challenging and resisting the perceived reneging on the prior Cold War social compact, or about its unjust or partial nature. But regional resistance to US authority, while vibrant, is ultimately constrained externally by the resilience of the meta-structures of its global hegemony, and intra-regionally by deep-seated moral and geopolitical contests. In unpacking the most promising avenue of economic regionalism in contemporary East Asia, Chapter 4 found limited prospects that the region might negotiate an alternative compact to resist and insulate itself from the crises engendered by the Western liberal global economic order. Financial regionalism faces two fundamental political impediments. First is the struggle over the internal hierarchy of the putative East Asian community: regionalism is constituted not only by intensifying regional interdependence, but also by a growing leadership and legitimization struggle between the world's second and third largest economies, China and Japan. Second, these regionalist efforts butt up against the resilient structures of the hegemonic global order. Fundamentally, the boundaries between the putative regional community and the global economic order are difficult to police. East Asian economic development is markedly externally oriented, foreclosing the option of any 'closed' regionalism project. For the leading economies of China and Japan, regional renegotiation of financial governance is also limited by their multiple aims in the ongoing reforms of the global economic order—to limit exposure to different types of risk commensurate with their financial profiles, to block each other's potential gains in status, and to preserve certain beneficial aspects of the existing order while reforming less desirable elements. Ultimately, Japan and China are unwilling or unable to monopolize the supply of regional financial public goods also because of capacity considerations. The US-led neoliberal economic order remains resilient in the face of crisis, not because the US-led global liberal ideology and institutions cannot be challenged, but rather because hegemonic institutions are extremely costly to replace. Chapter 4 thus showed East Asian states returning to partial support of the neoliberal economic orthodoxy and of international financial institutions shortly after the 1997 crisis. Indeed, East Asian financial regionalism has been aimed mainly at mediating the adverse effects of globalization, rather than undermining or replacing the global economic order. The result is thus not straightforward resistance, but a layering of regional financial safety nets as back-up and support for global arrangements in times of crisis.

The critical stumbling block posed by Sino-Japanese conflict to any new social compact is essentially about Japan's gradual alienation from the East Asian order, begun during the Meiji Restoration and solidified after the Second World War. What Chapter 5 made clear is that US regional hegemony is built upon this divorce. The cessation of the Cold War dampened the strategic imperatives for order sufficiently for the conflicting justice claims surrounding the partial collective memory regime about the war to surface within East Asia. Since the 1980s, attempts to renegotiate the balance of justice and order in this vital moral realm have accompanied the recovery of East Asia as a region. The contests over Japanese history textbooks, the Yasukuni shrine, and restitution for comfort women have caused the balance of order and justice to shift perceptibly: the justice claims of Asian war victims have been explicitly acknowledged; a vibrant regional public sphere of legitimate resistance based on deep-seated struggles for justice has been created; and the connections between order and justice claims have been forged. Yet entrenched moral opposition and domestic political reinforcement, as well as US interventions to uphold old fences of memory, serve to limit this renegotiation of the moral order. By stoking the tendency to choose imperatives of order over those of justice, this in turn reinforces Japan, China, and Korea's reliance on the United States as ring-holder.

My analysis of this rich empirical material points to three conclusions. First, the contested process of renegotiating the normative structure of regional society reflects a widespread regional inclination to sustain the most important element of the social structure: US preponderance. With the partial exception of China, East Asian states basically want to negotiate a new social compact that would consolidate US post-Cold War primacy within mutually agreed constraints. Having been forced to adjust the terms of the Cold War bargain with the United States, non-communist regional states have particularly worked to renegotiate the social compact underpinning US leadership, without challenging the state of this leadership itself. The nature of the resulting post-Cold War regional order is hegemonic, because US leadership extends beyond preponderance and is characterized by consensual normative structures and a more accessible process of negotiation involving other great powers and smaller states in regional society. The economic realm has seen most East Asian resistance to changing the Cold War bargain with the United States, and the new trade institutions and financial arrangements represent negotiated adjustments that still aim to protect regional economies from the type of full liberalization they had avoided in the past in exchange for strategic acquiescence. However, the pull exerted by the wider hegemonic global order is also hard for the leading East Asian economies to resist, and they rallied after recent crises to boost this hegemonic order in exchange for some reforms within it. Moreover, US hegemonic interposition into the regional social and moral realm is very marked, driven by existential order concerns that regional states are unable fundamentally to overturn thus far in spite of domestic and societal pressures. Most persuasive, though, is the US position of special privilege and authority within this crowded strategic region. In spite of various types of resistance and contestation, these dynamics take place within the boundaries of a near consensus about the critical deterrence that US military power provides in the region, and its vital position as ring-holder between Japan and its neighbours. Northeast Asian, especially Japanese and South Korean, security strategies continue to be constituted mainly by their alliances with the United States, while American authority as regional conflict manager traverses both the Northeast and Southeast Asian theatres.

In general, regional states consent to support or tolerate US hegemony because of their belief that the distribution of benefits, while not ideal, is preferable in this pluralist order to any alternatives they can devise. East Asian states might construct secondary safety nets—enmeshing China in the hopes of socializing it, cultivating regional community, inching towards moral reconciliation—but in the meantime, the strategic oxygen for such endeavours is perceived to flow from the hard deterrence and guarantor-ship that the United States alone can provide. The regional social compact with the United States is not so much geared at taming its preponderant power as it is at harnessing and channelling it into binding security commitments. This sits in contrast to East Asian approaches to China, which concentrate on constraining and balancing it, and socializing it into a different type of power capable of making compacts in the first place; and to the regional ambivalence over Japan and its identity and position in the region.

Second, the patterns of resistance that emerge from the foregoing analysis are noticeably partial. Certainly, resistance to US dominance, not just from

Conclusion: The Hierarchical East Asian Order

rising powers but also other states in East Asia, has been more sustained precisely because regional order has become more plural after the Cold War. The grand strategic vacuum, the initial loss of US strategic initiative, and China's rise all created grave uncertainty and room for alternatives and contesting models and values. Yet the kind of partial resistance shown in East Asia over the last two decades has helped to consolidate US hegemony. East Asian states have been complicit in sustaining US hegemony because they have not fundamentally resisted or rejected the normative values and structures preferred by Washington. Moreover, by their reliance on the United States as an extra-regional, apparently benign, 'broker', regional supporters of the Western vanguard (including Japan) resist from within East Asia a potential shift to a China-dominated regional society. For its part, China has failed to mount sustained resistance to the hegemonic order: rather than propagating an alternative social compact, China has instead allowed itself to be co-opted partially into the US-led international and regional order, thus partly naturalizing the prevailing power relations. In a Gramscian reading, for instance, the multilateral institutions that China subscribes to and upholds, and the international society that it is seen to have joined, are critical elements of the 'hegemonic historic bloc' dominated by the United States. The processes of individual and institutional socialization that have made China part of these institutions represent the 'passive revolution' by which a small group of elites—intellectuals, policy-makers, key office holders in international institutions—are co-opted into the hegemonic ideology.

Put less categorically, China's participation in numerous international and regional institutions, while legitimizing its own ascent, also crucially enmeshes it into key social compacts that sustain US primacy in the region. Washington has abetted this dynamic by selective efforts to co-opt China. In subcontracting to China some of the organizational and negotiating leadership for managing the North Korean nuclear problem, and in singling out Beijing's currency policy as responsible for global imbalances, US leaders have explicitly recognized China's special position as a great power in the region and in the world. But the terms of this recognition are relatively circumscribed; the offer of stakeholder-ship comes in exchange for China's accession into the existing international order largely as it stands. China has been able to push back and increase the friction against some aspects, such as the nature of the sanctions regime against North Korea, but not to shift the modes and norms of this order.

This leads us into the final conclusion, that the accommodation of rising powers is arguably the most confounding element of the ongoing negotiation of order in East Asia. Fundamentally, how are we to accept that US hegemony has been consolidated precisely during a period when one historical great power is resurgent and another may be gradually normalizing in

East Asia? The empirical analysis in this book suggests that the answer lies in multiple practices of layering: attempts to integrate differentiated authority, functions, and goals by easing them one on top of the other in order of priority. At the most general level, there emerges a distinction between the global tier consisting of the meta-structures of global strategic and economic order dominated by the United States and Western liberal states and ideology, and the regional tier. East Asian states contribute to the widespread consent and support undergirding the global order, by not creating a regional order that challenges it. Rather, as encapsulated in the financial realm, the regional tier is developing as a support layer under the global. Within the regional realm are further efforts at layering. China and Japan most actively engage in geopolitical and normative competition, and often act to deny each other status. Neither side regards the other as equal. Other regional states also do not manage their relationships with the United States with the same priority or in the same way as they do those with China or Japan. The developing bargains over institutions and conflict management most clearly illustrate this landscape of tiered unequal power and gradations of authority, as well as how regional attempts to justify them are the major political preoccupation.

In summary, the preceding analysis suggests that since 1989, East Asia has experienced parallel resurgence from the United States as well as China. However, my substantive investigation of the ongoing normative negotiations presented a narrative that departs from the near-universal spotlight on China cast within the literature: it found that US hegemony has been established during this period, and that other regional states—particularly Japan and the key Southeast Asian players—have been active in negotiating the terms of this hegemony. China's resistance to the US hegemonic agenda has been often indirect and sometimes subject to co-optation. Attempts to reconcile the demands of unequal power and clashing meanings, ideologies, and claims to justice have found outlet in practices of layering. But where does this leave us in furthering our understanding of East Asian order? I suggested at the start that regional order is constituted by a normative but also social structure. What does the social structure of this emerging regional society look like? Which states belong, and in what positions, with what status, rights, and responsibilities? What type of social processes do these messy normative negotiations lead to?

The Social Structure: Hegemony with Hierarchy

I suggest that the normative dynamics detailed in this volume pull towards the construction of a regional social structure approximating a hegemonic order with layered hierarchical characteristics. This novel proposition comes at the end rather than the beginning of this book because it is an interpretation of its complex findings, not an abstract model I wished to 'prove' by this undertaking. This interpretive framework may be regarded as an interim outcome of the ongoing order transition in East Asia, and a touchstone for further research in this fascinating and fast-evolving field.

Hegemony and Hierarchy

The basic idea is that the process of contestation and renegotiation in East Asia since the end of the Cold War has created a layered hierarchical order in East Asia. This order is hierarchical in two senses: US hegemonic authority exists; but below the United States there is also a rank ordering of other major regional powers. Critically, this hierarchy integrates China as a constrained, pro-status quo regional great power subordinate to the United States as global and regional hegemon. This hierarchical order represents an order transition rather than a power transition because the vital alterations reside in the renegotiated terms of the social compact that underpins US hegemony, not in the power distribution per se. Crucially, this new compact provides for gradations in authority and status among the major powers.

Referring basically to unequal relations, hierarchy ought to be a prevalent International Relations concept, for the international system is ridden with inequalities and differentiation. Yet the concept has enjoyed a revival of attention only in the past decade, partly because of the distracting dichotomization of anarchy and hierarchy as conditions marked by the presence or absence of overarching authority.[2] Recent scholarship has returned us to the notion of international hierarchies as the wide range of inequalities and differentiation in authority relations in the international system.[3] An anarchical system, then, can and usually does contain relations of hierarchy. Clearly, hegemony is one form of hierarchy. However, these two concepts have often suffered an artificial distinction. For instance, the most influential recent social contractual study of international hierarchy uses the hierarchy concept mainly to stress the consensual nature of the unequal authority relationships between the United States and its allies and to overcome the less pleasant connotations of realist understandings of the term hegemony.[4] The classic Gramscian notion of hegemony adopted here, explicitly acknowledging both coercion and consent, does not suffer from this problem. There is a tendency, too, to conceive of a singular hegemon exercising authority

---

[2] Waltz 1979.
[3] See e.g. Donnelly 2006.
[4] Lake 2007, 2011.

in a broadly two-layered system of hegemon-and-the others. In this regard, Clark's reworking of hegemony as an institution of international society is an important breakthrough: his understanding of hegemony turns on social legitimacy—so much so that we can move beyond the structural constraints of a single-power material primacy to conceive of 'collective hegemony' shared among a number of great powers or of 'coalitional hegemony' in which the actor is hegemonic insofar as it is able to legitimize its social order vis-à-vis a restricted audience.[5] If one accepts—as I do—Clark's argument that the most useful way of understanding hegemony is to privilege its social foundations as legitimate superordinate authority, then it is but a short step towards conceiving of a hegemonic order with hierarchical characteristics. There is an overarching consensus on the shared goals and values of the international society led by the hegemon, but this is an order with variegated layers of relationships of sub- and superordination among states. Such relationships stem in part from dependencies that arise from inequalities, be they military, economic, or political. More importantly, these layers of differentiated authority are in turn defined and sustained by accompanying differentiated social processes.

The notion of a layered hierarchical international order is more reflective of reality in general and of East Asian history in particular. Regional and international orders are seldom simply two-layered and even if there is one predominant power, there are usually a number of other states less powerful than the dominant, but significantly more powerful than others.[6] Moreover, as Kang usefully reminded the academy in a significant 2003 paper, East Asia perhaps exhibits most vividly such layered hierarchical political relations in the historical Sino-centric order.[7] This book's findings suggest that this hierarchical propensity is a more general tendency amongst states in the East Asian security complex. In recent history, when China has been relatively weak, this tradition was transposed into a context of US dominance after the Second World War, and key states have since worked to facilitate a US-centric regional hierarchical order after the Cold War.[8]

Social Processes

Two sets of social processes are vital to layered hierarchical orders: first, the identity formation processes and ordering principles that constitute the status and rankings of great power states; and second, the social dynamics of

---

[5] Clark 2011.
[6] This point is made by other scholars such as Buzan and Waever 2003; Lemke 2002.
[7] Kang 2003a.
[8] I have sketched this argument before, in Goh 2008.

Conclusion: The Hierarchical East Asian Order

complicity and resistance through which the hierarchical order is created and reproduced.

Conceiving of East Asian order as a multilayered hierarchy brings us back closer to the neo-classical realist roots of English School approaches, to earlier realist scholars who read the evolution of world order in terms of the rise and fall of a succession of hegemons, and to power transition theorists' emphasis on contests over hierarchies of power and prestige. My conceptualization of hegemony with hierarchy brings rank ordering back into East Asian regional society.[9] However, this book provides limited scope to address status and rank formation processes as such; it allows only the relatively general interpretation that the East Asian hierarchical order is variegated at the top. To illustrate, using Levy's classic three-part determination of great power status,[10] the foregoing analysis clearly demonstrates the superpower overlay of the United States in terms of its preponderant capabilities, proven willingness to employ them in managing regional crises and affairs, and in the social recognition it receives within the region. China's status as the major regional great power is growing on these three fronts, but it still lags significantly behind the United States. Most notably, China receives recognition from regional states that do not deny it a major regional role, even if they might not support it in a preponderant position. At the same time, Japan retains a prominent position in determining regional order, with its still-significant economic capabilities, and its security relationship with the United States, which makes it a vital hegemonic supporter and potential 'swing' state. As Figure 6.1 illustrates, the analysis here suggests the rank ordering, but there remains room for further work that will clarify the currently fuzzy areas between each layer. Nevertheless, there are two discernible breaks in this hierarchy corresponding to the vertical and horizontal dimensions of unequal power addressed in the preceding analysis: one dividing the United States as hegemon from the rest, and the other dividing the United States, China, and Japan from the non-great power states.

This book's analysis of the renegotiation of the regional social compact contributes most to understanding the social dynamics that animate and sustain such a layered hierarchical order. As is clear from the above discussion, hierarchical orders, especially hegemonic ones, are crucially constituted by complicity: without the consent and acquiescence of all states in the system, hierarchies cannot be sustained. At the same time, though, we also saw that the dynamics of complicity were accompanied by forces of

---

[9] See the related revival of interest in IR on status, e.g. Lebow 2008; Wohlforth 2009; Larson and Shevchenko 2010; Volgy et al. 2010. Much of this literature, though, is concerned with using status to explain conflict and cooperation, rather than with developing the notion of status or rank in and of itself.

[10] Levy 1983.

The Struggle for Order

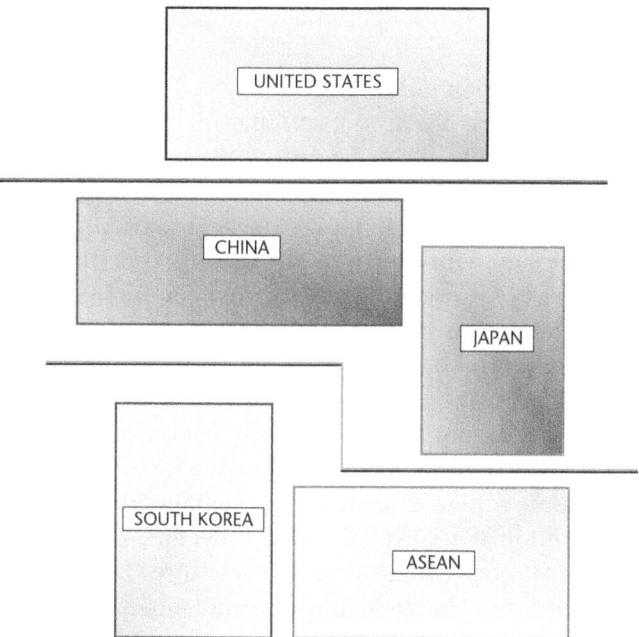

Figure 6.1. The East Asian hierarchical order

resistance—hierarchies are after all inequalities of power (even if they are institutionalized inequalities) that require the participation of subordinate groups. The analysis here suggests that the social dynamics of hierarchy can be conceived as an extension of the central balance of tensions surrounding unequal power we began with: on the one hand, the imperative of limiting or taming preponderant power so as to resist the worst of its potential excesses; and on the other, the exigency of maintaining and legitimizing—being complicit in the sustaining of—the preponderant power that undergirds international order. In post-Cold War East Asia, this balance thus far appears to swing in favour of complicity in sustaining US hegemony, but as the discussion below highlights, a number of other subtle and significant trends in dynamics of both resistance and complicity emerge from this book's analysis. The complex contestation and negotiations unpacked in the previous empirical chapters largely resolve themselves into these dynamics of resistance and complicity, and the layered hierarchy created by the resulting social compact is generating its own variegated social processes. With a degree of abstraction, I posit that these reciprocal processes are as follows.

Table 6.1 summarizes the dynamics of complicity and resistance in a hierarchical order. Taking into account the direction of these social processes, we can disaggregate complicity into upward deference by subordinate states

Conclusion: The Hierarchical East Asian Order

Table 6.1. The social dynamics of a layered hierarchical order

	Complicity	Resistance
Upwards ↑	Deference	Constraint/Revolt
Downwards ↓	Assurance	Comprehensive containment/Renegation

towards dominant states, and downward assurance by dominant states to subordinates. Resistance can similarly be separated into upward constraint and potential revolt posed by subordinates to superordinate power, and superordinate states' downward efforts to maintain order and resist significant demands for change by subordinates. There is at least one further dimension that must be highlighted for layered hierarchies, as illustrated in Figure 6.2. As noted throughout this book, there are more complex dynamics of complicity and resistance at the intermediate ranks of great powers below the hegemon but above non-great powers, which differ in significant ways from the dynamics between the hegemon and non-great power subordinates. Now that we have identified the multiple layers at the top of the hierarchy, I refine the previous working distinction between horizontal and vertical dimensions by assigning a 'short' vertical dimension to capture the hierarchical relations between the hegemon and the other great powers; as opposed to the 'long' vertical dimension that denotes the relations between the hegemon and all its subordinates.[11]

COMPLICITY

The contemporary East Asian case study here makes clear that at its core, the layered hegemonic order is sustained by assurance on the part of the dominant state, and deference on the part of subordinate states. The findings about US leadership point to four essential elements of hierarchical assurance over the *'long' vertical* dimension. First, as rationalists of the hegemonic stability school stress, the hegemon assures others of the stable provision of public goods: in East Asia, Washington directly assures its allies and partners of security and regional stability by its military preponderance and commitments, and of economic access and stability in conjunction with the global economic institutions. Second, the United States as hegemon credibly demonstrates its sustained benignity in assuring others of its lack of territorial ambitions, willingness to participate in some institutionalized restraints, and in extending long-term security and

---

[11] I am aware that we may also wish to consider a third dimension, that of relations between the dominant state/great powers as a group, and the non-great power states. But the foregoing analysis shows that the dynamics within the 'short' vertical dimension are more substantive than those between the disparate great powers and the rest.

The Struggle for Order

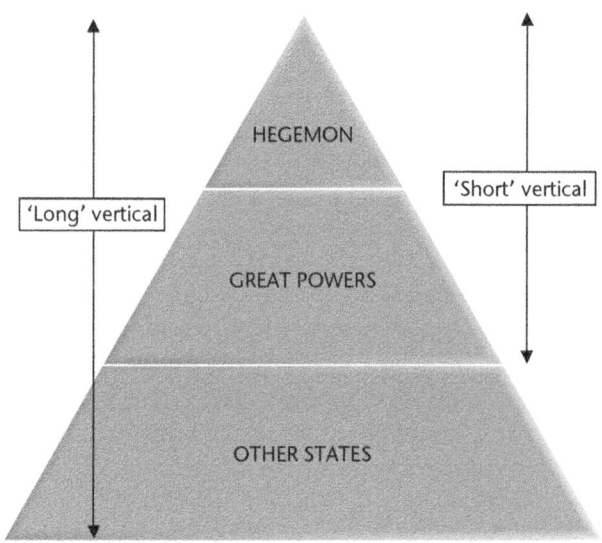

Figure 6.2. The vertical dimensions of hegemony with hierarchy

economic commitments to the region. Here, the most marked aspect is US commitment to its supporter states, more than the emphasis on self-restraint that liberal accounts prefer. Indeed, in the post-Cold War period, the United States has marked itself out as a hegemon responsive to allies' and partners' requests and strategic needs, even though the negotiation process may be fractious. Third, Washington provides leadership in the form of a normative framework—the broadly liberal socio-economic model and democratic political ideology—that other states at least appreciate and perceive to be of benefit to themselves, with some identifying with and emulating it. Finally, the key reason that the United States must ensure that its assurance strategies work is to uphold the imperative of maintaining the existing order. A commitment to the latter entails representation and legitimacy, including means of assimilating new great powers to the hierarchy and otherwise adjusting via renegotiating the social compact in response to strategic changes.

Post-Cold War transitions in the East Asian order strongly demonstrate the underlying (and overarching) dynamics of complicity in reinvigorating and maintaining the US-led regional hierarchy. Particularly important are regional consent, support, and active lobbying for, as well as deference to, US security commitments and relationships. The findings here about the majority of East Asian states' support of continued US leadership point to four reciprocal elements of hierarchical deference in the 'long' vertical dimension. First, these subordinate states' acquiescence and lack of opposition or

Conclusion: The Hierarchical East Asian Order

challenge to the US position as regional hegemon. Even though they avoid the term 'hegemony', as shown in this book's detailed analysis, smaller regional states have consistently adopted policies to reinforce the United States' primary position in the hierarchy, ranging from institutional bargains to justify its regional role, to facilitating its forward military projection. Second, subordinate states place greater priority on their relationship with the United States as hegemon than with any other great power. This is most marked among US allies; even for South Korea, which is subject to serious domestic divisions on how to handle the North and on increasing interdependent relations with China, the continued DPRK threat reinforced the alliance from 2008 onwards. Third, subordinate states accommodate the hegemon's core security imperatives. As shown by East Asian support of the US counter-terrorism agenda, this accommodation is calculated on the basis of the expected reciprocal benefits of buying continued US attention and commitment to the region. Finally, in return for hegemonic assurance, weaker states support the status quo, including US preponderance and the maintenance of the rank order below it.

But the variegated nature of complicity in a hierarchical hegemonic order is also evident in East Asian states' demonstrated secondary deference to China as the rising regional power. Realist scholars tend to read this simply as the politics of accommodation or bandwagoning, but they cannot account for the parallel (and greater) deference shown to the United States. As my analysis shows, there has been a surprising degree of activism on the part of subordinate states not only in helping to sustain US hierarchical leadership, but also in innovating so as to buttress the wider regional order. Their key innovation has been to try to facilitate the peaceful integration of China into the regional hierarchy, but without displacing US leadership or disrupting the US-led normative order. The seldom-voiced implication is that China has to be integrated at a level below that of the United States, and the other regional states have helped to negotiate a social compact with terms of differentiated complicity to ease this layering. According China status as a ranking great power entails social recognition, which East Asian states have extended in terms of inviting China to become a member of regional security institutions, creating high-level bilateral security exchanges, using consensual and informal institutional styles that Chinese officials are more comfortable with, and deferring formally to China's security imperatives especially on the status of Taiwan. To a large extent, these moves facilitated in turn Beijing's assurance strategies towards South Korea, Taiwan, and Southeast Asian states after 1995, creating a strong dynamic of complicity regarding integrating China into the regional order. These trends have led some authors to suggest that South Korea and Taiwan are even accommodating China's rise by trying to resolve their conflicts with Beijing and by adjusting their defence ties with the United States.[12] But my hegemony-with-hierarchy framework suggests that to make this argument, we would need to see these states move towards *primary* deference to China, by ending their security alliances with Washington and reorientating their force structure and planning away from US interests and towards China's. As my analysis shows, this has not happened.

The layered complicity processes become more pronounced when we focus on the *'short' vertical* dimension, which in the East Asian case involves the United States, China, and Japan. Here, hierarchical assurance from the hegemon to the great powers that rank below itself contains three specific additional emphases on status and rank assurance. First is the recognition of the latter's status and rights to special regard as great powers with exceptional capabilities and strategic interests that must be taken into account. Second, the United States as hegemon has granted China and Japan membership within the great power club in a number of ways, including some power sharing or subcontracting regarding public goods provision. This club membership grants the great powers rights as well as responsibilities along with a legitimate stake and privileged voice in maintaining the existing order. Essentially, such hegemonic assurance in the 'short' vertical realm is to reassure these potential competitors that their club membership is secure, and that the hegemon would not try deliberately to 'demote' them or expel them from the club. In return, though, the great powers are expected to demonstrate hierarchical deference to the hegemon and other higher-ranked powers. This deference consists critically of support for the status quo rank order, by undertaking specifically not to challenge the hegemon or try to overtake higher-ranked great powers. More generally, they support the existing order by agreeing not to exit from the great power club, which would constitute abdication from the hegemonic order.

Because hierarchical relations depend upon the consent of the subordinates through negotiated reciprocal understandings, hierarchical deference should be read as a result of choice more than simple path dependency. This is true especially within the 'short' vertical realm, where support for the hegemon is costly and may be based on normative (the logic of appropriateness that accompanies belief in legitimacy) rather than rationalist (for instance, the cost–benefit calculations based upon relative material strength that lead to bandwagoning)[13] motivations. In a layered hierarchy, deference from the other major powers ranked below the dominant state is most costly, as they might find themselves in possession of sufficient strength or status to challenge the hegemon or another state ranked above them, thereby

[12] Ross 2006b; Kang 2007.
[13] See, for instance, Schweller 2006.

Conclusion: The Hierarchical East Asian Order

improving their own ranking. This is also why hierarchical assurance plays a bigger role within the 'short' vertical dimension. The East Asian case presents two particularly notable characteristics in this regard. The first is how crucial US assurance of China is if the latter's incorporation into the regional hierarchy is to be successfully managed. Here, the creation of bilateral strategic dialogues, expectations of bilateral coordination and cooperation for key security issues, and Washington's inclusion of Beijing in the key regional conflict management mechanism of the Six Party Talks are all indicators of its recognition of China's great power status and membership in the great power club. However, hegemonic assurance aimed at China contains a strong emphasis on conditional reciprocity: Washington demands that China assures other states of its pro-status quo intentions, and its willingness to be bound by the norms of the existing order. This book's analysis points out that a central problem here is that China has been relatively unwilling to engage in the substantive elements of the strategic renegotiation, while the United States defines stakeholder-ship conservatively, requiring China to buy wholesale into the existing pro-US-weighted order. For the hegemon, therefore, an increasingly vital component of its assurance strategy is its ability to manage China's rise—successfully deterring Chinese adventurism using alliances while bringing China into regional order by partnership, stakeholder-ship, and concert on critical issues—without disrupting the normative order and its own position. Looking ahead, Washington's ability to do both these things well will crucially underpin its hegemony in the region.

The second notable point about complicity in the 'short' vertical dimension is Japan's crucial choices in rank and order terms. The updating and upgrading of the United States–Japan alliance after the Cold War critically helps to underwrite the United States' position as the dominant state in the regional hierarchy in two ways: it enhances US power projection both in the region and in the world; and it is a powerful symbol of the acquiescence and subordination of one of its two main potential challengers for regional hegemony. Yet, because of their alliance and its associated bilateral bargain, the nature of US assurance to Japan within the 'short' vertical is more asymmetrical, and Washington may not need to pay as much attention to assuring Japan about its great power club membership as in China's case. Yet, given Sino-Japanese rivalry, one challenge for the United States is how to assure Japan enough that it will not be bypassed by its ally en route to China. At the same time, Japan's case also epitomizes the way that East Asian preferences for maintaining US leadership go beyond what others have argued to be the simple imperative of intra-regional great power balancing.[14] Tokyo is

---

[14] See Wohlforth 1999; Walt 2009.

not simply trying to counter China's growing power using its alliance with the United States, but also to integrate China into the regional order. More interestingly, as illustrated by Tokyo's revised approach towards supplying financial regionalism during the 2000s, Japan seems to recognize a greater imperative of supporting the normative order propounded by the United States, to forestall normative challenges and shifts that would alter the nature of the regional and international order itself. In so doing, Japan's aims go beyond supporting US preponderance in that they focus upon sustaining the broader international order led by the United States. This indicates Japan's developing vanguardist role in potentially ensuring that hegemonic institutions outlast the power advantage of the hegemon itself.[15] Yet Tokyo's stance will depend absolutely upon the certainty of continued US commitment to the region and US leadership of the hierarchy. Japan's strategy also contains a strong element of resistance, to which we now turn.

RESISTANCE

It would be a mistake to read from the above discussion that hierarchical orders are generically stable and self-perpetuating. As this book makes clear, complicity is always accompanied by resistance in super-/subordinate relationships. The study of political resistance is deeply influenced by poststructuralist perspectives, which stress Foucault's position that resistance is inscribed into power relations as 'an irreducible opposite' and thus there is a 'multiplicity of points of resistance...present everywhere in the power network'.[16] Without necessarily resorting to this extreme, at the most basic level, we would expect hierarchical resistance to take the form of infringements of the social contract represented by the dynamics of assurance and deference discussed above. We would also expect resistance to be more prevalent 'upwards' than 'downwards' within the hierarchy, as subordinates react against the powerful.[17]

As power transition theorists emphasize, superordinate states may resist challenges posed by subordinates against the existing rank and normative order. Such 'downwards' resistance could take the form of politico-military containment or even pre-emptive war to hold at bay or destroy a potential hegemonic challenger. But it might also consist of institutional, economic, or discursive strategies to circumscribe, isolate, limit, or end attempts to compete with or replace their material and normative dominance. The analysis in this book shows the United States as incumbent superpower after

---

[15] Keohane 1984.
[16] Foucault 1976, 94.
[17] In much the same way as Barnett and Duvall 2005, 22–3, in their path-breaking work, suggest that specific forms of resistance mirror their categories of compulsory, institutional, structural, and productive power.

Conclusion: The Hierarchical East Asian Order

the Cold War consistently exercising downward resistance against potential challenges so as to maintain its dominant position and its favoured order. In military terms, the United States has been able to neutralize the potential threats to its position from Japan via a stronger alliance, and from China by encircling and deterring it with allied and friendly states that support American preponderance. In institutional terms, it has resisted moves towards East Asian regionalism that might exclude non-Asian states by promoting 'open regionalism' in the Asia-Pacific, using multilateral institutions as a means to consolidate and extend its preferred values, and to facilitate a 'new round of accessions to the existing order'.[18] Essentially, this category—what I term 'comprehensive containment'—refers to the business of rank and order maintenance that superordinate states are obliged to engage in, managing threats to their position and preferred norms and ideas. A more extreme form of downward resistance would be the breaking of the compact by the hegemon, a form of revolt by the rule maker itself. This type of hierarchical renegation is not studied as often as upward revolts, but examples would be found in the variety of historical instances of crumbling empires, for instance. But this book shows that despite worries about the delegitimating effects of the George W. Bush administration's actions and rhetoric, the danger of hegemonic renegation was never large in East Asia where there was ready complicity even with his agenda.

Traditionally, 'upward' resistance receives more attention in International Relations. Here, we may distinguish between two types of resistance in hierarchical orders: resistance as constraint (to 'tame' unequal power), as opposed to resistance as revolt (to overthrow the dominant or a higher-ranking power). Constraint and revolt are distinguished by their different effects on the hierarchy itself and therefore the order associated with it. The analysis in this book focuses significantly upon how subordinate states have tried to constrain or 'tame' the great powers by institutional 'binding'. As demonstrated in the case of China and ASEAN in the South China Sea disputes, superordinate states may engage in self-binding, but the element of resistance comes to the fore at points when subordinate states wish to increase these constraints on the more powerful. Another common form of upward constraint is normative censure. At times when the superordinate power is perceived to have flouted the terms of the contract allowing complicity, subordinate states may advance serious criticism and political opposition to its actions. These would censure the powerful state on normative grounds and would seek to delegitimize its actions, encouraging wider opposition and imposing political costs. The aim would be to persuade the superordinate

---

[18] Clark 2001, 183.

state to change its policy, since such opposition affects the legitimacy and ultimately the security of the superordinate state's special role. Within the renegotiation of East Asia's post-Cold War order, normative censure has been common at multiple levels: by smaller states towards China regarding its unilateral assertions of authority, by South Korea and China towards Japan regarding collective memory, and by China and many others towards US actions. Popularized by the debate on 'soft balancing', such policies indirectly constrain superordinate states by increasing the frictional forces that can 'delay, frustrate, and undermine' their agenda.[19]

The foregoing analysis spotlights particularly the dynamics of resistance in the *'short' vertical* realm, where East Asian great powers have resisted each other's potential rank elevation both by military modernization and alliance strengthening, and by competitive promotion and leadership of regional security institutions. Notably, China deploys wide-ranging modes of resistance against US hegemony and Japan's rank-seeking within the existing hierarchy. At one end of the spectrum, Chinese leaders have evinced clear ambitions to remove—if not explicitly to replace—the United States as the dominant state, whether in its harsh criticisms of US 'hegemony' and alliances in the Asia-Pacific in the early 1990s, or in laying the groundwork for a potential structural revolt in building loose coalitions with BRICS emergent economies and developing countries in issue areas such as global financial governance and climate change negotiations. Most worrying for many observers is China's growing military expenditure and modernization, and the People's Liberation Army's developing asymmetrical warfare and area denial strategies for the vital littoral areas of East Asia—much of which appears to be targeted at undermining superior US war-fighting capabilities in this theatre.[20] As shown in my analysis, though, in practice when China has attempted directly to challenge US military dominance in the region, it has met with very limited success. The key example is the way in which more assertive Chinese action to push the United States, Japan, and other regional claimants out of contested maritime territories since 2009 has engendered strong collective resistance from the United States and other regional states. The plethora of Chinese resistance activity tends towards more indirect means of resistance though constraint.[21] Beijing favours normative censure,

---

[19] Pape 2005, 10.

[20] American scholars have also increasingly emphasized the ideological elements of nationalist ambition providing additional purpose for potential deployments of China's growing material capabilities—see Ross 2009; Friedberg 2011.

[21] Indeed, even Chinese attempts to expand the club of world leaders through channels like the BRICS may be read primarily as voice creation opportunities within the existing order—or, as Schweller and Pu 2011, 52–4, observe, instances of 'rightful resistance' within the domestic context, 'in which weak actors partially accept the legitimacy of the hegemon but seize opportunities to grow and contest perceived injustice'.

Conclusion: The Hierarchical East Asian Order

for instance in trying to delegitimize Washington and stigmatize its neighbours for developing security partnerships with an antagonistic, outdated 'Cold War mentality'. The Chinese leadership has also pursued indirect means of undermining US imperatives in areas of strategic importance for China, such as in dealing with the region's 'rogue states', North Korea and Myanmar. As illustrated in conflict management, Beijing has strived to keep Pyongyang out of the US-led international and regional order by supplying food and energy to sustain the regime and its ability to resist US-led pressures.

But it is the middle sections of the hierarchy, in the fudged area where China, Japan, and South Korea overlap, where the dynamics of mutual resistance are most obvious. Towards Japan, which Chinese leaders regard as ranking below China in the regional hierarchy, Beijing has been more forthcoming in resisting potential rank elevation. Hence the strenuous Chinese opposition to Tokyo's bid for a permanent seat on the UN Security Council, as well as suspicion and criticism of potential revisions to its constitution that would allow Japan to play a more significant security role. For its part, Japan has generally avoided overt balancing or rank contest to displace China's position in the regional hierarchy, preferring to rely on its alliance guarantee with the United States as the ultimate deterrence of potential Chinese antagonism. These limits to Japan's willingness to antagonize Beijing are shared by others: for instance, the fledgling trilateral and quadrilateral security dialogues between the United States and its allies in the region have not developed significantly because the latter are deeply unwilling to antagonize China by creating the impression of formal encirclement. But Japan has resisted China's rank consolidation through 'institutional racing' and competitive regional aid and investment programmes. At the same time, rank competition between Japan and the ROK—seen for instance in their failure to see through even a fairly routine intelligence sharing initiative in 2012—limits their potential ability to jointly constrain China's rank elevation within the hierarchy.

Nevertheless, great power resistance in the short vertical realm has inbuilt limitations because of the layered nature of the hierarchy. For instance, if the processes of hierarchical assurance and deference were to operate absolutely, there ought not to be regional contestation over rival security institutions or membership of particular groupings—all subordinate states in the hierarchy ought to support and desire clear US-led institutions. Yet these states' perceived need to enmesh China into the regional order while retaining US leadership creates tensions that pit hegemonic complicity dynamics against the broader need to assure China its place within the regional order. The upside of the reliance on the US hegemon principally to contain China, though, is that there is no need for the other middle-ranking powers—Japan and perhaps South

Korea—to overdo their resistance. At heart, therefore, the prevalent dynamics of resistance at the middle levels do not challenge the existing hierarchy itself.

For any study of transition, the types of resistance that are most significant in terms of challenging the existing hierarchical order are ones which entail direct rank competition, direct or indirect normative challenges, or defection. This type of upward resistance, which I term 'revolt', is noticeably absent in the survey of post-Cold War East Asia conducted in this book. In theory, such revolt may take the following forms. First, the type of systemic revolt favoured by neo-realists, concentrating on direct assaults against the existing power hierarchy using instruments of military balancing, coalition formation, and ultimately systemic war to overthrow superordinate states. Second, institutional revolutions, in the form of major changes to the 'rules of the game', alterations to the agenda and nature of institutions, and/or the use of institutions for new purposes. Third, structural revolts akin to Gramsci's 'wars of position',[22] which would see the forging of coalitions across different subordinate groups of states to take solidaristic action to challenge the existing 'common sense' about international order.[23] Finally, a normative revolution would be represented by attempts to replace the existing normative order, or to resist 'productive' power by destabilizing actors' identities in ways that would undermine the existing hierarchy.[24] Examples of the latter would include overturning the notion that a 'normal' great power is necessarily one that must possess military superiority, or statehood as a prerequisite for full membership in international institutions. The difference between constraining and revolutionary forms of resistance in hierarchical orders is worth reiterating. Thus far, there has been no evidence of the latter form of resistance in East Asia, but the balance of tensions may conceivably reach a tipping point in future after which resistance is no longer about restraint only, but begins to focus on revolution, or the overthrow of the hegemon and/or the existing order. This discussion serves to provide indicators of what would constitute such a challenge to the regional layered hegemonic order itself, in contrast to the usual focus on power distribution and transition.

Further Research

Apart from making greater sense of the complex empirical material, conceiving of a hegemonic and hierarchical order in contemporary East Asia helps

---

[22] Gramsci 1971, 229–30. See also Cox 1983.

[23] An example would be China building bridges between itself and emergent and developing countries, trying to form loose coalitions in global governance reform negotiations.

[24] This derives from Foucauldian notions of productive power residing in broader social processes and practices that produce subjectivities and subjects' identities, and render them 'normal' and 'natural'.

Conclusion: The Hierarchical East Asian Order

to clarify a number of critical puzzles that have dogged the literature, and to reveal more salient questions for further research.

To begin with, there are two diametrically opposite ways to read my conclusion that power transition has not occurred in East Asia since the end of the Cold War. The first response is to focus on the processes of contestation and resistance, and to argue that these forces will gain traction over time: US hegemony will face steady and inevitable erosion; and the growing ideational prowess of China and other East Asian states, domestic resistance, and eventual revolt will determine the speed of the ultimate power transition. The alternative reading—the one supported here—is that the US-led hegemonic order will be reproduced for some time by the complex layers of complicity and partial resistance that does not challenge its fundamentals and that ends up being co-opted. The co-optation of rising China and East Asia into this hierarchical structure will strengthen the existing order, if not necessarily the hegemon. For those who see some value in my interpretation, the challenge then is to push beyond the empirical legwork and informed observation presented here that US hegemony has been established in post-Cold War East Asia. Too many pundits stop at the observation that China and other rising powers have failed to provide a grand strategic alternative or grand normative vision to replace that of the United States. Yet the more productive question is: has anything else changed within the parameters of US hegemony? The answer in this book is a detailed and resounding 'yes'. Moreover, my hierarchy framework suggests that the East Asian order transition now requires ever more subtle and potentially more costly negotiation and management. In this regard, three research areas require further attention.

First, on the social dynamics of maintaining US hegemony: how does the hierarchical nature of the current order affect US strategies of preponderance and leadership? My hierarchical order framework explains why those looking out for balancing behaviour against the United States after the Cold War have been barking up the wrong tree. Yet the absence of balancing does not mean that US hegemony is secure. Rather, understanding the social dimensions of power and recognizing the painful normative renegotiations that have led to this interim social structure highlight the constant struggle of legitimizing and taming this extreme preponderance of power. Sustaining hegemony in East Asia turns on Washington's ability to cultivate complicity and manage resistance. It faces the imperative of ensuring that its assurance strategies work both at the 'short' and 'long' vertical realms, and towards the twin constituencies of allies and potential adversaries. How have US alliance relationships in East Asia been renegotiated during this order transition? Do allies have a different type of social compact that sits apart from the regional one? What are the interactions between these unequal partnerships and the developing hierarchical regional order? Do these special relationships offer US allies special status within the regional hierarchy, and to what effect?

As China's power grows, Washington will need to pay more attention to how to extend assurance to and resist potential rank challenges from China. A large part of this task, though, should probably begin at home, with hard questions about the extent to which US leaders and strategists are willing to take on board the type of hegemonic assurance I suggest is critical in the 'short' vertical realm. Extending China great power recognition, rank assurance, and leadership opportunities within the existing order is a challenge that successive US administrations have elided since the end of the Cold War. Within the massive literature on United States–China relations is a significant lack of research on whether and how Washington has tried to renegotiate a strategic bargain with China in the current order transition. At the risk of generalization, the literature and discourse are dominated by realists who fear that 'an illiberal China [will] displace us as the preponderant player in Asia' and liberals who stress the importance of 'accommodat[ing] China by offering it status and position within the regional order in return for Beijing's acceptance and accommodation of Washington's core strategic interests', but do not see the problems entailed when these core interests include the United States 'remaining a dominant security provider within East Asia'.[25] As my hierarchical framework bluntly illustrates, the latter amounts to demanding that China be integrated as second-ranked power within a hegemonic US order. This is not necessarily impossible, but it will require vastly more significant American efforts at convincing and persuading Beijing why it ought to do so, rather than simply expecting Chinese decision-makers to fall into line. In other words, there is an urgent need to investigate the extent to which the United States as hegemon has been and may be open to socialization into an international order that privileges legitimacy and negotiated power sharing.

Yet we should not overestimate a hegemon's control or activism, or underestimate the conservatism of incumbent dominant powers. We tend to ascribe to hegemons more and more constant influence and control than they realistically wield or want to wield, especially in fraught and overworked periods of transition when policy agendas are fiercely contested domestically and priorities need to be set in global strategic policy. As is clear from this book, the trajectory of order renegotiation in East Asia has been set just as much by periods of US benign neglect, when it took its eye off the ball or when its attention was focused elsewhere, as it has been by the deliberate application of US hegemonic aims and agenda.

---

[25] Friedberg 2011, 8; Ikenberry 2011, 356.

Conclusion: The Hierarchical East Asian Order

The second focus for future research is thus the ripe arena of great power rank and status competition at the second and third tiers of the hierarchical order. Even assuming the sustainability of US hegemony on the basis of continued complicity from its supporter states in the region, these processes of rank competition, assurance, and integration will present the most important sources of order renegotiation in East Asia. The challenge will be how to analyse these dynamics in a useful way.

One obvious area that needs more careful work is Japan's vital role in the central East Asian strategic triangle. My analysis explains why Japan has not yet 'normalized' and suggests that this is unlikely to happen as long as US commitment to leading the regional hierarchy is assured. The nub is, of course, what form of and how much reassurance are necessary for Japan. Moreover, to what extent is Japan's unresolved regional identity and continued moral alienation from its immediate neighbours an impediment or a necessity to the existing hierarchical order? What other forms of subtler order maintenance is Tokyo engaged in to help perpetuate the existing hegemonic order? Might we conceivably contemplate a further order transition that involves the passing of the United States as hegemon but not the destruction of the normative order, in which Japan is critical?

This book also shows that searching for outright balancing behaviour against China in East Asia is not the most useful exercise. As the main rising power in the region, China has been working hardest on assurance, in order to gain the recognition and status that buy neighbouring states' complicity in integrating China into the existing hierarchy. Beijing's priority thus far has been to resist potential threats to its economic development imperative, but this has not prevented it from trying at the same time to constrain the more objectionable elements of US leadership and strategic imperatives, and Japanese rank-seeking. However, China has largely resisted both in indirect ways, aimed at undermining, rechannelling, or diluting their effects, rather than revolting against the existing order. Overall, China continues to face the imperative of 'long' and 'short' vertical assurance if it wishes to direct its resources and energies to national development. Thus deference to regional and international norms, muting conflicts, limited cooperation with Japan, and selective deference to US leadership will remain important parts of Beijing's strategy. However, we may confidently expect China to act more assertively to resist attempts to exclude it or demote it within the regional hierarchy, and to hold on to its entitlement to special status as the second-ranked but regionally legitimate power. In this regard, the most fruitful focus for research will be the evolving domestic debates within China. Chinese thinking and internal debates about future preferences and ambitions will escalate as China's material power and reach expand. The increasingly complex domestic political climate within China makes the outcome of these discursive contests difficult to predict.[26] But scholars should remain vigilant for how these Chinese debates are shaped significantly by the socio-structural context of choices and preferences of neighbouring states, whose overwhelming complicity with the US-led order renders the material and social costs of potential revolt for China particularly high.

The third and final avenue for further investigation relates to non-great power states within hierarchical orders. Their key challenge regarding unequal power is how to accept the privileges accorded great powers while maximizing the available leverage and ensuring sufficient autonomy to achieve their security and developmental imperatives. My proposed East Asian hierarchy will not be popular with most South Koreans or Southeast Asians, but the shared nature of their nation-building and integration imperatives is a clear reason why these states occupy a particular layer in the regional hierarchy. Future research should concentrate on the interactions between these existential and identity agendas and the strategic choices and innovations made by such states. Within East Asia, there is a special need to analyse the unfinished business of Korean reunification through longer lenses of regional order transition, and to pay attention to specific Southeast Asian countries that are emerging as more decisive or pivotal strategic actors outside the institutional framework of ASEAN.

Ultimately, this book reveals the complex renegotiation of the social compact within post-Cold War East Asia that has consolidated US hegemony, and integrated China and other regional states within a layered social hierarchy. Undeniably, the region has seen changes in the distribution of power, but most crucial thus far have been the normative renegotiations underscoring the authority of US leadership and its associated normative structures, the legitimate accommodation and binding of rising powers, and the satisfaction of the insecurities of the smaller states. The dynamics of complicity have been more marked than those of resistance because of a broad collective belief in the hegemonic commitment and in the East Asian powers' collective inability and unwillingness to forge an alternative, costlier structure. All this points to an overarching conservatism in the East Asian strategic landscape. Yet this may prove to be but a conservative interregnum. Any consensus reached is often uneasy: there has been more process than outcome thus far, and regional order in East Asia is likely to remain transitional for a long time. In the meantime, the demands on and potential stress points within the evolving hierarchical order are considerable. We shall be able to judge the strength and authority of this renegotiated social compact only when it has faced the significant tests that lie ahead.

---

[26] On the contested landscape of Chinese strategic thinking, see Schweller and Pu 2011, 57–70; Shambaugh 2011.

Bibliography

Acharya, Amitav. 1997a. Ideas, Identity, and Institution-building: From the 'ASEAN Way' to the 'Asia-Pacific Way'. *Pacific Review 10* (3): 319–49.
Acharya, Amitav. 1997b. *The ASEAN Regional Forum: Confidence-Building*. Ottawa: Department of Foreign Affairs and International Trade.
Acharya, Amitav. 2001. *Constructing a Security Community in Southeast Asia: ASEAN and the Problem of Regional Order*. London: Routledge.
Acharya, Amitav. 2003. Regional Institutions and Asian Security Order: Norms, Power, and Prospects for Peaceful Change. In *Asian Security Order: Instrumental and Normative Features*, edited by Muthiah Alagappa, 210–40. Stanford: Stanford University Press.
Acharya, Amitav. 2009a. *Whose Ideas Matter? Agency and Power in Asian Regionalism* (Ithaca: Cornell University Press, 2009).
Acharya, Amitav. 2009b. The Strong in the World of the Weak: Southeast Asia in Asia's Regional Architecture. In *Asia's New Multilateralism: Cooperation, Competition, and the Search for Community*, edited by Michael J. Green and Bates Gill, 172–92. New York: Columbia University Press.
Acharya, Amitav. 2011. Can Asia Lead? Power Ambitions and Global Governance in the Twenty-First Century. *International Affairs 87* (4): 851–69.
Acharya, Amitav and Evelyn Goh, eds. 2007. *Reassessing Security Cooperation in the Asia-Pacific: Competition, Congruence, and Transformation*. Cambridge, MA: MIT Press.
Acharya, Amitav and See Seng Tan. 2006. Betwixt Balance and Community: America, ASEAN, and the Security of Southeast Asia. *International Relations of the Asia-Pacific 6* (1): 37–59.
Aggarwal, Vinod K. and Min Gyo Koo. 2008. *Asia's New Institutional Architecture: Evolving Structures for Managing Trade, Financial, and Security Relations*. Berlin: Springer-Verlag.
Alagappa, Muthiah, ed. 2003. *Asian Security Order: Instrumental and Normative Features*. Stanford: Stanford University Press.
Alagappa, Muthiah. 2003. Constructing Security Order in Asia. In *Asian Security Order: Instrumental and Normative Features*, edited by Muthiah Alagappa, 72–8. Stanford: Stanford University Press.
Allen, Matthew. 2002. *Identity and Resistance in Okinawa*. Lanham: Rowman & Littlefield.
Almonte, Jose. 1997/8. Ensuring the 'ASEAN Way'. *Survival 39* (4): 80–92.
Altbach, Eric. 1997. The Asian Monetary Fund Proposal: A Case Study of Japanese Regional Leadership. In *JEI Report No. 47*. Washington DC: Japan Economic Institute.

Bibliography

Amyx, Jennifer. 2004. Japan and the Evolution of Regional Financial Arrangements in East Asia. In *Beyond Bilateralism: U.S.–Japan Relations in the New Asia-Pacific*, edited by Ellis S. Krauss and T. J. Pempel, 198–220. Stanford: Stanford University Press.

Amyx, Jennifer. 2008. Regional Financial Cooperation in East Asia since the Asian Financial Crisis. In *Crisis as Catalyst: Asia's Dynamic Political Economy*, edited by Andrew Macintyre, T. J. Pempel, and John Ravenhill, 117–39. Ithaca: Cornell University Press.

APEC. 1995. *The Osaka Action Plan: Road Map to Realising the APEC Vision, Report of the Pacific Business Forum 1995*. Singapore: APEC Secretariat.

Arase, David. 2010. Japanese Security Policy: From Soft to Hard Power. In *The U.S.–Japan Alliance: Balancing Soft and Hard Power in East Asia*, edited by David Arase and Tsuneo Akaha, 35–57. Abingdon: Routledge.

Armacost, Michael and Kenneth Pyle. 2001. Japan and the Unification of Korea: Challenges for U.S. Policy Coordination. In *Korea's Future and the Great Powers*, edited by Nicholas Eberstadt and Richard Ellings, 125–63. Seattle: University of Washington Press.

ASEAN. 1995. *The ASEAN Regional Forum: A Concept Paper*. Jakarta: ASEAN Secretariat.

ASEAN. 2002. *Final Report of the East Asia Study Group*. ASEAN+3 Summit, 4 November. Available at <http://www.asean.org/images/archive/pdf/easg.pdf>. Accessed 6 March 2013.

ASEAN-ISIS. 1991. *A Time for Initiative: Proposals for the Consideration of the Fourth ASEAN Summit* (4 June). Jakarta: ASEAN Institutes of Strategic and International Studies.

ASEAN Secretariat. 1992. *ASEAN Declaration on the South China Sea*. 22 July, Manila. Available at <http://cil.nus.edu.sg/1992/1992-asean-declaration-on-the-south-china-sea-signed-on-22-july-1992-in-manila-philippines-by-the-foreign-ministers/>. Accessed 6 March 2013.

ASEAN Secretariat. 2009. *ASEAN Plus Three Cooperation* (January). Available at < http://www.asean.org/images/archive/22206.pdf>. Accessed 6 March 2013.

Ashizawa, Kuniko. 2008. When Identity Matters: State Identity, Regional Institution-Building, and Japanese Foreign Policy. *International Studies Review 10*: 571–98.

Athurokala, Prema-chandra and Hal Hill. 2010. Asian Trade and Investment: Patterns and Trends. In *The Rise of Asia: Trade and Investment in Global Perspective*, edited by Prema-chandra Athukorala, 11–57. London: Routledge.

Athukorala, Prema-chandra and Nobuaki Yamashita. 2008. Patterns and Determinants of Production Fragmentation in World Manufacturing Trade. In *Globalisation, Regionalism and Economic Interdependence*, edited by Filippo do Mauro, Stephanie Dees, and Warwick McKibbin, 45–72. Cambridge: Cambridge University Press.

Atlantic Council Working Group on North Korea. 2007. *A Framework for Peace and Security in Korea and Northeast Asia* (April). Washington: Atlantic Council.

Augelli, Enrico and Craig Murphy. 1993. Gramsci and International Relations: A General Perspective and Example from Recent US Policy toward the Third World. In *Historical Materialism and International Relations*, edited by Stephen Gill, 127–47. Cambridge: Cambridge University Press.

Ba, Alice. 2003. China and ASEAN: Re-navigating Relations for a 21st Century Asia. *Asian Survey 43* (4): 630–8.

Bibliography

Ba, Alice. 2009. *[Re]Negotiating East and Southeast Asia: Region, Regionalism, and the Association of Southeast Asian Nations*. Stanford: Stanford University Press.

Babicz, Lionel. 2009. South Korea, Japan, and China: In Search of a Shared Historical Awareness. In *Global Korea: Old and New: Proceedings of the Sixth Biennial Conference Korean Studies Association of Australasia*, edited by Duk-soo Park, 115–27. Sydney: University of Sydney.

Baker, James. 1991/2. America in Asia: Emerging Architecture for a Pacific Community. *Foreign Affairs 70* (5): 1–18.

Baker, James. 1992. *Statement at the ASEAN–U.S. Dialogue Session*, Manila, Philippines, 26 July.

Baker, James and Thomas DeFrank. 1995. *The Politics of Diplomacy: Revolution, War, and Peace, 1989–1992*. New York: Putnam's.

Baker, Richard. 1998. The United States and APEC Regime Building. In *Asia-Pacific Crossroads: Regime Creation and the Future of APEC*, edited by Vinod Aggarwal and Charles Morrison, 165–89. New York: St. Martin's Press.

Banlaoi, Rommel C. 2002. The Role of Philippine–American Relations in the Global Campaign Against Terrorism: Implications for Regional Security. *Contemporary Southeast Asia 24* (2): 294–312.

Barmé, Geremie. 1993. History for the Masses. In *Using the Past to Serve the Present: Historiography and Politics in Contemporary China*, edited by Jonathan Unger, 260–86. Armonk: M. E. Sharpe.

Barnett, Michael and Raymond Duvall, eds. 2005. *Power in Global Governance*. Cambridge: Cambridge University Press.

Baviera, Aileen. 2012. The Influence of Domestic Politics on Philippine Foreign Policy: The Case of Philippines–China Relations since 2004. *RSIS Working Paper* 241 (5 June). Singapore: Rajaratnam School of International Studies.

Beckman, Robert. 2010. South China Sea: Worsening Disputes or Growing Clarity in Claims? *RSIS Commentary* (16 August).

Beckman, Robert. 2011. China, UNCLOS and the South China Sea. Paper presented to the Asian Society of International Law Third Biennial Conference, August, Beijing. Available at <http://cil.nus.edu.sg/wp/wp-content/uploads/2009/09/AsianSIL-Beckman-China-UNCLOS-and-the-South-China-Sea-26-July-2011.pdf>. Accessed 12 September 2012.

Beckman, Robert. 2012. Geopolitics, International Law and the South China Sea. Paper presented at the Trilateral Commission Plenary Meeting, April, Tokyo.

Beckman, Robert and Tara Davenport. 2010. CLCS Submissions and Claims in the South China Sea. Paper presented to the Second International Workshop on 'The South China Sea: Cooperation for Regional Security and Development', November, Ho Chi Minh City. Available at <http://cil.nus.edu.sg/wp/wp-content/uploads/2009/09/Beckman-Davenport-CLCS-HCMC-10-12Nov2010-1.pdf>. Accessed 12 September 2012.

Beeson, Mark. 2000. Mahathir and the Markets: Globalisation and the Pursuit of Economic Autonomy in Malaysia. *Pacific Affairs 73* (3): 335–51.

Beeson, Mark and Iyanatul Islam. 2005. Neo-liberalism and East Asia: Resisting the Washington Consensus. *Journal of Development Studies 41* (2): 197–219.

Bibliography

Bell, David. 1975. *Power, Influence, and Authority*. Oxford: Oxford University Press.

Benedict, Ruth. 1946. *The Chrysanthemum and the Sword: Patterns of Japanese Culture*. Boston: Houghton Mifflin.

Berger, Thomas U. 2002. The Power of Memory and Memories of Power: The Cultural Parameters of German Foreign Policy-Making since 1945. In *Memory and Power in Post-War Europe: Studies in the Presence of the Past*, edited by Jan-Werner Müller, 76–99. Cambridge: Cambridge University Press.

Berger, Thomas U. 2008. Dealing with Difficult Pasts: Japan's 'History Problem' from a Theoretical and Comparative Perspective. In *East Asia's Haunted Present: Historical Memories and the Resurgence of Nationalism*, edited by Tsuyoshi Hasegawa and Kazuhiko Togo, 17–41. Westport: Praeger.

Bernard, Mitchell and John Ravenhill. 1995a. Beyond Product Cycles and Flying Geese: Regionalization, Hierarchy, and the Industrialization of East Asia. *World Politics 47*: 171–209.

Bernard, Mitchell and John Ravenhill. 1995b. The Pursuit of Competitiveness in East Asia: Regionalization of Production and Its Consequences. In *National Competitiveness in a Global Economy*, edited by David Rapkin and William Avery, 103–31. Boulder: Lynne Rienner.

Best, Jacqueline. 2003. From the Top Down: The New Financial Architecture and the Re-Embedding of Global Finance. *New Political Economy 8* (3): 363–84.

Betts, Richard K. 1993/4. Wealth, Power and Instability: East Asia and the United States after the Cold War. *International Security 18* (3): 34–77.

Bhagwati, Jagdish and Hugh Patrick, eds. 1990. *Aggressive Unilateralism: America's 301 Trade Policy and the World Trading System*. Ann Arbor: University of Michigan Press.

Bobrow, Davis. 1999. Hegemony Management: The U.S. in the Asia-Pacific. *Pacific Review 12* (2): 173–97.

Boister, Neil and Robert Cryer. 2008. *The Tokyo International Military Tribunal: A Reappraisal*. Oxford: Oxford University Press.

Borodziej, Wlodzimierz. 2003. The German–Polish Textbook Dialogue. In *Sharing the Burden of the Past: Legacies of War in Europe, America and Asia*, edited by Andrew Horvat and Gebhard Hielscher, 35–8. Tokyo: Asia Foundation.

Borrus, Michael. 1997. Left for Dead: Asian Production Networks and the Revival of U.S. Electronics. In *The China Circle: Economics and Electronics in the PRC, Taiwan, and Hong Kong*, edited by Barry Naughton, 136–63. Washington DC: Brookings.

Borrus, Michael. 2000. The Resurgence of U.S. Electronics: Asian Production Networks and the Rise of Wintelism. In *International Production Networks in Asia: Rivalry or Riches*, edited by Michael Borrus, Dieter Ernst, and Stephen Haggard, 56–78. London: Routledge.

Bowles, Paul. 1997. ASEAN, AFTA and the 'New Regionalism'. *Pacific Affairs 70* (2): 219–34.

Breen, John, ed. 2008. *Yasukuni, the War Dead, and the Struggle for Japan's Past*. New York: Columbia University Press.

Breslin, Shaun. 2006. Theorising East Asian Regionalism(s). In *Advancing East Asian Regionalism*, edited by Melissa Curley and Nick Thomas, 26–51. London: Routledge.

Breslin, Shaun. 2007. An Alternative Look at the Forces Driving East Asian Community Building. *Policy Analysis Brief*, Stanley Foundation. Available at <http://www.stanleyfoundation.org/policyanalysis.cfm?id=268>. Accessed 20 August 2012.
Breslin, Shaun. 2007. *China and the Gobal Political Economy*. Basingstoke: Palgrave-Macmillan.
Breslin, Shaun. 2010. Comparative Theory, China, and the Future of East Asian Regionalism(S). *Review of International Studies* 36: 709–129.
Breslin, Shaun. 2011. East Asia and the Global/Transatlantic/Western Crisis. *Contemporary Politics* 17 (2): 109–17.
Brinkley, Douglas. 1998. *The Unfinished Presidency: Jimmy Carter's Quest for World Peace*. New York: Penguin.
Brooks, Stephen G. and William W. Wohlforth. 2008. *World Out of Balance: International Relations and the Challenge of American Primacy*. Princeton: Princeton University Press.
Brown, Gordon. 2010. *Beyond the Crash: Overcoming the First Crisis of Globalisation*. New York: Simon & Schuster.
Browne, Marjorie Ann. 2004. The Law of the Sea Convention and U.S. Policy. *Congressional Research Service* Issue Brief (2 June). Washington DC: U.S. Congress.
Bu, Ping. 2011. Zhongri gongtong lishi yanjiu zhong de lilun yu fangfa wenti [Theoretical and Methodological Issues in Sino-Japanese Joint History Research]. *Kangri zhanzheng yanjiu [The Journal of Studies on China's War of Resistance against Japan]* 1: 5–12.
Bukovansky, Mlada, Ian Clark, Robyn Eckersley, Richard Price, Christian Reus-Smit, and Nicholas Wheeler. 2012. *Special Responsibilities: Global Problems and American Power*. Cambridge: Cambridge University Press.
Bull, Benedicte. 1999. 'New Regionalism' in Central America. *Third World Quarterly* 20 (5): 957–70.
Bull, Hedley. 1977. *The Anarchical Society: A Study of Order in World Politics*. London: Macmillan.
Bull, Hedley. 2002. *The Anarchical Society: A Study of Order in World Politics*. 3rd edn. Basingstoke: Palgrave Macmillan.
Bull, Hedley and Adam Watson, eds. 1984. *The Expansion of International Society*. Oxford: Clarendon Press.
Bush, Richard C. 2004. *At Cross Purposes: U.S.–Taiwan Relations since 1942*. Armonk: M. E. Sharpe.
Busse, Nikolas. 1999. Constructivism and Southeast Asian Security. *Pacific Review* 12 (1): 39–60.
Buszynski, Leszek. 2003. ASEAN, the Declaration on Conduct, and the South China Sea. *Contemporary Southeast Asia* 25 (3): 434–63.
Buzan, Barry. 2004. *From International to World Society? English School Theory and the Social Structure of Globalisation*. Cambridge: Cambridge University Press.
Buzan, Barry. 2008. A Leader without Followers? The United States in World Politics after Bush. *International Politics* 45 (5): 554–70.
Buzan, Barry and Ole Waever, eds. 2003. *Regions and Powers: The Structure of International Security*. Cambridge: Cambridge University Press.

Bibliography

Buzan, Barry, Charles Jones, and Richard Little. 1993. *The Logic of Anarchy*. New York: Columbia University Press.

Calder, Kent. 1988. Japanese Foreign Policy Formation: Explaining the Reactive State. *World Politics 40* (4): 517–47.

Carlson, Allen. 2005. *Unifying China, Integrating the World: Securing Chinese Sovereignty in the Reform Era*. Stanford: Stanford University Press.

Carter, Ashton B., William J. Perry, and John D. Steinbruner. 1992. *A New Concept of Cooperative Security*. Washington DC: Brookings.

Cha, Victor. 2007. Winning Asia: Washington's Untold Story. *Foreign Affairs 86* (6): 98–113.

Cha, Victor. 2009/10. Powerplay: Origins of the U.S. Alliance System in Asia. *International Security 34* (3): 158–96.

Cha, Victor. 2011. Complex Patchworks: US Alliances as Part of Asia's Regional Architecture. *Asia Policy 11*: 27–50.

Cha, Victor. 2012. *The Impossible State: North Korea, Past and Future*. London: Bodley Head.

Cha, Victor D. and David C. Kang. 2003. *Nuclear North Korea: A Debate on Engagement Strategies*. New York: Columbia University Press.

Chan, Steve. 2004. Exploring Puzzles in Power Transition Theory: Implications for Sino-American Relations. *Security Studies 13* (3): 103–41.

Chatterjee, Partha. 2005. *The Politics of the Governed*. New York: Columbia University Press.

Chen, Lifei and Su Zhiliang. 2000. Zhongguo 'wei'anfu' wenti guoji xueshu yantao hui zongshu kuozhan gongneng [Review of the International Symposium on China's 'Comfort Women' Problem]. *Lishi Yanjiu [Historical Research]* 3.

Chey, Hyoung-kyu. 2009. The Changing Political Dynamics of East Asian Financial Cooperation: The Chiang Mai Initiative. *Asian Survey 49* (3): 450–67.

Chin, Gregory T. 2010. Remaking the Architecture: The Emerging Powers, Self-Insuring and Regional Insulation. *International Affairs 86* (3): 693–715.

Chin, Gregory T. 2011. Mediating Financial Instability: China, the BRICS and Continuing Rise. In *Global Economic Crises: National Response and Geopolitical Implications*, edited by John Kirton, Chiara Oldani, and Paolo Savano, 89–108. Aldershot: Ashgate.

Chinkin, Christine. 2001. Women's International Tribunal on Japanese Military Sexual Slavery. *American Journal of International Law 95* (2): 335–41.

Chong, Chin-song. 2004. *Ilbon'gun Song Noyeje: Ilbon'gun Wianbu munje ui silsang kwa ku haegyol ul wihan undong [Japanese Military Sexual Slavery: The Realities of the Comfort Women Problem and Movements toward a Solution]*. Seoul: Seoul National University Press.

Christensen, Thomas J. 1999. China, the US–Japan Alliance, and the Security Dilemma in East Asia. *International Security 23* (4): 49–80.

Chung, Chien-peng. 2010. *China's Multilateral Cooperation in Asia and the Pacific: Institutionalising Beijing's 'Good Neighbour Policy'*. Abingdon: Routledge.

Chung, Jae-Ho. 2006. China and the Korean Peninsula: From Interest Revaluation to Strategic Realignment. In *Power Shift: China and Asia's New Dynamics*, edited by David Shambaugh, 151–69. Berkeley: University of California Press.

Chung, Jae-jeong. 2011. Historical Conflict and Dialogue between Korea and Japan: A Focus on Japanese History Textbooks. In *Designing History in East Asian Textbooks: Identity, Politics and Transnational Aspirations*, edited by Gotelind Müller, 207–28. Abingdon: Routledge.

Ciorciari, John D. 2011. Chiang Mai Initiative Multilateralization: International Politics and Institution-Building in Asia. *Asian Survey 51* (5): 926–52.

Clark, Ian. 1977. *The Hierarchy of States: Reform and Resistance in the International Order*. New York: Cambridge University Press.

Clark, Ian. 2001. *The Post-Cold War Order: The Spoils of Peace*. Oxford: Oxford University Press.

Clark, Ian. 2011. *Hegemony in International Society*. Oxford: Oxford University Press.

Clegg, Jenny. 2011. Korean Denuclearization: A Test for China's Cooperative Security Strategy. In *Conflict Management and Dispute Settlement in East Asia*, edited by Ramses Amer and Zou Keyuan, 127–46. Farnham: Ashgate.

Clinton, Hillary Rodham. 2010. Remarks at press availability. Hanoi, Vietnam, 23 July. Available at <http://www.state.gov/secretary/rm/2010/07/145095.htm>. Accessed 12 September 2012.

Clinton, Hillary Rodham. 2011. America's Pacific Century. *Foreign Policy 189*: 56–63.

Clinton, William J. 1993. Fundamentals of Security for a New Pacific Century. Address before the National Assembly of the Republic of Korea, Seoul, 10 July.

Congressional Research Service. 2010. Implementation of UN Security Council Resolution 1874 (11 November). Washington DC: U.S. Congress. Available at <http://nautilus.org/napsnet/napsnet-special-reports/implementation-of-u-n-security-council-resolution-1874/>. Accessed 30 October 2012.

Conrad, Sebastian. 2003. Entangled Memories: Versions of the Past in Germany and Japan, 1945–2000. *Journal of Contemporary History 38* (1): 85–99.

Coomaraswamy, Radhika. 1996. *Report on the Mission to the Democratic People's Republic of Korea, the Republic of Korea and Japan on the Issue of Military Sexual Slavery in Wartime*. UN Economic and Social Council, Commission on Human Rights.

Cooper, Andrew. 2010. The G20 as an Improvised Crisis Committee and/or a Contested 'Steering Committee' for the World. *International Affairs 6* (3): 741–57.

Corning, Gregory P. 2009. Between Bilateralism and Regionalism in East Asia: The Asean–Japan Comprehensive Economic Partnership. *The Pacific Review 22* (5): 639–65.

Cossa, Ralph A. 2009. Evolving U.S. Views on Asia's Future Institutional Architecture. In *Asia's New Multilateralism: Cooperation, Competition, and the Search for Community*, edited by Michael J. Green and Bates Gill, 33–54. New York: Columbia University Press.

Cox, Michael. 1997. Whatever Happened to the 'New World Order'? *Critique 25*: 85–95.

Cox, Robert W. 1983. Gramsci, Hegemony and International Relations: An Essay in Method. *Millennium 12* (2): 162–75.

Cox, Robert W. 1987. *Production, Power and World Order: Social Forces in the Making of History*. New York: Cambridge University Press.

Cronin, Richard. 1992. *Japan, the United States and Prospects for the Asia-Pacific Century: Three Scenarios for the Future*. Singapore: ISEAS.

Bibliography

Cumings, Bruce. 1997. Japan and Northeast Asia into the Twenty-First Century. In *Network Power: Japan and Asia*, edited by Peter Katzenstein and Takashi Shiraishi, 136–68. Ithaca: Cornell University Press.

Cumings, Bruce. 1999. The Asian Crisis, Democracy, and the End of 'Late' Development. In *The Politics of the Asian Economic Crisis*, edited by T. J. Pempel, 17–44. Ithaca: Cornell University Press.

Curley, Melissa. 2006. The Role of Civil Society in East Asian Region Building. In *Advancing East Asian Regionalism*, edited by Melissa Curley and Nick Thomas, 179–201. London: Routledge.

De Castro, Renato Cruz. 2003. The Revitalized Philippine–U.S. Security Relations. *Asian Survey 43* (6): 971–88.

De Mesquita, Bruce Bueno. 1990. Pride of Place: The Origins of German Hegemony. *World Politics 43* (1): 28–52.

De Soysa, Indra, John O'Neal, and Yong-Hee Park. 1997. Testing Power Transition Theory Using Alternative Measures of National Capabilities. *Journal of Conflict Resolution 41* (4): 509–28.

Deans, Phil. 2007. Diminishing Returns? Prime Minister Koizumi's Visits to the Yasukuni Shrine in the Context of East Asian Nationalism. *East Asia 24*: 269–94.

Deng, Yong. 1997. *Promoting Asia-Pacific Economic Cooperation: Perspectives from East Asia*. New York: St. Martin's Press.

Deng, Yong. 1998. Managing China's Hegemonic Ascension: Engagement from Southeast Asia. *Journal of Strategic Studies 21* (1): 21–43.

Dewitt, David. 1994. Common, Comprehensive, and Cooperative Security. *Pacific Review 7* (1): 1–15.

Dewitt, David and Paul Evans. 1991. *The North Pacific Cooperation Security Dialogue: Setting the Research Agenda*. Toronto: York University.

DiCicco, Jonathan M. and Jack S. Levy. 2003. The Power Transition Research Program: A Lakatosian Analysis. In *Progress in International Relations Theory: Appraising the Field*, edited by Colin Elman and Miriam Fendius, 109–58. Cambridge: Belfer Center for Science and International Affairs.

DiFilippo, Anthony. 2012. Time for North Korea Peace Treaty. *The Diplomat* (11 April).

Djalal, Hasjim. 2002. *Preventive Diplomacy in Southeast Asia: Lessons Learned*. Jakarta: Habibie Centre.

Dobson, Hugo. 2010. Japan and the Changing Global Balance of Power: The View from the Summit. *Politics 30* (1): 33–42.

Dong, Runming. 1998. Yazhou jinrong weiji: Meiguo weihe fanying chidun [The Asian Financial Crisis: Why the US Was Slow to Respond]. *Guoji zhanwang [World Outlook] 2*: 13–14.

Donnelly, Jack. 2006. Sovereign Inequalities and Hierarchy in Anarchy: American Power and International Society. *European Journal of International Relations 12* (2): 139–70.

Dower, John. 1999. *Embracing Defeat: Japan in the Aftermath of World War II*. London: Penguin.

Drennan, William. 2003. *A Comprehensive Resolution of the Korean War. United States Institute of Peace Special Report No. 106* (May). Washington: USIP.

Drezner, Daniel. 2003. The Hidden Hand of Economic Coercion. *International Organization* 57 (3): 643–59.
Drezner, Daniel. 2009. Bad Debts: Assessing China's Financial Influence in Great Power Politics. *International Security* 34 (2): 7–45.
Drysdale, Peter. 1991. *Open Regionalism: A Key to East Asia's Economic Future. Pacific Economic Papers 197*. Canberra: ANU Australia–Japan Research Centre.
Drysdale, Peter. 2005. *Regional Cooperation in East Asia and FTA Strategies. Pacific Economic Papers 355*. Canberra: ANU Australia–Japan Research Centre.
Drysdale, Peter and Shiro Armstrong. 2010. International and Regional Cooperation: Asia's Role and Responsibilities. *EABER Working Paper Series, No. 62*.
Drysdale, Peter and Ross Garnaut. 1997. The Pacific: An Application of a General Theory of Economic Integration. In *Pacific Dynamism and the International Economic System*, edited by C. Fred Bergsten and Marcus Noland, 183–224. Washington DC: Institute for International Economics.
Dudden, Alexis. 2001. 'We Came to Tell the Truth': Reflections on the Tokyo Women's Tribunal. *Critical Asian Studies* 33 (4): 591–602.
Dudden, Alexis. 2008. *Troubled Apologies Among Japan, Korea, and the United States*. New York: Columbia University Press.
Duffield, John. 2003. Asia-Pacific Security Institutions in Comparative Perspective. In *International Relations Theory and the Asia-Pacific*, edited by G. John Ikenberry and Michael Mastanduno, 243–70. New York: Columbia University Press.
Dumbrell, John. 2008. *Clinton's Foreign Policy: Between the Bushes 1992–2000*. London: Routledge.
Dunaway, Steven. 2009. *Global Imbalances and the Financial Crisis. Council for Foreign Relations Special Report 44*. New York: CFR.
Dunaway, Steven. 2011. *The G20's Continuing Policy Drift. Expert Brief* (17 February). New York: Council for Foreign Relations.
Duncan, James. 2002. Embodying Colonialism? Domination and Resistance in Nineteenth-Century Ceylonese Coffee Plantations. *Journal of Historical Geography* 28 (3): 317–38.
Dunne, Tim. 1998. *Inventing International Society: A History of the English School*. Basingstoke: Macmillan.
Dunne, Tim. 2003. Society and Hierarchy in International Relations. *International Relations* 17(3): 303–20.
Edström, Bert. 1999. *Japan's Evolving Foreign Policy Doctrine: From Yoshida to Miyazawa*. Basingstoke: Macmillan.
EEZ Group 21. 2005. *Guidelines for Navigation and Overflight in the Exclusive Economic Zone* (16 September). Tokyo: Ocean Policy Research Foundation. Available at <http://www.sof.or.jp/en/report/pdf/200509_20051205_e.pdf>. Accessed 30 October 2012.
Elms, Deborah. 2012. Getting from Here to There: Stitching Together Goods Agreements in the Trans-Pacific Partnership (TPP) Agreement. *RSIS Working Paper 235*. Singapore: Rajaratnam School of International Studies.
Elrod, Richard B. 1976. The Concert of Europe: A Fresh Look at an International System. *World Politics* 28: 159–74.

Bibliography

Emmers, Ralf. 2003. *Cooperative Security and the Balance of Power in ASEAN and the ARF.* London: Routledge Curzon.

Emmers, Ralf. 2010a. *Geopolitics and Maritime Territorial Disputes in East Asia.* London: Routledge.

Emmers, Ralf. 2010b. The Changing Distribution of Power in the South China Sea: Implications for Conflict Management and Avoidance. *Political Science 62* (2): 118–31.

Emmers, Ralf. 2013. *Resource Management and Contested Territories in East Asia.* Basingstoke: Palgrave Macmillan.

Emmers, Ralf and John Ravenhill. 2011. The Asian and Global Financial Crises: Consequences for East Asian Regionalism. *Contemporary Politics 17* (2): 133–49.

Emmerson, Donald. 2010. Asian Regionalism and U.S. Policy: The Case for Creative Adaptation. *RSIS Working Paper 193* (March).

Ernst, Dieter. 2000a. Evolutionary Aspects: The Asian Production Networks of Japanese Electronics Firms. In *International Production Networks in Asia: Rivalry or Riches*, edited by Michael Borrus, Dieter Ernst, and Stephen Haggard, 79–107. London: Routledge.

Ernst, Dieter. 2000b. What Permits David to Grow in the Shadow of Goliath? The Taiwanese Model in the Computer Industry. In *International Production Networks in Asia: Rivalry or Riches*, edited by Michael Borrus, Dieter Ernst, and Stephen Haggard, 108–38. London: Routledge.

Evans, Gareth. 1990a. Address to the Committee for the Economic Development of Australia, Melbourne, 22 March.

Evans, Gareth. 1990b. Australia's Asian Future. Speech at Monash University, Melbourne, 19 July.

Evans, Paul. 1994. Building Security: The Council for Security Cooperation in the Asia-Pacific. *Pacific Review 7* (2): 125–39.

Fearon, James. 1995. Rationalist Explanations for War. *International Organization 49* (3): 379–414.

Findlay, Trevor. 1989. Confidence-Building Measures for the Asia-Pacific: The Relevance of the European Experience. In *Building Confidence—Resolving Conflicts*, edited by Muthiah Alagappa, 55–74. Kuala Lumpur: Institute for International and Strategic Studies.

Findlay, Trevor. 1990. *Asia-Pacific CSBMs: A Prospectus.* Canberra: Australian National University Peace Research Centre.

Findlay, Trevor. 1995. The European Cooperative Security Regime: New Lessons for the Asia-Pacific. In *Pacific Cooperation: Building Economic and Security Regimes in the Asia-Pacific Region*, edited by Andrew Mack and John Ravenhill, 209–32. Boulder: Westview.

Foot, Rosemary. 1998. China in the ASEAN Regional Forum: Organizational Processes and Domestic Modes of Thought. *Asian Survey 38* (5): 425–40.

Foot, Rosemary. 2003. Introduction. In *Order and Justice in International Relations*, edited by Rosemary Foot, John Gaddis, and Andrew Hurrell, 1–23. Oxford: Oxford University Press.

Foot, Rosemary. 2004. *Human Rights and Counter-Terrorism. Adelphi Paper 363.* London: IISS.

Foot, Rosemary. 2006. Chinese Strategies in a U.S.-Hegemonic Global Order: Accommodating and Hedging. *International Affairs 82* (1): 77–94.
Foot, Rosemary and Andrew Walter. 2011. *China, the United States, and Global Order.* New York: Cambridge University Press.
Foucault, Michel. 1970. *The Order of Things: An Archaeology of the Human Sciences.* New York: Pantheon.
Foucault, Michel. 1976. *The Will to Knowledge: The History of Sexuality* Volume 1. London: Penguin.
Foucault, Michel. 1986. *The History of Sexuality*. Trans. Robert Hurley. London: Pantheon.
Fravel, Taylor M. 2011. China's Strategy in the South China Sea. *Contemporary Southeast Asia 33* (3): 292–319.
Friedberg, Aaron. 2011. *A Contest for Supremacy: China. America. and the Struggle for Mastery in Asia*. New York: Norton.
Friedman, Thomas L. 2005. *The World is Flat: A Brief History of the Twenty-first Century.* New York: Farrar, Straus & Giroux.
Frost, Ellen. 2008. *Asia's New Regionalism*: Boulder: Lynne Rienner.
Funabashi, Yoichi. 1995. *Asia Pacific Fusion: Japan's Role in APEC*. Washington DC: Institute for International Economics.
Funabashi, Yoichi. 1996/7. Bridging Asia's Economic-Security Gap. *Survival 38* (4): 105–11.
Funabashi, Yoichi. 1999. *Alliance Adrift*. New York: Council on Foreign Relations.
Funabashi, Yoichi. 2007. *The Peninsula Question: A Chronicle of the Second Korean Nuclear Crisis*. Washington DC: Brookings.
G20. 2009a. Leaders' Statement: The Pittsburgh Summit. Reprinted in *Financial Times*, 25 September.
G20. 2009b. *Global Plan for Recovery and Reform. London summit meeting official communiqué*. Available at <http://www.g20.utoronto.ca/2009/2009communique 0402.html>. Accessed 30 October 2012.
G20. 2011. *Meeting of Finance Ministers and Central Bank Governors Communiqué*. Available at <http://www.reuters.com/article/2011/02/19/g20-text-idUSLDE71I0FN20110219>. Accessed 30 October 2012.
Gao, Haihong. 2004. Cong Qingmai xieyi dao yatai zhaiquan jijin [From the Chiang Mai Initiative to the Asian Bond Fund]. *Guoji jingji pinglun [International Economic Review]* 5: 21–6.
Gill, Stephen. 2003. *Power and Resistance in the New World Order*. Basingstoke: Palgrave-Macmillan.
Gilpin, Robert. 1988. The Theory of Hegemonic War. In *The Origin and Prevention of Major Wars*, edited by Robert Rotberg and Theodore Rabb, 15–37. Cambridge: Cambridge University Press.
Gilpin, Robert. 1997. APEC in a New International Order. In *From APEC to Xanadu: Creating a Viable Community in the Post-Cold War Pacific*, edited by Donald C. Hellmann and Kenneth B. Pyle, 14–36. Armonk: M. E. Sharpe.
Gilpin, Robert A. 1981. *War and Change in World Politics*. Cambridge: Cambridge University Press.

Bibliography

Gilson, Julie. 2007. Strategic Regionalism in East Asia. *Review of International Studies* 33: 145–63.

Glaser, Bonnie. 2009. China's Policy in the Wake of the Second DPRK Nuclear Test. *China Security* 5 (2). Available at <http://asiafoundation.org/resources/pdfs/GlaserChinaSecurity2.pdf>. Accessed 12 September 2012.

Glosny, Michael. 2010. China and the BRICS: A Real (but Limited) Partnership in a Unipolar World. *Polity* 42: 100–29.

Gluck, Carol. 2007. Operations of Memory: 'Comfort Women' and the World. In *Ruptured Histories: War, Memory, and the Post-Cold War in Asia*, edited by Sheila Miyoshi Jäger and Rana Mitter, 47–77. Cambridge, MA: Harvard University Press.

Goh, Evelyn. 2004. The ASEAN Regional Forum in United States East Asian Strategy. *Pacific Review* 17 (1): 47–69.

Goh, Evelyn. 2005a. The U.S.–China Relationship and Asia-Pacific Security: Negotiating Change. *Asian Security* 1 (3): 216–44.

Goh, Evelyn. 2005b. *Constructing the U.S. Rapprochement with China, 1961–1974: From Red Menace to Tacit Ally*. New York: Cambridge University Press, 2005.

Goh, Evelyn. 2005c. *Meeting the China Challenge: The U.S. in Southeast Asian Regional Security Strategies*. Washington DC: East–West Center Washington Policy Studies Monograph 16.

Goh, Evelyn. 2005d. The Bush Administration and Southeast Asian Regional Security Strategies. In *George W. Bush and Asia: A First Term Assessment*, edited by Robert Hathaway and Wilson Lee, 183–94. Washington DC: Woodrow Wilson Center.

Goh, Evelyn. 2007. Southeast Asian Perspectives on the China Challenge. *Journal of Strategic Studies* 30 (4): 809–32.

Goh, Evelyn. 2007/8. Great Powers and Hierarchical Order in Southeast Asia: Analyzing Regional Security Strategies. *International Security* 32 (3): 113–57.

Goh, Evelyn. 2008. Hierarchy and the Role of the United States in the East Asian Security Order. *International Relations of the Asia-Pacific* 8 (3): 353–77.

Goh, Evelyn. 2009. How is Global Architecture Likely to Evolve, and Can it Meet the World's Key Economic and Security Challenges. Paper presented at the Conference on the Asia-Pacific Community, Sydney, 4 December.

Goh, Evelyn. 2011a. How Japan Matters in the Evolving East Asian Security Order. *International Affairs* 87 (4): 887–902.

Goh, Evelyn. 2011b. Institutions and the Great Power Bargain in East Asia: ASEAN's Limited 'Brokerage' Role. *International Relations of the Asia-Pacific* 11 (3): 373–401.

Goh, Evelyn. 2011c. Rising Power...to Do What? Evaluating China's Power in Southeast Asia. *RSIS Working Paper 226*.

Goh, Evelyn. Forthcoming/a. Hierarchy and Regional Security Governance. In *Effective Multilateralism: Through the Looking Glass of East Asia*, edited by Jochen Prantl. Basingstoke: Palgrave Macmillan.

Goh, Evelyn. Forthcoming/b. East Asia as Regional International Society: The Problem of Great Power Management. In *International Society and East Asia: English School Theory at the Regional Level*, edited by Barry Buzan and Yongjin Zhang.

Bibliography

Goh, Evelyn and Amitav Acharya. 2006. The ASEAN Regional Forum and U.S.–China Relations: Comparing Chinese and American Positions. In *Advancing East Asian Regionalism*, edited by Melissa Curley and Nick Thomas, 96–115. London: Routledge.

Goh, Evelyn and Amitav Acharya. 2007. Introduction. In *Reassessing Security Cooperation in the Asia-Pacific: Competition, Congruence, and Transformation*, edited by Amitav Acharya and Evelyn Goh, 1–17. Cambridge, MA: MIT Press.

Goto, Ken'ichi. 2003. *Tensions of Empire*. Athens: Ohio University Press.

Gramsci, Antonio. 1971. *Selections from the Prison Notebooks*, translated and edited by Quintin Hoare and Geoffrey Nowell Smith. London: Lawrence &Wishart.

Grieco, Joseph. 1988. Anarchy and the Limits of Cooperation: A Realist Critique of the Newest Liberal Institutionalism. *International Organization 42* (3): 485–507.

Grieco, Joseph. 1999. Realism and Regionalism: American Power and German and Japanese Institutional Strategies During and After the Cold War. In *Unipolar Politics: Realism and State Strategies After the Cold War*, edited by Ethan Kapstein and Michael Mastanduno, 319–53. New York: Columbia University Press.

Gries, Peter Hays. 2005. China's 'New Thinking' on Japan. *The China Quarterly 184*: 831–50.

Grimes, William W. 2006. East Asian Financial Regionalism in Support of the Global Financial Architecture? The Political Economy of Regional Nesting. *Journal of East Asian Studies 6* (3): 353–80.

Grimes, William W. 2009a. *Currency and Contest in East Asia: The Great Power Politics of Financial Regionalism*. Ithaca: Cornell University Press.

Grimes, William W. 2009b. Japan Confronts the Global Economic Crisis. *Asia-Pacific Review 16* (2): 42–54.

Grimes, William W. 2011. The Asian Monetary Fund Reborn? Implications of Chiang Mai Initiative Multilateralization. *Asia Policy 11*: 79–104.

Grugel, Jean, Pia Riggirozzi, and Ben Thirkell-White. 2008. Beyond the Washington Consensus? Asia and Latin America in Search of More Autonomous Development. *International Affairs 84* (3): 499–517.

Haggard, Stephen and Marcus Noland. 2010. Sanctioning North Korea: The Political Economy of Denuclearisation and Proliferation. *Asian Survey 50* (3): 539–68.

Hagström, Linus. 2006. The Dogma of Japanese Insignificance: The Academic Discourse on North Korea Policy Coordination. *Pacific Affairs 79* (3): 387–410.

Hale, Thomas. 2011. The De Facto Preferential Trade Agreement in East Asia. *Review of International Political Economy 18* (3): 299–327.

Haley, P. Edward. 2006. *Strategies of Dominance: The Misdirection of U.S. Foreign Policy*. Washington DC: Woodrow Wilson Center Press & Johns Hopkins University Press.

Harold, James. 2011. International Order after the Financial Crisis. *International Affairs 87* (3): 525–37.

Harris, Sheldon H. 2002. *Factories of Death: Japanese Biological Warfare, 1932–45 and the American Cover-up*. 2nd edn. London: Routledge.

Hasegawa, Tsuyoshi and Kazuhiko Togo, eds. 2008. *East Asia's Haunted Present: Historical Memories and the Resurgence of Nationalism*. Westport: Praeger.

Hatch, Walter and Kozo Yamamura. 1996. *Asia in Japan's Embrace: Building a Regional Production Alliance*. Cambridge: Cambridge University Press.

Bibliography

Hayashi, Shigeko. 2006. *Japan and Asian Monetary Regionalism: Towards a Proactive Leadership Role*. London: Routledge.

He, Yinan. 2007. Remembering and Forgetting the War: Elite Myth-making, Mass Reaction and Sino-Japanese Relations, 1950–2006. *History and Memory 19* (2): 43–74.

He, Yinan. 2009. *The Search for Reconciliation: Sino-Japanese and German–Polish Relations since World War II*. Cambridge: Cambridge University Press.

Hein, Laura. 2003. War Compensation: Claims Against the Japanese Government and Japanese Corporations for War Crimes. In *Politics and the Past: On Repairing Historical Injustices*, edited by John Torpey, 127–47. Lanham: Rowman & Littlefield.

Hein, Laura and Mark Selden. 1998. Learning Citizenship from the Past: Textbook Nationalism, Global Context, and Social Change. *Bulletin of Concerned Asian Scholars 30* (2): 1–19.

Helleiner, Eric and Stefano Pagliari. 2011. The End of an Era in International Financial Regulation? *International Organization 65*: 169–200.

Hemmer, Christopher and Peter Katzenstein. 2002. Why is There No NATO in Asia? Collective Identity, Regionalism, and the Origins of Multilateralism. *International Organization 56* (3): 575–607.

Henning, C. Randall. 2002. *East Asian Financial Cooperation*. Washington DC: Institute for International Economics.

Henning, C. Randall. 2010. Asian Regional Financial Arrangements and the IMF. *East Asian Forum* (2 May). Available at <http://www.eastasiaforum.org/2011/05/02/asian-regional-financial-arrangements-and-the-imf/>. Accessed 31 October 2012.

Hettne, Björn, András Inotai, and Osvaldo Sunkel. 1999. *Globalism and the New Regionalism*. New York: St. Martin's Press.

Hettne, Björn, András Inotai, and Osvaldo Sunkel. 2000. *The New Regionalism and the Future of Security and Development*. New York: St. Martin's Press.

Higgott, Richard. 1997. De Facto and De Jure Regionalism: The Double Discourse of Regionalism in the Asia-Pacific. *Global Society 11* (2): 165–83.

Higgott, Richard. 1998. The Asian Economic Crisis: A Study in the Politics of Resentment. *New Political Economy 3* (3): 333–56.

Holmes, James. 2012. China's Small Stick Diplomacy. *The Diplomat* (21 May).

Holslag, Jonathan. 2011. China's Vulnerability Gap. *Survival 53* (2): 77–88.

Hosoya, Chihiro et al. eds. 1986. *The Tokyo War Crimes Trial: An International Symposium*. Tokyo: Kodanshan.

Hosoya, Chihiro and Tomohito Shinoda, eds. 1998. *Redefining the Partnership: The United States and Japan in East Asia*. Lanham: University Press of America.

Hughes, Christopher W. 2000. Japanese Policy and the East Asian Currency Crisis: Abject Defeat or Quiet Victory? *Review of International Political Economy 7* (2): 219–53.

Hughes, Christopher W. 2004a. *Japan's Security Agenda: Military, Economic, and Environmental Dimensions*. Boulder: Lynne Rienner.

Hughes, Christopher W. 2004b. *Japan's Re-emergence as a 'Normal' Military Power. Adelphi Paper 368–9*. London: IISS.

Hughes, Christopher W. 2009a. *Japan's Remilitarisation*. London: Routledge.

Hughes, Christopher W. 2009b. Japan's Response to China's Rise: Regional Engagement, Global Containment, Dangers of Collision. *International Affairs 85* (4): 837–56.

Hurrell, Andrew. 1995. Explaining the Resurgence of Regionalism in World Politics. *Review of International Studies 21* (4): 331–58.

Hurrell, Andrew. 2003. Order and Justice in International Relations: What is at Stake? In *Order and Justice in International Relations*, edited by Rosemary Foot, John Gaddis, and Andrew Hurrell, 24–48. Oxford: Oxford University Press.

Hurrell, Andrew. 2005. Power, Institutions, and the Production of Inequality. In *Power in Global Governance*, edited by Michael Barnett and Raymond Duvall, 33–58. Cambridge: Cambridge University Press.

Hurrell, Andrew. 2007. *On Global Order: Power, Values, and the Constitution of International Society*. Oxford: Oxford University Press.

Hyland, William. 1999. *Clinton's World: Remaking American Foreign Policy*. New York: Greenwood.

Ienaga, Saburō. 1993/4. The Glorification of War in Japanese Education. *International Security 18* (3): 113–33.

Ienaga, Saburō. 2001. *Japan's Past, Japan's Future: One Historian's Odessey*, translated by Richard Minear. Lanham: Rowman & Littlefield.

Igarashi, Yoshikuni. 2000. *Bodies of Memory: Narratives of War in Postwar Japanese Culture, 1945–1970*. Princeton: Princeton University Press.

Ikenberry, G. John. 2001. *After Victory: Institutions, Strategic Restraint, and the Rebuilding of International Order after Major Wars*. Princeton: Princeton University Press.

Ikenberry, G. John. 2008. A New Order in East Asia? In *East Asian Multilateralism: Prospects for Stability*, edited by Kent Calder and Francis Fukuyama, 217–33. Baltimore: Johns Hopkins University Press.

Ikenberry, G. John. 2009. Liberal Internationalism 3.0: America and the Dilemmas of Liberal World Order. *Perspectives on Politics 7* (1): 71–87.

Ikenberry, G. John. 2011. *Liberal Leviathan: The Origins, Crisis, and Transformation of the American World Order*. Princeton: Princeton University Press.

Ikenberry, G. John and Daniel Deudney. 1999. Structural Liberalism: The Nature and Sources of Postwar Western Political Order. *Review of International Studies 25*: 179–96.

Ikenberry, G. John and Michael Mastanduno, eds. 2003. *International Relations Theory and the Asia-Pacific*. New York: Columbia University Press.

Ikenberry, G. John and Jitsuo Tsuchiyama. 2002. Between Balance of Power and Community: The Future of Multilateral Security Cooperation in the Asia-Pacific. *International Relations of the Asia-Pacific 2* (1): 69–94.

Ingrao, Charles. 2009. Weapons of Mass Instruction: Schoolbooks and Democratization in Multiethnic Central Europe. *Journal of Educational Media, Memory and Society 1* (1): 180–9.

International Crisis Group. 2012. *Stirring up the South China Sea (I)*. Asia Report 223 (23 April).

Ito, Go. 2003. *Alliance in Anxiety: Détente and the Sino-American-Japanese Triangle*. New York: Routledge.

Jäger, Sheila Miyoshi and Rana Mitter. 2007. Introduction. In *Ruptured Histories: War, Memory, and the Post-Cold War in Asia*, edited by Sheila Miyoshi Jäger and Rana Mitter, 1–14. Cambridge, MA: Harvard University Press.

Bibliography

Japan Center for International Exchange. 2008. Korea–Japan Joint Committee for Promoting History Studies. Available at <http://www.jcie.or.jp/thinknet/forums/k-j_history.html>. Accessed 20 August 2012.

Japan MOFA. 2005. Basic Position of the Government of Japan Regarding Prime Minister Koizumi's Visits to Yasukuni Shrine. Available at <http://www.mofa.go.jp/policy/postwar/yasukuni/position.html>. Accessed 20 August 2012.

Japan MOFA. 2011. Japan–China Joint History Research Report (March). Available at <http://www.mofa.go.jp/region/asia-paci/china/pdfs/jcjhrr_mch_en1.pdf>. Accessed 20 August 2012.

Jayasuriya, Kanishka. 2004. *Governing the Asia Pacific: Beyond the 'New Regionalism'*. Basingstoke: Palgrave Macmillan.

Jervis, Robert. 1992. A Political Science Perspective on the Balance of Power and the Concert. *American Historical Review 97* (3): 716–24.

Ji, Guoxing. 2009. The Legality of the Impeccable Incident. *China Security 5* (2): 16–21.

Jiang, Yang. 2010a. China's Pursuit of Free Trade Agreements: Is China Exceptional? *Review of International Political Economy 17* (2): 238–61.

Jiang, Yang. 2010b. Response and Responsibility: China in East Asian Financial Cooperation. *The Pacific Review 23* (5): 603–23.

Jin, Qiu. 2006. The Politics of History in China–Japan Relations. *Journal of Chinese Political Science 11* (1): 25–53.

Joffe, Josef. 1995. Bismarck or Britain? Toward an American Grand Strategy after Bipolarity. *International Security 19* (4): 94–117.

Johnston, Alastair Iain. 2003. Socialization in International Institutions: The ASEAN Way and International Relations Theory. In *International Relations Theory and the Asia-Pacific*, edited by G. John Ikenberry and Michael Mastanduno, 107–62. New York: Columbia University Press.

Johnston, Alastair Iain. 2004. Beijing's Security Behavior in the Asia-Pacific: Is China a Dissatisfied Power? In *Rethinking Security in East Asia: Identity, Power, and Efficiency*, edited by Allen Carlson, Allen Katzenstein, and J. J. Suh, 34–96. Stanford: Stanford University Press.

Johnston, Alastair Iain. 2008. *Social States: China in International Institutions, 1980–2000*. Princeton: Princeton University Press.

Johnstone, Christopher. 1999. Strained Alliance: U.S.–Japan Diplomacy in the Asian Financial Crisis. *Survival 41* (2): 121–38.

Kang, David C. 2002. *Crony Capitalism: Corruption and Development in South Korea and the Philippines*. Cambridge: Cambridge University Press.

Kang, David C. 2003a. Getting Asia Wrong: The Need for New Analytical Frameworks. *International Security 27* (4): 57–85.

Kang, David C. 2003b. Hierarchy and Stability in Asian International Relations. In *International Relations Theory and the Asia-Pacific*, edited by G. John Ikenberry and Michael Mastanduno, 163–90. New York: Columbia University Press.

Kang, David C. 2007. *China Rising: Peace, Power, and Order in East Asia*. New York: Columbia University Press.

Kaplan, Ethan and Dani Rodrik. 2001. *Did the Malaysian Capital Controls Work? National Bureau of Economic Analysis Working Paper, no. 8142*. Available at <http://www.nber.org/papers/w8142>. Accessed 30 October 2012.

Katada, Saori. 2004. Japan's Counterweight Strategy: U.S.–Japan Cooperation and Competition in International Finance. In *Beyond Bilateralism: U.S.–Japan Relations in the New Asia-Pacific*, edited by Ellis S. Krauss and T. J. Pempel, 176–97. Stanford: Stanford University Press.

Katada, Saori. 2008. From a Supporter to a Challenger? Japan's Currency Leadership in Dollar-Denominated East Asia. *Review of International Political Economy* 15 (3): 399–417.

Katada, Saori. 2009. Politics That Constrains: The Logic of Fragmented Regionalism. *East Asian Institute Fellows Program Working Paper 21*.

Katzenstein, Peter J. 1997. Regionalism in Comparative Perspective. In *Network Power: Japan and Asia*, edited by Peter Katzenstein and Takashi Shiraishi, 1–46. Ithaca: Cornell University Press.

Katzenstein, Peter J. 2005. *A World of Regions: Asia and Europe in the American Imperium*. Ithaca: Cornell University Press.

Katzenstein, Peter and Nobuo Okawara. 2004. Japan and Asia-Pacific Security. In *Rethinking Security in East Asia: Identity, Power, and Efficiency*, edited by J. J. Suh, Peter J. Katzenstein, and Allen Carlson, 97–130. Stanford: Stanford University Press.

Kaul, Inger, Isabelle Grunberg, and Marc Stern, eds. 1999. *Global Public Goods: International Cooperation in the 21st Century*. New York: Oxford University Press.

Kelly, Brendan. 2009. China's Challenge to the International Monetary System: Incremental Steps and Long-Term Prospects for Internationalization of the Renminbi. *Issues and Insights 9* (June). Honolulu: Pacific Forum CSIS.

Kent, Ann. 2007. *Beyond Compliance: China, International Organizations, and Global Security*. Stanford: Stanford University Press.

Keohane, Robert O. 1984. *After Hegemony: Cooperation and Discord in the World Political Economy*. Princeton: Princeton University Press.

Kerr, Pauline, Andrew Mack, and Paul Evans. 1995. The Evolving Security Discourse in the Asia-Pacific. In *Pacific Cooperation: Building Economic and Security Regimes in the Asia-Pacific Region*, edited by Andrew Mack and John Ravenhill, 233–55. Boulder: Westview.

Khong, Yuen Foong and Helen Nesadurai. 2007. Hanging Together, Institutional Design, and Cooperation in Southeast Asia. In *Crafting Cooperation: Regional International Institutions in Comparative Perspective*, edited by Amitav Acharya and Alastair Iain Johnston, 32–82. Cambridge: Cambridge University Press.

Kim, Il Myon. 1976. *Tennō no guntai to Chōsenjin ianfu [The Emperor's Forces and Korean Comfort Women]*. Japanese trans. Tokyo: San-ichi Shobo.

Kim, Mikyoung. 2008. Myths, Milieu, and Facts: History Textbook Controversies in Northeast Asia. In *East Asia's Haunted Present: Historical Memories and the Resurgence of Nationalism*, edited by Tsuyoshi Hasegawa and Kazuhiko Togo, 95–118. Westport: Praeger.

Kim, Samuel S. 2006. *The Two Koreas and the Great Powers*. Cambridge: Cambridge University Press.

Kim, Samuel S. 2011. The Rivalry between the Two Koreas. In *Asian Rivalries: Conflict, Escalation, and Limitations on Two-Level Games*, edited by Sumit Ganguly and William R. Thompson, 145–75. Stanford: Stanford University Press.

Bibliography

Kim, Sung Chull and David C. Kang, eds. 2009. *Engagement with North Korea: A Viable Alternative*. Albany: SUNY Press.

Kim, Tae Hyung. 2009. South Korea's Missile Defense Policy: Dilemma and Opportunity for a Medium State. *Asian Politics and Policy 1* (3): 371–89.

Kim, Woosang. 1991. Alliance Transitions and Great Power War. *American Journal of Political Science 35* (4): 833–50.

Kim, Woosang and James Morrow. 1992. When Do Power Shifts Lead to War? *American Journal of Political Science 36* (4): 896–922.

Kindleberger, Charles P. 1986. *The World in Depression, 1929–1939*. Berkeley: University of California Press.

Kingston, Jeff. 2007. Awkward Talisman: War Memory, Reconciliation and Yasukuni. *East Asia 24*: 295–318.

Kirshner, Jonathan. 1995. *Currency and Coercion: The Political Economy of International Monetary Power*. Princeton: Princeton University Press.

Kirshner, Jonathan. 2008. Dollar Primacy and American Power: What's at Stake? *Review of International Political Economy 15*: 418–38.

Kitaoka, Shinichi. 2010. A Look Back on the Work of the Joint Japanese–Chinese History Research Committee. *Asia-Pacific Review 17* (1): 6–20.

Kitazawa, Takuya. 2001. Textbook History Repeats Itself. *Japan Quarterly 48* (3): 51–7.

Koh, Tommy. 2009. Rudd's Reckless Regional Rush. *The Australian* (18 December).

Koizumi, Jun'ichiro. 2002. Japan and ASEAN in East Asia: A Sincere and Open Partnership. Speech in Singapore, 14 January. Available at <http://www.kantei.go.jp/foreign/koizumispeech/2002/01/14speech_e.html>. Accessed 20 August 2012.

Konings, Martijn. 2009. The Construction of US Financial Power. *Review of International Studies 35* (1): 69–94.

Kornprobst, Markus. 2007. Argumentation and Compromise: Ireland's Selection of the Territorial Status Quo Norm. *International Organization 61* (1): 69–98.

Krauss, Ellis. 2004. The United States and Japan in APEC's EVSL Negotiations: Regional Multilateralism and Trade. In *Beyond Bilateralism: U.S.–Japan Relations in the New Asia-Pacific*, edited by Ellis Krauss and T. J. Pempel, 272–95. Stanford: Stanford University Press.

Kristensen, Hans M. 2002. Preemptive Posturing: What Happened to Deterrence? *Bulletin of the Atomic Scientists 58* (5): 15.

Kupchan, Charles. 1998. After Pax Americana: Benign Power, Regional Integration, and the Sources of a Stable Multipolarity. *International Security 23* (2): 40–79.

Kurlantzick, Joshua. 2007. *Charm Offensive: How China's Soft Power is Transforming the World*. New Haven: Yale University Press.

Kushner, Barak. 2007. Nationality and Nostalgia: The Manipulation of Memory in Japan, Taiwan, and China since 1990. *International History Review 29* (4): 709–944.

Lake, David A. 1993. Leadership, Hegemony, and the International Economy: Naked Emperor or Tattered Monarch with Potential? *International Studies Quarterly 37* (4): 459–89.

Lake, David A. 2007. Escape from the State of Nature: Authority and Hierarchy in World Politics. *International Security 32* (1): 47–79.

Lake, David A. 2011. *Hierarchy in International Relations*. Ithaca: Cornell University Press.
Langenbacher, Eric. 2010. Collective Memory as a Factor in Political Culture and International Relations. In *Power and the Past: Collective Memory and International Relations*, edited by Eric Langenbacher and Yossi Shain, 13–50. Washington DC: Georgetown University Press.
Langenbacher, Eric and Yossi Shain, eds. 2010. *Power and the Past: Collective Memory and International Relations*. Washington DC: Georgetown University Press.
Larson, Deborah Welch and Alexei Shevchenko. 2010. Status Seekers: Chinese and Russian Responses to U.S. Primacy. *International Security* 34 (4): 63–95.
Larson, Eric et al. 2004. *Ambivalent Allies? A Study of South Korean Attitudes toward the U.S.* Santa Monica: Rand.
Lebow, Richard Ned. 2008. *A Cultural Theory of International Politics*. Cambridge: Cambridge University Press.
Lee, Chae-Jin. 2006. *A Troubled Peace: U.S. Policy and the Two Koreas*. Baltimore: Johns Hopkins University Press.
Lee, Kuan Yew. 2010. China's Rise: A Shift in Global Influence. *Forbes Magazine* (20 December). Available at <http://www.forbes.com/forbes/2010/1220/opinions-lee-kuan-yew-current-events-china-rise.html>. Accessed 30 November 2012.
Lee, Lavina Rajendram. 2010. *U.S. Hegemony and International Legitimacy: Norms, Power and Followership in the Wars in Iraq*. London: Routledge.
Lee, Yong Wook. 2006. Japan and the Asian Monetary Fund: An Identity-Intention Approach. *International Studies Quarterly* 50 (2): 339–66.
Leifer, Michael. 1996. *The ASEAN Regional Forum: Extending ASEAN's Model of Regional Security*. Adelphi Paper 302. London: IISS.
Lemke, Douglas. 2002. *Regions of War and Peace*. Cambridge: Cambridge University Press.
Lemke, Douglas and William Reed. 1996. Regime Types and Status Quo Evaluations: Power Transition Theory and Democratic Peace. *International Interactions* 22 (2): 143–64.
Lemke, Douglas and Suzanne Werner. 1996. Power Parity, Commitment to Change and War. *International Studies Quarterly* 40 (2): 235–60.
Lessnoff, Michael, ed. 1990. *Social Contract Theory*. Oxford: Blackwell.
Levy, Jack S. 1983. *War in the Modern Great Power System*. Lexington: University Press of Kentucky.
Levy, Jack S. 1987. Declining Power and the Preventive Motivation for War. *World Politics* 40 (1): 82–107.
Levy, Jack S. 1996. Loss Aversion, Framing, and Bargaining: The Implications of Prospect Theory for International Conflict. *International Political Science Review* 17 (2): 179–95.
Li, Mingjiang. 2009. China and Asian Regionalism: Pragmatism Hinders Leadership. *RSIS Working Paper 179* (May).
Li, Mingjiang 2012. Chinese Debates of South China Sea Policy: Implications for Future Developments. *RSIS Working Paper 239* (17 May).
Lim, Robyn. 1998. The ASEAN Regional Forum: Building on Sand. *Contemporary Southeast Asia* 20: 115–36.

Bibliography

Lind, Jennifer. 2008. *Sorry States: Apologies in International Relations*. Ithaca: Cornell University Press.

Lipscy, Phillip. 2009. Explaining Institutional Change: Policy Areas, Outside Options and the Bretton Woods Institutions. Unpublished manuscript. Available at <http://www.stanford.edu/~plipscy/paperIMFWBoutsideoptions.pdf>. Accessed 30 October 2012.

Liu, Changli. 2010. Zhongri hezuo gongtong tuijin dongya gongtongti [Pushing forward of East Asian Community by Sino-Japan Cooperation]. *Dongbeiya luntan [Northeast Asia Forum]* 19 (2): 64–72.

Liu, Jiangyong. 2010. Tongxiang dongya gongtongti zhilu: hezuo yu chuangxin—xin xingshi xia de zonghexing zhanlue sikao [Towards East Asian Community: Cooperation and Innovation—A Comprehensive Strategy under New Circumstances]. *Waijiao xueyuan xuebao [Journal of Foreign Affairs College]* 2: 57–66.

Liu, Jianren. 2008. Cong dongmeng yitihua jincheng kan dongya yitihua fangxiang [Viewing the Direction of East Asian Integration from the Vantage Point of the ASEAN Integration Process]. *Dangdai Yatai [Contemporary Asia-Pacific]* 1: 21–35.

Lukes, Steven. 2005. *Power: A Radical View*. 2nd edition. Basingstoke: Palgrave Macmillan.

Ma, Licheng. 2002. Duiri guanxi xinsiwei—zhongri minjian zhiyou [New Thinking on Relations with Japan—Sino-Japanese Peoples' Concerns]. *Zhanlüe yu guanli [Strategy & Management]* 6: 41–7.

Ma, Yanbing. 2000. Dongmeng diqu luntan de chuangjian, fazhan ji qianjing [The Development, Progress and Prospects of the ARF]. *Heping yu Fazhan [Peace and Development]* 4: 22–6.

McCormack, Gavan. 2007a. North Korea and the Birth Pangs of a New Northeast Asian Order. *Asia-Pacific Journal* (24 October). Available at <http://japanfocus.org/-gavan-McCormack/2555>. Accessed 30 October 2012.

McCormack, Gavan. 2007b. *Client State: Japan in the American Embrace*. London: Verso.

McDougall, Gay. 1998. Final Report on Systemic Rape, Sexual Slavery and Slavery-Like Practices during Armed Conflict. UN Sub-Commission on Prevention of Discrimination and Protection of Minorities.

McIntyre, Andrew and Barry Naughton. 2005. The Decline of the Japan-Led Model of the East Asian Economy. In *Remapping East Asia: The Construction of a Region*, edited by T. J. Pempel, 77–100. Ithaca: Cornell University Press.

MacIntyre, Andrew, T. J. Pempel, and John Ravenhill, eds. 2008. *Crisis as Catalyst: Asia's Dynamic Political Economy*. Ithaca: Cornell University Press.

Mahbubani, Kishore. 2008. *The New Asian Hemisphere: The Irresistible Shift of Global Power to the East*. New York: Public Affairs.

Mann, James. 1998. *About Face: A History of America's Curious Relationship with China, From Nixon to Clinton*. New York: Vintage.

Manyin, Mark. 2003. *Japan–North Korea Relations: Selected Issues. Congressional Research Service Report for Congress* (26 November). Washington DC: U.S. Congress.

Martin, Lisa. 1993. The Rational State Choice of Multilateralism. In *Multilateralism Matters: The Theory and Praxis of an Institutional Form*, edited by John Gerald Ruggie, 91–124. New York: Columbia University Press.

Mastanduno, Michael. 1997. Preserving the Unipolar Moment: Realist Theories and U.S. Grand Strategy after the Cold War. *International Security 21* (4): 49–88.

Mastanduno, Michael. 1999. A Realist View: Three Images of the Coming International Order. In *International Order and the Future of World Politics*, edited by T. V. Paul and John A. Hall, 19–40. Cambridge: Cambridge University Press.

Mastanduno, Michael. 2003. Incomplete Hegemony: The United States and Security Order in Asia. In *Asian Security Order: Instrumental and Normative Features*, edited by Muthiah Alagappa, 141–70. Stanford: Stanford University Press.

Mayo, Marlene. 1984. Civil Censorship and Media Control in Early Occupied Japan. In *Americans as Proconsuls: United States Military Government in Germany and Japan, 1944–1952*, edited by Robert Wolfe, 263–320. Carbondale: Southern Illinois University Press.

Mearsheimer, John J. 1994/5. The False Promise of International Institutions. *International Security 19* (3): 5–49.

Mearsheimer, John J. 2006. China's Unpeaceful Rise. *Current History 105*: 160–2.

Menon, Rajan. 1989. New Thinking and Northeast Asian Security. *Problems of Communism 38* (2/3): 1–29.

Midford, Paul. 2000. Japan's Leadership Role in East Asian Security Multilateralism: The Nakayama Proposal and the Logic of Reassurance. *Pacific Review 13* (3): 367–97.

Milner, Anthony. 2003. Asia-Pacific Perceptions of the Financial Crisis. *Contemporary Southeast Asia 25* (2): 284–305.

Minear, Richard. 2001. *Victor's Justice: The Tokyo War Crimes Trial*. Ann Arbor: Center for Japanese Studies, University of Michigan.

Mitter, Rana. 2000. Behind the Scenes at the Museum: Nationalism, History and Memory in the Beijing War of Resistance Museum, 1987–1997. *The China Quarterly 161*: 279–93.

Mitter, Rana and Aaron William Moore. 2011. China in World War II, 1937–1945: Experience, Memory, and Legacy. *Modern Asian Studies 45* (2): 225–40.

Mochizuki, Mike. 2003. Terms of Engagement: The U.S.–Japan Alliance and the Rise of China. In *Beyond Bilateralism: U.S.–Japan Relations in the New Asia-Pacific*, edited by Ellis Krauss, 87–114. Stanford: Stanford University Press.

Modelski, George and William Thompson. 1989. Long Cycles and Global War. In *Handbook of War Studies*, edited by Manus Midlarsky, 23–54. Boston: Unwin Hyman.

Moon, Chung-In and Jong-Yun Bae. 2004. The Bush Doctrine and the North Korean Nuclear Crisis. In *Confronting the Bush Doctrine: Critical Views from the Asia-Pacific*, edited by Melvin Gurtov and Peter Van Ness, 39–62. London: Routledge.

Moore, Gregory. 2008. America's Failed North Korea Nuclear Policy: A New Approach. *Asian Perspectives 32* (4): 9–27.

Most, Benjamin and Harvey Starr. 1989. *Inquiry, Logic, and International Politics*. Columbia: University of South Carolina Press.

Mukae, Ryuji. 1996. Japan's Diet Resolution on World War Two: Keeping History at Bay. *Asian Survey 36* (10): 1011–30.

Müller, Jan Werner, ed. 2002. *Memory and Power in Post-war Europe*. Cambridge: Cambridge University Press.

Bibliography

Murata, Kōji. 2006. Domestic Sources of Japan's Policy Towards China. In *Japan's Relations with China*, edited by Lam Peng-Er, 37–49. Abingdon: Routledge.

Musharraf, Pervez. 2006. *In the Line of Fire: A Memoir*. New York: Free Press.

Nair, Deepak. 2009. Regionalism in the Asia-Pacific/East Asia: A Frustrated Regionalism? *Contemporary Southeast Asia 31* (1): 110–42.

Nair, Deepak. 2010. Do Stated Goals Matter? Regional Institutions in East Asia and the Dynamic of Unstated Goals. *RSIS Working Paper 199*.

Nakasone, Yasuhiro. 2001. Watashi ga Yasukuni-Jinga Koshiki-Sanpei wo Dannen Shita Riyu [Why I gave up official visits to Yasukuni Shrine]. *Seiron* (September): 100–11.

Nelson, John. 2002. Tempest in a Textbook: A Report on the New Middle School History Textbook in Japan. *Critical Asian Studies 34* (1): 129–48.

Nelson, John. 2003. Social Memory as Ritual Practice: Commemorating Spirits of the Dead at Yasukuni Shinto Shrine. *Journal of Asian Studies 62* (2): 443–67.

Nesadurai, Helen. 1996. APEC: A Tool for U.S. Domination? *Pacific Review 9* (1): 31–57.

Nesadurai, Helen. 2003. *Globalisation, Domestic Politics, and Regionalism: The ASEAN Free Trade Area*. London: Routledge.

Nesadurai, Helen. 2006. APEC and East Asia: The Challenge of Remaining Relevant. In *APEC and the Search for Relevance: 2007 and Beyond*, edited by Lorraine Elliott, 16–25. Canberra: ANU.

Nesadurai, Helen. 2009. ASEAN and Regional Governance after the Cold War: From Regional Order to Regional Community? *Pacific Review 22* (1): 91–118.

Nikitin, Mary Beth. 2008. *The Proliferation Security Initiative. Congressional Research Service Report for Congress* (4 February). Washington.

Ninkovich, Frank. 2007. History and Memory in Postwar U.S.–Japanese Relations. In *The Unpredictability of the Past: Memories of the Pacific War in U.S.–East Asian Relations*, edited by Marc Gallicchio, 85–120. Durham: Duke University Press.

Noble, Gregory. 2008. Japanese and American Perspectives on East Asian Regionalism. *International Relations of the Asia-Pacific 8*: 247–62.

Noble, Gregory and John Ravenhill, eds. 2000. *The Asian Financial Crises and the Global Financial Architecture*. Cambridge: Cambridge University Press.

Noland, Marcus. 2009. The (Non-)Impact of Sanctions on North Korea. *Asia Policy 7*: 61–88.

Norrlof, Carla. 2010. *America's Global Advantage: US Hegemony and International Cooperation*. New York: Cambridge University Press.

Nozaki, Yoshiko. 2003. 'I'm Here Alive': History, Testimony, and the Japanese Controversy over 'Comfort Women'. *World History Connected 1* (1). Available at <http://worldhistoryconnected.press.illinois.edu/1.1/nozaki.html>. Accessed 20 August 2012.

Nozaki, Yoshiko. 2005. Japanese Politics and the History Textbook Controversy, 1945–2001. In *History Education and National Identity in East Asia*, edited by Edward Vickers and Alisa Jones, 275–305. London: Routledge.

Nozaki, Yoshiko. 2008. *War Memory, Nationalism and Education in Postwar Japan, 1945–2007*. London: Routledge.

Nozaki, Yoshiko and Hiromitsu Inokuchi. 2000. Japanese Education, Nationalism, and Ienaga Saburō's Textbook Lawsuits. In *Censoring History: Citizenship and Memory in Japan, Germany, and the United States*, edited by Laura Hein and Mark Selden, 96–126. Armonk: M. E. Sharpe.

Nozaki, Yoshiko and Mark Selden. 2009. Japanese Textbook Controversies, Nationalism, and Historical Memory: Intra- and Inter-national Conflicts. *The Asia-Pacific Journal* (15 June). Available at <http://japanfocus.org/-Yoshiko-Nozaki/3173>. Accessed 20 August 2012.

Nye, Joseph. 1995. The Case for Deep Engagement. *Foreign Affairs 74* (4): 90–102.

Nye, Joseph. 2001. The 'Nye Report': Six Years Later. *International Relations of the Asia-Pacific 1* (1): 95–103.

O'Dwyer, Shaun. 2010. The Yasukuni Shrine and the Competing Patriotic Pasts of East Asia. *History and Memory 22* (2): 147–77.

O'Neal, John, Indra de Soysa, and Yong-hee Park. 1998. But Power and Wealth are Satisfying: A Reply to Lemke and Reed. *Journal of Conflict Resolution 42* (4): 518.

Ogata, Sadako. 1988. *Normalization with China: A Comparative Study of U.S. and Japanese Processes*. Berkeley: University of California Press.

Organski, A. F. K. 1958. *World Politics*. New York: Knopf.

Organski, A. F. K. and Jacek Kugler. 1980. *The War Ledger*. Chicago: University of Chicago Press.

Oxman, Bernard. 1981. The Third United Nations Conference on the Law of the Sea: The Ninth Session. *American Journal of International Law 75*: 211–56.

Palmer, Glenn and T. Clifton Morgan. 2007. Power Transition, the Two-Good Theory, and Neorealism: A Comparison with Comments on Recent U.S. Foreign Policy. *International Interactions 33*: 329–46.

Pan, Chengxin. 2012. Normative Convergence and Cross-Strait Divergence: Westphalian Sovereignty as an Ideational Source of the Taiwan Conflict. In *New Thinking about the Taiwan Issue*, edited by Jean-Marc Blanchard and Dennis Hickey, 45–64. Abingdon: Routledge.

Panetta, Leon. 2012. The U.S. Rebalance towards the Asia-Pacific. Speech delivered at the Shangri-La Dialogue, Singapore (2 June). Available at <http://www.iiss.org/conferences/the-shangri-la-dialogue/shangri-la-dialogue-2012/speeches/first-plenary-session/leon-panetta/>. Accessed 12 September 2012.

Pang, Zhongying. 2003. Diquhua, diquxing yu diqu zhuyi [Regionalisation, Regional Identity, and Regionalism]. *Shijie Jingji yu Zhengzhi [World Economics and Politics] 11*: 3–10.

Pang, Zhongying. 2011. Rebalancing Relations between East Asian and Trans-Pacific Institutions: Evolving Regional Architectural Features. In *APEC and the Rise of China*, edited by Lok Sang Ho and John Wong, 45–63. Singapore: World Scientific.

Pape, Robert. 2005. Soft Balancing against the United States. *International Security 30* (1): 7–45.

Park, Y. C. and K. Shin. 2009. Economic Integration and Changes in the Business Cycle in East Asia: Is the Region Decoupling from the Rest of the World? *Asian Economic Papers 8* (1): 107–40.

Patton, Paul. 1998. Foucault's Subject of Power. In *The Later Foucault*, edited by Jeremy Moss, 64–77. London: Sage.

Bibliography

Payne, Anthony. 2010. How Many Gs Are There in 'Global Governance' after the Crisis? The Perspectives of the 'Marginal Majority' of the World's States. *International Affairs 6* (3): 729–40.

Pempel, T. J. 1998. *Regime Shift: Comparative Dynamics of the Japanese Political Economy*. Ithaca: Cornell University Press.

Pempel, T. J. 2005. Introduction. In *Remapping East Asia: The Construction of a Region*, edited by T. J. Pempel, 1–31. Ithaca: Cornell University Press.

Pempel, T. J. 2007. Northeast Asian Economic Integration: A Region in Flux. *Asia-Pacific Review 14* (2): 45–61.

Peng, Dajin. 2002. Invisible Linkages: A Regional Perspective of East Asian Political Economy. *International Studies Quarterly 46* (3): 423–47.

Phillips, Andrew. 2010. *War, Religion and Empire: The Transformation of International Orders*. Cambridge: Cambridge University Press.

Piccigallo, Philip. 1979. *The Japanese on Trial: Allied War Crimes Operations in the East, 1945–1951*. Austin: University of Texas Press.

Pincus, Jonathan and Jeffrey Winters. 1999. *Reinventing the World Bank*. Ithaca: Cornell University Press.

Pingel, Falk. 2008. Can Truth Be Negotiated? History Textbook Revision as a Means to Reconciliation. *Annals of the American Academy 617*: 181–98.

Powell, Robert. 1999. *In the Shadow of Power: States and Strategies in International Politics*. Princeton: Princeton University Press.

Powell, Robert. 2002. Bargaining Theory and International Conflict. *Annual Review of Political Science 5*: 1–30.

Powell, Robert. 2006. War as a Commitment Problem. *International Organization 60*: 169–203.

Pritchard, Charles L. 2007. *Failed Diplomacy: The Tragic Story of How North Korea Got the Bomb*. Washington: Brookings.

Pye, Lucian. 1996. Memory, Imagination, and National Myths. In *Remembering and Forgetting the Legacy of War and Peace in East Asia*, edited by Gerrit W. Gong, 19–37. Washington DC: CSIS.

Qi, Huaigao. 2010. Guoji zhidu bianqian yu dongya tixi heping zhuanxing—yizhong zhidu zhuyi shijiao fenxi [Institutional Change in the International System and the Peaceful Transition in East Asia: An Institutional Perspective]. *Shijie jingji yu zhengzhi [World Economics and Politics] 4*: 54–68.

Qin, Yaqing and Wei Ling. 2008. Structures, Processes, and the Socialization of Power: East Asian Community-building and the Rise of China. In *China's Ascent: Power, Security, and the Future of International Politics*, edited by Robert Ross and Zhu Feng, 115–38. Ithaca: Cornell University Press.

Qin, Zhilai. 2008. Zunque lijie diqu zhuyi de 'kaifangxing'—yi dongya diqu hezuo weili [Properly Understanding the Openness of Regionalism: A Case Study on Regional Cooperation in East Asia]. *Shijie jingji yu zhengzhi [World Economics and Politics] 12*: 71–6.

Radelet, Steven and Jeffrey Sachs. 1998. The East Asian Financial Crisis: Diagnosis, Remedies, Prospects. *Brookings Papers on Economic Activity, no. 1*. Available at <http://www.earth.columbia.edu/sitefiles/file/about/director/documents/BPEA1998_1with Radelet-TheEastAsianFinancialCrisis.pdf. Accessed 30 October 2012.

Ramo, Joshua Cooper. 2004. *The Beijing Consensus*. London: Foreign Policy Centre.
Rana, Pradumma. 2010. Reform of the International Financial Architecture: How Can Asia Have a Greater Impact in the G20? *RSIS Working Paper, No. 201*.
Rana, Pradumma. 2012. The Evolving Multi-layered Global Financial Safety Net: Role of Asia. *RSIS Working Paper, No. 238*.
Rapkin, David. 1995. Leadership and Cooperative Institutions in the Asia-Pacific. In *Pacific Cooperation: Building Economic and Security Regimes in the Asia-Pacific Region*, edited by Andrew Mack and John Ravenhill, 98–129. Boulder: Westview.
Rapkin, David P. 2001. The United States, Japan, and the Power to Block: The APEC and AMF Cases. *The Pacific Review 14* (3): 373–410.
Rapkin, David and William Thompson. 2003. Power Transition, Challenge and the (Re)Emergence of China. *International Interactions 29*: 315–42.
Ravenhill, John. 1993. The 'Japan Problem' in Pacific Trade. In *Pacific Economic Relations in 1990s: Cooperation or Conflict?* edited by Richard Higgott, Richard Leaver, and John Ravenhill, 106–32. Sydney: Allen & Unwin.
Ravenhill, John. 1999. Japanese and U.S. Subsidiaries in East Asia: Host-Economy Effects. In *Japanese Multinationals in Asia: Regional Operations in Comparative Perspective*, edited by Dennis Encarnation, 261–84. New York: Oxford University Press.
Ravenhill, John. 2000. APEC Adrift: Implications for Economic Regionalism in Asia and the Pacific. *Pacific Review 13* (2): 319–33.
Ravenhill, John. 2001. *APEC and the Construction of Pacific Rim Regionalism*. Cambridge: Cambridge University Press.
Ravenhill, John. 2007a. From Poster Child to Orphan: The Rise and Demise of APEC. *UNISCI Discussion Papers 13*. Available at <http://redalyc.uaemex.mx/pdf/767/76701307.pdf>. Accessed 20 August 2012.
Ravenhill, John. 2007b. Mission Creep or Mission Impossible? APEC and Security. In *Reassessing Security Cooperation in the Asia-Pacific: Competition, Congruence, and Transformation*, edited by Amitav Acharya and Evelyn Goh, 135–54. Cambridge, MA: MIT Press.
Ravenhill, John. 2010. The 'New East Asian Regionalism': A Political Domino Effect. *Review of International Political Economy 17* (2): 178–208.
Reilly, James. 2011a. Remember History, Not Hatred: Collective Remembrance of China's War of Resistance to Japan. *Modern Asian Studies 45* (2): 463–90.
Reilly, James. 2011b. *Strong Society, Weak State: The Rise of Public Opinion in China's Japan Policy*. New York: Columbia University Press.
Reus-Smit, Christian. 2004. *American Power and World Order*. Cambridge: Polity.
Rose, Caroline. 1998. *Interpreting History in Sino-Japanese Relations: A Case Study in Political Decision-Making*. London: Routledge.
Rose, Caroline. 2005. *Sino-Japanese Relations: Facing the Past, Looking to the Future?* London: Routledge Curzon.
Rosenau, James N. and Ernst-Otto Czempiel, eds. 1992. *Governance without Government: Order and Change in World Politics*. Cambridge: Cambridge University Press.
Ross, Robert A. 2006a. Comparative Deterrence: The Taiwan Strait and the Korean Peninsula. In *New Directions in the Study of China's Foreign Policy*, edited by Alastair Iain Johnston and Robert A. Ross, 13–49. Stanford: Stanford University Press.

Bibliography

Ross, Robert S. 2006b. Balance of Power Politics and the Rise of China: Accommodation and Balancing in East Asia. *Security Studies 15* (3): 355–95.

Ross, Robert S. 2009. China's Naval Nationalism. *International Security 34* (2): 46–81.

Roy, Denny. 2012. South China Sea: Not Just about 'Free Navigation'. *Asia-Pacific Bulletin* (4 September).

Rozman, Gilbert. 2007. *Strategic Thinking about the Korean Nuclear Crisis: Four Parties Caught between North Korea and the United States*. New York: Palgrave Macmillan.

Rozman, Gilbert. 2008. South Korean Strategic Thought toward Japan. In *South Korean Strategic Thought toward Asia*, edited by Gilbert Rozman, In-Taek Hyun, and Shin-wha Lee, 179–201. New York: Palgrave Macmillan.

Ruan, Zongze. 2005. Shixian Zhongguowaijiao 'Huayuquan' [Achieving 'Discursive Power' in China's Foreign Relations]. *Liaowang [Outlook] 32*: 26–8.

Samuels, Richard. 2007. *Securing Japan: Tokyo's Grand Strategy and the Future of East Asia*. Ithaca: Cornell University Press.

Samuels, Richard. 2007/8. 'New Fighting Power!' Japan's Growing Maritime Capabilities and East Asian Security. *International Security 32* (3): 84–112.

Satoh, Yukio. 1993. The Japanese Role. In *Asian-Pacific Security after the Cold War*, edited by T. B. Millar and James Walter. Canberra: Allen & Unwin.

Schachte, William. 2008. The Unvarnished Truth: The Debate on the Law of the Sea Convention. *Naval War College Review 61*: 119–27.

Schneider, Claudia. 2008. The Japanese History Textbook Controversy in East Asian Perspective. *Annals of the American Academy of Political and Social Science 617*: 107–22.

Schofield, Clive and Ian Storey. 2009. *The South China Sea Dispute: Increasing Stakes and Rising Tensions*. Washington DC: Jamestown Foundation.

Schonberger, Howard. 1989. *Aftermath of War: Americans and the Remaking of Japan, 1945–1952*. Kent, OH: Kent State University Press.

Schwartz, Barry and Mikyoung Kim, eds. 2010. *Northeast Asia's Difficult Past: Essays in Collective Memory*. Basingstoke: Palgrave Macmillan.

Schweller, Randall. 2006. *Unanswered Threats: Political Constraints on the Balance of Power*. Princeton: Princeton University Press.

Schweller, Randall and Xiaoyu Pu. 2011. After Unipolarity: China's Visions of International Order in an Era of U.S. Decline. *International Security 36* (1): 41–72.

Sebastian, Leonard. 2012. Indonesia's Regional Diplomacy: Imperative to Maintain ASEAN Cohesion. *RSIS Commentaries* (23 July).

Selden, Mark. 1997. China, Japan, and the Regional Political Economy of East Asia, 1945–1995. In *Network Power: Japan and Asia*, edited by Peter Katzenstein and Takashi Shiraishi, 306–40. Ithaca: Cornell University Press.

Senda, Kakō. 1973. *Jōgun Ianfu [Military Comfort Women]*. Tokyo: Futabasha.

Seraphim, Franziska. 2007. Relocating War Memory at Century's End: Japan's Postwar Responsibility and Global Public Culture. In *Ruptured Histories: War, Memory, and the Post-Cold War in Asia*, edited by Sheila Miyoshi Jäger and Rana Mitter, 15–46. Cambridge, MA: Harvard University Press.

Setser, Brad. 2008. *Sovereign Wealth and Sovereign Power: The Strategic Consequences of American Indebtedness*. New York: Council on Foreign Relations.

Severino, Rodolfo. 2006. *Southeast Asia in Search of an ASEAN Community*. Singapore: ISEAS.

Shambaugh, David. 2003. China and the Korean Peninsula: Playing for the Long Term. *The Washington Quarterly 26* (2): 43–56.

Shambaugh, David. 2004/5. China Engages Asia: Reshaping the Regional Order. *International Security 29* (3): 64–99.

Shambaugh, David. 2011. Coping with a Conflicted China. *Washington Quarterly 34* (1): 7–27.

Shen, Dingli. 2009. Cooperative Denuclearization toward North Korea. *Washington Quarterly 32* (4): 175–88.

Shi, Yinhong. 2003. Zhongri jiejin yu 'waijiao geming' [Sino-Japanese rapprochement and a 'diplomatic revolution']. *Zhanlüe yu guanli [Strategy and Management] 2*: 71–5.

Shi, Yinhong. 2010. Yizhili de jingjiu jiaoliang: ruogan lishi fanli toushi [The Prolonged Contest of Willpower: A Number of Historical Examples in Perspective]. *Xiandai guoji guanxi [Contemporary International Relations] 8*: 1–8.

Shibuichi, Daiki. 2005. The Yasukuni Shrine Dispute and the Politics of Identity in Japan. *Asian Survey 45* (2): 197–215.

Shreer, Benjamin and Brendan Taylor. 2011. The Korean Crises and Sino-American Rivalry. *Survival 53* (1): 13–19.

Sigal, Leon V. 1998. *Disarming Strangers: Nuclear Diplomacy with North Korea*. Princeton: Princeton University Press.

Simon, Sheldon. 1998. Security Prospects in Southeast Asia. *Pacific Review 11* (2): 195–212.

Simon, Sheldon. 2007. Whither Security Regionalism? ASEAN and the ARF in the Face of New Security Challenges. In *Reassessing Security Cooperation in the Asia-Pacific: Competition, Congruence, and Transformation*, edited by Amitav Acharya and Evelyn Goh, 113–33. Cambridge, MA: MIT Press.

Smith, Robert W. 2010. Maritime Delimitation in the South China Sea: Potentiality and Challenges. *Ocean Development & International Law 41*: 214–36.

Snidal, Duncan. 1985. The Limits of Hegemonic Stability Theory. *International Organization 39* (4): 579–614.

Snyder, Scott. 2007. Responses to North Korea's Nuclear Test: Capitulation or Collective Action? *The Washington Quarterly 30* (4): 33–43.

Soeya, Yoshihide. 1994. The Evolution of Japanese Thinking and Polices on Cooperative Security in the 1980s and 1990s. *Australian Journal of International Affairs 48* (1): 87–95.

Soh, C. Sarah. 2003. Japan's National/Asian Women's Fund for 'Comfort Women'. *Pacific Affairs 76* (2): 209–33.

Soh, C. Sarah. 2008. *The Comfort Women: Sexual Violence and Postcolonial Memory in Korea and Japan*. Chicago: University of Chicago Press.

Sohn, Yul. 2010. Japan's New Regionalism: China Shock, Values, and the East Asian Community. *Asian Survey 50* (3): 497–519.

Song, Guoyou. 2010. Meiguo chongfan dongya qianjing ruhe? [Future Prospects for America's Return to Asia]. *Dangzheng luntan [Party & Government Forum]* (31 October): 37.

Song, Jing. 2011. Meiguo yinsu yingxiang xia de yatai, dongya hezuo jizhi zhi zheng [American Influence over the Competition Between Asia Pacific and East Asia

Bibliography

Cooperative Mechanisms]. *Shijie jingji yu zhengzhi luntan [Forum of World Economics and Politics]* 1: 48–57.

Song, Jooyoung. 2011. Understanding China's Response to North Korea's Provocations: The Dual Threats Model. *Asian Survey* 51 (6): 1134–55.

Song, Qiang et al. 1996. *Zhongguo haishi nengshuo bu [China Can Still Say No]*. Beijing: Zhongguo Wenlian Chubanshe.

Song, Yann-Huei. 2005. Declarations and Statements with Respect to the 1982 UNCLOS: Potential Legal Disputes between the United States and China after U.S. Accession to the Convention. *Ocean Development & International Law* 36: 261–89.

Song, Yann-Huei. 2010. The Application of Article 121 of the Law of the Sea Convention to Selected Geographical Features Situated in the Pacific Ocean. *Chinese Journal of International Law* 9: 663–98.

Stiglitz, Joseph. 2002. *Globalization and Its Discontents*. New York: Norton.

Stubbs, Richard. 2002. ASEAN Plus Three: Emergent East Asian Regionalism? *Asian Survey* 42 (3): 440–55.

Su, Hao. 2006. Dongya kaifang diqu zhuyi de yanjin yu zhongguo de zuoyong [China's Role in the Evolution of Open Regionalism in East Asia]. *Shijie jingji yu zhengzhi [World Economics and Politics]* 9: 43–51.

Su, Hao. 2008. Hutao moxing: 10+3 yu dongya fenghui shuangceng quyu hezuo jiegou fenxi [The Walnut Model: A Structural Analysis of Two-layered Regional Cooperation in ASEAN+3 and the East Asian Summit]. *Shijie jingji yu zhengzhi [World Economics and Politics]* 10: 31–4.

Su, Zhiliang. 2000. *Rijun Xingnüli: Zhongguo 'weianfu' zhenxiang [Japanese Army Sex Slaves: The Truth about Chinese 'Comfort Women']*. Beijing: Renmin Chubanshe.

Su, Zhiliang. 2001, *Riben lishi jiaokeshu fenbo de zhenxiang [The Truth about the Japanese Textbook Crisis]*. Beijing: Renmin Chubanshe.

Subacchi, Paola. 2008. New Power Centres and New Power Brokers: Are They Shaping a New Economic Order? *International Affairs* 84 (3): 485–98.

Suh, J. J. 2007. War-like History or Diplomatic History? Contentions over the Past and Regional Orders in Northeast Asia. *Australian Journal of International Affairs* 61 (3): 382–402.

Suh, J. J., Peter J. Katzenstein, and Allen Carlson, eds. 2004. *Rethinking Security in East Asia: Identity, Power, and Efficiency*. Stanford: Stanford University Press.

Sun, Ge. 2011. The Predicament of Compiling Textbooks on the History of East Asia. In *Designing History in East Asian Textbooks: Identity, Politics and Transnational Aspirations*, edited by Gotelind Müller, 9–31. Abingdon: Routledge.

Suzuki, Shogo. 2008. Ontological Security in Sino-Japanese Relations. Unpublished manuscript.

Suzuki, Shogo. 2009. *Civilisation and Empire: China and Japan's Encounter with European International Society*. London: Routledge.

Suzuki, Shogo. 2011. The Competition to Attain Justice for Past Wrongs: The 'Comfort Women' Issue in Taiwan. *Pacific Affairs* 84 (2): 223–44.

Swaine, Michael. 2011. China's Assertive Behaviour Part One: On 'Core Interests'. *China Leadership Monitor* 34 (Winter).

Swaine, Michael and Taylor Fravel. 2011. China's Assertive Behaviour Part Two: The Maritime Periphery. *China Leadership Monitor* 35 (Summer).

Swaine, Michael and Ashley Tellis. 2000. *Interpreting China's Grand Strategy*. Santa Monica: RAND.

Takagi, Shinji. 2010. The G20 and IMF Reform. East Asia Forum. Available at <http://www.eastasiaforum.org/2010/11/06/the-g20-and-international-monetary-fund-reform/>. Accessed 30 October 2012.

Takashima, Shuji. 2006. Japan's War Dead and the Yasukuni Shrine. *Japan Echo 33* (5).

Takayama, Keita. 2009. Globalizing Critical Studies of 'Official' Knowledge: Lessons from the Japanese History Textbook Controversy over 'Comfort Women'. *British Journal of Sociology of Education 30* (5): 577–89.

Tamaki, Taku. 2010. *Deconstructing Japan's Image of South Korea*. Basingstoke: Palgrave Macmillan.

Tanaka, Akihiko. 2006. The Development of the ASEAN+3 Framework. In *Advancing East Asian Regionalism*, edited by Melissa Curley and Nick Thomas, 52–73. London: Routledge.

Tanaka, Akihiko. 2008. The Yasukuni Issue and Japan's International Relations. In *East Asia's Haunted Present: Historical Memories and the Resurgence of Nationalism*, edited by Tsuyoshi Hasegawa and Kazuhiko Togo, 119–41. Westport: Praeger.

Tang, Yizhou, Liu Shaohua, and Chen Benhong. 2003. *Zhongguo yu zhoubian guojia guanxi [China's Relations with Neighbouring Countries]*. Beijing: Zhongguo Shehui Kexue Chubanshe.

Taylor, Brendan. 2010. *American Sanctions in the Asia-Pacific*. London: Routledge.

Taylor, Brendan. 2010. *Sanctions as Grand Strategy*. Adelphi Paper 411. London: IISS.

Terada, Takashi. 2003. Constructing an 'East Asian' Concept and Growing Regional Identity: From EAEC to ASEAN+3. *Pacific Review 16* (2): 251–77.

Terada, Takashi. 2006. Forming an East Asian Community: A Site for Japan–China Power Struggles. *Japanese Studies 26* (1): 5–17.

Terada, Takashi. 2010. The Origins of ASEAN+6 and Japan's Initiatives: China's Rise and the Agent-Structure Analysis. *Pacific Review 23* (1): 71–92.

Thakur, Yoko H. 1995. History Textbook Reform in Allied Occupied Japan, 1945–52. *History of Education Quarterly 35* (3): 261–78.

Thayer, Carlyle. 2011a. Sovereignty Disputes in the South China Sea: Diplomacy, Legal Regimes and *Realpolitik*. Paper presented to International Conference on Topical Regional Security Issues in East Asia, St Petersburg, 6–7 April.

Thayer, Carlyle. 2011b. The Tyranny of Geography: Vietnamese Strategies to Constrain China in the South China Sea. *Contemporary Southeast Asia 33* (3): 348–69.

Thirkell-White, Ben. 2005. *The IMF and the Politics of Financial Globalisation*. Basingstoke: Palgrave Macmillan.

Tian, Huan. 1997. *Zhanhou zhongri guanxi wenxianji [A Documentary Record of Post-war Sino-Japanese Relations] Volume 2: 1971–1995*. Beijing: Zhongguo Shehui Kexue Chubanshe.

Tianda yanjiu keti zu. 2010. Hou jinrong weiji shidai guoji jinrong tixi gaige—zhongguo de Zhanlue yu xuanze [Post-Financial Crisis Reform of the International Financial System: China's Strategy and Choices]. *Jingji yanjiu cankao [Review of Economic Research] 9*: 2–32.

Togo, Kazuhiko. 2008. Comfort Women: Deep Polarisation in Japan on Facts and on Morality. In *East Asia's Haunted Present: Historical Memories and the Resurgence of*

Nationalism, edited by Tsuyoshi Hasegawa and Kazuhiko Togo, 142–63. Westport: Praeger.

Tokunaga, Shojiro. 1992. Japan's FDI-promoting Systems and Intra-Asia Networks: New Investment and Trade Systems Created by the Borderless Economy. In *Japan's Foreign Investment and Asian Economic Interdependence*, edited by Shojiro Tokunaga, 5–47. Tokyo: University of Tokyo Press.

Tonnesson, Stein. 2002. Why are the Disputes in the South China Sea so Intractable? A Historical Approach. *Asian Journal of Social Sciences 30* (3): 570–601.

Totani, Yuma. 2008. *The Tokyo War Crimes Trial: The Pursuit of Justice after World War II*. Cambridge, MA: Harvard University Press.

Tow, William. 2008. *The Trilateral Strategic Dialogue: Facilitating Community-building or Revisiting Containment? NBR Special Report No.16*. Available at <http://www.aei.org/docLib/20090122_NBR.pdf>. Accessed 1 April 2012.

Tow, William T. 2001. *Asia-Pacific Strategic Relations: Seeking Convergent Security*. Cambridge: Cambridge University Press.

Tow, William T. and Brendan Taylor. 2010. What is Asian Security Architecture? *Review of International Studies 36* (1): 95–116.

Toye, John. 1987. *Dilemmas of Development: Reflections on the Counter-Revolution in Development Theory and Practice*. Oxford: Blackwell.

Tucker, Nancy Bernkopf. 2009. *Strait Talk: United States–Taiwan Relations and the Crisis with China*. Cambridge, MA: Harvard University Press.

Twomey, Christopher. 2008. Explaining Chinese Foreign Policy toward North Korea: Navigating the Scylla and Charybdis of Proliferation and Instability. *Journal of Contemporary China 17* (56): 401–23.

Tyler, Patrick. 1999. *A Great Wall: Six Presidents and China*. New York: Public Affairs.

Ueno, Chizuko. 1999. The Politics of Memory: Nation, Individual and Self. *History & Memory 11* (2): 129–52.

United Nations. 2009. Report of the Commission of Experts of the President of the UN General Assembly on Reforms of the International Monetary and Financial System. New York.

Uriu, Robert. 2009. *Clinton and Japan: The Impact of Revisionism on U.S. Trade Policy*. Oxford: Oxford University Press.

U.S. Congress. 2000. *International Financial Institutions Advisory Commission. Report*. Washington DC: U.S. Congress.

U.S. Department of Defense. 1990. *A Strategic Framework for the Asian Pacific Rim: Report to Congress* (April). Washington DC: DoD.

U.S. Department of Defense. 1992. *Report to Congress: A Strategic Framework for the Asian Pacific Rim*. Washington DC: USGPO.

U.S. Department of Defense. 1993. *Report of the Secretary of Defense to the President and the Congress*. Washington DC: USGPO.

U.S. Department of Defense. 2012. *Sustaining U.S. Global Leadership: Priorities for 21st Century Defense*. Washington DC: DoD.

U.S. Department of State Press Statement. 2012. *South China Sea* (3 August). Washington DC: DoS. Available at <http://www.state.gov/r/pa/prs/ps/2012/08/196022.htm>. Accessed 12 September 2012.

Valencia, Mark J. 2005. *The Proliferation Security Initiative: Making Waves in Asia. Adelphi Paper 376*. London: IISS.
Valencia, Mark J. 2008. The Philippines' Spratly 'Bungle': Blessing in Disguise? Nautilus Institute Policy Forum Online (18 March). Available at <http://www.nautilus.org/fora/security/08022Valencia.html>. Accessed 12 September 2012.
Valencia, Mark J. 2009a. The Impeccable Incident: Truth and Consequences. *China Security* 5 (2): 22–8.
Valencia, Mark J. 2009b. The South China Sea Hydra. Nautilus Institute Policy Forum Online (24 July). Available at <http://www.nautilus.org/fora/security/08057Valencia.html>. Accessed 30 October 2012.
Valencia, Mark J., Jon M. Van Dyke, and Noel A. Ludwig. 1997. *Sharing the Resources of the South China Sea*. Netherlands: Kluwer Law International.
Van Dyke, Jon M. 2005. The Disappearing Right to Navigational Freedom in the EEZ. *Marine Policy 29*: 107–21.
Van Dyke, Jon M. and Robert A. Brooks. 1983. Uninhabited Islands: Their Impact on the Ownerships of the Oceans. *Ocean Development & International Law 12*: 265–300.
Vines, David. 2011. The Global Imperatives for Macroeconomic Policy Coordination. East Asia Forum (20 February). Available at <http://www.eastasiaforum.org/2011/02/20/global-imperative-of-macroeconomic-policy-coordination/>. Accessed 30 October 2012.
Volgy, Thomas J., Renato Corbetta, Keith A. Grant, and Ryan G. Baird. 2010. *Major Powers and the Quest for Status in International Politics: Global and Regional Perspectives*. New York: Palgrave Macmillan.
Volz, Ulrich. 2010. A Regional Solution to Global Imbalances: We Need a Beijing Accord. East Asia Forum (15 October). Available at <http://www.eastasiaforum.org/2010/10/15/a-regional-solution-to-global-imbalances-we-need-a-beijing-accord/>. Accessed 30 October 2012.
Wade, Robert. 1996. Japan, the World Bank, and the Art of Paradigm Maintenance. *New Left Review 217*: 3–36.
Wade, Robert. 1998. From 'Miracle' to 'Cronyism': Explaining the Great Asian Slump. *Cambridge Review of Economics 22* (6): 693–706.
Wakamiya, Yoshibumi. 1999. *The Postwar Conservative View of Asia*. Tokyo: LTCB International Library Foundation.
Wakeman, Frederic and Richard L. Edmonds, eds. 2000. *Reappraising Republican China*. Oxford: Oxford University Press.
Waldron, Arthur. 1996. China's New Remembering of World War II: The Case of Zhang Zizhong. *Modern Asian Studies 30* (4): 945–78.
Walker, William. 2004. *Weapons of Mass Destruction and International Order. Adelphi Paper No. 370*. Oxford: Oxford University Press.
Wallace, Helen. 2002. Europeanisation and Globalisation: Complementary or Contradictory Trends? In *New Regionalisms in the Global Political Economy: Theories and Cases*, edited by Shaun Breslin et al. 137–49. Abingdon: Routledge.
Walt, Stephen M. 2009. Alliances in a Unipolar World. *World Politics 61* (1): 86–120.
Walter, Andrew. 2008. *Governing Finance: East Asia's Adoption of International Standards*. Ithaca: Cornell University Press.
Waltz, Kenneth. 1979. *Theory of International Politics*. Reading, MA: Addison-Wesley.

Bibliography

Wan, Ming. 2010. The Great Recession and China's Policy toward Asian Regionalism. *Asian Survey 50* (3): 520–38.

Wanandi, Jusuf. 1996. ASEAN's China Strategy: Towards Deeper Engagement. *Survival 38* (3): 117–28.

Wang, Gungwu. 2008. China and the International Order: Some Historical Perspectives. In *China and the New International Order*, edited by Wang Gungwu and Zheng Yongnian, 21–31. London: Routledge.

Wang, Jisi 2004. China's Changing Role in Asia. In *The Rise of China and a Changing East Asian Order*, edited by Kokubun Ryosei and Wang Jisi, 3–21. Tokyo: Japan Centre for International Exchange.

Wang, Jisi. 2009. Dangdai shijie zhengzhi fazhan qushi yu Zhonggu de quanqiu juese [Trends in Contemporary World Politics and China's Global Role]. *Beijing Daxue Xuebao [Peking University Journal] 46*.

Wang, Xuxiang, 1999. Cong yazhou jinrong weiji toushi guoji huobi jijin zuzhi de fanwei ji gongneng [Examining the IMF's Remit and Ability through the Asian Financial Crisis]. *Shanghai Jinrong Gaodeng Zhuanke Xueyuan Xuebao [Journal of Shanghai Finance College] 3*: 13–16.

Wang, Yuanlong. 2011. Guoji jinrong tixi gaige de Zhongguo celue [China's Strategy in the Reform of the International Financial System]. *Jinrong bolan [Financial Digest]* 4: 30–1.

Wang, Zheng. 2008. National Humiliation, History Education, and the Politics of Historical Memory: Patriotic Education Campaign in China. *International Studies Quarterly 52* (4): 783–806.

Wang, Zheng. 2009. Old Wounds, New Narratives: Joint History Textbook Writing and Peacebuilding in East Asia. *History & Memory 21* (1): 101–26.

Watanabe, Akio and Tsutomo Kikuchi. 1997. Japan's Perspective on APEC: Community or Association? In *From APEC to Xanadu: Creating a Viable Community in the Post-Cold War Pacific*, edited by Donald Hellmann and Kenneth Pyle, 126–47. Armonk: M. E. Sharpe.

Watson, Adam. 1992. *The Evolution of International Society*. London: Routledge.

Wei, Ling. 2010. Guifan, zhidu, gongtongti—dongya hezuo de jiegou yu fangxiang [Norms, Institutions and Community—Architecture and Direction of East Asian Cooperation].*Waijiao xueyuan xuebao [Journal of Foreign Affairs College] 2*: 67–81.

Weldes, Jutta. 1996. Constructing National Interests. *European Journal of International Relations 2* (3): 275–318.

Wendt, Alexander and Daniel Friedheim. 1996. Hierarchy under Anarchy: Informal Empire and the East German State. In *State Sovereignty as Social Construct*, edited by Thomas Biersteker and Cynthia Weber, 240–77. Cambridge: Cambridge University Press.

Werner, Suzanne and Jacek Kugler. 1996. Power Transitions and Military Buildups: Resolving the Relationship between Arms Buildups and War. In *Parity and War: Evaluations and Extensions of The War Ledger*, edited by Jacek Kugler and Douglas Lemke, 187–210. Ann Arbor: University of Michigan Press.

White House. 2002. *National Security Strategy* (September). Available at <http://georgewbush-whitehouse.archives.gov/nsc/nss/2002/>. Accessed 12 September 2012.

White, Hugh. 2008/9. Why War in Asia Remains Thinkable. *Survival 50* (6): 85–104.

Bibliography

White, Hugh. 2012. *The China Choice: Why America Should Share Power*. Melbourne: Black Inc.

Wight, Martin. 1991. *International Relations: The Three Traditions*. Leicester: Leicester University Press.

Williamson, John. 1999. What Washington Means by Policy Reform. In *Latin American Development: How Much Has Changed?*, edited by John Williamson. Washington DC: Institute for International Economics.

Wilson, Brian and James Kraska. 2009. American Security and Law of the Sea. *Ocean Development & International Law 40*: 268–90.

Wiseman, Geoffrey. 1992. Common Security in the Asia-Pacific Region. *Pacific Review 5* (1): 42–59.

Wit, Joel S., Daniel B. Poneman, and Robert L. Gallucci. 2004. *Going Critical: The First North Korean Nuclear Crisis*. Washington DC: Brookings.

Wohlforth, William C. 1999. The Stability of a Unipolar World. *International Security 24* (1): 5–41.

Wohlforth, William C. 2009. Unipolarity, Status Competition, and Great Power War. *World Politics 61* (1): 28–57.

Wong, Poh Kam. 2000. Riding the Waves: Technological Change, Competing U.S.–Japan Production Networks, and Singapore's Electronics Industry. In *International Production Networks in Asia: Rivalry or Riches*, edited by Michael Borrus, Dieter Ernst, and Stephen Haggard, 174–94. London: Routledge.

Woods, Ngaire. 2008. Whose Aid? Whose Influence? China, Emerging Donors and the Silent Revolution in Development Assistance. *International Affairs 84* (6): 1205–21.

Woodward, Bob. 2002. *Bush at War*. New York: Simon & Schuster.

Woolcott, Richard. 2009. An Asia-Pacific Community: An Idea Whose Time is Coming. East Asia Forum (18 October). Available at <http://www.eastasiaforum.org/2009/10/18/an-asia-pacific-community-an-idea-whose-time-is-coming/>. Accessed 6 March 2013.

Woolf, Amy. 2012. *Non-proliferation and Threat Reduction Assistance. Congressional Research Service Report* (6 March). Washington: U.S. Congress.

Wright, Thomas. 2012. Outlaw of the Sea. *Foreign Affairs* (7 August). Available at <http://www.virginia.edu/colp/pdf/Wright-Outlaw-of-the-Sea.pdf>. Accessed 6 March 2013.

Wu, Shicun and Ren Huaifeng. 2003. More Than a Declaration: A Commentary on the Background and Significance of the Declaration on the Conduct of Parties in the South China Sea. *Chinese Journal of International Law 2* (1): 311–20.

Xia, Liping. 2006. U.S. Policy toward the Korean Peninsula and the North Korean Nuclear Issue: Chinese Perspectives. *Korea & World Affairs 30* (1): 83–5.

Xiao, Jiwen. 1998. *Riben: Yige buken fuzui de guojia [Japan: A Country that Refuses to Admit its Guilt]*. Nanjing: Jiangsu Renmin Chubanshe.

Yamazaki, Jane. 2006. *Japanese Apologies for World War II: A Rhetorical Study*. Abingdon: Routledge.

Yang, Kuisong. 2007. Zhongguo xindaishi yanjiu zhong de jige wenti [A Number of Questions Regarding the Study of Modern Chinese History]. *Nandu Zhoubao [Nandu Weekly]* 152.

Bibliography

Yang, Zewei. 2012. Freedom of Navigation in South China Sea: An Ideal or Reality? *Global Review* (Summer): 52–60.

Yeung, Wai-chung Henry. 2009. Regional Development and the Competitive Dynamics of Global Production Networks: An East Asian Perspective. *Regional Studies 43* (3): 325–51.

Yoshimi, Yoshiaki. 2000. *Sexual Slavery in the Japanese Military during World War II*, translated by S. O'Brien. New York: Columbia University Press.

Yu, Meihua 1997. Xin shiqi Mei-Ri-Er dui chaoxian bandao zhengce tedian jiqi zoushi [The New Era and Future Trajectory of U.S., Japanese and Russian Policies towards the Korean Peninsula]. *Xiandai Guoji Guanxi [Contemporary International Relations] 1*: 32–5.

Yuan, Weishi. 2006. Xiandaihua yu lishi jiaokeshu [Modernisation and History Textbooks]. *Bingdian* (weekly supplement to *China Youth Daily*) (11 January).

Zha, Daojiong. 1999. Chinese Considerations of 'Economic Security'. *Journal of Chinese Political Science 5* (1): 69–87.

Zhai, Kun. 2002. What Underlies the U.S.–Philippine Joint Military Exercise? *Beijing Review* (14 March).

Zhang, Liangui. 2004. Chaoxian bandao de tongyi yu Zhongguo [Korean Reunification and China]. *Dangdai Yatai [Contemporary Asia-Pacific] 5*: 29–36.

Zhang, Yunling, ed. 2003. *Weilai 10–15 nian Zhongguo zai Yatai diqu bianling de guoji huanjing [China's International Environment in the Asia-Pacific over the Next 10–15 Years]*. Beijing: Zhongguo Shehui Kexue Chubanshe.

Zhang, Yunling and Tang Shiping. 2005. China's Regional Strategy. In *Power Shift: China and Asia's New Dynamics*, edited by David Shambaugh, 48–70. Berkeley: University of California Press.

Zhao, Quansheng. 2006. Moving Toward a Co-Management Approach: China's Policy Towards North Korea and Taiwan. *Asian Perspective 30* (1): 39–78.

Zhebin, Alexander. 2004. The Bush Doctrine, Russia, and Korea. In *Confronting the Bush Doctrine: Critical Views from the Asia-Pacific*, edited by Melvin Gurtov and Peter Van Ness, 130–52. New York: Routledge.

Zheng, Xianwu. 2007. 'Dongya gongtongti' yuanjing de xuhuanxing xilun [East Asian Community: Reality or Illusion?]. *Xiandai guoji guanxi [Contemporary International Relations] 4*: 53–60.

Zhu, Shilong. 2011. Ershiguo jituan yus hijie jingji zhixu [G20 and the Global Economic Order]. *Shijie jingji yu zhengzhi luntan [World Economics and Politics] 2*: 42–56.

Zou, Keyuan. 1999. The Chinese Traditional Maritime Boundary Line in the South China Sea and its Legal Consequences for Resolution of the Dispute over the Spratly Islands. *International Journal of Maritime and Coastal Law 14* (1): 27–55.

Index

11 September terrorist attacks 54, 57–9, 61

Abe, Shinzo 95, 139, 197
Alagappa, Muthiah 11, 30, 31
Aquino, Beningno 108, 112
ASEAN
  Defence Ministers meeting 68n, 106, 110
  in hierarchical order 212, 226
  and institutional bargains 29, 40, 46–52, 68–71
  regionalism 121
  role in East Asia 35, 51, 63–4, 212, 226
  and South China Sea 100, 104–7, 110–1, 113–14
  Treaty of Amity and Cooperation (TAC) 50n, 51, 62–6, 104–5
  way 40, 47–8
ASEAN–China relations 62, 65, 105, 152, 219
  FTA 56, 141, 120n
ASEAN–Japan relations 64, 141
ASEAN–United States relations 34, 43, 50, 58, 61, 65–6, 115
ASEAN Plus Three (APT) 54–7, 62–5, 68n, 69, 71, 131, 133, 136–8, 141
ASEAN Regional Forum (ARF) 38, 40, 55n
Asia–Pacific Economic Cooperation forum (APEC) 35–41, 48, 55, 58, 61, 68n
Asian Development Bank (ADB) 131, 150, 155

Asian financial crisis 25, 29, 39–40, 53, 56, 118, 120, 121, 138, 156, 205
  causes 54–5, 129, 134
  impacts 131, 143, 148–9
  Japan's role 127–31, 134–5
Asian Monetary Fund (AMF) 25, 54, 128–31, 134–5, 137, 142, 147–8, 155
Asian Women's Fund (AWF) 193
Australia 37–8, 41–2, 46–9, 51, 61n, 63, 67–8, 71, 90n, 102n, 112–13, 130, 150n, 151n
authority
  and conflict management 24–5, 74–80, 87, 98–9, 107, 110–17
  definition 75
  and hegemony 76, 209, 226
  hierarchical 27, 208–9
  and institutional bargains 33–4

Ba, Alice 69
Baker, James 40, 42
Ban, Ki Moon 155
Beijing consensus 133
Brazil 55, 143n, 145, 149n, 150, 151n, 152n
Breslin, Shaun 63, 155
BRIC 150–1
BRICS 150, 152, 155, 220
Brunei 61n, 99n, 105
Bull, Hedley 7, 10, 30, 74
Bush, George H. W. 20, 35, 40, 42–3, 46, 82, 87, 194, 219
Bush, George W. 57, 59–61, 84–6, 89–90, 94–6

261

Index

Cambodia 107, 113, 159n
Canada 38, 46–7, 49n, 61n, 90n, 149n
Carter, Jimmy 88
Cha, Victor 85n, 94
China, People's Republic (PRC)
  and conflict management 24–5, 74–9, 98–9, 114–17, 204
  and hegemony 2–3, 123, 151–3, 156–8, 207–8, 217
  and hierarchy 1–2, 8, 27, 209–12, 215–17
  and institutional bargains 23, 29, 54, 57, 66–70, 203
  People's Liberation Army 109, 220
  and regional order 3, 13, 206–8
  and Six Party Talks 80, 87, 90–6
  threat 20–1, 44, 53, 105
  see also South China Sea
China–ASEAN relations *see* ASEAN–China relations
China–Japan relations 111, 208, 217–18
  and history 26–7, 159–63, 166–7, 170, 172, 174–6, 178, 180, 184–9, 193, 197–9
  and institutions 61–70
  and Korean peninsula 90–1, 93, 95, 97, 116
  and US hegemony 157–60, 163–4, 201, 205–6, 218
  see also regionalism
China–North Korea relations 74, 88, 91–4, 96–8, 114, 116, 204, 207
  see also Six Party Talks
China–South Korea relations 68, 92–3, 95
China–South Korea–Japan trilateral summit 68, 71, 185, 200
China–United States relations 1–5, 13, 20–1, 34–5, 45, 60, 72, 76–9, 93–6, 113–14, 144–5, 207, 217, 221, 224
Chinese Communist Party (CCP) 171, 186–7
Chiang Mai Initiative (CMI) 25, 56, 131–7, 139, 141–2
  multilateralization 133, 135–7, 146, 153
Clark, Ian 10, 33n, 35–6, 210

Clinton, William Jefferson 20, 36, 44–5, 51–2, 56, 83–4, 87–9, 92, 94
Clinton, Hillary Rodham 110–12
collective memory regime 161–6, 168–71, 173
  complicity 161, 166, 170–1, 173, 192, 194
  contestation 26, 172–94
  renegotiation 194–8
  US role 26–7, 160–1, 166–9, 198–201
  see also China–Japan relations, history, power, social compact
comfort women 26, 162, 168, 173–4, 177–9, 185, 189–94
Conference on Security and Cooperation in Europe (CSCE) 46–9

Democratic Republic of Korea *see* North Korea
Deng, Xiaoping 186–7

East Asian Community (EAC) 61–3, 65, 118, 120, 204
East Asian Economic Group (EAEG) 35, 38–40, 55
East Asian Free Trade Area (EAFTA) 62
East Asian Summit (EAS) 62–5, 67–9, 71
English School 7, 10, 17, 30, 202, 211
European Union (EU) 35, 37, 40, 49n, 89, 150n, 153
exclusive economic zone (EEZ) 99, 101–2, 108

Foucault, Michel 12, 218, 222n
France 67, 69, 90n, 149n, 151

G7/G8 67, 149, 150, 154
  Financial Stability Board 150, 154
  Financial Stability Forum 150
G20 135, 145, 147, 149–51, 153–5
General Agreement on Tariffs and Trade (GATT) 34, 41
Germany 67, 69, 90n, 135, 147, 149n, 151n, 153
global financial crisis 3, 132, 138, 144–6, 150, 153, 155

Index

global war on terrorism 54, 58, 60, 95
Gluck, Carol 168
Gramsci, Antonio 6, 12, 30, 207, 209, 222
great powers
  bargain 159, 162, 203
  concert 2, 16–17, 33n, 67, 75, 80, 92, 96, 98, 217
  and institutional bargains 28–34, 50–2, 67–8, 71, 219
  legitimacy 3, 8
  management 17–18, 21n, 34, 72–5, 113, 115–17
  and public goods provision 8–9, 24–5, 76–7, 114, 203–4
  and regionalism 118–20, 128, 154–7
  special responsibilities 8–9, 11, 21–4, 74n, 216
  status 90, 93, 123, 142, 157, 208, 210–11, 216–17, 224–5
Grimes, William W. 135

He, Yinan 170
hegemonic stability theory 76
hegemony
  collective 2, 210
  and complicity 5, 75, 96, 112, 115–16, 204–5, 225
  consensual 22, 31
  definition 5n, 6, 9, 30n
  Gramscian 6n, 12, 209
  and hierarchy 30, 209–12, 214, 216
  liberal 2–3, 13, 16
  resilience of 19, 123, 143–5, 156–7, 205, 223, 225
  and resistance 5, 12n, 21–3, 25–27, 118, 122, 128, 130, 134–7, 162, 165, 200–1, 203, 207–8, 212, 220–1, 223
  and social compact 9–10, 27
  US 1–9, 11, 13, 36, 42, 73–4, 76, 100, 113, 115–16, 131, 159–60, 163–4, 201–2, 204–8, 215, 217, 226
hierarchical order 10, 27, 124, 163, 209–13, 218–19, 222–6
hierarchy
  and complicity 211–18
  definition 75, 209–10

East Asian 7–8, 27, 210–11
  and English School 211
  and institutional bargains 29, 71
  and regionalism 120–1, 127
  and resistance 211–13, 218–22
Hirohito, Emperor 167, 174, 183
history 26, 91n, 159, 162, 210
  joint projects 163, 180, 195–8
  textbooks 26, 162, 174–80, 205
  see also collective memory regime
Hong Kong 38, 125, 128, 133n, 136, 152
Hu, Jintao 197
Hughes, Christopher W. 64–5
Hurrell, Andrew 10–11, 33, 66

Ienaga, Saburō 177–8
Ikenberry, G. John 2n, 10n, 24, 30–3, 41, 67
India 3, 8, 18, 48, 53, 63, 67, 102n, 143n, 145, 150, 151n
Indonesia 1n, 59, 64, 67, 102n, 104, 113, 129, 132–3, 149, 150n, 152n, 170n, 189
International Atomic Energy Agency (IAEA) 79, 81, 83–8, 91
International Monetary Fund (IMF) 54, 128–37, 139, 143, 145–6, 149–51, 153–4
international society 7–8
  East Asian 8–9, 35, 51, 118, 122, 162, 211
  great powers in 8–10, 17
  institutions of 14, 30, 74–5, 210
  normative structure 21–3, 202–8
  social structure 16, 21, 27, 208–10
  solidarist and pluralist 28, 161
  see also English School, order, social compact

Japan
  alliance with US 18, 35, 42–5, 59–60, 98, 115, 160, 200–1, 206, 217, 219
  and global governance 143–7, 150–8

263

Index

Japan (*Cont.*)
  in hierarchical order 124, 127, 212, 216–18, 220–2
  and institutional bargains 23, 29, 34–41, 47–9, 52, 54, 66, 68, 70, 203
  political parties 172, 174, 176–9, 181–4, 188, 190, 193
  and regional order 26–7, 139, 141, 159–63, 205–7, 211, 225
  and regionalization 119–20, 123–7
  Self-Defence Forces (JSDF) 59, 168, 184
  and Six Party Talks 90–2, 95, 97
  see also Asian financial crisis, Asian Monetary Fund, Chiang Mai Initiative, collective memory regime, history, regionalism
Japan–ASEAN relations *see* ASEAN–Japan relations
Japan–China relations *see* China–Japan relations
Japan–North Korea relations 44, 59, 84–6, 89, 92, 95, 97, 117, 171n
Japan–South Korea relations 68n, 98, 160–2, 171–2, 174–6, 178, 180, 185–6, 190–1, 193, 195–7, 200–1, 221
Japan–United States relations 37–8, 56, 118
Japanese Society for History Textbook Reform (JSHTR) 179–80, 188, 196

Kang, David C. 21n, 210
Kim, Dae-jung 82, 193
Kim, Hak-sun 190
Kim, Il Sung 88
Kim, Jong Il 82, 94, 171n
Kim, Jong-un 98
Kindleberger, Charles P. 75
Koizumi, Jun'ichirō 59, 63n, 68n, 95, 139, 180–1, 184–5
Kōno, Yohei 190, 192
Kuomintang (KMT) 171, 186

Lake, David A. 10n, 75
Lee, Hsien Loong 111
Lee, Myung Bak 82, 96–7
Lukes, Steven 12

Macau 86, 152
Mahathir, Mohamad 38
Malaysia 38–9, 40n, 55, 59, 61n, 99, 103, 105n, 107, 131, 133, 152n
Mastanduno, Michael 30
Miyazawa, Kiichi 190, 192
Murayama, Tomiichi 178, 179n, 193, 196
Myanmar 48, 221

Nakasone, Yasuhiro 183–4
Nakayama, Taro 47, 52
Nanjing massacre 174, 177, 179
Nesadurai, Helen 121
New Miyazawa Initiative 131, 134, 137, 153
New Zealand 49n, 61n, 63, 90n, 152n
North American Free Trade Area (NAFTA) 35, 37, 40
North Atlantic Treaty Organization (NATO) 35, 97
North Korea (DPRK) 48, 79, 138
  peace settlement 81, 83, 85, 92, 168
  see also public goods
North Korea–China relations *see* China–North Korea relations
North Korea–Japan relations *see* Japan–North Korea relations
North Korea–South Korea relations 81–2, 89, 92, 95–8, 116
  see also Six Party Talks, South Korea
North Korea–United State relations *see* United States–North Korea relations
North Korean nuclear weapons programme 80–1
  Agreed Framework 83, 89
  complete, verifiable, and irreversible dismantlement (CVID) 83, 85–6, 97
  crises 44, 54, 83, 87–8
  Four Party Talks 84

Korean Energy Development
  Organization (KEDO) 79, 89
  missile tests 59, 84, 86, 96–7
  nuclear tests 84, 86, 91, 95–7
  uranium enrichment programme 85–6
  see also IAEA, Six Party Talks
Nye, Joseph S. 45

Obama, Barack 61, 65, 97, 109–3
order
  creation and maintenance 11, 17,
    21, 73
  definition 7, 17, 21, 28
  economic 25–6, 35, 37, 41, 61, 118,
    123, 125–7, 149, 152, 204–5
  hegemonic 5–7, 9, 149, 204, 206
  hierarchical 10, 27, 123, 126, 202,
    208–10
  and institutions 22, 30–2
  and justice 22, 26–7, 159, 161–3, 166,
    180, 193, 197, 199–201, 205
  regional and global 1–3, 11, 71,
    121–3, 128, 134, 138, 142, 147, 155,
    202, 208
  regulative and distributive 29,
    53–4, 67
  see also English School, international
    society
order transition 7, 13, 16–19, 21, 27, 76,
  143, 159–62, 203
  East Asia's 19–27, 209, 223–6
  and power transition 17–19, 27, 202
Organisation for Economic Co-operation
  and Development (OECD) 64

Park, Chung-hee 171
Pempel, T. J. 132
Philippines 1n, 42–3, 58, 99, 102n,
  103–9, 111n, 112–13, 159n, 170n
Powell, Robert A. 15
power
  and authority 75
  balance and balancing 2, 4, 30, 34, 36,
    44–5, 48, 50n, 52, 75, 138, 199, 217
  and institutions 28–34

legitimizing 5, 8, 13, 23–5, 28
  and memory 165
  preponderant 1, 3–6, 9, 14, 24, 31, 42,
    50, 67, 75, 115–16, 202–6, 213, 215,
    218–19, 223
  productive 19, 218n, 222
  taming 6, 22–4
  third dimension of 12
power transition 3, 6–7, 11, 154,
  161, 223
  theory 13–16, 211, 218
  see also order transition
Proliferation Security Initiative (PSI) 79,
  89–90, 96–7
public goods 1n, 23–5, 72–5, 79, 115,
  203–4
  definition 76–7
  financial 122–3, 142, 157, 205
  and hegemon 24, 76, 213, 216
  Korean peninsula 80–3, 85–7, 91–3,
    95, 98, 114, 116
  South China Sea 99–100, 110
  see also great powers

Ravenhill, John 141
regionalism 11n, 21, 69, 118, 203–4, 218
  and China–Japan relations 25–6,
    65–7, 119–122, 131, 134–40, 142,
    152–8, 204–5
  closed/exclusive 56, 64, 127, 137, 204
  financial 23, 25–6, 128–58, 218
  and global order 121, 142–57, 205
  'new' 120–1
  'open' 40–1, 60, 64, 121–2, 219
  and regionalization 119, 141
  regulatory 132, 134
  as resistance 118–20, 121–2, 128, 134,
    142–3, 147–50, 152, 157–8
  see also ASEAN, great powers,
    hierarchy, Japan, social compact
Republic of Korea *see* South Korea
Roh, Moo-hyun 94n, 97n
Roh Tae-Woo 171
Russia 3, 48, 50, 55, 67–8, 85n, 89–93,
  102n, 143n, 145, 149n, 151n

265

Index

San Francisco Peace Treaty (SFPT) 161, 166, 168–70, 181, 183, 192
San Francisco system 42–3, 58
Second World War 2, 18, 23, 26–7, 32, 35–6, 42, 46, 67, 81, 118, 142, 159–66, 174–6, 182, 188, 191, 201, 205, 210
Singapore 1n, 42n, 43, 49–50, 52n, 59, 61, 64, 67, 78, 90n, 111–13, 125–6, 128, 133, 135n, 152
Six Party Talks (6PT) 24, 79–80, 84–6, 90–8, 115
Su, Hao 71
Supreme Commander of the Allied Powers (SCAP) 166–70
social compact 6–7, 9–11, 13, 20–1, 28, 202–6, 209, 211–15, 223–5
  and collective memory 27, 161–4, 175, 199–200
  and institutional bargains 22, 28, 31–4, 53
  and regionalism 118
South China Sea 23–4, 73, 76, 79, 98–9, 204, 219
  and China 43, 51, 53, 74, 100–2, 104–9, 114–15
  Code of Conduct (CoC) 105, 107, 110, 113–14
  Declaration on the Conduct of Parties (DoC) 62, 79, 105–7, 113
  joint development 100, 105, 107, 117
  and Philippines 58, 102–3, 106, 108–9, 113
  sovereignty claims 99, 103–4, 107
  and United States 99–102, 109–14, 116–17
  and Vietnam 102–3, 106, 109, 113
  see also ASEAN, public goods, UNCLOS
South Korea (ROK) 38, 55, 67, 90n, 102n, 124, 149n, 150n, 152n
  alliance with US 34, 42, 68, 83, 87–8, 94, 97–8, 115, 160, 206
  demilitarized zone 88–9, 94
  in hierarchical order 212, 215, 220–1, 226
  and regionalism 56, 126, 131–3, 138, 146
  and Six Party Talks 84, 90–1, 93
  sunshine policy 82, 93, 96
South Korea–China relations see China–South Korea relations, Six Party Talks
South Korea–Japan relations see collective memory regime, comfort women, history, Japan–South Korea relations
South Korea–North Korea relations see North Korea–South Korea relations
Soviet Union 20, 33–5, 43, 47, 87, 170, 186

Taiwan 1n, 38, 44, 60, 72, 76–9, 93, 98–9, 104–7, 124–7, 124–6, 128, 138, 189, 192–3, 198, 215
Thailand 1n, 42, 58, 129, 133, 149, 159
Trans-Pacific Partnership (TPP) 61, 66, 120n, 139n
Treaty on the Non-Proliferation of Nuclear Weapons (NPT) 80–3, 85–8, 90, 93, 97

United Nations 35, 58, 82, 89–90, 120n, 146, 155, 191
  Charter 62n, 95–6, 101, 105
  Commission on the Limits on the Continental Shelf (CLCS) 103–4
  Convention on the Law of the Sea (UNCLOS) 79, 101–5, 111
  Educational, Scientific and Cultural Organization (UNESCO) 197
  Security Council (UNSC) 89, 91, 93, 96, 180, 188, 221
United States of America
  in hierarchical order 209–20, 223–5
  and institutional bargains 38–41, 45–6, 50, 58, 60–1, 66–7, 69–71

pivot/rebalance to Asia 110–13
reassertion 69, 79, 96–8, 112, 114, 131
as regional security guarantor 6, 25, 42, 53, 59, 69, 72–4, 107, 111–12, 114, 116, 203–4, 206
and regionalism 122–3, 125–6, 130–1, 134, 142, 144–5, 156–8
strategic bargains 34–5, 37–8, 40, 45, 76, 205
strategy for East Asia 42–5, 52
see also authority, collective memory regime, global financial crisis, great powers, hegemony, order transition, South China Sea
United States–ASEAN relations *see* ASEAN–United States relations
United States–China relations *see* China–United States relations
United States–Japan relations *see* Japan, Japan–United States relations
United States–North Korea relations 80–2, 83, 84, 87, 91–2, 94–5, 116
bilateral talks 84
sanctions 88–9, 94–6, 207
United States–South Korea relations *see* South Korea

Vietnam 1n, 5, 48, 58, 61n, 99, 102n, 103–10, 112–13, 170n, 178

war crimes 170, 173, 191–2
trials 161, 166–8, 170, 181, 183, 189n, 190–1, 195, 200
Washington consensus 148–9
weapons of mass destruction (WMD) 59, 89, 91, 96
World Bank 54, 128, 144, 149–50, 154
World Trade Organization (WTO) 41, 56, 148, 154

Yasukuni shrine 26, 68n, 162, 173, 180–5, 188, 199, 205

Zhu, Rongji 56

Printed and bound by CPI Group (UK) Ltd, Croydon, CR0 4YY